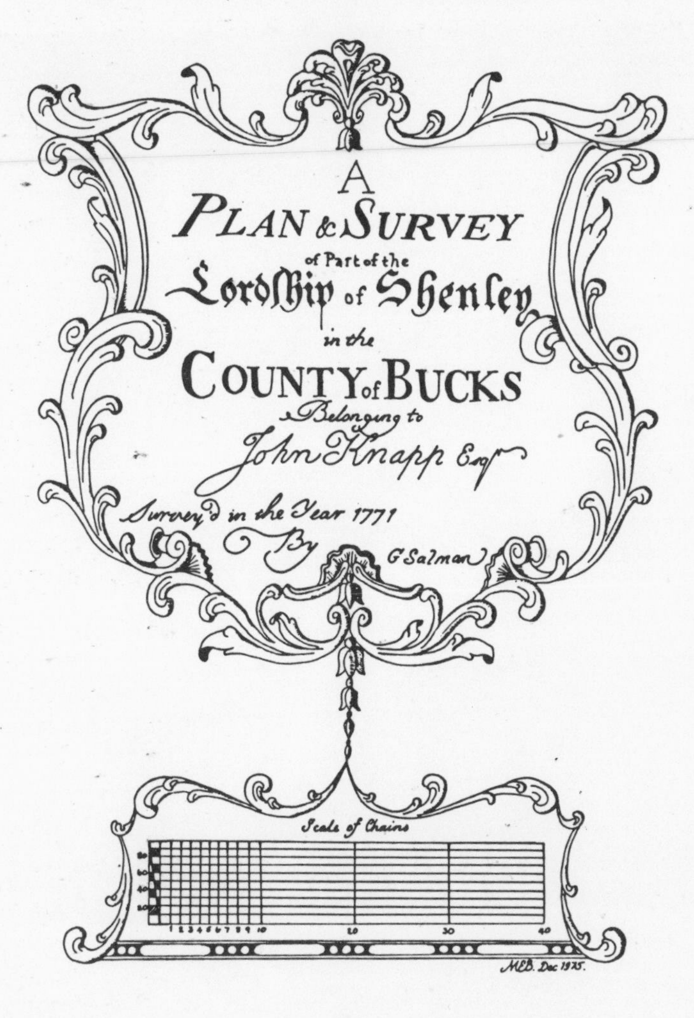

TABLE of Refer…

Nº	Names of Tenants & Grounds		
	King		
2	Part of Cottage Close		
3	New Close		
4	Furze Close		
5	Banky Ground		
6	Simpsons Close		
7	Mowing Close		
10	Wheat Closes		
8	Grazeing Ground		
9	Home Dº		
11	Home Close		
12	Harvey's Long Mead		5 3 18
13	Square Close		4 0 11
14	Parrots Field Meadow		4 0 20
15	Parrots Field		13 2 27
16	Long Close		4 1 36
		Total	106 2 03
	John Sibthorp		
26	Chads Pightle		2 0 37
30	Holines Field	(Late Lees)	15 3 08
31	Field Mead	Ditto	3 18
32	Long Field	Dº	13 0 03
33	Bankey Ground	Dº	9 2 36
34	Middle Ground	Dº	8 0 11
35	Furzey Ground	Dº	8 0 23
37	Spinney Close	Dº	1 0 24
38	Smallow Hill	(Late Clark's)	16 6 15
39	White Close	(Late Clark's)	13 1 03
40	Fulwell Lane Pightle	(Late Lees)	1 1 13
49	Far Ground	Dº	12 1 08
51	Far Knowles	(Late Clarks)	8 0 13
52	Oak hill Lane	Dº	6 3 33
53	Pricked Knowles	Dº	4 2 37
54	Home Ditto	Dº	13 2 70
55	Blacknage	Dº	45 3 24
56	Upper Kents Ground	Dº	10 0 39
57	Lower Dº	Dº	11 1 30
58	Grange hill Mead	Dº	5 0 25
59	Grange hill	Dº	28 2 78
60	Kents home Ground	Dº	22 0 14
61	Part of Green Lane	Dº	3 0 00
62	Lower Ten Acres	Dº	9 2 09
63	Homestead & Garden	Dº	0 2 18
64	Orchard	Dº	0 1 36
65	Upper Ten Acres	Dº	9 1 16
66	Oak hill Close	Dº	8 2 00
36	Hazeley's Pightle	Dº	2 0 00
84	Pightle & Green Lane		1 1 39
		Total	297 1 28
	Isaac Whitmey		
73	Homested & Orchard		0 3 11
72	Wood Common		25 1 29
69	Lower Lane		13 0 02
68	Mowing Dº		5 2 14
67	Furze Dº		13 1 24
70	Oakhill Lane		4 2 07
71	Dº Wood Riding		0 3 38
76	Dº Close		9 3 02
75	Upper Meadow		11 0 04
77	Middle Dº		7 0 13
78	Lower Dº		2 3 09
		Total	94 1 33
	Richarde Newman		
28	Fathom Grounds		20 2 25
29	Down Slade		9 2 26
27	New Close (in Loughton Parish)		6 2 10
25	Stubbs's South Field		9 2 19
24	Dº Field (Late Simpson's)		10 3 39
23	Late Dancers Farm Leys		6 0 10
22	Square Crownhill		3 0 01
17	Lower Dº		6 3 36
18	Side Dº		7 0 17
21	Upper Dº		8 2 34
20	Crown hill Meadow		1 3 12
		Total	91 0 29
	Jaycock		
47	Furze Ground		11 2 22
42	Long Close		3 0 38
43	Lower Middle Ground		5 2 06
44	Middle Ground		5 2 20
45	Far Ground		9 0 28
		Total	35 0 34
	Edward Clarke		
46	Ground & Calverton Common		10 1 32
	Hicks		
50	Long Ground		5 3 39
	James Sibthorp		
94	Home Close & Homestead		8 0 06
95	Overthwart Close		2 3 26
96	Middle Ground		10 1 26
97	Upper Dº		5 3 28
89	Lanes Close		1 3 00
88	Home Close (Late Lees)		1 2 32
87	North Close Dº		1 0 11
86	Calves Pightle		0 3 20
85	Torthill		9 2 24
83	Green Lane		12 0 35
		Total	54 2 08
			0 2 17
			5 0 12
			9 1 22
			3 0 35
			4 0 07
			3 2 37
			2 2 00
			4 1 38
			3 0 21
			7 3 16
			9 2 36
			2 3 22
			5 2 18
	William Brice		
109	Fulmoor Close		28 1 27
114	Homestead		0 1 35
113	Home Close		5 1 24
112	Rabbet Close		3 0 05
111	Mozon's Close		7 2 28
110	Moons Close		3 1 19
108	Peartree Close		4 3 01
107	Mary Close		22 2 11
142	Upper Meadow		20 0 32
140	Kibbs Hadeland Meadow		14 2 26
139	Furze Field		21 1 15
141	Middle Field		25 3 12
143	Barn Field		21 3 12
		Total	173 2 01
	John Clarke		
120	Homestead & Garden		1 0 25
121	Home Close		3 2 39
122	Curtis's Dº		3 0 28
117	Jenkens's Close		9 2 36
115	Dº Orchard & Yard		2 1 00
116	Late Simpsons Piece		7 1 32
118	Ironmongers Close		8 0 13
119	East Green		11 2 32
126	Dº Close		3 3 24
125	Medwich's Close with Spinney		13 2 38
123	Late Dudley's Close		4 3 13
124	Field under Medwich's Close		14 1 35
128	Ditto Spinney		30 3 09
127	Old Street Furlong Field		24 3 39
129	Bridge Furlong Field		36 2 39
		Total	176 3 22
	Joseph James		
130	Bridge Meadow		13 3 33
131	Upper Moor		21 0 14
132	North Fur Ground		27 1 06
133	Dº Home Ground		21 3 28
134	South Far Ground		18 1 38
135	Dº Home Ground		18 0 02
136	Sand Furlong Field		20 2 39
137	Stoney Ford Meadow		17 1 02
138	Furze Ground		38 1 07
		Total	198 0 09
	Henry Josseys		
104	Riding Close		4 2 06
86	Toothill Moat & Island		0 2 38
81	Shenley Wood		77 0 21
80	Oakhill Dº South		32 0 02
79	Dº North		102 0 26
82	Shenley Wood Riding (John Rutland)		2 2 10
1	The Cottagers Close		10 2 26
41	Shepherds Spinny		13 0 04
	Total of Mr Kings Farm		106 2 03
	Dº Jnº Sibthorp's		297 1 28
	Dº Isaac Whitney's		94 1 33
	Dº Richard Newmans		91 0 29
	Dº Jaycock's		35 0 34
	Dº Edward Clarke's		10 1 32
	Dº Hicks's		5 3 39
	Dº James Sibthorp's		54 2 08
	Dº John Billington		95 2 10
	Dº Willm Brice		173 2 01
	Dº John Clark		176 3 22
	Dº Joseph James		198 0 09
	Dº Henry Jossey's		4 2 06
		Total of Plan	757 2 30

Milton Keynes: Image and Reality

Presented by

Milton Keynes Development Corporation

to

Des Ramsden

---

a member of the team which helped
the Corporation to complete
its work

1992

Milton Keynes: Image and Reality

Terence Bendixson and John Platt

Granta Editions

Published by Granta Editions, 47 Norfolk Street, Cambridge CB1 2LE

Granta Editions is an imprint of The Book Concern Limited

A CIP catalogue record is available for this book from the British Library.

ISBN 0 906782 72 4

Designed by Jim Reader
Design, editorial and production in association with Book Production Consultants, 47 Norfolk Street, Cambridge CB1 2LE

Printed and bound by Grillford Limited, Milton Keynes

FRONTISPIECE: *Old and new at Milton Keynes.*

Contents

PREFACE

'Earth has not anything to show more fair', wrote Wordsworth, looking down the Thames from Westminster Bridge. London to him was a place where

> Ships, towers, domes, theatres, and temples lie
> Open unto the fields, and to the sky ...

Milton Keynes too has its admirers. The best-known is almost certainly the television cameraman who depicted the boy running with the red balloon. Seldom, if ever, has a new town been portrayed in such a romantic, evocative and hopeful light. And not since the 1930s, when the London Underground commissioned posters urging people to 'Come out to Metroland', has the ideal of suburban living been so seductively painted.

Yet, it has to be acknowledged that new towns are not universally loved. On the contrary they are feared, disliked and treated by some with snobbish disdain. Country people see them, to quote Frederic Osborn, as 'the storm troops of the urban invasion'.[1] Lord Hinchingbrooke, speaking in Parliament during a debate on what was to become the New Towns Act 1946, saw in them something much more sinister. The Bill was, he said, 'a state experiment in the life and happiness of our people and in my opinion like all state experiments, it will work havoc, bitterness, and grave social damage'.[2]

As if that were not damning enough, new towns are also a product of planning – seemingly a most un-British activity. They flow more from the mind than the heart: they stir an uneasiness that goes back at least to William Blake, whom Kathleen Raine describes as 'of all English poets the supreme poet of the City'.

Blake saw no beauty in Wordsworth's London of 'ships, towers, domes'. He was concerned about the city as people and about spirituality:

> I wander thro' each charter'd street
> Near where the charter'd Thames does flow,
> And mark in every face I meet
> Marks of weakness, marks of woe.

Where we see pretty, pink-brick Georgian England, Blake, as a Romantic, saw aridity. His contemporaries, the philosophers Bacon and Locke and the mathematician Newton, seemed to him to have created a 'world of hate', where reason had banished brotherhood and art. St Paul's Cathedral, designed by the calculating Wren, was cold and soulless. Babylon was his label for the efficient, well-equipped London of his day. Today he would, no doubt, attach the tag to Milton Keynes.

Kathleen Raine, poet and sharer of the Blakean vision, is a reminder that the Romantic tradition is alive and well. 'What is notably lacking in cities built without the vision of the "heavenly original" is any trace of beauty, where the eyes can rest and find peace or delight', she writes. 'There may be stupendous works in terms of size, productivity, efficiency, but the soul is starved.'[3]

It may seem ridiculous to suggest that Milton Keynes in any way fits this description. Françoise Choay praises the garden city idea as 'one of the last and most influential utopian models to come out of the nineteenth century'.[4] And Milton Keynes is one of the finest – if not the finest – expressions of that ideal. A historian of this extraordinary city therefore finds in his subject a paradox. The topic is contentious and contradictory. Those looking at the place from one angle, like the inhabitants of one of Calvino's fantasies, experience something different from those looking at it from another.[5]

But Blake does help to explain the paradox. When he wrote about 'dark Satanic mills' he was not writing about buildings; he was looking through them to their underlying ideology – materialism based on machine production. And, like it or not, that ideology pervades every well-planned, tree-lined corner of modern England.

Thus, Milton Keynes, being a quintessential part of that England, is not a place for us when we are in the mood for the quaint, the mystical and the old. It is bold, new, shiny, rational, progressive and materialist. (Is that why the Japanese like it?) It symbolises a society that is, as Kathleen Raine puts it, 'still in the power of its machines'. And that, I think, is one reason that the new city, for all its magnificence and beauty, comes in for knocks. The rational in us admires its logic. The romantic in us fears its order.

John Platt says that this book is about Milton Keynes seen over the shoulder of the chairman of Milton Keynes Development Corporation. He is right. It is only very indirectly about the people who live in the city (the 'golden builders' as Blake would have called

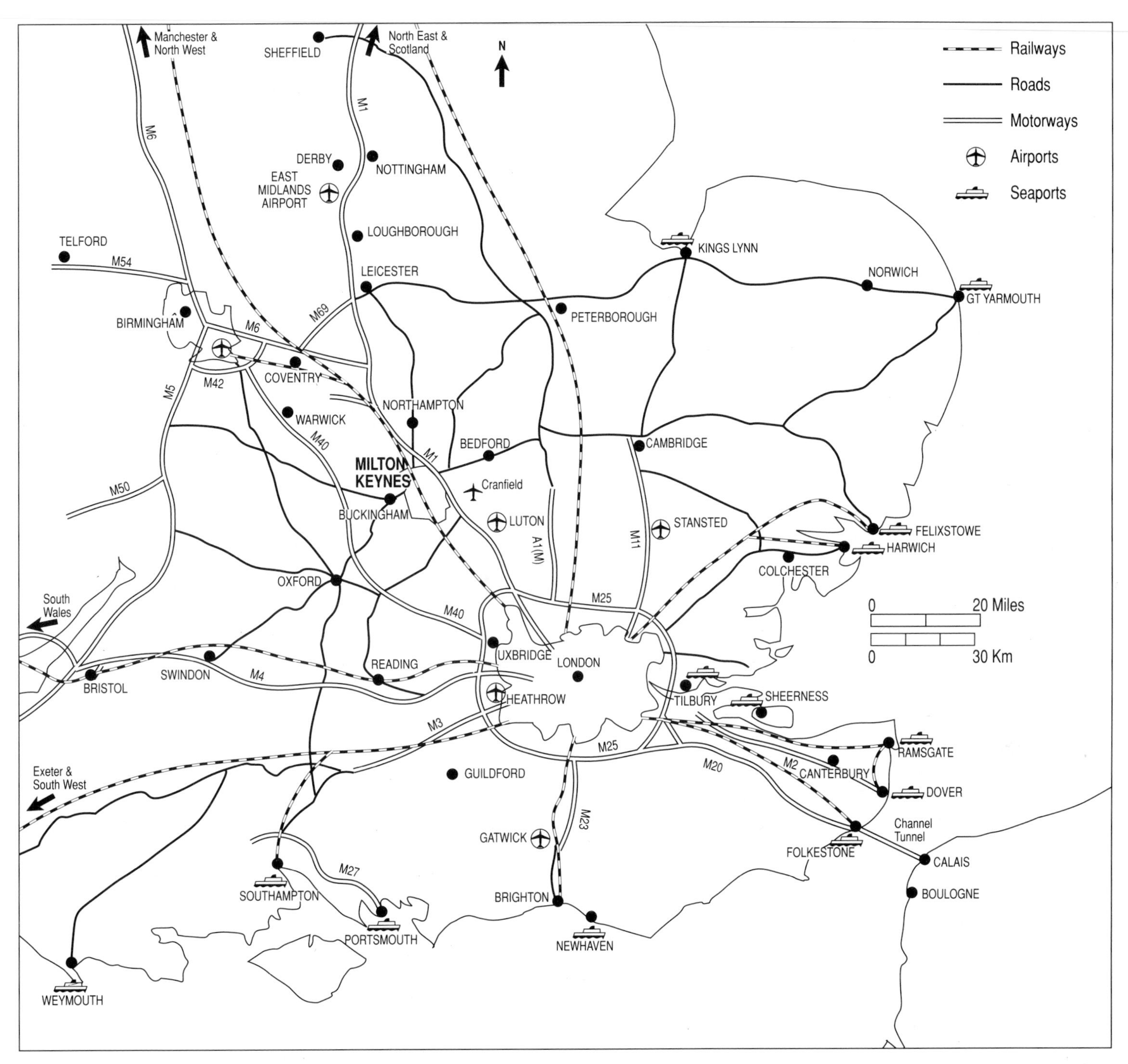

The location of Milton Keynes showing the main roads and railways as they were in 1991.

them). It is more about the aims, hopes and prejudices of the members of the board of the corporation, the small band of men and women to whom the executive reported. I suspect it gives the chairmen too much prominence and their colleagues too little. I know it is completely silent about some individuals - board members, officers and civil servants - who made major contributions to the city. That is my responsibility but it is not due to any malice towards them; history has always been partly about what is left out.

The book's foundation stones are the corporation's minutes through which John Platt trawled and in which I sought themes. These minutes were confidential when they were written and, covered as they are by the thirty-year secrecy rule governing all public records, are still inaccessible to the public - though copies no doubt exist amongst the private papers of individual board members.

Other sources include books, reports and articles about Milton Keynes, some produced by the corporation, some by observers and some by critics. I also interviewed a very limited number of individuals closely connected to the new city. These were, above all, the two chairmen, Lords Campbell and Chilver, and two of the three general managers, Fred Roche and Frank Henshaw. I met Peter Shore, the Environment Secretary who started the rundown of the new towns; Bill Benyon, MP for Buckingham and then for Milton Keynes from 1970 to the present; and finally the two chief executives of Milton Keynes Borough Council, Erroll Ray and Michael Murray. A small number of past and present members of the corporation's staff were kind enough to discuss Milton Keynes with me or read chapters of the book in draft. I am grateful to all of them but particularly to John Platt and Frank Henshaw. The book could not have been written without them. As for its faults and omissions, they are mine.

1

Birth of a City

The future city of Milton Keynes first became a site on a map on Thursday 13 January 1966. Prior to that everything about it was nebulous. Clouds of uncertainty hung over its location, its form, its timing and its financing. Many doubted whether it would be built at all. The clouds were finally blown away by Richard Crossman MP, Minister of Housing and Local Government in Harold Wilson's first Labour Government. Crossman held a press briefing in Whitehall at which the Ministry produced a map depicting the boundaries of the future city. Although later to be modified, they resembled, then as now, a huge pocket handkerchief tossed casually across about forty undulating square miles of North Buckinghamshire. And, to everyone's surprise, the handkerchief was so large that it covered Wolverton as well as Bletchley.

Crossman said the North Bucks project would be bigger than any previous new town and would one day be lived in by a quarter of a million people. It would cover 21,000 rural acres and 6,000 urban ones. (Not long after, a Wolverton councillor, determined to banish any idea that residents in the new city would be 'living like rabbits', observed that Manchester, with about the same area, had nearly a million residents.) The great extent of the proposed city was intended to avoid problems beginning to emerge at other new towns.[1] These included unsuccessful attempts to extend Stevenage, which was bursting at the seams, and providing for 100,000 people on a mere 7,234 acres at Runcorn in Cheshire.

The Minister forecast that the project would cost £400 million and that, with luck, 60,000 to 70,000 newcomers would be living in the city within ten years. He hoped to appoint the members of a development corporation by the end of 1966. Planning would take a further year to eighteen months. Crossman added a warning. Providing houses for Londoners on such a huge scale was not going to be easy. 'We are,' he said, 'now completely relooking at... incentives to move people and industry to new towns.'[2]

Crossman, by this time, was enjoying himself at the Housing Ministry. His battles with

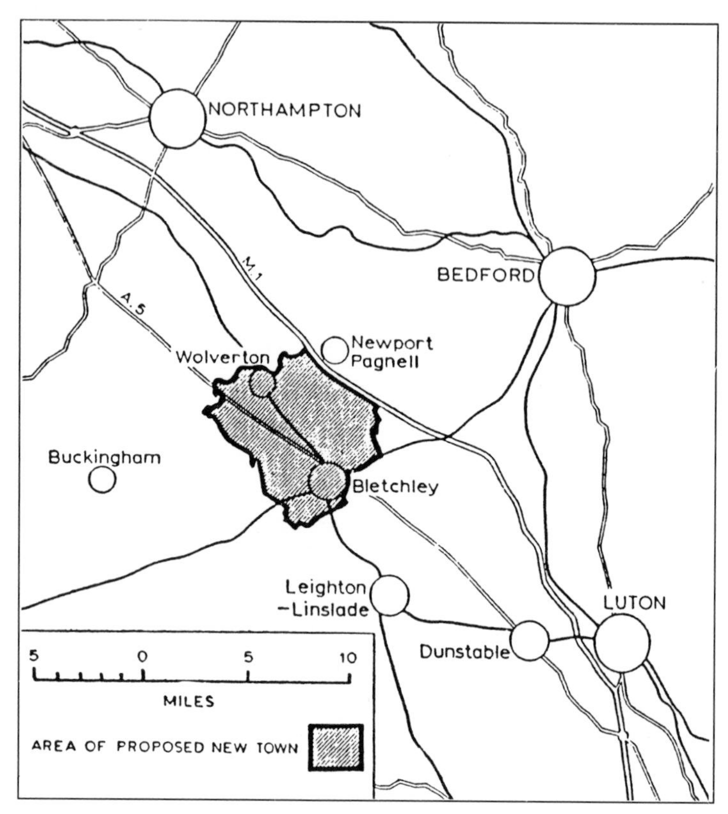

The site of the North Bucks new town announced by Richard Crossman in 1966. It covered 27,000 acres of which Wolverton and Bletchley accounted for about 6,000.

Dame Evelyn (later Baroness) Sharp, the first woman to reach Whitehall's top rank, and his deep distrust of all civil servants had not abated, but he had developed an excellent working relationship with John Delafons, his private secretary, and even with 'the Dame'.

Dame Evelyn, a towering personality and a mandarin of immense experience, was possibly less certain about this than Crossman. 'He would *not* listen,' she told Simon Jenkins in an interview in 1975. 'He distrusted us from the start and made that clear. He was a bully. Meetings with him were simply a turmoil. He was a bull in a china shop and he felt like a bull in a china shop. I think he *wanted* to be a bull in a china shop, he wanted to hear the china smashing.'[3]

Alun Sylvester-Evans, Under-secretary in charge of the Ministry's new towns directorate and godfather to Milton Keynes, saw Crossman in a different light. 'I enjoyed working with him. He loved disputation. He would hammer you into the ground with outrageous arguments.' Before a meeting with local officials 'you would wonder what on earth he was going to say ... only to find him putting over the departmental line crisply and cogently'. He liked to test ideas to destruction, but officials who realised this and 'were prepared to argue back forcefully' found he could be very stimulating.[4]

Crossman's Milton Keynes announcement, coming as it did after months of speculation, prompted Robert Maxwell, Labour MP for Buckingham, to give thanks for the end of 'stultifying uncertainty' and then to put in a plea for adequate compensation for tenant farmers. The *Wolverton Express* took up their cause a week later. 'Years of careful husbandry, stretching back in many instances for several generations, will be destroyed by the necessity to provide homes for Londoners,' the editor wrote. 'This social need must be balanced by adequate provision for those who will themselves be made homeless and jobless.'[5]

When the local authorities reacted to the prospect of a central government cuckoo descending on their mostly rural nest, they divided not along party but town and country lines. Bletchley Council, which had during the previous fifteen years provided homes for 15,000 Londoners under a local expansion scheme, voted unanimously in favour of the new city, although councillors wanted reassurance that their projects could continue until they were assimilated into it.

Newport Pagnell and Wolverton Urban Districts were likewise in favour of the new city, although Newport was deeply worried at the prospect of losing half of its 'golden goose' – the western part of the motorway service station on the M1. The exception was Newport Pagnell Rural District. Although the councillors had earlier been in favour of a new town, sight of the Minister's proposals caused them to do a U-turn. The opposition was led by Arthur Snaith who represented Loughton: he described the new town as a 'hearse for North Bucks'.[6] For tenant farmers it must have seemed just that. The Agricultural Holdings Act 1948 provided dispossessed tenants with compensation for improvements and 'unexhausted manures' plus one or, in exceptional cases, two years' rent. It was brutally unfair.

Two months after he had set plans for the future Milton Keynes in motion (and a fortnight before the general election at which Labour increased its majority in the House of Commons from four to forty-eight seats) Dick Crossman visited North Bucks to see the site and meet members of the county and district councils. He was, so he told the press, prompted by the unprecedented scale of the project to take this unusual step. He had the impression, he added, that the city raised no strong objections. However, when J. R. (Jimmy) James, chief planner at the Housing Ministry, described the farmland in the proposed site as 'second or lower class', someone at the meeting shouted 'Rubbish!'. Such conflict was

something Crossman was keen to avoid. He wanted the new city, but he also wanted 'both good buildings and good relations with local people'.[7]

March also saw the retirement of Dame Evelyn Sharp. She was succeeded as permanent secretary by Sir Matthew Stevenson, bleakly characterised by Crossman as 'an insurance representative from the Prudential'.[8] Notwithstanding this staff change, progress at the Ministry over the succeeding months was fast. In April, following representations by the local authorities, the Ministry published a 'draft designation order' which trimmed 1,800 acres off the original site. Newport Urban District was one of the gainers. It was allowed to retain both parts of the M1 service station – its 'golden goose'.[9]

April also saw the formation of a North Bucks Association by the twelve rural parishes that lay within the 'pocket handkerchief'. They had decided to fight the new city. At an inaugural meeting at Loughton their president Sir Frank Markham, Maxwell's Tory predecessor as MP for Buckingham, argued that Norfolk, Aldershot or Southampton, with their indifferent agricultural land, would all be good city sites. North Buckinghamshire contained, so he said, some of the best farmland in the country. It was crossed by roads like the A5, which could not possibly accommodate an additional 70,000 cars. As for the River Ouse, it 'just oozes along and has a job to get rid of the rain water'. Faced with the run-off from 25,000 acres of concrete and buildings, it would not be able to cope.

Arthur Snaith, the Association's secretary, once again found a funereal metaphor to fit the occasion. The great swathe of cities between London and Birmingham was, he reminded his audience, called 'the coffin', and North Bucks was its only respite from buildings. 'This new town, if it comes, will complete the belt of urbanity that goes right across the centre of the country. It will,' he said, 'be the last nail in the coffin.'[10]

The public inquiry into the new city began at Wilton Hall in Bletchley on 4 July. It was a modest affair, considering the huge scale of the proposal and the impact that it would have throughout the south Midlands. The Housing Ministry did not even have to submit itself to cross-examination. It presented a statement and sent down a battery of senior officials to answer questions. Lawyers were not involved at all. The lucrative concept of the 'planning bar' still lay in the future.

The inspector chosen by the Ministry (which was still judge and jury in its own court) was Geoffrey Godber, clerk of Shropshire County Council. One of the first witnesses was Aron Owen, speaking on behalf of the North Bucks Association. Owen asserted that a decision to build the new city had already been made. He then quoted Robert Maxwell who had accused the Minister of saying: 'I have a completely open mind – and nothing you say will make me change it.' This nettled Godber who denied that a decision had been

LEFT: Milton Keynes: the original village.

made. He had, he assured the inquiry, better things to do than waste his time presiding over a foregone conclusion. And, in a thinly veiled allusion to the Labour MP, he added: 'These are frolics for irresponsible politicians.'

Amongst the other eighty-five objectors were the National Farmers Union and the Country Landowners' Association. A voice was heard from Bedford too. The town, thirty-five meandering miles further down the Ouse, drew its drinking water from the river and the water board was worried about the effect of additional effluent. James Marchant, a resident of Loughton, added a depressing personal note. He said he would move, possibly emigrate, if the development went ahead.

When it came the turn of the big guns to fire, Buckinghamshire gave its wholehearted support to the Government's proposal. Not only would a new city help to relieve pressure in London; it promised as well to provide a safety valve for towns such as Slough and High Wycombe in the county's fast-growing southern extremity. Bletchley too was in favour but lodged an objection because the council was determined that its town should, for several years to come, be the centre of the new city. Bletchley was the only place of substance within the draft designated area, said Jim Cassidy, chairman of the town development committee. 'Bletchley must surely form the core...'[11]

Councillor Cassidy's plea was much to the point. The Whitehall view was that the new city would be 'multicentred'. Alun Sylvester-Evans enlarged on this at the inquiry. He spoke of new principles of design that were to be used. The population density would be lower than the thirteen-to-the-acre average for earlier new towns. (The Minister's statement, which had been sent to all who had lodged written objections, said the overall density would be 9.9 persons per acre, the same as Dawley in Shropshire where the proposed population was 90,000.) Shopping and business would not be so concentrated as in traditional cities. Such concentration would, he said, lead to 'a demand for roads on a scale which is too costly and ruins the environment of the city'. This had been made clear by a recent study of Leicester. It had shown that roads sixteen lanes wide would be needed to enable all car owners to drive into the city centre. Town planners were, therefore, increasingly in favour of dispersing shops and jobs.

(Crossman himself played an important part in deciding on the form of the new city. Sylvester-Evans later recalled that, during the Minister's March visit, 'both John Delafons and I noted how Crossman in his exuberance became firmer and firmer about the design of the new town at each successive meeting. He had virtually designed [it] by the end of the day.'[12] Crossman's preference was for dispersal.)

None of the earlier new towns had been treated in a multicentred way, Sylvester-Evans told the inquiry. The Minister did not, however, want a shapeless urban sprawl. Wolverton, Stony Stratford and Bletchley would be allowed to retain their identities. But none of them

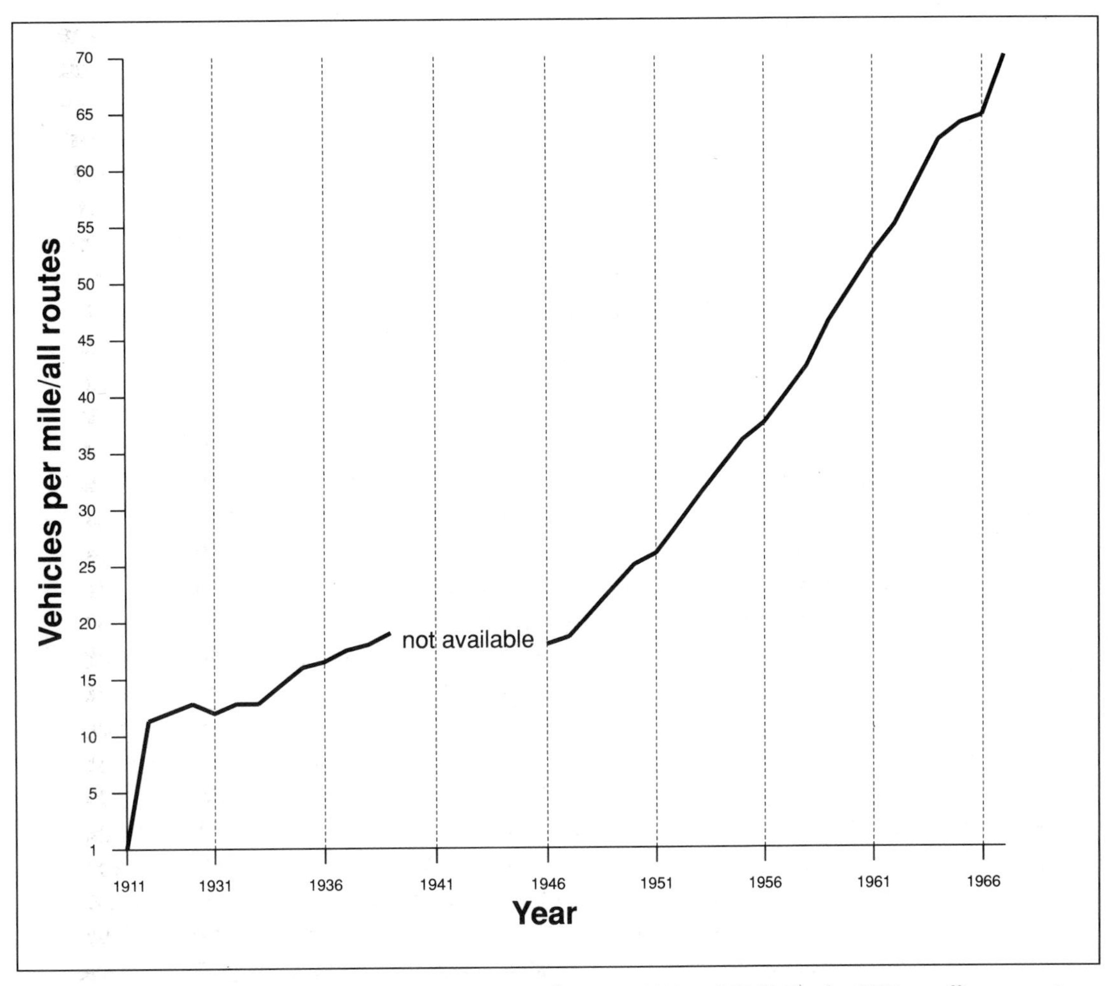

The growth in vehicles per mile of road in Britain between 1911 and 1967. By the 1960s traffic congestion was becoming serious in the wealthy counties of the south east.

was to be pre-eminent.[13] Bletchley, it seemed, far from being the centre of a far greater city, was going to be shunted into a siding.

The inquiry ended on a Monday evening, a mere four days after it had begun. Geoffrey Godber said he hoped to deliver his report to the Minister within a month. In a footnote the *Wolverton Express* observed that Bletchley had taken fifteen years to increase its population by 15,000. Yet if the Government went ahead with its plan to bring 75,000

157
GYR

Londoners to North Bucks by 1981, it would involve almost five times as much growth in thirteen years.[14]

True to his word Godber sent his report to the Minister before the end of August but, for one reason or another, Whitehall failed to keep to Crossman's proposed timetable. The Draft North Buckinghamshire New Town (Designation Order) was not made until 11 January 1967. The job of announcing it, and of naming the new city Milton Keynes, fell to Anthony Greenwood, who succeeded Crossman as Housing Minister.

The inspector's report is unlikely to have been welcomed in Whitehall. Godber suggested that an expanded Bletchley, half the size of the proposed new city, would have been more generally acceptable. He thought the proposed density too low and drew attention to the serious engineering problems raised by drainage. Urging cuts of 6,738 acres from the proposed site he said: 'If my recommendations are adopted the result will be a designated area of about 18,600 acres, appreciably bigger than Leicester with its population of 267,000. This is sufficient to accommodate 279,000 people at 15 to the acre – not at all a high overall density – or 223,200 at 12 to the acre.'[15]

The Ministry of Housing disregarded Godber's cautious proposals. Officials were determined that the huge new development they had in mind should not be strangled by lack of space. The Ministry's forceful designation letter was signed by John Palmer, an assistant secretary in the new towns division. 'The amount of land required for development on the scale proposed here,' he wrote, 'cannot be settled by simple comparison with the new towns of smaller size already started, still less with existing towns which show such formidable problems of traffic congestion because of their centralised structure.'[16]

Palmer also made clear that the Ministry wanted a site large enough to incorporate Bletchley, Wolverton and Stony Stratford in the new city 'in a manner which preserves rather than obliterates their strong and individual sense of local community'. Thus, only 3,300 acres were lopped off the original site, reducing it from 25,200 to 21,900 acres, or about thirty-four square miles. Within this site the Government proposed homes and jobs for 150,000 Londoners, 70,000 of them by 1981. For Arthur Snaith, secretary of the North Bucks Association (as for the National Farmers Union), the decision was a bitter disappointment, but he met it with magnanimity: 'it is now up to everyone to play their part in making it a happy community,' he told the local paper.[17]

The advent of the new city was widely reported by Fleet Street but only the *Guardian* asked: 'Dawley, Crawley, Corby and now Milton Keynes. Who chooses new town names?'

LEFT: Bletchley Park, 1860–1906, once the centre of Bletchley social life: during World War II it was Britain's cypher-cracking hub.

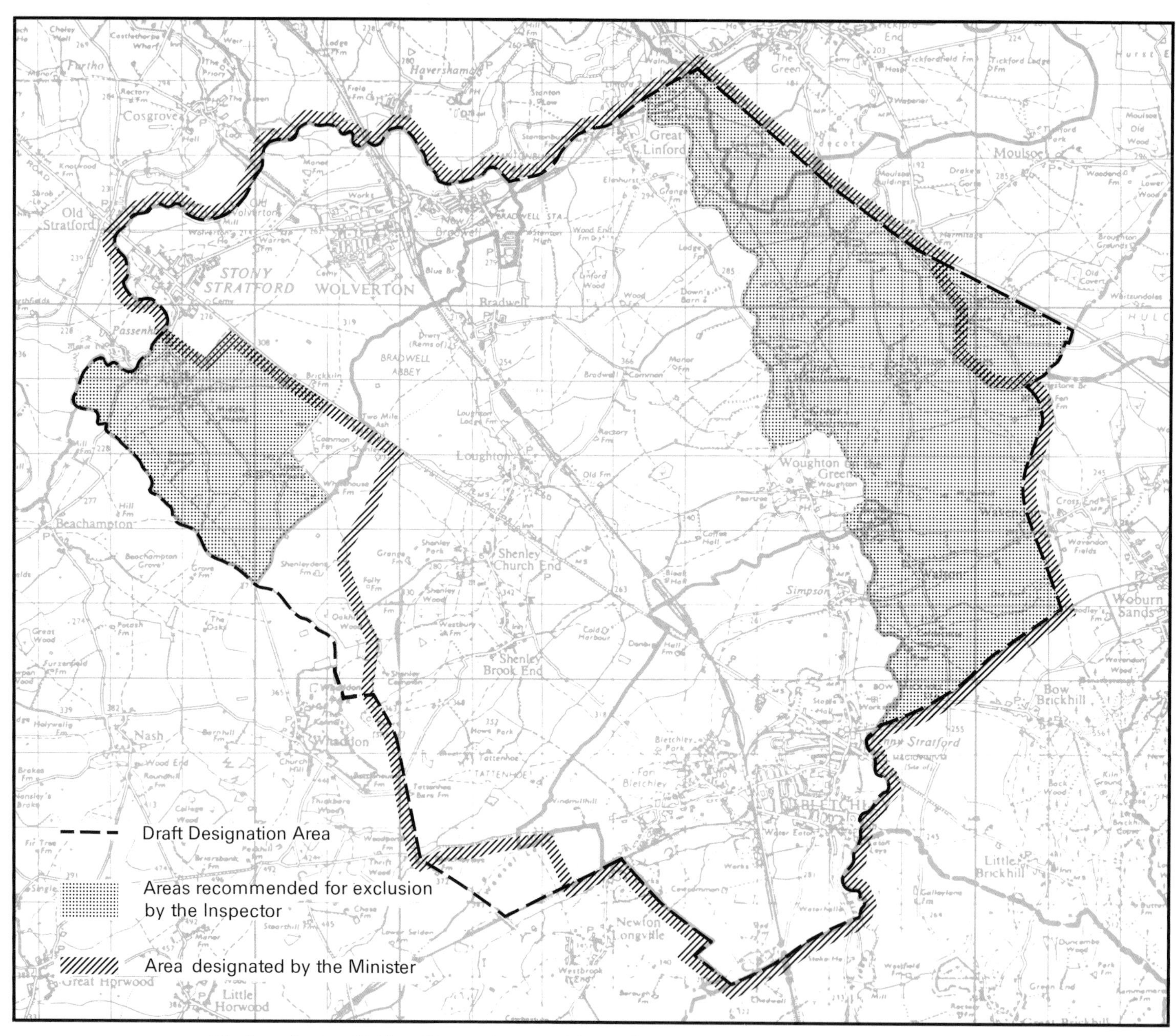

The boundaries of Milton Keynes designated by Anthony Greenwood in 1967. Huge cuts were recommended by the inspector who ran the public inquiry. Most of these were rejected by the Government.

The answer, corroborated by Sylvester-Evans, was none other than Tony Greenwood. He 'selected the name of a tiny village engulfed by the new city because the three old towns due for absorption ... all seemed too touchy about local pride'.[18]

Milton Keynes was formally designated a new town on 23 January 1967; it took until March to establish a development corporation, and on 1 April 1967 Anthony Greenwood announced that Lord Campbell of Eskan would be its first chairman. Was it true, as Aron Owen had argued, that the project had long since been unstoppable? Many believed so. Evidence submitted in November 1966 to the Royal Commission on Local Government by Newport Pagnell Urban and Rural District Councils, for instance, assumed that the new city was on the way. Yet new towns have been strangled at birth. Ipswich already had a master plan and had been through a public inquiry into its draft designation order when the Treasury, in the throes of a sterling crisis, killed it off in 1969.[19] Geoffrey Godber was right. Up to the time of its formal designation, Milton Keynes might have been stifled.

The Ministry pushed on with it because the country was faced with a population explosion. As the ration-book 1940s had given way to the more hopeful 1950s, Britons had begun to have more babies. By 1964 the population was growing as it had not done for decades. The facts were spelt out by Alun Sylvester-Evans at the North Bucks inquiry: Britain's population was forecast to grow by 20 million by the year 2000 and the epicentre of this expanding human cloud was the London metropolitan region. Room for these people had to be found somewhere. But why was North Bucks thought suitable? Why not, as Sir Frank Markham argued, expand in Norfolk or at Aldershot?

PETROL
GARAGE
HIGH STREET

2

Antecedents

Few people were better equipped to answer that question than Sir Frank himself. An Oxford don turned MP, who had been born in Stony Stratford and become the historian of Milton Keynes, he well knew that North Bucks, although unmarked by great medieval or eighteenth century monuments, had time and again felt the feet of surveyors intent on changing the economic geography of Britain. The Roman legions came first in about AD 50 and established a camp called Magiovinium. They were building Watling Street which went straight as an arrow from London to Chester. It was, Markham says, 'probably the most important road in Romanised Britain'.[1]

The route the Romans established never lost its importance. Following centuries of use by riders and packmen, stage-coaches began regular service in 1673, and by the end of the eighteenth century forty a day, pulled by up to six horses, streamed in and out of Stony Stratford. A similar number of inns and ale houses grew up to cater for travellers ranging from bishops to salesmen. London gossip was little over five hours old when it got to North Bucks. A 'stage' departing from near St Paul's at 8.30 a.m. arrived at Stony Stratford by 1.47 p.m. By 5 a.m. the following morning it was in Manchester.

Where the Roman legions led, the canal surveyors eventually followed. The Oxford Canal, the first waterway to connect London and Birmingham, went circuitously by way of the Thames and was in use as early as 1780. It took the engineers another twenty-five years to cut a more direct route. (Tunnels of 2,000 and 3,000 yards were needed at Braunston and Blisworth and the Ouse required an aqueduct.) But when they succeeded, the opening of the Grand Junction transformed North Bucks. Canal barges were the motorway juggernauts of their time. They cut transport costs.

Left: Stony Stratford High Street in 1910: stage-coaches once stopped at inns in the town en route for Manchester and Holyhead.

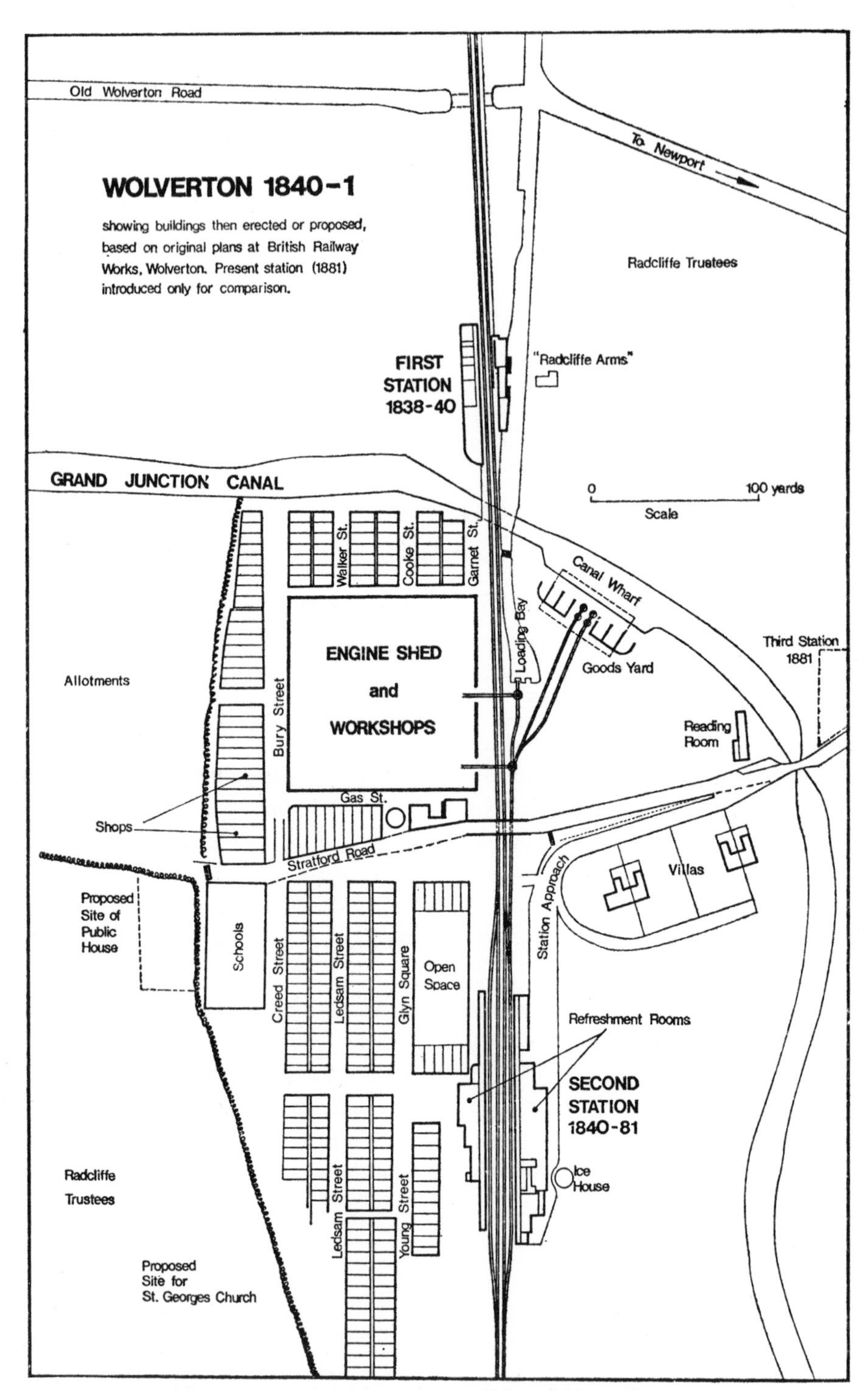
WOLVERTON 1840-1
showing buildings then erected or proposed, based on original plans at British Railway Works, Wolverton. Present station (1881) introduced only for comparison.
Old Wolverton Road
To Newport
Radcliffe Trustees
FIRST STATION 1838-40
"Radcliffe Arms"
GRAND JUNCTION CANAL
0
100 yards
Scale
Walker St.
Cooke St.
Garnet St.
Canal Wharf
Loading Bay
Goods Yard
Third Station 1881
ENGINE SHED and WORKSHOPS
Allotments
Bury Street
Reading Room
Gas St.
Shops
Stratford Road
Villas
Station Approach
Proposed Site of Public House
Schools
Creed Street
Ledsam Street
Glyn Square
Open Space
Refreshment Rooms
SECOND STATION 1840-81
Ice House
Radcliffe Trustees
Ledsam Street
Young Street
Proposed Site for St. Georges Church

Wolverton in the early 1840s: a planned railway town.

The heyday of the Grand Junction was, however, brief. The £100 shares in the company stood at £242 in 1832 and paid thirteen per cent interest. A few years later trade was down by a half, the stage-coach business had been decimated and the industrialisation of North Bucks had begun. A new generation of surveyors was on the way. George Stephenson and his son Robert examined the lie of the land in 1831 and only seven years later a double-track railway stretched the full 112 miles between London and Birmingham.

The London & Birmingham chose Wolverton for its central engine repair works in 1836. It was a choice with far-reaching consequences, as was foreseen four years later by the *London & Birmingham Railway Guide*. The authors, after noting the 'grand central depot', added: 'This station is an extensive establishment, and will probably give rise to the formation of a new town.'[2]

They were right. With the coming of steam, engineering transformed North Bucks. The L & B began by building railwaymen's houses in a way never seen before in this hitherto remote rural backwater. They were lined up on a grid of streets. The engine works then expanded into engine design and, in particular, to making McConnell's 'bloomer' engines. (Just as Mrs Bloomer's pantaloons showed off a lady's legs so these express locomotives showed off their wheels.) Printing arrived next, as demand for railway timetables (and the presence of employable railwaymen's daughters) drew in McCorquodales from Lancashire. A planned Victorian town was arising in North Bucks.

Bletchley's development was more variegated. It was a mere village when the Stephensons decided to put a station between it and the staging post at Fenny Stratford. Bletchley station subsequently became a junction when cross-country lines were opened to Oxford in 1851 and to Bedford and Cambridge eleven years later. The railways attracted brickworks, brushworks and smoke-filled engine sheds and, gradually, the two settlements coalesced. Yet even though the railways dominated Bletchley, it was never, like Wolverton, a company town.

The 1920s saw, for the first time, a fall in railway jobs in Wolverton and presumably at Bletchley too. Things picked up in the 1930s and Ron Staniford, the young editor of the newly founded *Bletchley District Gazette* began to campaign for a 'bigger, better, brighter Bletchley'. The county council was positive too and commissioned a report which identified the railway junction as the most suitable growth point in North Bucks. Development of an unplanned kind followed. Then World War II came and turned Bletchley station into a troop train interchange while Bletchley Park was filled with huts and top secrets. 'Ultra' was based there and the huts housed the hundreds of cryptographers who broke the cyphers of the Nazi high command.

The war years, which threw sombre light on the unwieldiness of London and saw government take unprecedented powers to move people, requisition property and direct

Wolverton as proposed by the futuristic Geoffrey Jellicoe in 1945. 'The old town has gone. Tall buildings separated by gay and spacious gardens have taken its place.'

industry, also gave respectability to regional planning. It cropped up everywhere. In London, in the midst of the bombing, the county council somehow found time to commission Sir Patrick Abercrombie to prepare a plan for the metropolis. In Wolverton two councillors, inspired in 1943 by a Town and Country Planning Association conference, urged their colleagues to expand the town by 30,000 people.

Wolverton took the idea seriously and commissioned Geoffrey (later Sir Geoffrey) Jellicoe to advise them. His plan, published in 1945, identified the town's main shortcomings as 'insufficient variety in population' (the company town syndrome) and 'a lack of harmony between the urban features and their rural setting' (the place was too bricky). Jellicoe, who was a landscape architect, a planner and a futurist, couched his proposal in two stages. First came the down-to-earth part – 1,300 new houses and a 'landscape way' for strolling and cycling. The more visionary stage called for the bulldozing of the existing town and its replacement by a *ville radieuse* of towers that almost certainly owed its inspiration to Le Corbusier.

According to Francis Hyde a storm of controversy blew up when the local paper published Jellicoe's futurist drawing. 'It showed,' he added enigmatically, 'how keenly interested the people still are in the future of their town, how conscious they are of its imperfections, and how determined they are to grasp at every opportunity for its improvement.'[3]

RIGHT: Great Linford Manor, built in 1688/9 and remodelled in the eighteenth century, stands in the north of the city adjacent to the Grand Union Canal.

None of Jellicoe's proposals was carried out. The 'problems of implementation were too daunting' for a small urban district. Wolverton decided instead to build prefabs at New Bradwell.[4]

Wolverton fared no better from Abercrombie's Greater London Plan of 1944, which contained proposals for ten close-in satellite towns, ten remoter developments (including Aylesbury and Bletchley) and a list of 109 towns that might be suitable for expansion. Bletchley, with its 'excellent communications', was recommended for a new town of 50,000 people. Wolverton got not a crumb.

Decisions were, nevertheless, being made in Westminster that were to have far-reaching consequences for North Bucks. Clement Attlee's Government was determined to try to correct the prewar imbalance of job opportunities between north and south, and also had to do something about the country's overcrowded cities. Three seminal actions followed. The first, the Distribution of Industry Act 1945, created 'development areas' in the smokestack regions of the north and gave Whitehall power to control industrial expansion in the south. The second, the New Towns Act 1946, empowered the Government to provide for 'overspill' from congested cities by setting up Treasury-financed new town development corporations. The third occurred when Alfred Barnes, the Transport Minister, had a diagram of 800 miles of motor roads displayed in the Members' tea room in the House of Commons in May 1946. As David Starkie notes, this 'tea room plan', which outlined the hourglass-shaped M1, M4, M5, M6 and M62 network, was acted upon by a Conservative government a decade later.[5]

Bletchley, as intent as ever on becoming 'bigger, better and brighter', watched these developments closely and prepared a plan for a new town of 60,000 people. The Labour-controlled council seemed to have grounds for optimism. It was 'probably the most co-operative and go-ahead urban district council in the country'.[6] And at Westminster Lewis Silkin MP, Attlee's Minister of Town and Country Planning, was keen to get moving with some of his innovatory development corporations.

However, when Silkin published a 'Memorandum on the Greater London Plan' in May 1947, he made no mention of a Bletchley new town. He proposed, instead, expansion from 7,500 to 40,000 people. Yet when he stopped in for tea with the councillors the following year he could confirm nothing. Meanwhile Buckinghamshire was having doubts and the town of Bedford was worried about contamination of the Ouse. The following year the Ministry announced that large-scale development at Bletchley was impractical. It was precluded by water and sewage problems locally and by a balance of payments crisis at Westminster. A disappointed Silkin told an even more disappointed deputation of councillors that the town would have to limit its growth to 20,000 souls.

Bletchley, which by 1950 had built no fewer than 500 postwar houses, may have been bloodied but it was unbowed. After asking Whitehall to allow expansion *by* 20,000 (the Minister, officials replied, had said expansion *to* 20,000), a revised town map was prepared and agreed with the county council. It provided for growth from 10,248 in 1950 to 19,300 in 1970. Meanwhile Bletchley was hard at work with ministers and officials pushing for town development powers. Some way had to be found to reduce the cost to the ratepayers of accelerated growth, a delegation told Miss Evelyn Sharp, deputy secretary at the Housing Ministry. She sympathised, said that new powers depended on new legislation, and urged Bletchley to get ready for it.

Bletchley's pushy but pragmatic Labour councillors were constantly in London during 1951 while the details of the Bill were being settled. One concern was whether they would be able to buy land for better-class private houses. They feared that if they failed to attract the relatively well-to-do, the result would be a loss of rateable income and the impoverishment of the town's social life.

The council and in particular John Smithie, its engineer and surveyor, were not, however, prepared to follow Miss Sharp's advice about waiting. They drew up a plan to build 300 houses a year and began on the first 100 at Whiteley Crescent on land they did not own and without approval from the Ministry. Their choice of a steel-frame and brick building technology underscores their willingness to experiment and their determination to get on.

The general election of October 1951 brought down Clement Attlee, returned Winston Churchill to Downing Street and ushered in thirteen years of Conservative government. Harold Macmillan was made Housing Minister, found Silkin's Town Development Bill in his in-tray and promptly enacted it. He was looking for ways to redeem a promise to build 300,000 houses a year. The Town Development Act 1952 promised to help. It empowered cities to contribute to the cost of building houses in outlying towns so that overcrowded families could move out. It also contained special retroactive provisions to cover the cost of work already under way in Bletchley. The energetic railwaymen had, at long last, found a basis for financing the expansion of their town.

Yet, although Whitehall demanded that Bletchley produce capital expenditure estimates for the first stage of its expansion, Pat Mortimer notes with surprise that no comparable request was made for a town plan:

> ... it is difficult to see why a small town, with so little planning expertise, should have been allowed and encouraged to embark on its own scheme without ... an overall master plan ... Many of the unsatisfactory aspects of Bletchley's layout could have been avoided if, at this stage, the ministry had insisted on ... [a plan] ... It may be that here the honourable tradition of not interfering unduly with the way local authorities worked was paramount.[7]

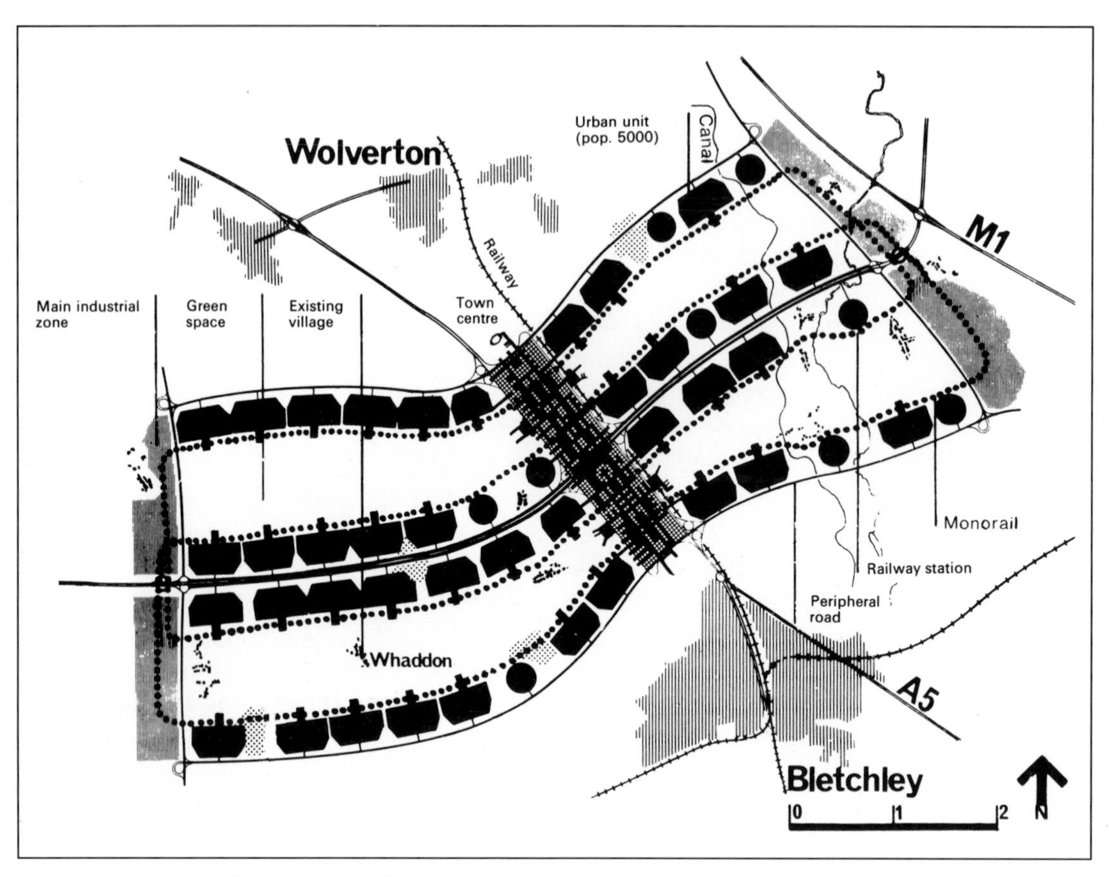

Fred Pooley's plan for a monorail-based new town in North Bucks. The town centre would have been a multi-decked structure with the A5 Holyhead Road running beneath it. The residents would have lived in 'townships'.

Plans were, it seems, for Wolverton. Bletchley was a place of action.

Throughout the 1950s the council drove ahead with its pioneering town development scheme, although the annual output of houses was always closer to 200 than the intended 300. In 1957, following a developer's proposal for an eighty-acre industrial estate to the north of Watling Street (then the A5), the Ministry proposed a 're-appraisement' by the general manager of Crawley new town. The result was a report critical in some respects but sufficiently complimentary in others for the district council, the county and then the Minister to agree the following year that expansion should proceed to 23,700.

But if Bletchley was consistently expansionist during the 1950s, the county council was more changeable. Its first development plan (required by the Town and Country Planning Act 1947) duly incorporated Bletchley's intentions but made no mention of any new town. Indeed, in July 1951, the chairman of the planning committee emphasised that nowhere in Buckinghamshire was suitable for one.

However, by the time the county plan came up for review in 1959, Fred Pooley, who had been appointed chief architect and planning officer in 1954, was in charge. Pooley, a purring, tweedy, aitch-dropping teddy-bear of a man, was one of the outstanding county technical officers of his generation. With an anti-development lobby growing up in the Chilterns in South Bucks and with the brand-new M1 motorway opening up the county's 'frozen north' (traffic zoomed on to the first seventy-two miles in 1959), he drew up a plan for a new city of 250,000 people between Bletchley and Wolverton.

A series of reports on the design of the new city was published by Pooley and his personal assistant Bill Berrett in 1962. In them these visionary architects argued that 'it was impossible at reasonable costs' to plan a city satisfactorily 'for 100 per cent motor car use' and that 'public transport should be seriously investigated'.[8]

Proposals followed for a city based on a 'free' monorail to be paid for out of the rates. Townships of 5,000 to 7,000 people were to be placed along the overhead railway, like 'beads on a string', with no house more than seven minutes' walk from a station. In 1964 the county council agreed a new plan. Pooley was well aware of the ambitions of Bletchley and had, therefore, taken care to allow for 'major expansions for existing towns'. But the plan also provided for the monorail city. No county council had before done anything like it – and none has since. Pooley, in launching his extraordinary high-tech project and in convincing his councillors to back it, had laid foundations for the future city of Milton Keynes.

3

WHERE WILL THE PEOPLE LIVE?

The 1960s were a period when Britain thought big. They were years of rising expectations, motorways, the Beatles, hippies and the Campaign for Nuclear Disarmament. In government, they saw national and regional planning elevated to unprecedented importance. The *Manchester Guardian*, reflecting the spirit of the times, appointed a planning correspondent. It was the first national newspaper to do so and the job was given to Brian Redhead.

At the Ministry of Housing and Local Government Miss Sharp was made permanent secretary, and became Dame Evelyn. Together with J. D. Jones, her deputy, and Jimmy James, the chief planner, she led a team of talented officials which was responsible for an unprecedented outpouring of town and regional plans.

After the general election of 1964, Harold Wilson took the process further, creating a Department of Economic Affairs and charging George Brown, its first Minister, to produce a national plan. Shortly afterwards regional economic planning councils were set up throughout England. Economic analysis and planned urban development were seen as companion mechanisms for directing public investment. The object was to create an efficient and equitable Britain. London would be managed. The north would be revived. Public investment would lead the way.

The 1960s also saw a steep rise in motor-car ownership and with it the coming of congested roads. Travel in towns, where traffic management was virtually unknown and parking still a free-for-all, became steadily more difficult and led to public outcry. Ernest Marples, the Transport Minister, responded by commissioning two reports of far-reaching consequence. One, 'Road pricing: the economic and technical possibilities', made an eloquent case for pay-as-you-drive road charges. The other, Sir Colin Buchanan's better-known 'Traffic in towns', advocated the building of urban motorways *and* demonstrated the scale of the roads that would be needed in dense, old-fashioned cities if everyone were to drive to work.

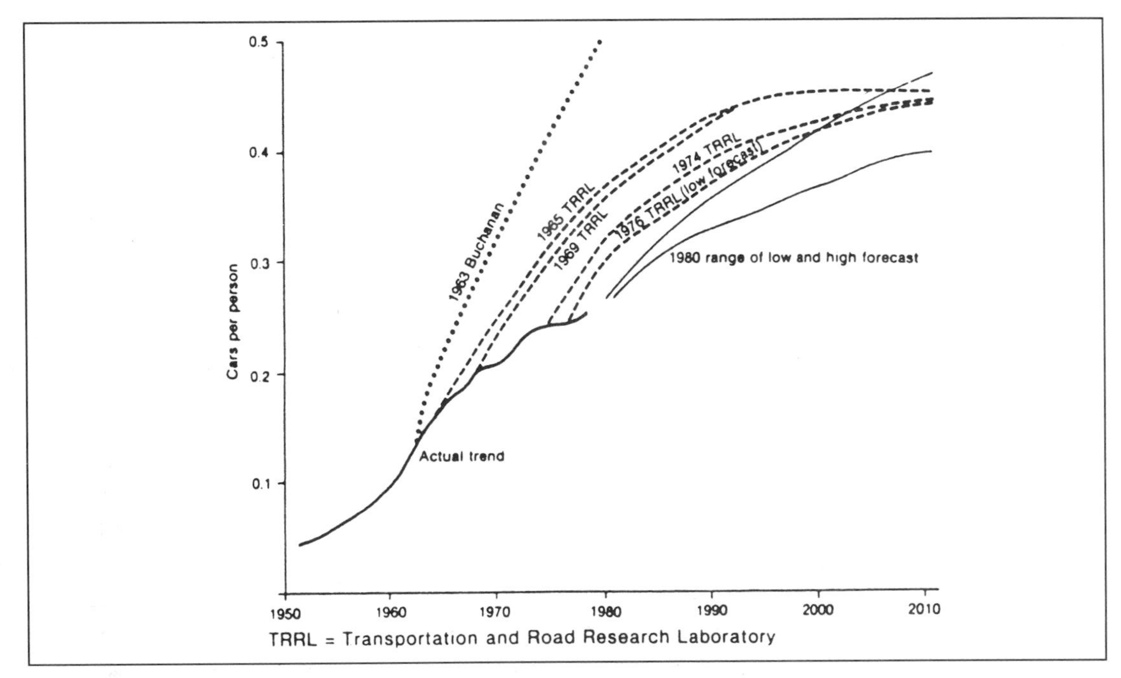

Cars per person in Britain in the 1960s and 1970s: Buchanan and the Transport and Road Research Laboratory may have forecast growth rates too high but overcrowded roads were still very common.

Computers were coming into use too and urban-transport planners used them to analyse hitherto unmanageable amounts of data. London pioneered the new methodology but, because of its size, took years to obtain results. Leicester was another pioneer and, being smaller, was first to produce a computer-based plan. The print-outs made clear that cars were going to create huge problems for old-fashioned cities.

The new city of Milton Keynes, conceived by Buckinghamshire County Council and brought into being by Harold Wilson's Labour Government, was a product of this exciting, postwar, motor-age Britain, but population pressure was its ultimate justification.

Twenty years before, when the people of Britain were being scrutinised by a Royal Commission on the Industrial Population (Cmd 6153 of 1940), it was not their numbers but their *distribution* that gave rise to concern. Births were typically 600,000 a year in that period. They climbed to 881,000 in 1947 – the peak of the postwar baby boom – and then, reassuringly for the government actuary, fell back in the 1950s to prewar levels. Suddenly the unforeseen began to happen. Perhaps because Britons, in Harold Macmillan's perceptive

and, at the time, shocking phrase, had 'never had it so good', the number of births started climbing again and by 1962 it was 839,000. Not surprisingly concern switched to population *growth*.

The government actuary scrambled to revise his population projections and, determined not to undershoot again, assumed that births would exceed 850,000 a year in the mid-1960s and rise to 1.1 million a year after 1967. A factor in these calculations was immigration from the West Indies, India and Pakistan prior to the Commonwealth Immigrants Act 1962. The resulting forecast was that the population of England and Wales would grow by 7 million over the two decades up to 1981. Such growth was unprecedented. It had certainly not been catered for by the counties in their development plans.

Warning bells sounded at the Ministry of Housing and Local Government. Where was this incoming tide of people going to live? The Ministry sought answers in a series of regional assessments the first of which, *The South East Study*, was logical, lucid and daring. Its drafting bore the unmistakable mark of Jimmy James, the chief planner, whom Crossman described as 'absolutely first rate'. Its working assumptions were that over the twenty years up to 1981 the population of the south east – in those days a region bounded by Dover, Weymouth and the Wash – would grow naturally by 2.4 million. Migration from other parts of the country and abroad was forecast to boost that figure to 3.5 million. Beyond 1981 the demographers saw even more growth – another 3.5 million by the end of the century.[1]

These were not comfortable prospects. They flew in the face of years of effort to stop the 'drift to the south': furthermore, as the study acknowledged, the figures on which they were based were forecasts and might well turn out to be as exaggerated as those of the 1940s had been understated. But Jimmy James was never a man to be chicken-hearted. 'If the forecast ... proves wrong ... ,' the study argued, 'it is more likely to be an underestimate than an overestimate.' Hard-headed practicality underlay this assertion. In building towns the pace of development can always be slowed down; it is infinitely harder to speed it up.

Yet even in the much-planned 1960s James and his colleagues found it necessary to ask whether or not the shaping of the metropolis might be left to market forces. They had to acknowledge that it could be, but at a cost of cuts in the green belt and 'continuous sprawl'. Road problems 'when multiplied by the increase in traffic' would have been 'enormous'. Overall the effects would have been 'intolerable, inefficient and expensive'.

Far from accepting market forces, the planners aimed to refashion the thrust of London's development. In this they were not alone. Had not *The Economist*, seeking ways to break London's unhealthy dominance of Britain, recently advocated moving Parliament to

LEFT: Willen Church and Manor Farm seen from the old Newport–Bletchley road in 1972. The viewpoint today is on the edge of Willen Lake.

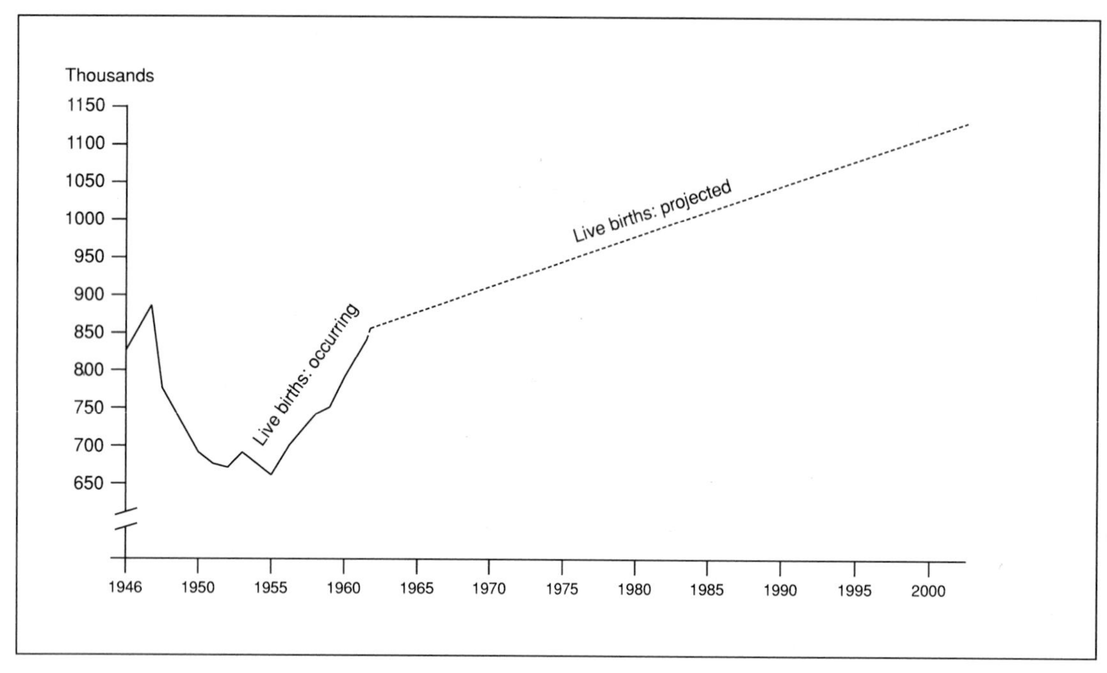

The forecast of population growth underlying The South East Study *which led to decisions to build new towns at Milton Keynes, Northampton and Peterborough.*

'Elizabetha', a new city in Yorkshire? As *The South East Study* put it, satellite new towns and expansions, as advocated by Abercrombie in 1944, were able to receive London's human overflow. But, given their relatively small size, they 'do nothing to turn off the tap'. The problem was the overpowering magnetism of the London job market. It followed, the study said, that 'a big change in the economic balance within the south east is needed to modify the dominance of London and to get a more even distribution of growth'.

'The aim should be to develop centres of growth alternative to London.' The biggest would rank as 'cities of the future'. They would have to be 'large and strong'. The authors of the study then got down to figures, warning that many were tentative, and that there 'may be surprises'. Of the forecast total of 3.5 million people, the county planners were given responsibility for allocating land for 2 million. Responsibility for the remainder – between 1 million and 1.25 million – would be shouldered by the Government. This nationally planned development would provide, in particular, for low-income Londoners driven out by bulldozers (urban renewal was in full swing) and for migrants attracted to London by the prospects of jobs.

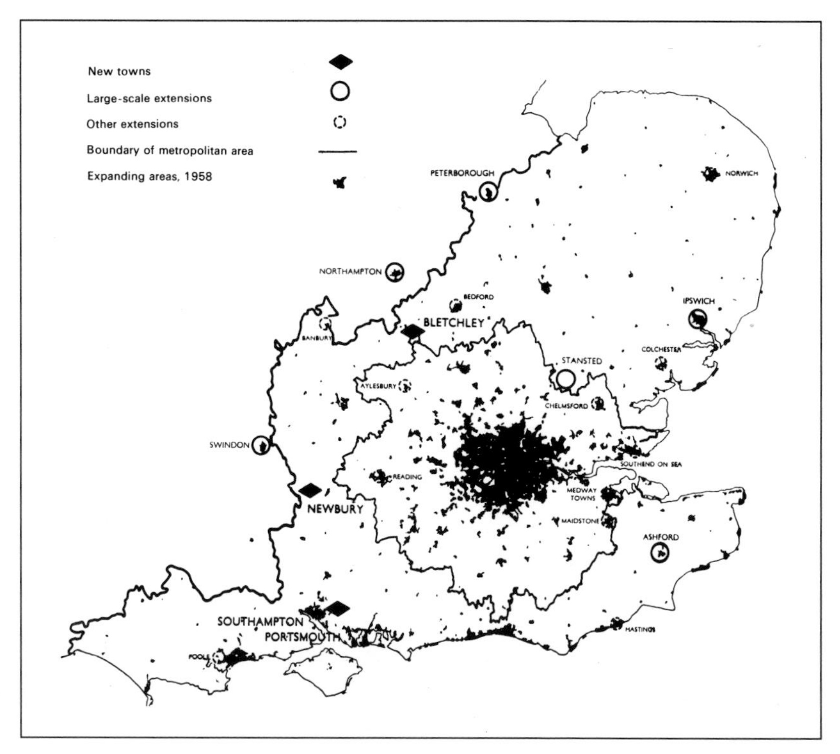

The developments proposed in The South East Study. *'Counter-magnets' or new cities at Newbury and at Southampton–Portsmouth were never implemented: nor were new towns at Stansted and Ashford.*

However, the authors of the study warned against trying to label too firmly who would live where. The scale and location of development was the key point to get right. Sites should be well away from London and selected not because, for instance, they made use of derelict land, but because they promised success. Big schemes promised better than small ones. They would attract large firms, provide the school-leavers needed by office firms and sustain large shopping centres. Furthermore, the 'cost per head of providing basic services should fall with size'.

The specification for the big schemes did not end there. They should be located 'where both industry and commerce can be expected to thrive'. Links with London, ports and airports would be important. Roads were of 'primary importance'. Ebenezer Howard's turn-of-the-century thinking about small-scale satellites was firmly put aside. *The South East Study* advocated 'counter-magnets' – alternatives to London that would offer much of what could be found in the metropolis itself. Southampton–Portsmouth, Bletchley and

Newbury–Hungerford were all identified as potential locations for counter-magnets.

Bletchley, already served by the newly opened M1 and about to welcome British Rail's shiny new InterCity electrics (the first regular 100 m.p.h. service in Europe), was given high praise. 'It would be hard to find an area which would be more attractive to industrialists. There is plenty of room for building, and, in the very long term, a new city of a quarter of a million might arise.' In the meantime homes for 75,000 could be built by 1981.

George Cyriax, writing in *The Financial Times*, observed that Bletchley 'has some of the best communications of any region outside London. It has some of the least attractive surroundings. And it has thrown up no organised opposition ... to the idea of creating a city of 250,000...' Turning to the question of implementation he added: 'The Bucks County Council do not conceal their desire that the new city at Bletchley should be a mainly county affair, with the participation of private property developers ... The authorities in London are much more cautious, and tend to see the new towns, with their autonomous corporations, as a much closer model.'[2]

The reaction of North Bucks to *The South East Study* was varied. The *Wolverton Express* suspected that it marked the end for Fred Pooley's plan. Announcing the report it said: 'City expansion for the Bletchley area. Not even a mention for Wolverton or Newport Pagnell. And what seems to be the quick good-bye to dreams of an ultra-modern monorail city somewhere in the Whaddon Chase country.'[3]

For Bletchley councillors one section of the study undid, in a few words, the aspirations of twenty years. Bletchley's 1961 population of 16,900 was, the study commented, 'not a sufficient base for building up the area by means of [town] expansion'. It is hard not to feel sympathy for the good burghers of Bletchley. Strive as they might to turn their modest railway junction into a town, they had been snubbed first by Buckinghamshire County Council and then by the Government.

On 31 August 1964, at the Park Lane Hotel in London, Bletchley Council struck back. Jim Cassidy, the chairman, unveiled a plan prepared by Bernard Engle and Partners of Lincoln's Inn which showed how the railway town itself, and not the 'area' of North Bucks, might be expanded to house 150,000 people. It was a daring scheme in which grotty brickpits were to be turned to good account. An architect's drawing showed them as a dinghy-dotted marina, the glistening waters of which reflected the outlines of five slender skyscrapers.

Bletchley's initiative was widely reported and *The Financial Times* noted that it was 'in direct conflict with the county council's plan'. The paper went on to spell out Cassidy's opposition to a free-standing city. It would have no roots and no social facilities. It was 'completely ludicrous'.[4]

LEFT: *The site of the new city.*

Bletchley's bid for a place in the sun. The 1964 Engle plan proposed to expand the town to 150,000 people at a cost of £195m. Flats tower beside a marina.

The conflict was expanded upon by the *Chronicle & Echo* in a report of a special council meeting. 'It would,' said Bill Caldwell, chairman of the development committee, 'be disastrous for [Bletchley] if the new city is built six miles out of the town ... the amount of money put into Bletchley warrants further ... expansions and the line we take in the new plan has the backing of the Chamber of Trade.'[5]

Clifford Clarke, moving a motion to reject the Engle plan, was reported to have 'urged the council to forget the past and petty jealousies and to reopen negotiations ... with the county council for a more balanced, sane and sensible development of Bletchley'. Notwithstanding the councillor's fears that the district council lacked the resources to promote so huge a project, the voting went in favour of it.

Sparring between the local authorities spluttered on for the rest of 1964. The county busied itself locally, reassuring towns like Wolverton and Olney that they could be thriving satellites of the monorail city, and in Whitehall, where it pressed the Ministry of Housing to give it a major role in creating the 'counter-magnet'. Robert Maxwell, newly elected as MP for Buckingham, urged the councils to stop squabbling and prepare for expansion alongside a new town development corporation. 'Look forward: be bold,' he said.[6] The Ministry, meanwhile, was concerned about the impact a new city might have on its surroundings. Richard Crossman, the Housing Minister, therefore appointed Hugh Wilson to report to him on how to handle development in a triangle bounded by Bletchley, Northampton and Bedford. (Wilson, a distinguished architect-planner, had earlier prepared master plans for new towns at Cumbernauld near Glasgow, and Skelmersdale near Liverpool.)

Finally, following a meeting in December between John Smithie, Bletchley's engineer, and Fred Pooley, the county planning officer, the two authorities agreed to take Maxwell's advice. Bletchley would withdraw its opposition to the monorail city. The county would prepare a new town map that would give Bletchley room to grow to 40,000 people by 1981.

The winter of 1964/5 was, economically speaking, a gloomy one. The Labour Government's huge programme of public expenditure created a lack of confidence in the pound. James Callaghan, the Chancellor, pushed interest rates up to seven per cent yet still the spending went on. On 3 February, Richard Crossman recorded in his diary that he had made 'my second major statement of my career as Minister: this was about London overspill and the use of new towns to deal with it. I announced the new town at Bletchley.' He went on to announce the doubling of the populations of Northampton, Peterborough and Ipswich by setting up development corporations alongside the 'three famous boroughs'.[7]

Crossman told the House of Commons that the existing London new towns were filling up and that 'immediate decisions' were necessary if 'a disastrous gap in housing for Londoners' was to be avoided. He added that the Bletchley new town would be the largest since 1945 and, replying to a question from Robert Maxwell, said that discussions were still taking place with the county about whether or not to set up a development corporation. Crossman gave no hint of the location of the proposed town.[8]

Discussion about machinery went on until May when the county finally decided that, in the absence of financial guarantees from Westminster, building a new city was too great a risk to impose on the ratepayers. 'We have spent a lot of time and imagination and effort on this,' announced a disappointed Ralph Verney, chairman of the county's development subcommittee. 'We really think it would be a wonderful scheme. We believe in the monorail. We believe in the new city site.' But given uncertainties about the growth of the town, loan charges might rise above a 6d (old pence) rate. That was a risk the council dared not take. The new city would have to be built by the central government.[9]

But where should the city be built – on virgin land or adjacent to Bletchley? This issue continued to generate much passion. The county persisted with what had come to be known as 'Pooleyville'. Robert Maxwell, by contrast, was insistent that new should be grafted onto old. Yet rumour had it that Crossman favoured a free-standing new town. Jim Cassidy, chairman of Bletchley Council, lobbied furiously against such an idea and in favour of expanding the existing town. 'To build the new town away from Bletchley would be the biggest mistake Dick Crossman could make,' he told the London *Evening News* on the eve of a visit to Bletchley by Prime Minister Harold Wilson.[10]

'No one wants the new town,' Cassidy continued, 'not our people in Bletchley, not the industrialists in the area, not the farmers and landowners in the countryside around ... no one in fact but the planners at the Housing Ministry.'

4

The Chairman, the Board and the Consultants

The first hint of a solution that would satisfy both Jim Cassidy and Richard Crossman emerged with the publication late in 1965 of Hugh Wilson's report on development in the Bletchley-Northampton-Bedford triangle. The report was full of maps showing what looked like caterpillars crawling over the south Midlands but it also made clear the full extent of a town of 250,000 people. It showed three shaded circles extending from Bletchley to the northern towns.

The *Wolverton Express* was observant. In its account of the Wilson report it wrote: 'Wolverton, Bletchley and Newport Pagnell may be almost physically part of the ... new city at a site near Bletchley.'[1] The local paper's insight was confirmed four weeks later when Richard Crossman, publishing the provisional boundaries of the new city, revealed that they would embrace 25,200 acres - far more than any previous new town and larger than the 22,000 acres proposed by Fred Pooley for the monorail city.

The events that took place between Crossman's announcement of January 1966 and the appointment in April 1967 of Lord Campbell as first chairman of Milton Keynes Development Corporation are covered in Chapter 1. It is now time to pick up those threads again and look at Milton Keynes in its formative months. Board members, staff and master plan consultants all had to be appointed. Decisions had be taken whether or not, in the absence of a master plan, to freeze all development in the designated area. And above all, good working relations needed to be established with the local councils.

In all of this Jock Campbell, humanist, chairman of the *New Statesman*, ex-chairman of Bookers (originally sugar merchants in Demerara but latterly a trading conglomerate best known for its literary prize) played a dominant role. Crossman considered that Campbell's only equal as a left-wing tycoon was Robert Maxwell. Admittedly he found such 'idealistic, businessmen socialists ... a little bit of an embarrassment' but confessed to a real fondness

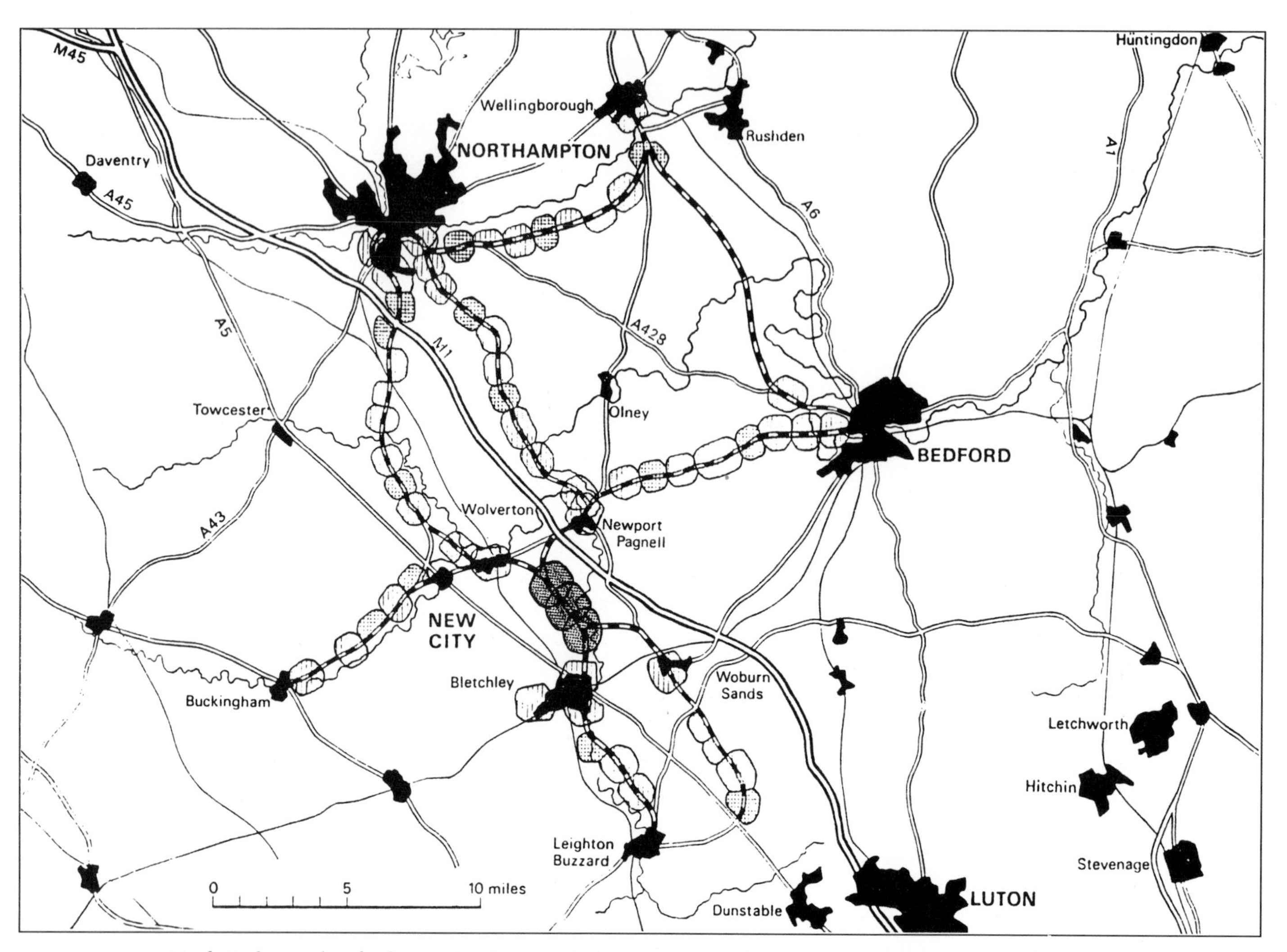

Hugh Wilson's plan for linear development linking the towns of the south Midlands. Trams or buses on busways would have enabled people to travel swiftly between new towns strung along the lines of existing roads.

for Campbell and his wife. He recorded: 'within his lights Jock remains a correct, high-minded socialist who enjoys having long talks about the morality of possessions and the taxation of wealth.' Campbell was clear, Crossman added, that Roy Jenkins' 1968 budget 'was against the wealthy socialists and welcomed it warmly'.[2]

Campbell's political convictions were born in Ireland, nurtured in Kent and matured in the plantations of Guyana. The process began in County Limerick where he was sent by his parents in 1916 to be out of the way of zeppelin raids. There, living with his grandparents, he spent, as was not unusual for a child in a big house, 'a lot of time with the servants and gamekeepers'. And from them he 'discovered that different people could describe the same events in totally different terms'. Back in Kent he discovered further contrasts between the life of 'great glamour' recounted by his mother and father on returning from visits to Demerara, and that of the servants, which took place behind the green baize door.

After Oxford, although keen to become a civil servant (he worked briefly in the Colonial Office), Campbell was persuaded to look at the sugar industry. 'I was fascinated by what I found,' he recalled, 'but also shocked ... by the appalling conditions in which people lived and worked.' The upshot was 'strong political feelings' about the need for Caribbean independence and a jelling of his conviction that people are more important than 'shops and ships and sugar estates'.

Campbell concluded from these experiences that if things were left 'to the tender mercies of the Conservatives – however good – you wouldn't have votes for women; you'd still be hanging sheep stealers'. He therefore joined the Labour party as well as deciding to make a business career in Bookers, thus, in two quick moves, qualifying himself to undertake a major commercial and industrial job for a left-wing government.

Sir Matthew Stevenson, permanent secretary at the Housing Ministry, was first to tell Campbell about Milton Keynes. The two men were at Lancaster House and Campbell later recalled being asked whether he 'knew anybody who would take on the chairmanship of the biggest new town in Europe'. Campbell suggested himself, explaining how that very morning he had decided to retire from Bookers. Stevenson showed interest but, to Campbell's surprise, never followed it up.

Not long afterwards, when at lunch with Tony Greenwood, Campbell found himself again being asked about Milton Keynes. Stevenson had, it transpired, said nothing about the Lancaster House meeting. Greenwood phoned later and said, 'Stevenson thought you were a respectable businessman but when he discovered you were in the Labour party, he absolutely clammed up about it.'[3] Campbell's appointment to be the first chairman of Milton Keynes followed shortly afterwards.

The new town's first month saw the Minister start to fill the places on the board. First, at Campbell's request, came Walter Ismay, 45, director and chief engineer of Yorkshire Imperial Metals. Ismay was made deputy chairman and, for the first time ever in a new town, full-time chief executive, at a salary of £10,000. His appointment was followed by that of a 'financial' member – Sandy Meikle, general manager of the Woolwich Equitable Building Society.

Then came four people connected with North Bucks, a local representation which,

John Menzies
PRICERITE
M & M. FRUITERERS.

Campbell noted, was 'exceptional' amongst new towns. Jim Cassidy, chairman of Bletchley Council, was Dundee-born and had himself arrived in Bletchley from London because his firm had migrated there. Ray Bellchambers, chief stores foreman at Wolverton Carriage Works, was chairman of Newport Pagnell Rural District and a Labour party member with trades union experience of farming.

The Minister's first woman appointee was Margaret Durbridge, a London-born magistrate, school governor and a founder of the North Bucks branch of the Council for the Preservation of Rural England. She had represented Newport Pagnell on Bucks County Council for six years and, characteristically for country districts in the 1960s, had recently been re-elected unopposed. The local paper reported that she believed in the need for an imaginative plan for transport and that 'the monorail system could well be the answer'.

The fourth local appointee was Ralph Verney of Steeple Claydon, a county alderman and the political force behind Pooley's plan for a new city. Major (later Sir Ralph) Verney's family had lived at Claydon House for 400 years and he himself had connections reaching far and wide across the county. Like Margaret Durbridge, Verney told the press that 'a monorail system will be the best for the proposed new city. We ... worked the cost out at two shillings a week a home with each home being only minutes away from the service.'[4]

London, which was intended to be the source of so many inhabitants of the new city, was represented by Horace Cutler, deputy leader and housing committee chairman on the Conservative-controlled Greater London Council (GLC), and Lady Serota, Labour's chief whip on the same council. Poor Wolverton once again suffered neglect. None of its town councillors was appointed.

Jock Campbell called his first board meeting on 15 June 1967 at Milton Keynes Community Centre. The new city must, he said, be made a place for people. 'We must try to offer them an environment as conducive as possible to good health, happiness, stimulation and satisfaction during their youth and working lives, and contentment and care in their old age.'

He went on to set out the board's top priorities: to build strong relationships with the local authorities and the GLC; to get the appointment of master planners right and to create a plan based on consultation (the minutes say: 'This master-planning by consultation might well be the special hallmark of the new Milton Keynes'); and to encourage the local authorities to go on building as fast as possible. The rest of the agenda was long and wide ranging.

The board discussed the vexed issue of compensation for tenant farmers and agreed to use section 22 of the Agriculture (Miscellaneous Provisions) Act 1963 to make discretionary

LEFT: *Queensway, Bletchley, in the early 1970s, when it was the main shopping centre in Milton Keynes.*

payments to tenants for disturbance and removal expenses. The Government had, since 1963, been urging corporations to use this powerfully and sympathetically.

The board invited Fred Pooley to join as a part-time special adviser – an act wrongly interpreted by the press as a good omen for the monorail city. It sorted out a procedure whereby the corporation could vet development proposals – and, where necessary, arrest them – and decided to ask the future master planners to give speedy advice on where a start could be made on building the town.[5]

Walter Ismay lost no time in executing the board's instruction to cultivate the local authorities. Within weeks of his appointment he accepted an invitation to open Bletchley's 3,600th house, and while doing so complimented the council on installing central heating.[6] It was the first of many contacts. He was to play a key role in gaining for the corporation the confidence of the residents, local authorities and the press.

Campbell's 'two first and greatest difficulties' concerned the appointment of Richard Llewelyn-Davies and the non-appointment of Pooley as master planner. (Pooley was determined that the new city should be designed by his team in the county planning department.) Campbell, who had met Llewelyn-Davies in Trinidad and 'got to know him very well because we shared a lot of political ideas', wanted to appoint him to plan the new city but was told by the Ministry that he must hold a competition.

The board, therefore, chose four firms of architect-planners and sent them a brief of the history and purpose of the city. The brief set out 'five fundamental requirements' and stated that 'solving the problems of transportation will be a prime factor in the physical success of the city'. Campbell had already had long discussions with Llewelyn-Davies about the need to plan for change and so the brief demanded proposals 'flexible enough to accommodate future changes in ways of living, working and playing, due for example to the rising standards of living and technological changes'.[7]

The four firms were Colin Buchanan and Partners; Shankland Cox and Associates; Wilson and Womersley; and Llewelyn-Davies Weeks Forestier-Walker and Bor. All were leaders in their field. Walter Bor, a Prague-trained architect who had joined Llewelyn-Davies the previous year after being Liverpool's city planning officer, recalled how his firm got what *The Sunday Times* labelled 'the most important job in British architecture and planning since the war'.[8]

Colin Buchanan, having decided to join Constantine Doxiadis (coiner of the word 'oecumenopolis') on a Mediterranean cruise, failed to represent his firm. Graeme Shankland gave the impression of being too argumentative. And Sir Hugh Wilson confined his presentation to slides of his firm's work instead of responding to Campbell's brief. This left Lord Llewelyn-Davies (he was created a life peer in 1964), of whom Bor said, 'he had the best brain of any man I ever came across', to sweep the field.[9] It was not quite as simple as

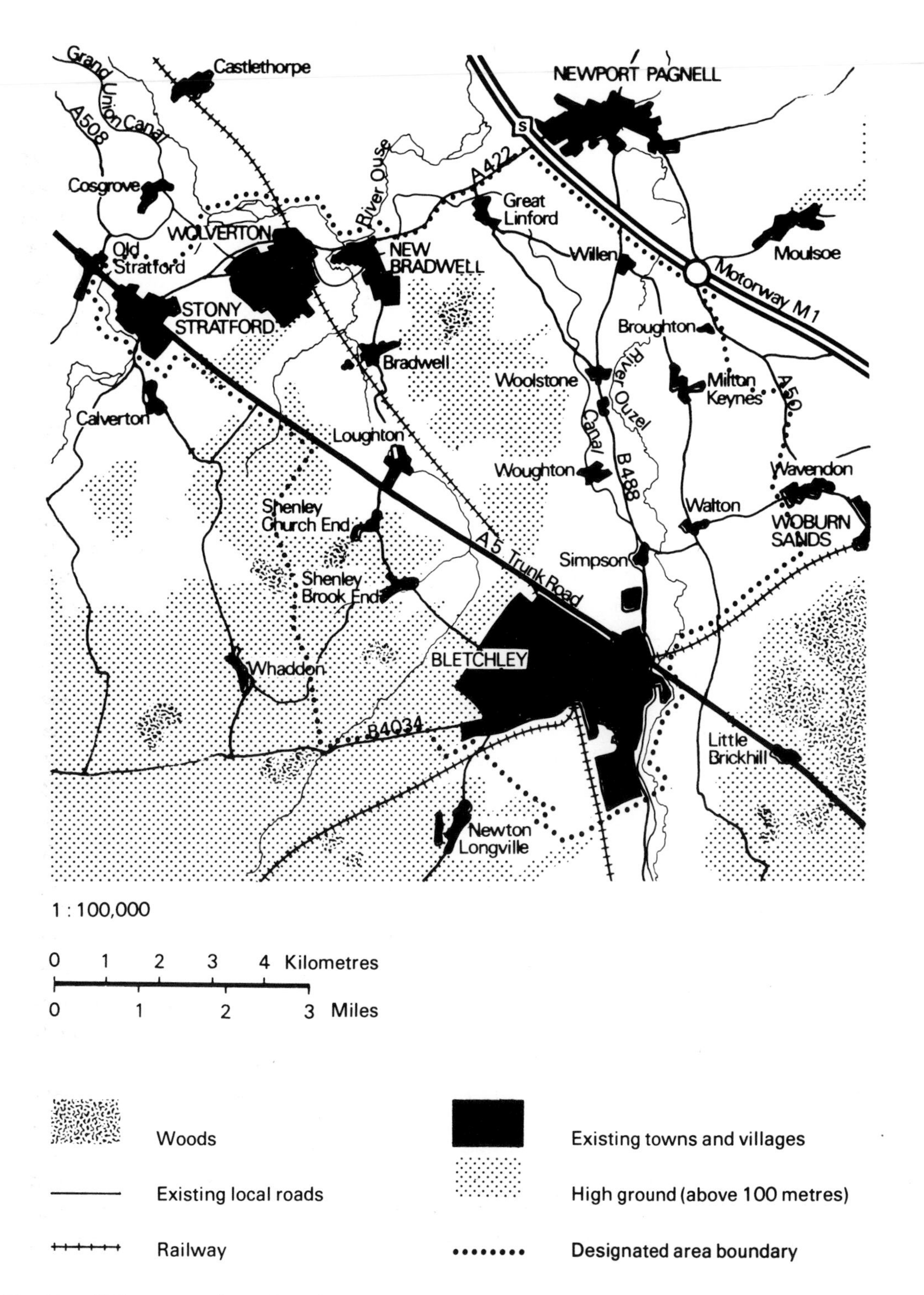

Bletchley, Wolverton and nearby villages, rivers and hills during the period when the master planners were designing Milton Keynes.

that but, as Campbell was later to acknowledge, he would have been in great difficulties had one of the competing firms put up a strong showing. As it was, 'the others really *did* rule themselves out'.

The man chosen to prepare the master plan for Milton Keynes was exceptional. His parents, his schooling – everything about him was larger than life. His mother, who was Irish, spent time in jail for supporting Sinn Fein while his father was a great friend of the philosopher Bertrand Russell. Until he went to Cambridge to qualify first as an engineer and then as an architect, Richard's education was accordingly largely conducted by Russell.[10]

Nicholas Taylor, writing in *The Sunday Times*, correctly described Llewelyn-Davies as 'the intellectual leader of the "scientific wing" of English architects … His suitability for Milton Keynes is enhanced by his habit of collaborating with experts in other professions.'[11] He was architect of buildings for *The Times*, the Stock Exchange and the Tate Gallery, and the planner of Washington New Town in County Durham.

'He was an incredibly attractive, enormously civilised man,' Jock Campbell recalled. But he was also 'fairly unpopular … because he was a member of the Labour Party and very iconoclastic'. The two were made for one another. Both were socialists. Both were intellectuals. Both loved arguments that ranged wide and deep. Milton Keynes presented them with one of the most important challenges of their respective careers – and both were to rise to it.[12]

The appointment of the master planners set in motion two years of research into urban form without precedent in British town planning. Happenstance helped to make this possible. The plans of all new towns created after Milton Keynes were, to save time, commissioned by Whitehall. Campbell was thus the last chairman to play a dominating role in shaping a new town. This fortuitous event, coupled with the size of the project, the intellectual strengths of Campbell and his colleagues, and the quality of the consultants, helped to give Milton Keynes the master plan *par excellence* of British new towns.

On 25 September 1967 the Press was told that Llewelyn-Davies had been given the job. (The *Guardian*'s planning correspondent had, a few weeks before, tipped the wrong firm.) Campbell got off to a fast start and promised an interim report by the end of 1968 and a final report twelve months later. Yet barely had the planners got to work than the South East Economic Planning Council published *A Strategy for the South East* and demonstrated the slipperiness of the demographic data on which the new city was to rest.

The problem, as Richard Crossman had complained two years before, was that the Registrar-General (who came under the Housing Ministry) did not have a computer. 'I

RIGHT: High Street, Stony Stratford, in the early 1970s: flares were fashionable.

Koda
PRODUCTS
CHEMIS
W.E.WILYM
OPTICIA
D.W. ROBERT
CHEMIST
CENTRE PHARMACY
CALOR GAS
THE
OLD
GEORGE
RESTAURANT

managed to get some fascinating facts ... about how vital figures from the (1961) census, which we need for our housing policy, won't be available four years from now,' he wrote. The reason was that '*my* ministry comes at the bottom of the list for borrowing the War Office's computer. Every time the War Office wants to compute its wages, our programme has to be taken out.'[13]

In the end the data surfaced in 1966 – two years earlier than Crossman expected – and enabled the South East Planning Council to portray a future different from that foreseen by *The South East Study*. The 'drift to the south' had virtually stopped. Birth rates, far from rising, were falling. The consequences were that, over the two decades to 1981, the population of the south east was expected to grow, not by 3.5 million, but by only 2.6 million.[14]

Gradually the significance of these figures began to sink in. The 1966 census confirmed the downward trends and prompted Bill Benyon, prospective Conservative parliamentary candidate for North Bucks, (seeking, no doubt, to make a splash) to call for a review of the future of Milton Keynes. Referring to the period 1964 to 1981 (shorter by three years than the one used in *The South East Study*) he said, 'It now appears ... that the most likely increase will be about 1.6 million.' Benyon went on to relate the unforeseen fall in greater London's population to the prospect of resulting labour shortages in the capital and thus of overcrowded commuter lines.

A cloud had appeared on the horizon the size of a man's hand. On it could be detected the words 'inner city problems'. That cloud was to grow and grow over the lifetime of the development corporation. Benyon, who ousted Robert Maxwell as MP for Buckingham in 1970, had sighted it. He offered two responses: speed up the building of Milton Keynes or scrap it. 'I favour the former,' he told his audience of Wolverton Young Conservatives, adding that the compromise of reduced expenditure and slower growth would be 'absolutely fatal'.[15] It was a judgement he was not to regret.

5

GOALS

It took over two years to prepare the Milton Keynes master plan. The task facing the board was akin to designing Concorde or the QE2. They and the executive slogged away at it, tried to keep the local authorities happy, assembled staff and, much to their surprise, found an adjacent site being chosen as a possible third London airport. It was bound to take time – and although the corporation 'fast-tracked' certain projects, for some people it was not fast enough. If they had known that Rome was not built in a day, they had forgotten it. The board's first warning about local restlessness came as little as six months after their initial meeting.

The multicentredness of the city caused trouble too. Wolverton, hypersensitive as ever, thought it had got wind of a shift in policy. Peter Cosford, a Wolverton councillor, asserted, and the Press duly reported, that such a change would be nothing less than a 'confidence trick of great magnitude'.[1] Letters steamed between the council offices at Stony Stratford and Bucklersbury House in London, Bookers' Cannon Street office and the corporation's temporary home. Jock Campbell, peeved at having his sincerity impugned but habitually polite, asked Wolverton's chairman whether he would be prepared 'to correct the unfortunate, and I think unfair, impression which the article will be bound to make upon many people?'[2]

Campbell tried to nail the matter once and for all when speaking to the Press after the board's meeting on 25 September. 'While wishing to avoid preconceptions as to number and size of town centres,' he said, 'the board confirms views previously expressed that the new city must avoid dependence on one monolithic centre. The existing centres of Bletchley, Wolverton and Stony Stratford must not only be preserved, but enhanced in their role in the new city,' he added.[3]

Three months later Bletchley made a bid for a place in the sun by publishing a roads plan for a population of 70,000. The plan was designed to establish Bletchley's dominance

in the new city and the council made no effort to consult the corporation about it. John Smithie, who by this time had become town manager, told local businessmen that Bletchley must be made a 'very important part' of Milton Keynes. 'Bletchley station is the key,' he said. 'Further north you can only get half the service.'[4] Fifteen years later Central Milton Keynes station was open and by 1991 nearly 200 trains a day stopped there. John Smithie, like other residents in the locality, seems to have had no inkling of the scale of the changes ahead. Or perhaps it was just not in his interest to contemplate them.

The board meanwhile 'expressed surprise and disappointment' that Bletchley's road proposals, which clearly impinged on the master plan, should have been broadcast without consultation. Walter Ismay was asked to convey these concerns to the council. Jim Cassidy supported the action and promised to use his influence to prevent any recurrence of 'this unfortunate incident'.[5]

A special study of Bletchley was commissioned later that year from Richard Llewelyn-Davies. The board's aim was to find ways to integrate the town into the new city. The consultants were asked to look, in particular, at Bletchley's social facilities, to compare them with those in other towns of the same size, and consider whether additions to them were necessary or desirable.[6]

During 1967 the corporation moved into Wavendon Tower and its staff grew from a nucleus of two in early May – Ismay and his secretary Win Heald – to about twenty at the end of the year. Ernest Pye and Alan Ashton, chief engineer and estates officer respectively, were the first senior technical appointments – reminders that new towns start with drains, roads and buying land.

Kenneth Wren, chief finance officer, came next in February 1968 but it was not until July that Gerald West, seconded from Llewelyn-Davies, joined as architectural project manager. Bill Berrett, Fred Pooley's associate on the monorail city, joined soon after. Eighteen months later, numbers had risen to 170 and the establishment committee forecast that, with investment likely to be running at £15m a year, a staff of 500 would be needed by April 1971 and ultimately 'at least 700'.[7] The corporation's appetite for architects was prodigious. By November 1970 the committee was forecasting a need for 254 of them – compared with an average of 100 at Runcorn, Redditch and Washington.[8]

Staff growth at this pace put intense pressure on Wavendon Tower which was being expanded almost continuously. By November 1970 further room was needed and Derek Walker, who had joined earlier in the year as chief architect and planning officer, proposed to solve the problem in part with 'temporary air structure offices'. The board, sceptical of

LEFT: A prototype factory at Wavendon Tower, the corporation's headquarters 1967–84: occupied first by the architects, it later became the corporation's publicity centre.

rubber rooms puffed up by giant Hoovers agreed to 'temporary offices, though not necessarily air structures'. It was their first taste of Derek Walker's love of the new, a passion that was to fill the world's architectural magazines with images of Milton Keynes.[9]

How do people design a city virtually from scratch? The planners of Milton Keynes started with a site, a population target, three towns, thirteen villages and certain guidelines, but they had to arrange them in some kind of pattern, be it that of a Canberra, a Brasilia or anywhere else. How should they set about it? The then conventional answer was 'ask the people'. 'All the development corporations wanted their towns to be beautiful,' Sir Frederick Gibberd, Harlow's architect-planner, observed in 1970, 'but they believed that their formal characteristics should be developed from function – which is itself determined by the needs of society.'[10] Frank Schaffer, another new-towns luminary, said even more unequivocally: 'The planner must understand people and anticipate their every need.'[11]

But how does one find out what 'the people' – in this case many of them still unborn – want? Richard Llewelyn-Davies and his principal colleagues, Walter Bor and John and Sue de Monchaux, decided to bring in experts and use them to bounce ideas off the board members. The aim was to generate a set of social objectives that would guide the hands of the physical designers – the town planners, engineers and architects. Llewelyn-Davies acknowledged that the resulting 'goals' were 'relatively tame', though he added that 'if even half can be achieved, this will be a major accomplishment'.[12]

Establishing the goals involved countless meetings and two board-level seminars. Introducing the first seminar in December 1967, Llewelyn-Davies said the object was to consider 'some of the likely form-giving elements of future urban situations' and to inspect aspects such as health and education 'not normally given prominence in new town design'. He went on: 'We hope in three months from now that we shall have a picture of the society for which we might be providing in Milton Keynes.' He described the seminar as 'the start of a dynamic process of goal formulation'.

Experts introduced papers on topics ranging from the future of the family to the state of agriculture. David Donnison, professor of social administration at London School of Economics, whom Crossman reckoned 'outstandingly intelligent and lively',[13] circulated a chilling analysis of the existing towns. Wolverton was a working-class community 'rather shut in upon itself'. Bletchley, with its London overspill, was growing rapidly but, Donnison observed: 'The more successful newcomers move on to buy houses outside the area; the less successful often find it hard to put down roots. Bleak and ill-planned, it is less confined by tradition than the other centres but it is in danger of becoming something of a transit camp.' It was a gloomy foreshadowing of what Milton Keynes might be.

Melvin Webber, professor of urban and regional development at the Berkeley campus of the University of California, then spoke about the urban society of the future. He began by suggesting that whereas the earlier new towns – symbolised by coal – were products of the 'middle-industrial era', Milton Keynes would be part of 'a post-industrial era' (symbolised by the transistor radio) 'in which the nature of the city is radically changing'.

The 'knowledge industries of education, research and development, decision making, information handling and systems analysis' were becoming the fastest growing parts of the economy. 'Milton Keynes will be, in a sense, a spearhead of this changing phase in urban civilisation,' Webber argued. He went on to suggest that this had profound implications. 'Contemporary planning is … the generation of … deliberate innovations and catalysts, and the planned invention of the future.' Urban planners, he seemed to be saying, were not servants of change but entrepreneurs and risk-takers. They should be forcing the pace.[14]

By the time of the second seminar, the consultants had begun to formulate goals and indicate how they might shape the city. Milton Keynes should be 'a city of opportunities' providing 'a variety of options for all its residents – and for those living outside it'. It

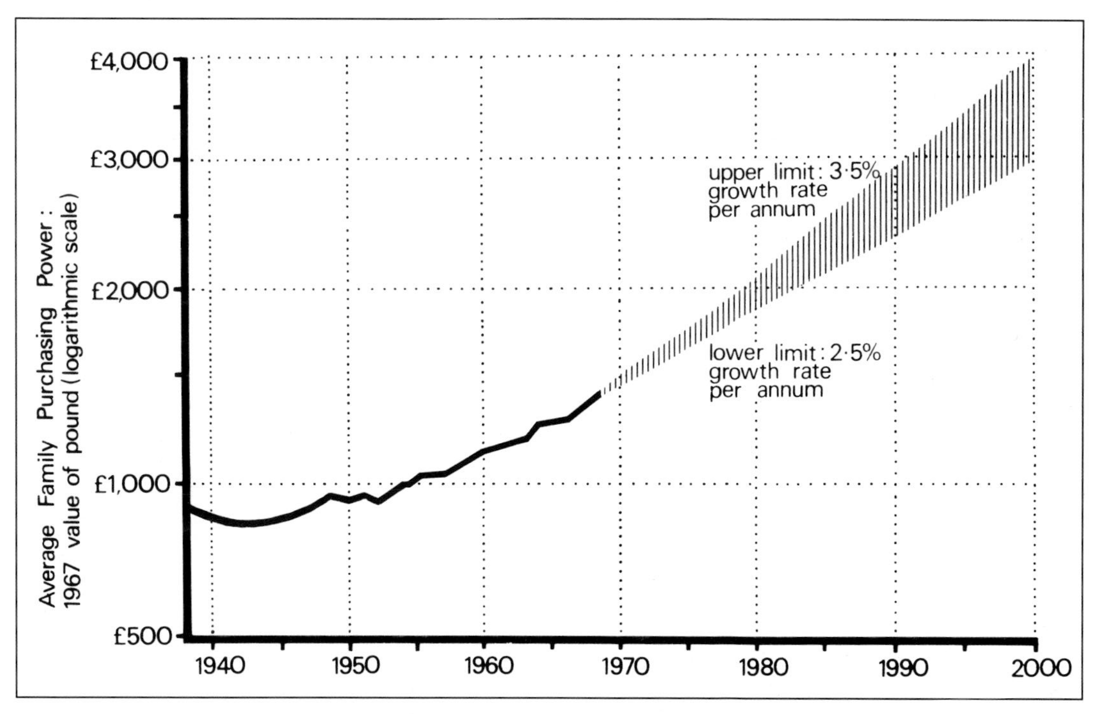

The growth of family purchasing power (in 1967 pounds) as forecast by the master planners. With the prospect that incomes would more than double by the year 2000 the planners were convinced that Milton Keynes should be designed for middle-class living.

should derive 'the maximum benefit from the resources put into it'. It 'should be an alive and attractive city ... Everywhere would be a special "place" and moving through the city would be an attractive as well as an informative experience.' Finally, Milton Keynes 'should be aware of its problems and be able to deal with them'.[15]

A few days after the second seminar Jock Campbell circulated a paper summarising his view of how things stood. True to form, he put his finger on a number of key issues. Wasn't there a conflict between the skills of the Londoners the city was due to house and Professor Webber's view of a science- and knowledge-based economy? 'It would be necessary to provide for the present inhabitants, for the first newcomers, and for future generations' even though 'their needs and interests would not necessarily be the same,' he suggested.

Turning to town centres Campbell asked about the location of such amenities as a theatre, a concert hall and a Marks & Spencer – 'of which there would only be one'. Where should *they* go? And, mindful of the touchiness of Wolverton and Bletchley, he added: 'Great thought and care would have to be devoted to the ultimate presentation of these decisions.'

The choice between 'planning for an egalitarian, one-class city' or 'providing for minority groups – whether executives or coloured people,' seemed to him to be the key social development issue. As for transport, Campbell's paper made clear that this was a subject which aroused strong passions. 'Mr Pooley had said that to provide for all the cars people would want to use in the city would result in a concrete jungle; therefore good public transport was required.' But Campbell was clearly dubious about the idea of a dense, monorail city. He hoped the board would ask the planners 'to provide for maximum, rather than minimum, use of motor cars in the city during the next seven to ten years. We should not start,' he said, 'by trying to induce congestion and frustrate motorists by inadequate roads and parking facilities: very much the reverse.'[16]

April saw the board trying to give their preferred goals physical form. As the consultants pointed out, and as Campbell reminded his colleagues, this meant dealing with three still unresolved issues: the city's mix of rich and poor; the role of cars and public transport; and the pattern of town centres.

Members easily dealt with the city's social mix and the town centres. They knew the new city would be catering for low- to middle-income Londoners but, as Ralph Verney put it: 'Milton Keynes should be a city in which the managers wanted to live as much as the clerical and manual workers.' A university (Walter Bor's suggestion), London commuters and high-tech industries should therefore all be attracted. There was wide agreement too that a big, alive-at-night, civic and commercial city centre need not involve the running down of the centres of Bletchley or Wolverton.

ABOVE LEFT AND ABOVE RIGHT: The powerful imagery of a monorail city: Gorden Cullen's drawings.

LEFT: In Cullen's monorail city many people would have been housed in towers of flats or in nests of houses to put them within a short walk of a station.

Transport proved to be the tricky issue but the feeling that the future lay with public transport was widespread. Ralph Verney, Margaret Durbridge and Fred Pooley all backed a fast, segregated system. Walter Ismay noted that 'over 100,000 people at Milton Keynes would be from wage-earning families – say £15–30 a week at present levels. These people would find it difficult to make ends meet ... and every penny would count.' He saw none of them having cars and thought the corporation 'was obliged to provide a really good public (transport) service'. Alan Ashton, the chief estates officer, warned that if early capital investment were car-related, it would close off options. People were looking for something new in urban development. 'This could possibly be the transport system.'

Monorails cropped up repeatedly in architectural and planning journals during the 1960s. One of the most seductive presentations of their potential appeared in a series of

SCALE 1:500

advertisements drawn by Gordon Cullen for Alcan, the Canadian aluminium company. Employing a deft mix of prose and images, Cullen and his co-author Richard Matthews played skilfully on the fear that England was due to vanish under a carpet of concrete. 'At present, the drift is towards the vast Los Angeles-type suburbs,' they wrote and went on to show how a 'reappraisal of housing' could make possible 'the salvation of the landscape'.[17]

But what did Cullen mean by reappraisal and salvation? Like Nash in London's Regent's Park (or Le Corbusier in his plan for a *ville radieuse*), Cullen prized the theatrical contrast of open parkland adjacent to dense clusters of buildings. Conventional suburbs or new towns with their spaced-out houses and gardens were the cancer that was consuming England's green and pleasant land. They were, as the *Architectural Review* termed it, an urban contagion; they were 'subtopia'. Monorail-based cities offered an escape from the twin evils of urban sprawl and domination by motor cars.

Ernest Pye, the corporation's chief engineer, took a different line. He did not want to see parking charges or deliberately contrived congestion used to limit the use of cars and he threw doubt on the often-repeated view that 'full motor car usage' was physically impractical. He was also dubious whether any new kinds of transport would be available within ten years. He therefore argued that the corporation should promote walking and public transport by giving them 'more direct routes' than cars. (Redditch and Runcorn new towns, both designated in 1964, were based upon such an approach.) Kenneth Wren, the chief finance officer, was another monorail sceptic. He drew attention to the high cost of providing both a transit system and roads.

By April 1968, most of the board (though not the officers) seemed to have convinced themselves that Milton Keynes should be based on public transport. The position of Richard Llewelyn-Davies is less clear. The minutes record him saying nothing specific about transport. Instead, he did his best to dispel the idea that the city would be working class. He spoke of it having many middle-income residents and 'upwardly mobile wage earners'. He also speculated that if, like their opposite numbers in New York, London firms decided to move out to parkland settings, Milton Keynes 'might well offer great attractions'. He was not explicit but he seems to have had in mind a middle-class, drive-in city.

Jock Campbell, sensing the way his colleagues' feelings were running, 'explained that when he spoke about the maximisation of the use of the private motor car, he never contemplated that this would be to the sacrifice of the best possible transport system. He appreciated that probably a third of the population of the city would in any circumstances need public transport.' He added that while he tended to favour a road to a rail system, 'he

LEFT: A township in Pooley's monorail city: slabs of flats rise above a station and form a link to a nearby carpet of terrace houses.

still had an open mind'. The economics of the various systems would, however, be of the greatest importance.[18]

The summer brought no resolution to this issue and Campbell decided to bring into the open the 'conflict ... between those favouring a relatively rigid transport system (a monorail or light railway) with relatively high density development; and those seeking a more flexible and diffused pattern of development based on rubber-tyred transport'.[19]

In this the corporation was, of course, grappling with one of the twentieth century's two or three most intractable urban problems but one to which, at the time, monorails seemed a possible answer. Safege, a French firm, had a prototype running at full scale near Paris and had licensed Taylor Woodrow to sell it in Britain. The virtues of monorails seemed so obvious. They were not troglodytic like undergrounds, yet they could not get snarled up in traffic.

At Milton Keynes the decision facing the board was made more difficult by the persuasiveness of Fred Pooley. Far from being a car-hater, his strength was that he was on the side of the motorist. 'The day has arrived when every family will not only want its car but its cars, and no new city plan which does not cater for this can be successful. Cars represent not only the desire for more mobility but are also a status symbol. Once bought they are used to justify their purchase. If one is to succeed in providing an alternative for in-city travel the alternative must be not only as convenient as the car, but must save real money over the actual cost of petrol and oil which a car would use.'

Pooley argued that such an alternative did exist. It 'was a monorail at a cost of £1m per mile to build and equip fully, ready for operation'. He went on to argue that for two shillings (ten pence) a week on the rates, the service could be free. 'The satisfactory alternative to the motor car is less expensive than the motor car itself. Have we,' he asked, 'the courage to accept and develop it?'[20]

Right: Bletchley Leisure Centre, built 1972–74 by Bletchley Urban District Council just before it vanished in the reform of local government.

6

Master Plan

Planning is an exercise that requires thinking. Imagination, prediction and analysis are also involved and then, if there is to be action, thinking has, at a certain stage, to give way to decision. Planning becomes the plan. The linkage between the two can, as Calvino suggests in *Invisible Cities*, be obscure or even mystical.

> 'What meaning does your construction have?' he asks ... 'Where is the plan you are following, the blueprint?'
>
> 'We will show it to you as soon as the working day is over; we cannot interrupt our work now,' they answer.
>
> Work stops at sunset. Darkness falls over the building site. The sky is filled with stars. 'There is the blueprint,' they say.[1]

The plan for the future city of Milton Keynes began to take shape at a board meeting which extended over two days in the autumn of 1968. On this momentous occasion members saw, for the first time, a drawing showing the characteristic warp and weft of main roads weaving through the soft south Midlands landscape. This layout, later to be castigated by some as a little Los Angeles, was quintessentially English. The hard, mechanical line of ruler and set-square was nowhere to be seen. The form of the future city was adapted to the land. It was how a Capability Brown or a Repton would have done it. The board members saw too a variant of this drive-in city plan. It showed loops of monorail overlaying a road grid.

Jock Campbell left his colleagues in no doubt that they had got to make up their minds about the consultants' proposals. They were faced by a choice between a high-density monorail city and a diffused, road-based one. He acknowledged responsibility for the

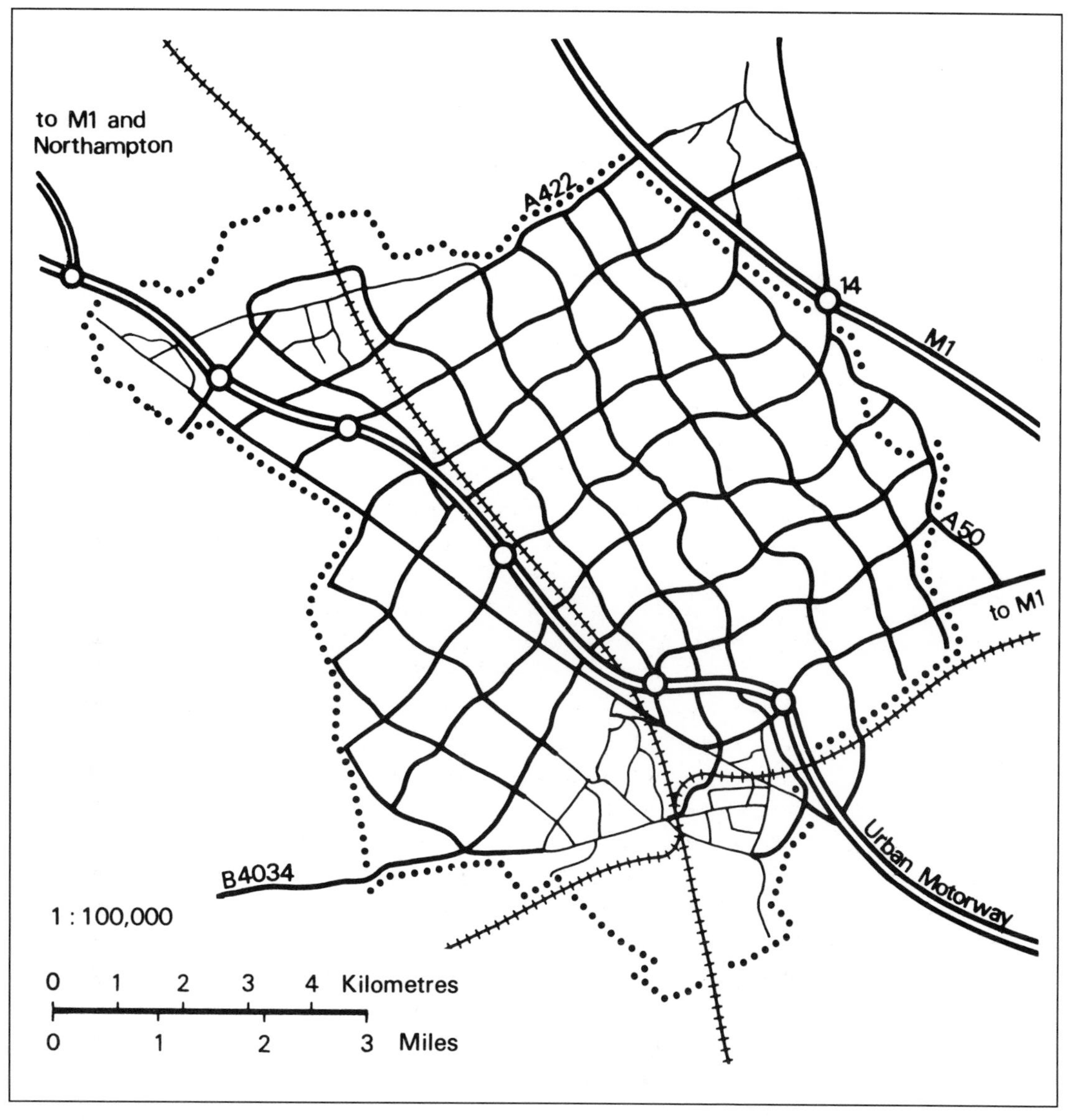

Milton Keynes' original fishnet of roads. When the time came to build them, they were somewhat straightened out and signal-controlled crossings were replaced by roundabouts.

The plan for Milton Keynes 1970 took the principle of decentralised land uses, based on a grid of main roads, further than in any previous new town.

emphasis given to the latter solution. 'The resolution of the conflict, and a decision on this question (one of the most important the corporation would have to make) could not be postponed for many weeks,' Campbell said. He 'had hoped that some compromise might emerge in the consultants' report; but as it had not, he had thought it right to precipitate a full debate now rather than later'.[2]

Richard Llewelyn-Davies introduced the report and made three points: the existing towns would need to be enhanced (he suggested a higher education campus for Stony Stratford); a very strong city centre should be created on high ground between the villages of Milton Keynes and Loughton; and 'macroform' considerations made it desirable for a linear park to be run along the city's eastern side.

He stressed too the importance of giving the city a pattern 'people could carry in their minds'. This was rare for a large city. Indeed some cities had been given loop road patterns 'which deprived residents of any sense of direction'. The consultants had tried to avoid this by the adoption of a road grid. After careful study it had been decided that a grid enclosing one-kilometre squares would be the most satisfactory.[3]

The report which the board was to discuss dealt first with the interaction of transport and urban form and then with the city's social and economic development. It began by setting out a series of 'goals for movement and activity'. They were:

a high degree of accessibility amongst all activities
freedom of choice between public and private transport
high-quality public transport
congestion-free driving
transport that allowed for expansion and change.

The problem encapsulated by these goals involved reconciling the low housing densities and high car use expected to result from 'increasing affluence' with the need for a high quality of public transport for those who 'are not so affluent'. It was a tough challenge. Some would say it involved squaring the circle.

In order to help the board in their deliberations, the consultants had worked out the annual construction, maintenance and operating costs per mile of a variety of forms of transport. They showed car use costs with and without the inclusion of a purchase price. Monorails did not show up well. If the city's buildings were packed around stations, a monorail might at peak times attract 9,000 passengers an hour giving a cost as low as £10 per mile. But given the scenario of affluence leading to demand for houses with gardens, many residents would have a walk of half a mile or even more to a stop. As a result fewer than 1,800 travellers an hour would be attracted to the service and costs would rise to £90 per mile. Furthermore, fitting any kind of railway into Bletchley and Wolverton would be tricky.

Minibuses, on the other hand, could readily serve concentrated and dispersed development, be quickly deployed in existing and new parts of the city and adapt easily to change. Furthermore, they would be better than big buses because they would run more often, be able to use all roads and offer a cosy ride.

The costs were:

Form of transport	*Cost per mile in £*
private cars	40 to 60
taxis	140
shared taxis	80
minibuses	35 to 55
80-passenger buses	12
a monorail	10 to 90
buses on bus-only roads	15

Llewelyn-Davies told the board that he favoured the idea of a minibus service (coming at five-minute intervals), although he recognised it might require subsidy. Fred Pooley had, however, made a case for looking at the city's public transport 'in terms of social costs as a whole and not simply in terms of its fare structure'. Llewelyn-Davies agreed with him.

The report then examined a series of five theoretical forms for Milton Keynes and, from them, arrived at two possible layouts. Plan A aimed at concentrating homes and jobs close to a rail transit system. The report acknowledged that such a system would provide the city with a 'unifying image', but went on to identify a serious drawback. Rail transit 'is not

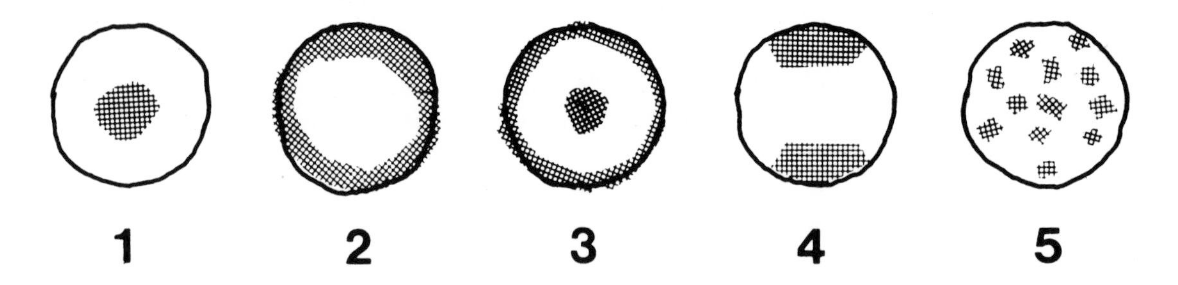

Five ways in which employment might have been distributed in the new city. Diagram five, which diffuses it evenly, was chosen.

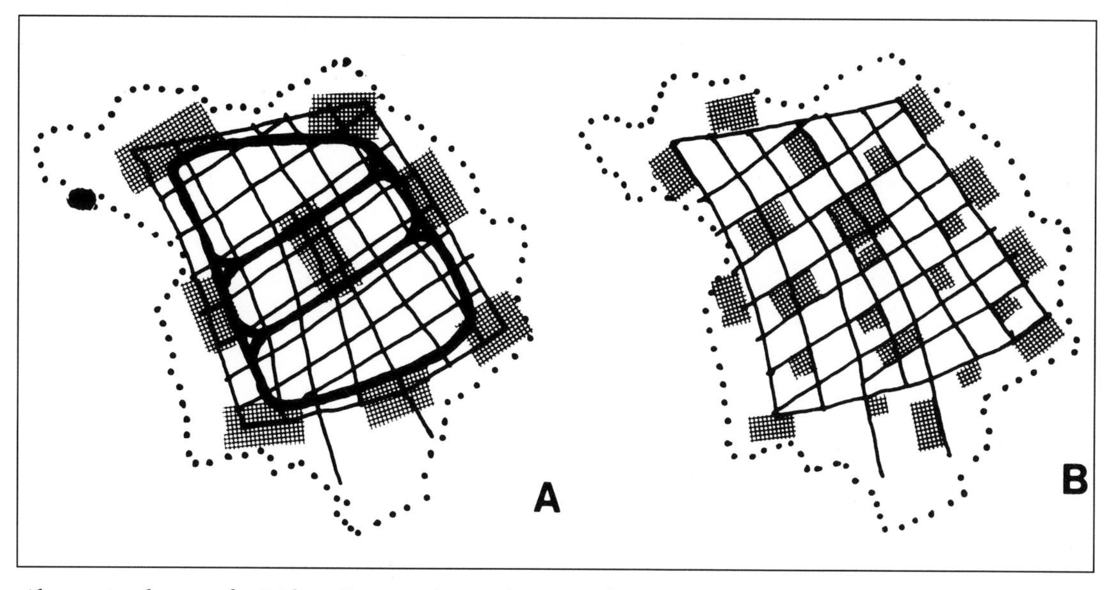

Alternative layouts for Milton Keynes: plan A shows employment in concentrations beside tracked public transport routes plus a grid of roads; plan B shows employment diffused across a grid of roads suitable for both cars and buses.

the most convenient form for people not owning or driving cars' and might well lead to ghettoes of the elderly and less affluent growing up around stations. And even if ways could be found to mix the poor and the well-to-do, the former would probably find themselves ill-served by transit.

Plan B was Milton Keynes almost as built. Houses and jobs would be spread along roads used by both cars and minibuses. Such a layout was seen to be compatible with 'high quality public transport', to provide opportunity and freedom and, although 'it may not provide so easily memorable an idea for the city ... we believe,' the planners said, 'that the image of the city as a coherent framework for ... life ... can be equally strongly fostered'.

Other factors favouring Plan B were costs and adaptability. Minibuses, with about one in five people using them to go to work, would be less expensive than rail and busway systems. A fixed-track system, by comparison, had to be built in large and costly lengths that would be under-used if built in advance or unavailable when first wanted if built only when justified by demand. Plan A was, in a single damning phrase, 'irreconcilable with the goals'.

The consultants, therefore, recommended their idea of a road grid at one-kilometre intervals. All the roads would be on the ground, though some might one day have to be dualled, and the squares they enclosed would accommodate all manner of facilities. Public transport based on subsidised minibuses might seem 'unorthodox' but, the consultants said, 'we have given sufficient thought to this to be confident that the concept ... is technically sound and feasible'.

Having dealt with transport, the planners turned to matters of flesh and blood. They urged a fast intake: 150,000 people from London and South Bucks by 1990. They also stressed a need to 'set out to attract and provide for the middle-aged, the old, the unskilled and the poor as these are the groups likely to be underrepresented unless very special efforts are made' on their behalf.

The average density of the city was envisaged as ten houses to the acre to start with (as was then characteristic of Bletchley), falling to eight to the acre in the year 2000 when Milton Keynes would be a city of 250,000. Manufacturing industry would account for thirty-five to fifty per cent of jobs in 1991. An early start would be needed on a main shopping centre but the only district centres would be the high streets of the existing towns. The planners then dealt with education, 'a major instrument of social development', as well as health and recreation (including allotments) before turning to the design of residential areas.

The goal of freedom of choice had a powerful effect on the layout of Milton Keynes. If residents were to be able to select the local schools and shops they liked, it would not do to treat every square as a self-contained neighbourhood and to lock into it those who happened to live there. Local shops and primary schools would, therefore, be located, not in the midst of squares, but would *bestride the roads* between them. Pedestrian underpasses or bridges would provide links between adjacent squares at these 'local activity centres'.

The planners decided that it was equally important to have local roads running across the main town roads from square to square. Such roads would improve access for drivers and would be essential if public transport were to approach door-to-door quality. The risk that short-cutting drivers might create a nuisance on such routes was recognised as a problem but not an insoluble one.[4]

Walter Bor told members that the city's existing villages, which would be important sources of character, would be little affected by main roads which would run through 'generous landscape'. He added: 'Great care would be taken to reduce noise to a minimum

RIGHT: Railwaymen's houses built at New Bradwell in the 1860s: more senior staff occupied the larger houses.

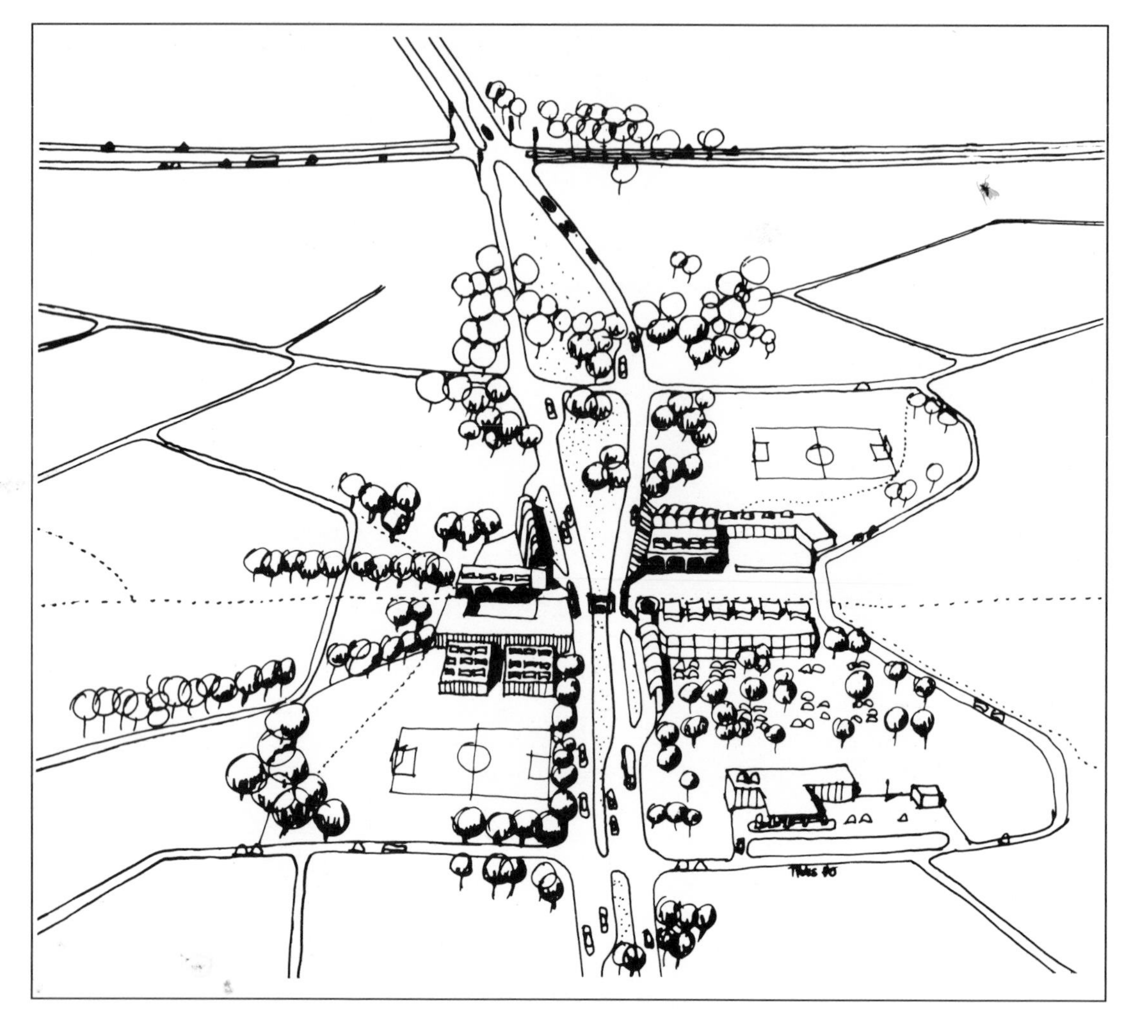

A local centre straddling a main road and crossed by a pedestrian route.

and to keep housing well away from the kilometre roads. Where non-residential buildings faced roads, they would form a buffer.'

Jock Campbell then asked Fred Pooley, 'recognising his long-standing interest in a rail transport system', to comment on the consultants' report. Pooley said at once that he was not happy with Plan B. There would have to be traffic lights at the main road junctions. Traffic lights would also be needed at the points of entry and exit from the squares –

particularly those with industry in them. 'He believed that with lights at intervals of one third of a kilometre a constraint would be built into the city pattern. This would also be detrimental to the city's image.' He concluded that 'a typical American city with a poor environment might be the result'.

Pooley also criticised Plan B on cost grounds. To him the advantages of Plan A were 'as much in economic terms as in terms of convenience and attraction'. A road solution, including the consultants' motorway-standard 'regional roads', would cost £63m. A transit-based solution, which would require £29m for roads, 'allowing 100 per cent car use', and £21m for a light railway, would cost £50m.

Pooley was answered by Brian Helm, of Peat Marwick Kates & Co., whom Llewelyn-Davies had brought in for his transatlantic expertise. Helm agreed that traffic signals would be needed at many exits from the squares but did not envisage any problems: but even with light rail there would be a need for signals though he doubted whether investment in such a system could be justified. In existing cities 'where one could observe a freedom of choice approaching the kind desired for Milton Keynes, the maximum use of public transport was thirty per cent. This rate of usage was declining and with the advent of two-car families could well lead to a maximum of twenty per cent.'

Moving on to the cost of different transit technologies, and thinking no doubt of the busway system being created by another new town development corporation at Runcorn, Helm said that urban rail systems had to be compared with buses running *on their own ways*. On this basis, buses were as cheap as trains or monorails but had the advantage of being able to leave their 'tracks' and, should patronage be at the twenty per cent level, were just as competitive. But with typical bus journeys being only 2.5 miles, fixed busways did not make sense. It was therefore necessary to look at buses running on the roads.

This was the consultants' preferred solution. It was the cheapest and would be capable of getting the closest to the origins and destinations of travellers' trips. Helm added that by the end of the century those without cars would not necessarily be the poor. If such residents were to be as well provided for as those with cars 'as much should be spent on public transport per person as was spent on the roads'. If this were accepted it pointed to ten- to twenty-seat minibuses that were easy to board and more attractive than conventional buses. 'The smaller the number of passengers carried, the greater the probability of a direct service being possible between two points.' This, Helm concluded, was 'the final stage of the consultants' thinking'.

A lengthy debate amongst the members then began. Ralph Verney was puzzled by the talk of 1,500-yard walks to rail stops and asked why the plan was not based on fifty per cent of travel by public transport. In Fred Pooley's monorail city no one would have needed to walk more than seven minutes. Brian Helm replied that 'he doubted whether it would be possible to achieve even fifty per cent without changing the whole density concept of the city'.

Opinion seemed to be swinging in favour of the minibus solution until Helm observed that it might require 500 buses. This caused Margaret Durbridge to point out that they would need a very large number of drivers, and Roy Parker to raise the matter of air pollution. Jim Cassidy then voiced doubts whether a rail system could be inserted into the existing towns and Walter Bor observed that a rail system could not be made financially viable in the early years. Lunch was taken and Margaret Durbridge reopened the debate with doubts whether the road plan would have an exciting image and whether the minibus idea would work. Ray Bellchambers thought that minibuses would be practical only if the corporation ran them and if they received a subsidy. Horace Cutler urged compromise – provide for cars and for a rail system to the extent that it could be justified.

Near the end of the afternoon Richard Llewelyn-Davies said that the two plans did not differ profoundly. It was less important for the corporation to choose between them than to decide its policy on transport subsidies and on what would be practical. This could be done either by choosing the cheapest option or by going for the best buy with the money available. He thought that 'a minibus service would be both cheaper and efficient'.

The first person to signal a major change of position was Walter Ismay. He had come to recognise that people's needs would not be met by a railway because of their reluctance to walk to pick-up points; their determination to use private cars to an increasing extent; their wish to live in low-rise, low-density dwellings and, not least, because of climatic conditions which, for much of the time, called for door-to-door transport. He therefore favoured working up Plan B. The meeting ended with Ralph Verney proposing that Fred Pooley and the consultants get together and iron out their differences. A final decision on the great transport debate was put off until the board's October meeting.[5]

7

DECISION

Fred Pooley conceded defeat at the board's meeting in October 1968. He had spent a great deal of the previous four weeks with the consultants and they, with their array of experts, had persuaded him to drop his advocacy of a high-density, monorail-based city. They had convinced him that a kilometre-grid of roads would cope with the city's traffic and he had acknowledged the difficulties of fitting tracks into Bletchley and Wolverton. All were agreed that some form of rail system might, however, be justified in the future. The minutes report that Pooley 'was quite happy to support Plan B with provision for a fixed-track system ... This was not a compromise, but rather a compound plan'. It was a plan designed to enable the corporation to adapt to technical and social changes which Pooley was confident would arise in the future.

The board accordingly accepted Plan B modified to provide for the following possibilities:

a) a 'dial-a-bus' service
b) a rapid transit service between Milton Keynes and other growth points in the region
c) rights of way along the kilometre roads to permit a tracked transport system.

It is a measure of the consultants' relentless futurism that, in agreeing to reserve paths for tracked vehicles, they included StaRRcar in their list of potential systems. Having decided on a city of verdant suburbs, they were confident that a monorail, which was no more than an aerial tram, would never be economic. StaRRcar, an ingenious capsule designed to be driven on residential roads and to be guided automatically on main ones, seemed an ideal technology.

The question of air quality was dealt with at the same meeting. Richard Llewelyn-

Davies adroitly observed that, even with 'full car ownership', vehicle emissions in Bletchley 'would be very small in comparison with the pollution … from the brick works already in the area'. Concern about the contribution to global warming of motor vehicles in general was still over a decade away.

He also reported on discussions about minibuses with the Ministry of Transport and the National Bus Company. Both had said they would 'be prepared to help where they could. The NBC, in particular, was keen to collaborate with the corporation and establish a Milton Keynes Bus Company as the corporation's agent … [It] would also be willing to consider subsidising the internal city services from regional operations.'[1]

By December an interim plan was ready and largely cleared by the Ministry of Housing and Local Government. Jock Campbell reminded his colleagues that 'it was not a definitive plan for building Milton Keynes'. It had two roles. One was to enable limited amounts of building to be initiated. The other was 'to enable, indeed to encourage, the basic ideas we are developing … to be discussed and considered at an early stage by the public and all the authorities concerned'.[2]

Tony Greenwood was present on 4 February 1969 when the report was launched in a splash of publicity which cost £15,000. As many as twenty-five packed-out public meetings were held. Most of the venues were within the boundaries of the future city, but Buckingham and Newport Pagnell were included as well.

The launch could not have come at a less auspicious time. The Labour Government had

Bletchley's Queensway redeveloped and with a monorail: the urban district hoped by this means to secure for itself a dominant position in the new city but also revealed the problems of fitting overhead tracks into an existing town.

just been forced into a morale-lowering devaluation. Five typists in Surbiton volunteered to work an extra half-hour a day without pay – which led to a jingoistic 'I'm backing Britain' campaign. It was not the moment to announce a giant public-sector investment and Jock Campbell was asked by the Press how the country could afford the £600m the city was by then forecast to cost. 'The last few decades have taught us that new towns are very financially beneficial indeed,' he answered valiantly, '... we have no fears about being unable to attract enough private money to the area to make it a great success.'

Yet the corporation had grounds for self-satisfaction. The interim report did, of course, attract some criticism. Bert Weatherhead, president of the Bletchley Chamber of Trade, doubted whether people would become as wealthy and leisured as the consultants suggested; he thought the city centre would 'act as a terrific traffic madness'; and, as for the dial-a-bus idea, he thought vandalism and malicious false calls would make it unworkable. Yet the reaction of the *Wolverton Express* was more typical. The editor summed it up in a single word, 'Exciting'. The death of Pooley's monorail city was little remarked. It seems that the local papers had long foreseen its demise.[3]

The technical press in London was more combative. The *Architects' Journal*[4] and *New Society*,[5] in particular, tore into the interim report. 'Non-plan ... unimaginative ... shying away completely from planning ... needing a more experimental spirit,' the two journals cried. Milton Keynes was getting a first taste of being a hate object amongst certain cadres of the metropolitan intelligentsia.

It was partly the old problem of architects longing for powerful imagery and great buildings. But it was also because town planning was in a state of flux. The prosperity of the 1960s had brought in train a host of changes in thinking and living to which the bureaucratic and centralised procedures of planning were ill-adapted. Advocates of reform called for a looser and more open-ended style of town planning. Reyner Banham urged 'non-plan' and Melvin Webber coined the term 'permissive planning'. Both were part of what Hugh Roper called a 'quiet revolution ... in the planning process', of which the Milton Keynes interim report was a state-of-the-art example. Unlike Pooley's monorail city, it could not be conveyed by vivid images. It was instead a set of human goals associated with a loose diagram. Roper was impressed by the report and found in it a 'vital balance of vision and humility' that had been absent in the plans of the preceding decade. He admired too its lack of 'architectural determinism' – that belief, widely held by architects, that the good life is a product of physical design.[6]

However, he also had some useful questions to ask. What, for instance, would happen when the city reached its 'target population'? Was its role in its subregion adequately reflected in proposals for transport? And what about a 'social development plan' – as proposed two years earlier by the Central Housing Advisory Committee?[7] The consultants

BABY SWEETUMS
DRINKS & WETS

had indeed pointed out that 'growth at the scale envisaged in the brief requires very careful social management'. But the interim report failed to carry this thinking forward. Roper explained why: 'it appears that nobody yet really knows what a social development plan should be, and how it can be prepared and implemented'.

Roper's observations make clear that the Milton Keynes interim report was a milestone in British town planning. Signs can even be found in it of the *laissez-faire*, enterprise-zone thinking urged a few years later by such proto-Thatcherites as Professor Peter Hall and Geoffrey Howe. However, if some planners were trying to be more permissive, the new social management seemed to a Tory squire like Ralph Verney more dangerous even than the physical planning which preceded it.

'I think you have to bear in mind as you approach this formidable document,' he told a meeting of the Wolverton Chamber of Trade, 'that the New Towns Act was passed in 1947 [sic] by a postwar Labour government and that the whole concept of new towns is a socialist concept which tends, unless it is very carefully worded, to place more emphasis on security than it does on competition and opportunity.'[8] Amongst Verney's fears were state control through the sale of houses leasehold rather than freehold and the idea that freedom in education meant a choice of comprehensive schools. What, he asked, if some residents want their children to have a different sort of education? As for social development planning, Verney saw it as a further extension of state-provided security.

When reporters buttonholed Verney after the meeting to ask him whether he proposed to resign from the corporation, he told them 'laughingly' that the chairman and other members were already well aware of what he thought. No doubt they were.

The local authorities had concerns about the interim report that were less ideological. Wolverton, worried as always about the future of its high street, grumbled: 'The size of the new city centre as proposed is questionable. There is too much disparity between [it] and the proposed town centres.' Wolverton's councillors were suspicious too about the new road proposed as a bypass to Watling Street, the minibus plan and the idea for a big industrial estate to the south of Stony Stratford.[9] Underlying their discontent was their continuing resentment towards the Minister for passing them over in his appointments to the corporation.

Bletchley was altogether happier. Joint meetings of members, officers and consultants were held in June, and Jock Campbell was able to report that they were 'very friendly and constructive'. The council's greatest concern 'appeared to be the need to get on with town centre redevelopment'. The joint working party under Ismay was, therefore, asked to make this task a priority.[10]

LEFT: Bletchley market before it was moved to a new building in the Queensway pedestrian area.

Much of 1969 was devoted to turning the interim report into a master plan, but in response to a forecast that the M1 would, by 1981, be overloaded, the Department of Transport decided that drivers should not be allowed to use the national motorway for local trips. An expressway running east-west from junction 14 to the proposed A5 bypass had, therefore, to be deleted. A threat to confine access to the city to junctions 13 and 15 has, however, not so far been implemented.[11]

The country's falling birth rate continued to haunt Milton Keynes. Buckingham Borough Council condemned the city as 'no longer necessary because of the failure of the expected population explosion to materialise'. Councillors complained that they 'could not afford to maintain roads properly', and that they had to put up with a 'tatty little hospital'. One went so far as to say that they were stagnating 'because we can't have funds, which are going to a still-born Milton Keynes'. A resolution on scrapping the new city was passed by an overwhelming majority and sent to Anthony Greenwood, the Housing Minister.[12]

The *Wolverton Express* took an interest in the same question but came to a somewhat different conclusion. Noting that Milton Keynes was not inevitable and could be stopped, the editor observed that the Minister had to decide 'whether the *need* for the new city is as vital now as when the 21,000 acres of North Bucks were designated'. What was the position? Two hundred thousand families were waiting for the Greater London Council to provide them with houses. These were people that Milton Keynes was designed to help. 'There is no real sign that anything has happened to change that situation,' the editor wrote.[13]

The causes of development in the south east were, however, changing. The population growth that had driven it in the early 1960s was giving way to something else equally potent. Young people were moving away from home earlier; more marriages were ending in divorce; elderly people were living longer; and lots of people wanted, and could afford, more room to live in. The effect was that more houses were going to be needed for a thousand people in the 1970s than had been needed for the same number in the 1960s. A new engine for urban development was getting up steam in the south east.

The final version of the master plan for the new city, *The Plan for Milton Keynes*, was published on 17 March 1970. It was set out in two volumes bound in green and was widely reported by the media. Jock Campbell wrote a letter to the staff thanking them for all their hard work. He himself received an appreciative letter from Anthony Greenwood.

The scale of what was proposed sent a shiver of anxiety through Wolverton Council and prompted the chairman of the finance committee to issue a warning. 'I think it is perhaps as well to make it quite clear that the plans, however excellent, cannot be brought into operation without a large burden falling on the ratepayers of the area,' Aileen Button told a meeting in March. 'I think there is rather too much emphasis on how delightful it

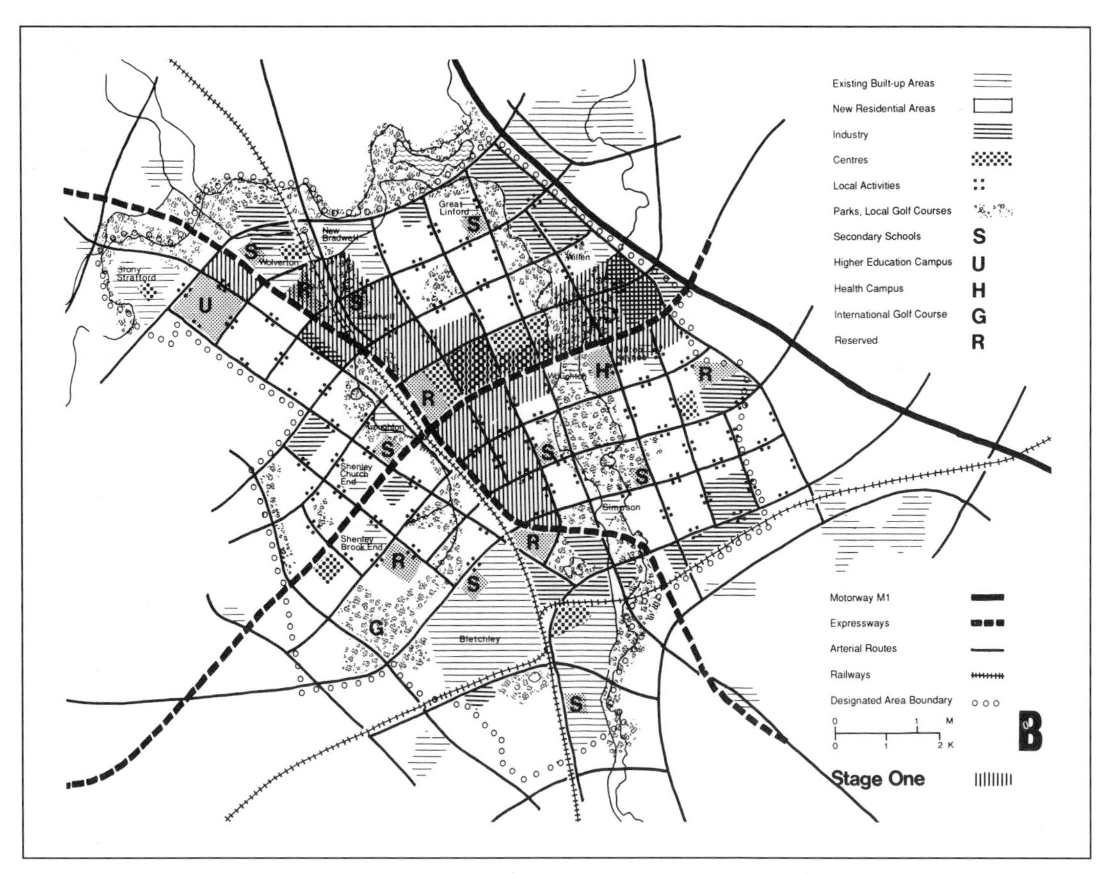

The master planners envisaged Milton Keynes with two motorway-type expressways but only the north–south one was built. The Ministry of Transport feared the other one would overload the Ml.

will all be, perhaps with over-optimism in some quarters.'[14]

Buckingham councillors were worried, too, because they believed that the new city would bring 'chaotic traffic' to the town's streets. However, as the corporation's staff analysed the objections they found that most were concerned with local matters; others (like Buckingham's) were about roads or the threat of a third London airport. None seemed to undermine the principles of the master plan.[15]

The public inquiry into the plan took ten days and ended on 26 June 1970. Walter Ismay reported to the board that the main objections concerned the size of the city centre, the location of the city's sewage works at Willen and the alignment of the southernmost road link between the city and the M1. As the corporation's counsel had told the inspector, most of the points were not objections to the plan as such but to its implementation. The Minister subsequently upheld the objections to the sewage works which was placed next to the motorway.[16]

Following Ismay's report, the board agreed to get on with the job and 'pursue a vigorous policy of building quickly to maintain confidence and to counter the uncertainty' of the immediate past. Their guide was a master plan without parallel in the history of British new towns. The new city's goals were:

opportunity and freedom of choice
easy movement and access
good communications
balance and variety
an attractive city
public awareness and participation
efficient and imaginative use of resources.

If the interim plan had aroused the ire of certain architects, the master plan was warmly received by Sir Frederic Osborn, who had not only inherited the mantle of Ebenezer Howard but was also the former estate manager of Welwyn Garden City and, for many years, chairman of the Town and Country Planning Association. Osborn was Mr Garden City and, despite being partisan, was a fair analyst. 'The broad concept promises a very good plan for the new city,' he wrote with Arnold Whittick. 'The aim is spacious development with good landscaping and a generous provision of open space and is largely a return to the garden city concept. The intention is to try to give people what they want, to encourage participation at every level, and to interpret people's wishes as carefully as possible.'[17]

RIGHT: Linford Wood: a relic of the past landscape of North Buckinghamshire now criss-crossed by footpaths, bridleways and a 'trim-trail'.

8

University and Airport

Late in 1968 the chairman of the Open University (OU) planning committee visited Milton Keynes to look at Walton Hall, then occupied by the corporation's architects and planners. At the time not one of Britain's twenty-six new towns contained a university and, bearing in mind the prestige attached to higher education, the board agreed 'that every effort should be made to encourage the Open University to come ... including possibly a reduction of the rent below normal commercial level'.[1]

Jock Campbell may not have seen himself as a tout. 'I did very little touting. I am not at all a good touter,' he said later, but he was not a man to miss a good opportunity. 'I knew Geoffrey Crowther well and when he became the chairman of Trusthouse Forte – we wanted to get a hotel in Milton Keynes – I rang him up and asked if I could see him. In my taxi on the way, I read in my *Times* that he had been made treasurer of the OU.' A few minutes later Campbell was telling Crowther, 'What I was coming to get was a hotel. What I now want is a university.'[2]

The idea of a 'university of the air' dated from the 1920s – the first age of radio. Harold Wilson outlined a scheme for such an institution in a campaign speech in 1963. It became a minor issue in the general election of 1964 and following Labour's victory, Wilson gave the task of husbanding his dream to Jennie (later Baroness) Lee. She was junior Minister for Education and Science.

A white paper called *A University of the Air* appeared in 1966. Twelve months later Sir Peter Venables, vice-chancellor of the University of Aston in Birmingham, was appointed to turn the dream into reality. Venables had a reputation for being 'a chairman of remarkable skill in the swift transaction of important business without inhibiting discussion'. His OU planning committee decided that a university could not be sustained on broadcasting alone and designed the institution largely as it is today.[3]

Venables moved quickly and by February 1969 Milton Keynes had been selected. He wanted the university to be under way by September and was pushing to have Fry and Drew, his architects, given a free hand in designing additions to Walton Hall. Members were uneasy about this. They feared it would set a precedent that could be seized upon by industrial firms.

Jock Campbell said that 'the decision of the OU whether or not to come to Milton Keynes was still finely balanced'; they had been offered 'an attractive alternative site at Didcot'. He felt that the corporation 'should be prepared to put itself to some inconvenience to tip the scales in favour of Milton Keynes'. Political views about it might differ, but the OU would stimulate publicity and, above all, ensure that 'a group of professional men and women [would be] living in attractive houses [in the city] right at the start'.

Richard Llewelyn-Davies added his advocacy to Campbell's by speaking up for Fry and Drew, the OU's 'distinguished architects'. (Maxwell Fry and Jane Drew had been pioneers of the Bauhaus style in England in the 1930s and later collaborated with Le Corbusier on Chandigarh, the 'City of Silver' and capital of the Punjab.)

The board was won over. They decided that inconvenience for their architects was justified to attract such a prize and allocated £2,000 to enable staff to move from Walton Hall. They also agreed that houses should be built for the incoming academics.[4]

Landing the OU as its first tenant was a coup for the corporation. The university was a new national institution and part of the 'white heat of technology' promised by Harold Wilson before the general election of 1964. Moreover, it was an electronic university that fitted every 1960s cliché about life in the late twentieth century. It was at the 'cutting edge of the knowledge society': and it was due to be an example *par excellence* of what Mel Webber called a 'non-place realm' – a community linked by wire rather than bounded by space.

In time the university got a reputation in some circles for being ultraleft in its politics. 'How is that awful OU of yours?' Mrs Thatcher once asked Campbell. (He had got to know her through being a trustee of Chequers.) 'It isn't mine and it isn't awful, Prime Minister,' Campbell retorted. 'Yes it is. It is a nest of Marxists. Anyone who got an 'O' level in divinity would get a degree there.' 'It simply isn't true, Prime Minister.' Mrs Thatcher put her hand on Campbell's shoulder: 'No, Jock,' she said, 'I know. I'm simply being feminine.'[5]

Left-wing or not, the new university took the new city to its bosom. In his inaugural address as chancellor, Geoffrey (later Lord) Crowther described the new institution as open to people, methods, ideas and places. 'This University has no cloisters – a word meaning closed. Hardly ever shall we have a campus. By a very happy chance, our only local habitation will be in the new city that is to bear two of the widest ranging names in the history of English thought, Milton Keynes.'[6]

MYE 13P
JMJ 558Y

A far less welcome event of 1969 was the selection of two sites near Milton Keynes as contenders for the role of London's third airport. They were Cublington (also called Wing), a bare five miles to the south of the city, and Thurleigh, less worryingly, some twenty miles away to the north east in Bedfordshire.

The search for a site for a third airport had been going on for nearly a decade before Milton Keynes was involved. Stansted started off as the front runner but after many vicissitudes, including accusations that the Government was acting in bad faith, a commission was set up to investigate the problem afresh. The Hon. Mr Justice Roskill was appointed chairman. A list of seventy-eight possible sites was drawn up and boiled down to a short list of four. To the joy of the Essex lobby this 'objective assessment' eliminated Stansted. Milton Keynes, on the other hand, acquired what the corporation decided were potentially two very unwelcome neighbours.[7]

The Roskill Commission undertook cost-benefit analysis and public hearings on a then unheard-of scale. The final report lists a secretariat of thirty-six, a research team of twenty-three and a cost of £1.1m. Hearings took place in London and at all the selected sites. The corporation gave evidence at local inquiries into both Cublington and Thurleigh and the likely effects of the former were judged to be so severe that Campbell and Ismay appeared in person before the commission.

The corporation's case was based on quotations from statements by ministers and officials at the time of the city's inception. The corporation had been set up to create a 'balanced community ... to the high standard to be looked for in a town of the importance envisaged'. The Minister had also spoken of a need for 'special co-ordination' of development in the south Midlands because of its position between London and Birmingham. An airport would change all that. It would reshape the way the subregion was growing, change the incoming flow of jobs and people and 'dramatically change the city'. The work already done on planning the city would be nullified.[8]

Sustaining the corporation's case presented real difficulties. Not only was it hard to show why the philosophy of adaptability espoused by the interim report should stop short at adapting to an airport, but the latest regional plan for the south east was consistent with having an airport there.[9] There was the additional problem that if the corporation turned the airport into too much of an ogre, it would frighten away potential investors.

None of this escaped the Roskill Commission. Wilfred Burns, chief planner at the Housing Ministry, saw no particular problems in adapting Milton Keynes to a city region or to an airport. Burns acknowledged that 'some rethinking' of the city's plan would be

LEFT: The Open University, for many years the city's largest employer, established itself at Walton Hall in 1969.

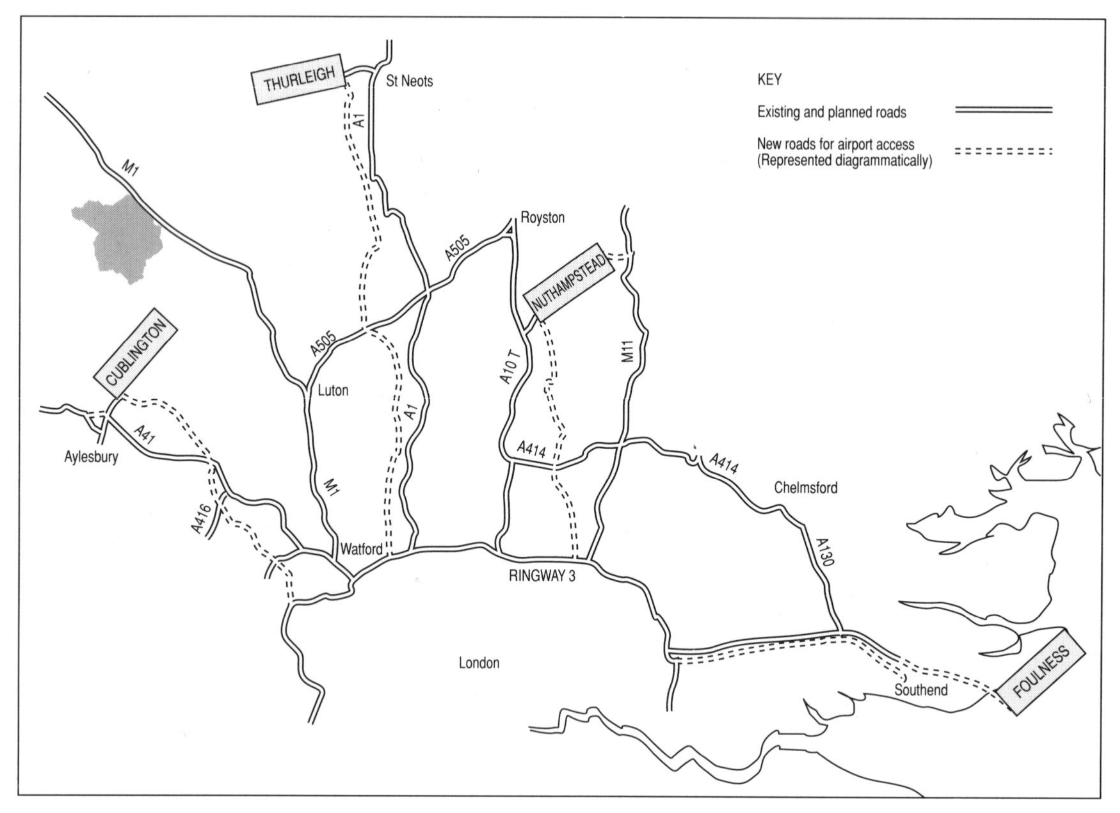

The four sites looked at in detail by the Roskill Commission on the third London airport. Stansted was never on the short list.

required but he 'thought that it would be possible to continue with the construction of the city in parallel with changing the plans'. The Greater London Council was equally unflappable. It 'looked to Milton Keynes as a nucleus of urban development to support the airport in its early years'.

Worse still, the interim report on the city, which was carefully researched by Roskill's ferrets, was found to contain a damaging admission – a reference to the 'considerable benefits which would accrue to Milton Keynes from an airport at Silverstone'.[10] Jock Campbell summed up the situation in a letter to the Bishop of Buckingham: 'Yes, we could [build an airport city], but we don't want to.' He felt sufficiently strongly to see it as a resignation issue. 'I personally wouldn't be interested in being chairman of an airport city,' he told the bishop.[11]

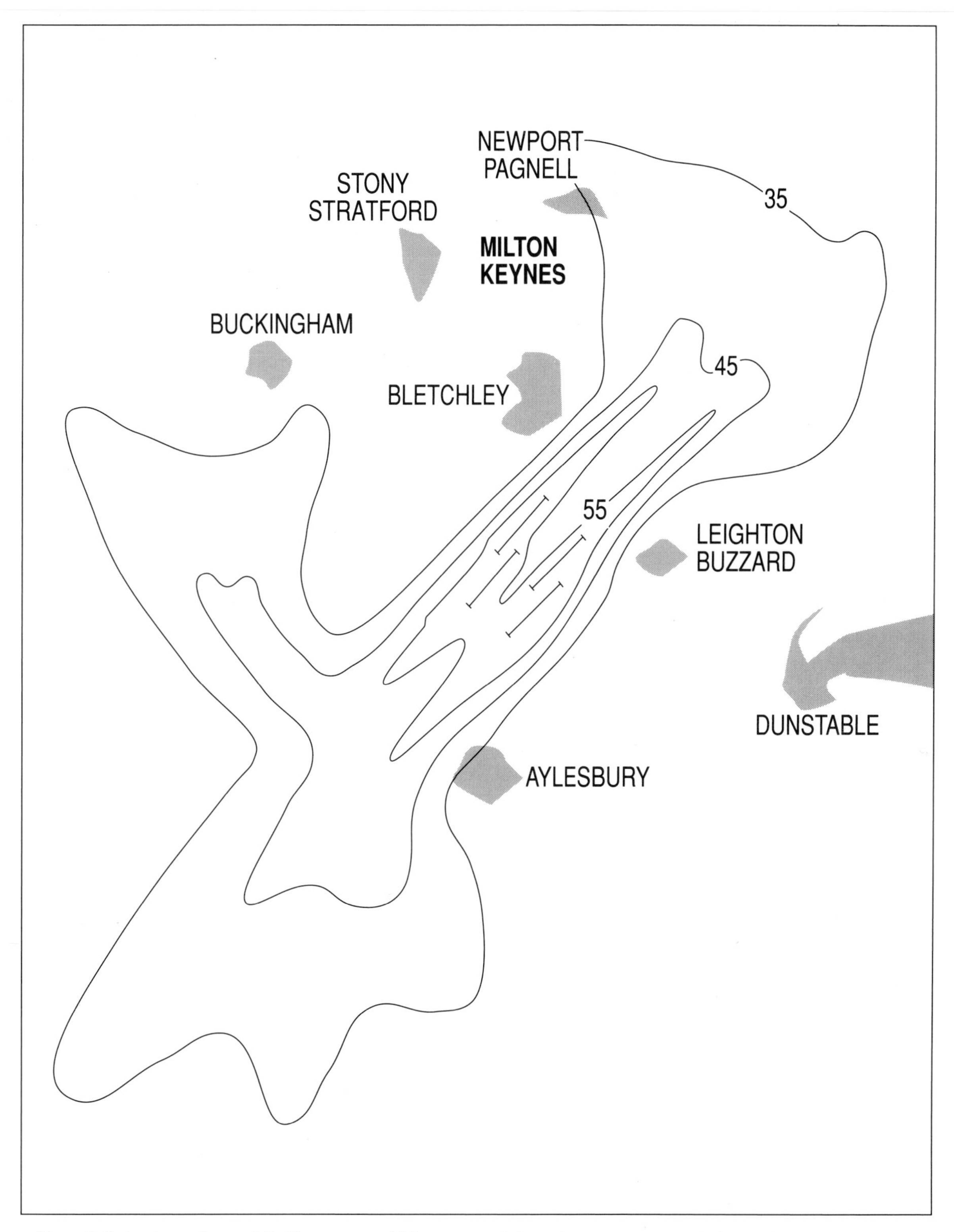

Aircraft flying in and out of Cublington would have spread disturbing noise around the south and east sides of Milton Keynes. The diagram shows proposed runways and noise number index predictions.

Campbell's passion was understandable. He was not a regional planner viewing North Bucks from a lofty office in Whitehall. He had his heart in Milton Keynes and feared that a four-runway airport would be a brutal neighbour. He had, after all, seen Roskill's maps of landing and take-off noise at the different sites. There was something strangely menacing about the contours of these 'noise footprints'. They were the shape of huge tiger sharks whose fins and snouts jabbed at the boundaries of Milton Keynes. The blight of noise could not have been given a more violent portrayal.

Early in 1970 the indefatigable Roskill published plans showing how the four sites might be equipped with related 'airport cities'. (Cublington had by then had its runways slightly realigned so as to reduce noise over Aylesbury and worsen it over Milton Keynes.) Graeme Shankland, Roskill's consultant for Cublington, after looking at various ways of providing for airport-related development, opted to expand Milton Keynes westwards from Bletchley through Winslow. He foresaw an ultimate population of 410,000 for this £566m airport city.[12]

Uncertainty, coupled with the possibility of a 'thunder cloud' of aircraft noise, cast its shadow across the launching of the master plan. Grafting Cublington-related development onto the young Milton Keynes would result in 'a monstrous mongrel city,' Campbell told councillors.[13]

A few days later *The Daily Telegraph* devoted almost two columns to the corporation's statement to Roskill prior to the commission's final session. 'Cublington would make at least fifteen per cent of the eastern part of the city unsuitable for development,' the paper reported. If an airport were built at Thurleigh 'the attractions of living in Milton Keynes would be seriously diminished by the ... blighting of a large part of the rural areas around the city'. The corporation's belief that the third airport should be at Foulness in the Thames estuary was also reported.[14] Campbell was determined to shift the airport out of his back yard.

Roskill reported to the Secretary of State for Trade and Industry in December 1970 and his first choice 'in the overall national interest' was Cublington. A deeply shocked board issued a statement saying that 'Milton Keynes is incompatible with a major airport nearby; and a major airport nearby is incompatible with the Minister's brief to the corporation'.[15]

The knight in shining armour who rescued the maiden city from the dragon of Cublington was a professor of transport at London's Imperial College of Science and Technology. Colin Buchanan, an ascetic engineer (he was also qualified as an architect and a town planner), had once before been cast in the role of national saviour. As an inquiry

RIGHT: Had London's third airport been built at Cublington, runways would have replaced Stewkley's Norman church.

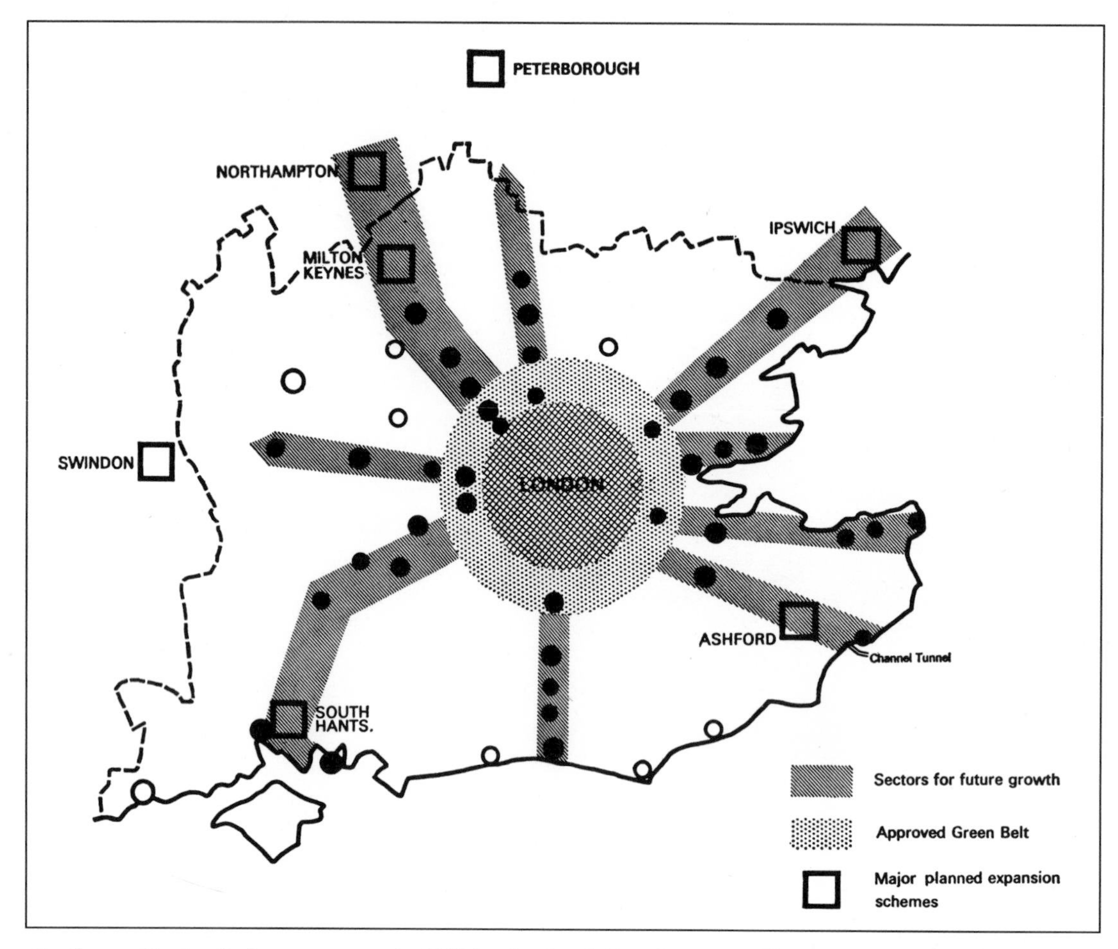

South-east England's future as seen in 1967 by the South East Economic Planning Council. Milton Keynes was to be one of a constellation of developments running from Luton to Northampton.

inspector he had frustrated the ambitions of a crass developer at Piccadilly Circus. This time, as a member of the Roskill Commission, he found himself forced by the adherence of his colleagues to cost-benefit analysis to write a dissenting report.

In eleven pages of eloquent and emotive prose, Buchanan destroyed two years of analytical labour. Yet he was as clinical as they were clumsy. He had taken the trouble to visit every grove, every dell and every eminence within Roskill's three inland sites. He had prowled the villages and gazed in awe at the country houses. Under his pen the little churches, within 'the zone of destruction', were transformed into helpless children. Airport noise became the fall-out of a new Hiroshima.

He played too on those immemorial English fears about London sprawling out of control. Scanning north-westwards from some vantage point on the Chilterns and cursing Didcot power station for its despoliation of the Vale of White Horse, he portrayed Cublington as yet another link in a chain of development that threatened to shackle the metropolis. 'I do not believe the next generation would thank us, if Cublington were chosen ... rather would they regard it as an act of madness.'

It was superb pleading. The Press loved it and was overwhelmingly on Buchanan's side. The wretched Roskill was rubbished. Four months later in April 1971 the Government decided in favour of siting the airport at Foulness in the Thames estuary. In May the master plan for Milton Keynes was accepted. The airport issue had given the board three anxious years and had inhibited progress on the new city but, at long last, the dragon had been slain.[16]

9

TROUBLES AT WESTMINSTER

New-town development corporations are executive arms of Westminster. When government policy changes, willy-nilly, corporation policy changes too. There is always room for manoeuvre and for lobbying as, over the years, Milton Keynes regularly demonstrated, but no room for outright defiance. Ultimately, the diktat of ministers and control by Whitehall officials is absolute. Permission is needed by corporations for all major development plans and spending proposals.

In the course of the twenty-five years between the foundation and winding up of the Milton Keynes Development Corporation, the demands of the Government changed significantly. First, while the master plan was being debated, there was a honeymoon. It seems that Whitehall then became impatient and told the corporation to stop planning and get on with building. A third stage followed during which government officials and the corporation had a common interest in getting the city built. This lasted right through the period when ministers were deciding to divert resources from new towns to inner cities.

But government resolve was weakening. It started to flag during Peter Shore's new-towns policy review in 1976. By the early 1980s, the Department of the Environment under Michael Heseltine became so concerned with limiting the growth of public expenditure and with trimming back the frontiers of the state, that the corporation began to feel it was no longer loved.

Getting a project as big as Milton Keynes going did not prove easy. Following Edward Heath's defeat of Harold Wilson in June 1970 (and Bob Maxwell's defeat by Bill Benyon as MP for Buckingham), Whitehall's energies were temporarily occupied with creating the

LEFT: The corporation wanted golf courses to be open to all. Abbey Hill course, with housing at Hodge Lea on the horizon, was laid out in the early 1970s.

megaministries demanded by the new Prime Minister. Applications by Hoechst and Kodak to build factories in the new city accordingly languished at the new Department of Trade and Industry while over at the gigantic new Department of the Environment (DoE) the Secretary of State (Peter Walker) sat on Roskill's recommendation to build London's third airport at Cublington.

The board minutes say nothing about pressure from Whitehall, but in February 1971 Jock Campbell saw Sir Michael Cary, the DoE's permanent secretary. The subject of the meeting was progress and two months later Fred Roche took over from Walter Ismay as general manager.[1] Roche recalled this period eight years later: 'I don't think that a lot of people who lived in the area thought [Milton Keynes] was going to happen ... I think that central government were beginning to get worried that it was not going to happen.' Getting Milton Keynes going was 'rather like starting off a very heavy vehicle: you need all your revs'.[2]

Roche successfully found the accelerator pedal, revved the corporation up and gave it momentum. By the end of his first year, in a report of Churchillian brevity, he set out the dimensions of the job. He listed eleven achievements: they included restructuring the corporation and establishing good relations with the DoE. He went on to list seven failures including 'the volume of paper used' (Roche was no bureaucrat), and seven priorities for 1972/3. Expanding the building industry labour force and 'the avoidance of bureaucracy' were amongst his priorities.[3]

The board too underwent change. The resignation in 1971 of Walter Ismay and of Professor Roy Parker, a sociologist, left vacancies which Peter Walker filled at the end of the year. The new members were Evelyn de Rothschild, merchant banker, and Peter Willcock, a senior property executive at Commercial Union. Rothschild was appointed deputy chairman and became chairman of a new financial policy committee. Campbell told the staff that his new deputy was 'a highly cultured man as well as a banker'.[4]

The next three years were as turbulent as any in the corporation's history. The 1973 decision of the oil-producing countries to bump up their prices led to the first of the board's many experiences of public expenditure cuts. But there was a glimmer of hope. Sir Idwal Pugh, who by then had replaced Michael Cary as the DoE's permanent secretary, visited the new city during the summer of 1973 and was impressed by it and, in particular, by the quality of the houses being built. 'He had accepted,' the board were told, 'that Milton Keynes had special problems and that to avoid jeopardising [the] government's investment in the city, and the charge that the plan was a false prospectus, DoE would have to support special treatment in certain areas of expenditure.' In view of the subsequent history of delay over hospital investment, it is no little irony that there was specific mention of special treatment over health service expenditure.[5]

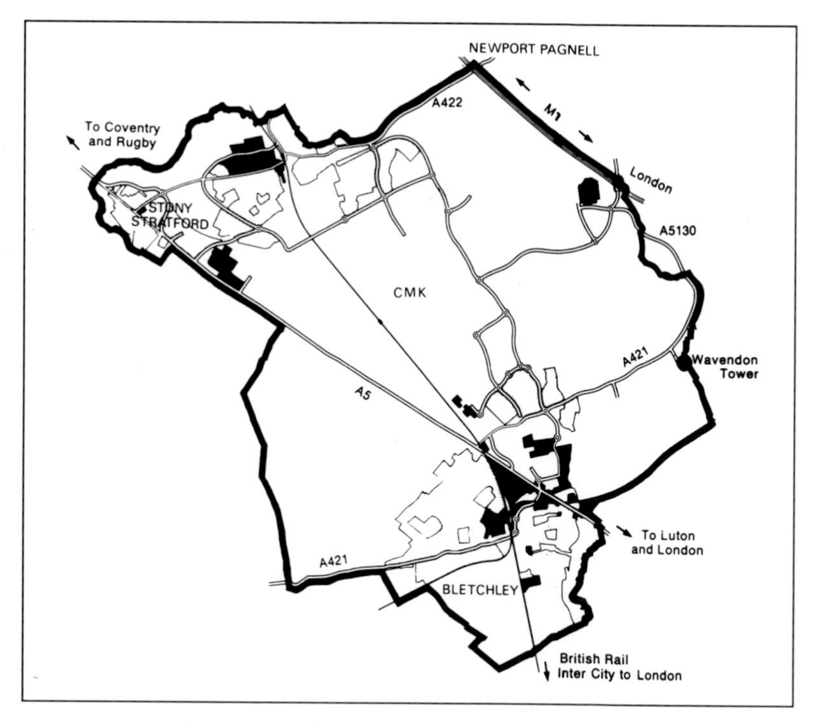

Milton Keynes begins to take shape: the first roads.

By January 1974 the miners' strike was in progress and the corporation was plunged into the three-day weeks. Electric light was available at Wavendon Tower only on Thursdays, Fridays and Saturdays. The minutes record: 'On lightless days office hours would be from 9 a.m. to 4 p.m. until increasing daylight permitted later closing.'[6]

The cuts were due to fall in the financial year 1974/5. The corporation calculated that by rephasing some projects and delaying the removal of trees killed by Dutch elm disease, £5.1m could be saved. And in order to keep the £7.5m district general hospital in the programme it was proposed to go partly for private finance for the city centre shopping building. The cuts were not going to make life easy. The different components of the city threatened to get out of phase, the confidence of investors seemed likely to flag and, worst of all, Sir Stanley Morton 'doubted that insurance companies and other financial institutions, although continuing to attract funds, would be in any hurry, in view of the high interest rates available, to invest in what [they] for the moment would regard as a somewhat speculative project'.[7]

In the end the board was obliged to offer a cut of £11.7m but approval was given to the plan to go for private finance for the city centre. Should the corporation, Fred Roche asked, give away the profits it would make on Central Milton Keynes in order to get the hospital? 'It could be a substantial sacrifice.' The board decided it had no choice.[8]

By May 1974 the miners' strike had destroyed Mr Heath's Conservative administration and a new Labour Government was in power with John Silkin as Minister for Planning and Local Government. The new broom, whose father had piloted the first New Towns Act through Parliament in 1946, at once set up a policy review. Fred Roche had high hopes of it and Campbell, after his first official meeting with Silkin on May Day, told the board that the Minister had 'expressed his total commitment to the new town movement'. However, as a socialist, Silkin was opposed to private property. He therefore announced his intention to review the split between houses to let and sell, the sale of rented houses to tenants, and the sale of land to developers. Campbell, as was his style, invited his colleagues to comment on these matters. He wanted to be sure he was properly representing them when 'leading the discussion with the Minister on behalf of the [new-town] chairmen's conference on 4 June'.

The members recognised that economic shifts made it necessary to be flexible on housing but agreed that a fifty-fifty split remained their objective. They were, however, reluctant to give up selling houses to tenants. Such sales 'gave an added incentive to build housing for rent well', and broke down the differences between the two 'worlds'. The Minister should, therefore, 'be pressed to continue to allow tenants to purchase their own homes'.

Selling land to developers raised more complex issues. The corporation, prompted by Conservative members of the board and, in particular, by Ralph Verney, had by this time abandoned its earlier dedication to leasehold disposals. Most developers were offered freeholds. Silkin was, however, understood to have other ideas. He was 'opposed to the alienation to private developers of assets created by public expenditure'. Did this mean that the building of private houses would have to stop? The board was relieved to find that if builders were assigned licences to sites, the freeholds of the resulting houses could pass directly from the corporation to purchasers. This promised to keep the Government happy since 'the developer would not then be speculating in corporation land'.[9]

Campbell met Silkin not once but three times – privately over lunch, during a whole-day visit to Milton Keynes on 20 May and then jointly with the other new-town chairmen. 'Despite the most cogent social arguments put forward by chairmen,' Campbell reported, 'the Minister had remained adamant that in present circumstances the sale of rented houses must stop.' The sale of land to developers was also stopped – to be replaced by building licences. And the Minister was 'adamant that assets should not be sold to raise money for new developments'.

RIGHT: Privately owned houses at Hanmer Road, Simpson, promoted by the corporation in the early 1970s.

Hanmer Road

The corporation did its best to finesse the first instruction. Silkin had added that houses might be sold to tenants where 'legal and moral obligations to sell' existed. The board interpreted this as widely as possible to include 100 tenants who were already negotiating to buy and all who had begun their tenancies before 29 April.[10]

In December 1974, when Silkin published *New Towns in England and Wales*, a consultation document, it was becoming clear that his ear had been bent by jealous Labour local authorities. They did not like the business style of development corporations and they were envious of the resources dispatched to them by Westminster. Silkin was keen to do their bidding. He proposed to wind up the early new towns; to transfer to local authorities the houses of the more recently started ones; and, following the reform of local government in 1974 (which had created fewer and bigger authorities), to transfer many other development corporation functions as well. Silkin proposed too that there should be more councillors on corporation boards and that board meetings be open to the public.

Milton Keynes was in the forefront of the battle to defend the new towns against the local authority predators. Fred Roche wrote a paper 'New towns legislation – the future' which was 'greeted with acclaim' by the other new-town chairmen. It advocated 'a concerted initiative against erosion of the powers of new towns'. However, not all the chairmen were willing to make a stand. There were, Campbell told the board, almost as many views about Silkin's document as there were chairmen, 'and some were not prepared to subscribe to any attitude of confrontation with the Minister'.

The upshot was, in Campbell's eyes, an inadequate response to the consultation document. Adroit chairmen have, of course, ways of dealing with such difficulties. In this case it was a covering letter. Campbell, who had prepared it in consultation with three of his more robust new-town colleagues, read a draft of it to the board. It drew Silkin's attention to the danger of confusing the division of responsibility between corporations and local authorities by 'shotgun weddings or by so over-representing local authorities on development corporations that they became shadow local authorities'.[11]

The campaign against the Government in which Milton Keynes played a leading role was largely successful. When the new-town chairmen met Silkin in May he told them (Campbell later reported) that he 'accepted that domination of a corporation by a local authority was not a sensible proposition'. He also suggested that 'it might soon be possible to relax the ban on the sale of rented housing to sitting tenants, and possibly to look again at the 75/25 rent/sale target'.[12]

Campbell and his fellow chairmen met Silkin once more in October, by which time the Minister 'raised no question whatever about the continuance of housing programmes unabated' or about the need for financing supporting services. He repeated his earlier promise to look into sales to tenants and agreed that the transfer of new-town houses raised 'the problem of the local authority's monopoly landlordism'. He had therefore asked his officials to look at alternatives.[13]

The dominant role played by Milton Keynes in the battle against the Labour Government's 1974 consultation document was, as Fred Roche later recalled, partly a matter of chance. The corporation was always bound to be influential. It had the strengths of its great size and the high quality of its members and officers. But it was 'Buggins's turn' that gave Campbell and Roche leadership roles, during that period. They were respectively chairmen of the new-towns' chairmen and general managers. Happenstance thus put them in key positions to shape new-towns policy and doubled the number of occasions on which they saw ministers and senior officials. Milton Keynes benefited greatly.

Silkin's policy review nevertheless highlighted differences not only between Wavendon Tower and Westminster but also between the corporation and the borough council. The critical issue was selling houses to tenants. Frank Atter, former Wolverton council chairman and by then a member of the big new 1974 Milton Keynes Borough Council, advised the board that his authority 'would not adopt a policy of selling rented houses to sitting tenants. In their experience it created management problems and the owners found it difficult to sell ... The feeling was that segregation was better for owners and management.'

Other members of the board disagreed. They 'felt that a policy of segregation was unacceptable in its long-term implications'. The corporation's aim was to blur the lines of demarcation, 'and in any case a tenant who wished to purchase did not normally want to move'. As the 1970s turned into the 1980s and the corporation was faced with a need to find new owners for its houses, such differences in point of view between the board and the council were to become progressively more troublesome.

Roger Parker-Jervis, a county councillor since 1967, raised a different local authority problem at the same board meeting. Buckinghamshire was beginning to be crippled by the cost of its contributions to the new city. The rates had recently been increased by thirty per cent and, in order to stop its finances from getting out of control, the county was proposing substantial cuts in its 1976/7 social services budget. 'The oncost of Milton Keynes was now clearly visible to ratepayers,' Parker-Jervis told his colleagues. 'And, owing to the inflation of interest rates, the city would not show a surplus on the rates in the lifetime of many ratepayers.' Opposition to the new city was growing in the south of the county.

It was a tricky problem since, as Parker-Jervis added, 'the county needed Milton Keynes and Milton Keynes needed the county. Neither could allow the city to fail ... both should press the Minister for special allocations' of money. Here, however, there was no split between the two bodies. Jock Campbell acknowledged that the county's position was 'politically untenable' and it was agreed to put a strong case to the DoE.[14]

In July 1976 Silkin informed the new-town chairmen that he wanted to meet them again and chose to do so at Milton Keynes. A message came from the DoE's permanent secretary that 'the minister and officials were concerned about the evident uneasiness amongst staff and even board members about the future of the [new-towns] movement and the importance which the government attached to it'. They wanted to understand and allay misgivings and seek views on ways in which new towns 'might be adapted to future needs, including the application of new town techniques to inner areas'.[15]

When the conference took place Silkin said encouragingly that new towns 'would continue to be built'. The use of development corporations in inner cities was discussed and the Minister agreed to allow the sale of houses to sitting tenants under certain conditions. These were that the waiting time for applicants for rented houses should not exceed three months; that there should be discussion between corporations and their local authorities; and discounts (twenty per cent) would be available only after four years' occupation – subject to the price being no less than the cost. Campbell told the board he thought the conference was 'extremely successful'.[16]

However, with the International Monetary Fund in London telling the Chancellor of the Exchequer to put his house in order, budget cuts were also on the board's agenda. One likely project was the Watling Street bypass. It was agreed that a postponement of eighteen months would be acceptable but Campbell said 'it was vital that the corporation should give absolute priority in expenditure to maintaining the housing programme and ancillary facilities, as any dip in the programme would destroy the confidence of investors'.[17]

The cuts, when they came, were nothing like as bad as they might have been. The corporation's bid to build 3,945 houses in 1977 was cut to 2,874. But assuming that houses for sale provided for thirty per cent of completions, the reduced total would still be on target to create, by 1980, a catchment population for the shopping building of 100,000.

Fred Roche was cautiously optimistic. Provided the corporation achieved its allocation of starts 'and continued to attract the necessary employment and to make substantial efforts to house deprived families from London, the allocation in 1978 was likely to be the same as in 1977'. He said a sophisticated monitoring system would be set up to see that there was no slippage.[18]

The other new towns were incensed. Milton Keynes had scooped twenty-eight per cent of the entire new-town housing allocation. Campbell reported 'considerable resentment' at the chairmen's September meeting. 'The view had been almost unanimously expressed,' he told the board, 'that the allocation was illogical and inequitable.'[19]

10

'Good Design'

The Greater London Council's (GLC's) architects were sufficiently proud of their Water Eaton estate at Bletchley to show it, together with others at Andover and Newmarket, to the Press. All three consisted of houses with gardens laid out according to traffic-segregation principles pioneered at Radburn, New Jersey, in 1929. The houses had garage courts on one side (the back entrance) and gardens opening on to parks on the other. Footpaths ran out from the front gardens through the parks to the local shops and schools. Wherever these paths met roads they dipped into underpasses. This was 'Radburn' planning and, by the mid-1960s, it was what progressive housing authorities were building.

Commenting on the three estates, the architectural correspondent of *The Financial Times* observed: 'the absence of any flat dwellings above three storeys shows how far the pendulum has swung from the times when high flats were considered to provide necessary punctuation in any scheme whether in the open country or in a city centre'.[1] Tower blocks had, of course, been prominent in both the 1945 Jellicoe plan for Wolverton and the 1964 Engle plan for Bletchley.

It fell to two exceptional individuals to decide whether or not Milton Keynes was going to be Water Eaton writ large. The first was Fred Lloyd Roche, the 39-year-old architect from Runcorn new town who had been appointed director of design and production in September 1970. Judy Hillman, in a piece about Roche in the *Guardian*, remarked on his 'proven ability'. He believed in new towns and was adventurous: at Runcorn he had got Jim Stirling, the then *enfant terrible* of British architecture, to design some houses. (Stirling later did the Tate Gallery extension and the Tate of the North although, sadly, his Runcorn houses were demolished in 1991.) Roche 'continually emphasises that [Runcorn] has been a team job,' Hillman wrote. He 'believes in speed, greenery, cutting red tape, consistency in materials and, quite simply, good design'.[2]

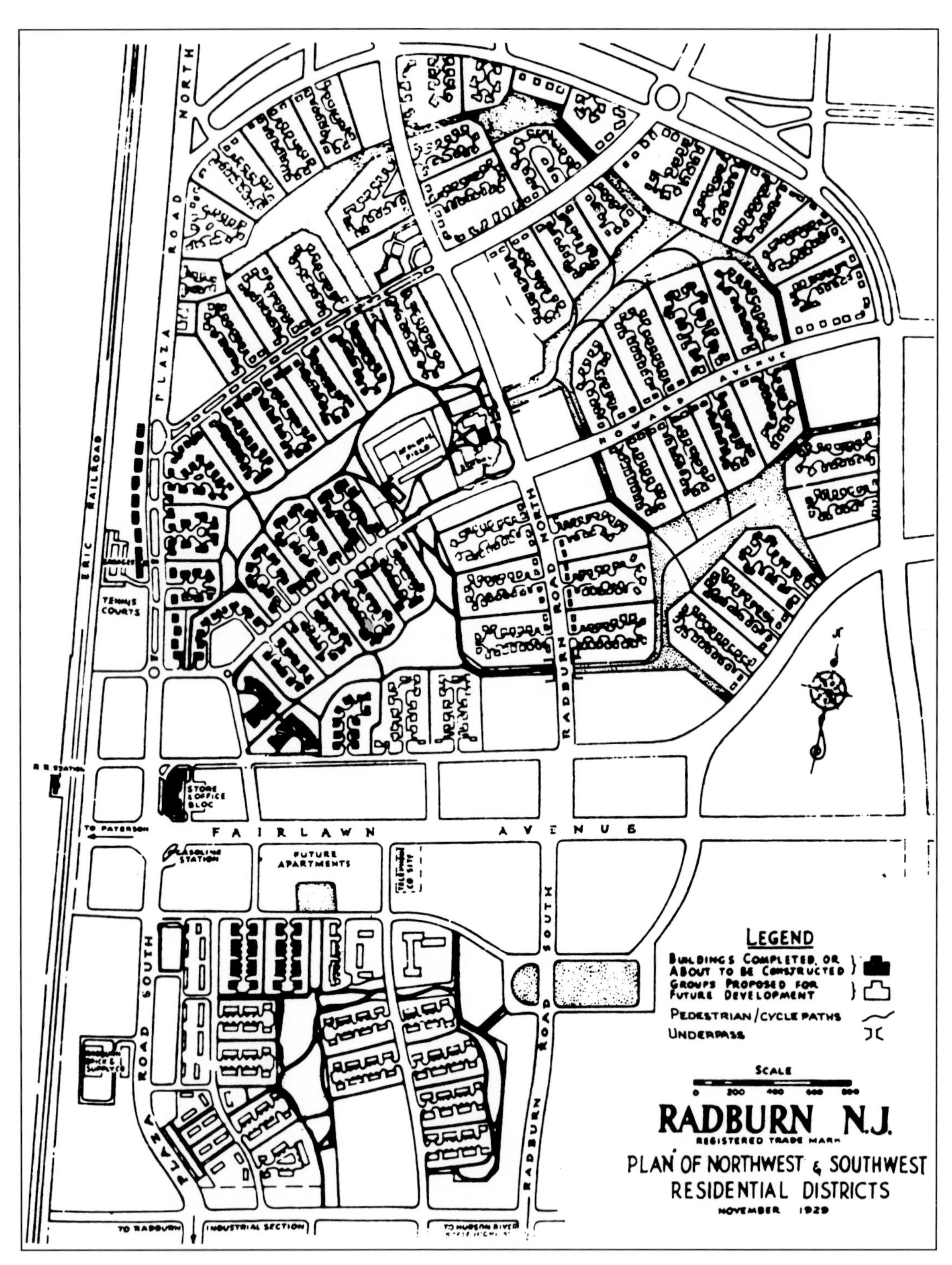

Part of the layout of Radburn, New Jersey, showing how the houses had cul-de-sacs for cars on one frontage and parks and footways on the other.

The second master builder was Derek Walker. He had worked as a consultant for Roche at Runcorn. He too was an architect and Roche persuaded him to give up his own practice and become the corporation's chief architect and planner. Between them, Roche and Walker made Milton Keynes a place of pilgrimage for architects.

No sooner had Roche taken over from Ismay as chief executive than he began to demonstrate his skill at getting things done. Walker, who remembered him 'lining up the DoE' and dealing with the 'county problem' – Pooley – called him 'an absolute political animal – an operator'. Milton Keynes folklore has it that Roche would choose Christmas Eve to take housing schemes down to Whitehall for final approval – and not leave until the officials he was visiting gave it.

Walker, young but already respected as a designer, set out to attract the best architects in the country. Like Leslie Martin at the London County Council in the 1950s, he aimed to create a temple of talent. He was astonishingly successful. His conviction was that 'if a place generated good design, you would attract good designers'. Ed Jones, Jeremy Dixon, Pierre Botschi, Mike Gold, Andrew Mahaddie and many others joined the Milton Keynes design team. Many went on to win architectural competitions. Their work in turn helped Walker to bring in the cream of Britain's private architects as consultants. Richard MacCormac, Ivor Smith, Martin Richardson, Norman Foster, Archigram, Edward Cullinan and Peter Phippen were only some of the stars whose buildings adorn Milton Keynes.[3]

Given all this talent, inter-professional rivalry was almost inevitable. According to Jeff Bishop who, in the early years of Milton Keynes, analysed 'the balance of power ... between planners and architects', it was the architects who began to get the upper hand. 'In particular the corporation became the home for a group of young architects ... known in MK as "the undertakers" because of their penchant for black suits ... For them, this new town was the classic sheet of blank paper ... They won out to the extent that each was "given" a grid square to design and they did just that – starting from scratch as if nothing else would ever exist.'[4]

This freedom was augmented by the lack, at least in the early days, of residents and of feedback. 'There was no client. You were writing your own brief,' Derek Walker recalled. Furthermore, 'it was a very socialist utopia we were talking about'.

This then was the intellectual climate in the glorious, optimistic days when the architects got to work on designing Milton Keynes. North Bucks was a *tabula rasa* of green fields. The master plan left wide discretion to those charged with implementing it. Architecture was in the hands of a posse of brilliant young artists and a pair of executives dedicated to 'good design'.

What was this 'good design' that tingled the spines of radical, mid-twentieth-century architects? Tom Wolfe, the American cultural historian, pinpoints its source in *From*

Bauhaus to Our House. It originated in 1927 in Weimar Germany at a worker-housing exhibition, the Stuttgart Weissenhof Werkbund project. Its creators included Mies van der Rohe, Le Corbusier and Walter Gropius. It was both a political ideology and an aesthetic. The ideology emanated from the writings of Marx and the victory of Lenin. This explains how blocks of 'worker housing' came to be the cathedrals of the new style and why anything 'bourgeois' was viewed with lordly contempt.

And how, Wolfe asks, did worker housing look? 'It looked non-bourgeois within an inch of its life: the flat roofs, with no cornices, sheer walls, with no window architraves or raised lintels, no capitals or pediments, no colors, just ... white, beige, gray and black ... The interiors had pure white rooms stripped, purged, liberated ... They had open floor plans, ending the old individualistic, bourgeois obsessions with privacy. There was no wallpaper, no "drapes" ... no doilies, knick-knacks, mantlepieces, headboards, or radiator covers. Radiator coils were left bare as honest, abstract sculptural objects. And no upholstered furniture.'[5]

This was the all-powerful, all-consuming, all-embracing 'international style'. Wolfe called it a movement 'with a set of inviolable aesthetic and moral principles'. It was revolutionary and socialist. It alone was good design. Jeff Bishop, looking at it from a social development perspective, saw something else. He characterised it as 'design by helicopter' because it was so self-sufficient and remote and because of Helmut Jacoby's brilliant aerial perspective of 'Central Milton Keynes in 1990' – with a helicopter up front.

For young architects filled with 'moral principles', Jock Campbell was an ideal chairman. He may not have been indoctrinated at the Architectural Association but he believed passionately in socialist housing. He told Richard Crossman he wanted 'a properly planned, publicly-owned new town like the others' and not one, as the Treasury was insisting (and as the brief had stipulated), in which Wates and Costains would build half the houses. 'Here is Jock,' Crossman commented, 'a big businessman, who is also a very idealistic socialist who really believed that the job of this Wilson Government was to introduce new socialist planning and who is beginning to be bitterly disappointed.'[6]

Netherfield, the first grid-square to be designed as a unity, and Coffee Hall, likewise a complete square, date from the heroic first years. Derek Walker's whiz-kids were way ahead of the GLC architects with their stuffy old Radburn. They were rediscovering the street. The houses of the two estates, therefore, faced one another across wide avenues and ran across the land in terraces as straight as railway tracks.

Netherfield, designed by Ed Jones, Chris Cross, Jeremy Dixon and Mike Gold, was built

RIGHT: The architectural model-makers at Milton Keynes had few equals. Their 1972 model of Netherfield showed terraces running for half a mile across an undulating landscape.

Helmut Jacoby's westward-looking, helicopter-eye-view of what Central Milton Keynes might look like by 1990.

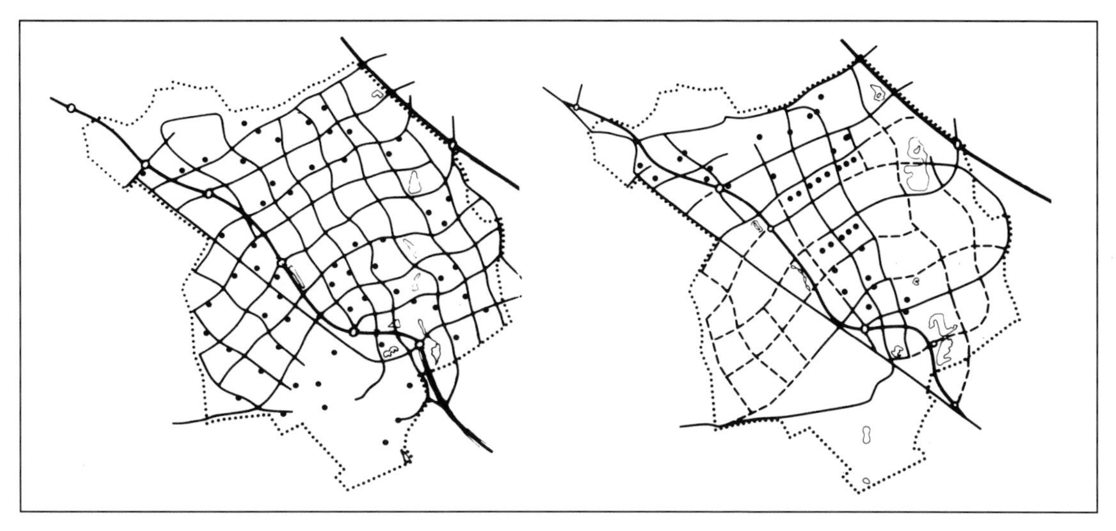

The location of local centres, as intended and initially as built.

with timber walls and aluminium roofing. Plastic fins 'expressed' (stuck out from) the walls between the individual houses. (For an architect with moral principles this was about as far as one could go in decorating a building. Had not Adolf Loos written about 'ornament and crime'?) The resulting design yielded to neither sentiment nor landscape. Netherfield's roofs stretched as flat as runways from side to side of the grid-square. Where the land flowed underneath in gentle undulations it was accommodated by varying the heights of the houses *under the roofs*.

Netherfield and Coffee Hall were not at all what was envisaged in the master plan. These huge, repetitive 'worker housing' schemes reduced choice while the siting, for reasons of architectural form, of pubs, shops and schools away from the main roads isolated each square from its neighbours.

The master planners, aiming to link adjacent squares and create interest and landmarks for motorists had, by contrast, put the local shops next to the main roads. 'As you drive along a main road your view will alternate between parkland and buildings, as local activity centres are passed,' Richard Llewelyn-Davies explained.[7] In such a location the local shops – always on a financial razor's edge – might even have attracted passing trade.

Netherfield, unfortunately showing signs of deterioration by 1991, was a striking and original piece of architecture but for Roger Kitchen, a corporation community worker, it was an enigma. 'Is this the classic piece of architectural conceit fitting people to houses

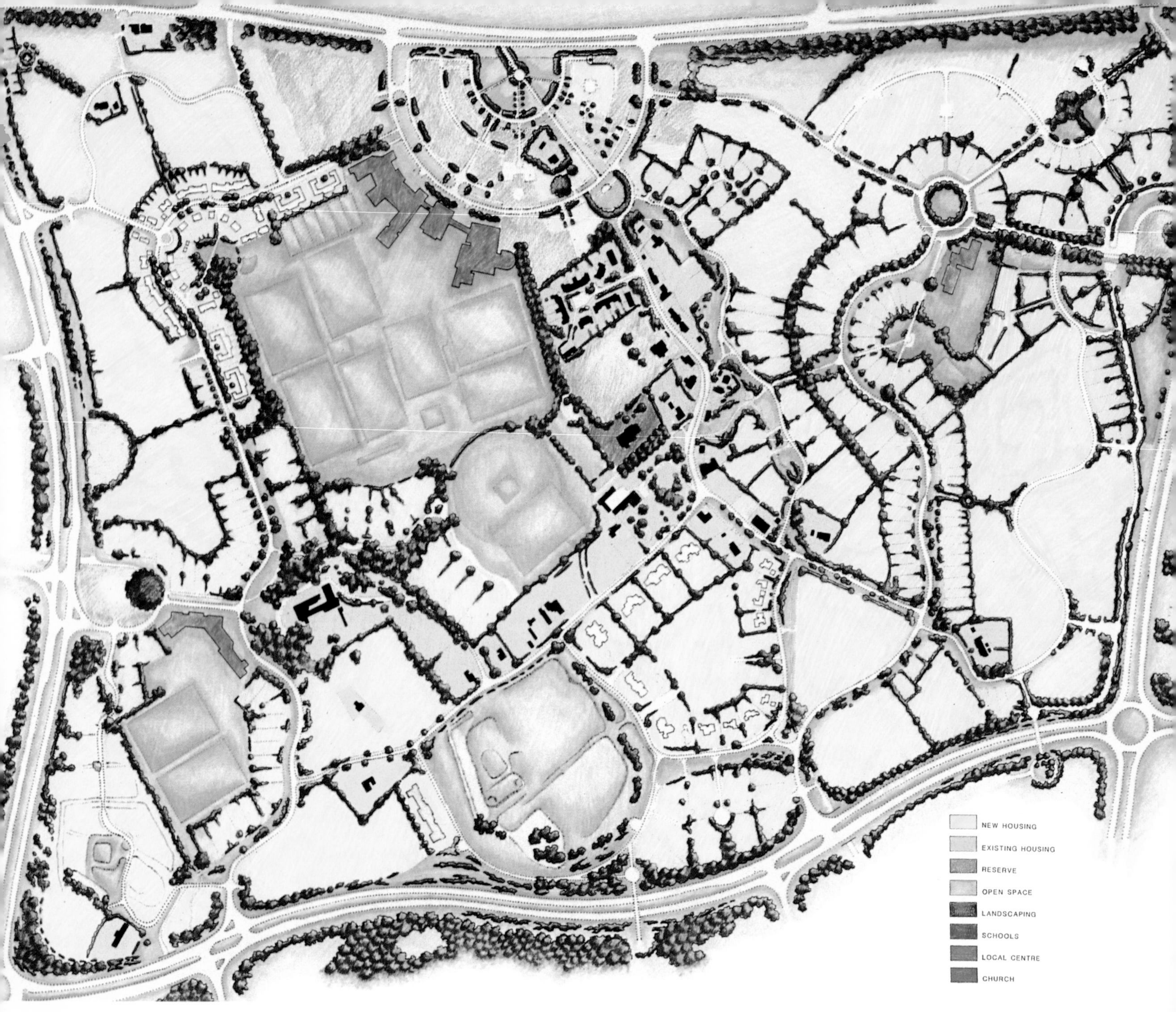

Shenley Church End, designed in the 1980s, showed a more curvilinear approach to town-making.

rather than fitting houses around people?' he asked. Or perhaps its role was to provoke anger and 'community action'.

Kitchen did not pass a final judgement on Netherfield but, in considering early Milton Keynes housing in general, he expressed doubts about its user-friendliness. While many 'failures' in design undoubtedly stemmed from the tight budgets to which the architects were tied, many did not. Complaints about 'noise, lack of privacy, condensation ... non-provision of drying areas for the elderly, location of parking spaces can be said to be truly self-inflicted wounds,' he observed. As Kitchen saw it, the problem lay in the tendency for architects to rate appearances higher than livability. They considered 'design' more important than 'integrated, balanced, social architecture'.[8]

Yet the designers themselves believed they were producing social architecture. They worked very hard at it. Were they not carefully ridding their schemes of every sign of bourgeois individualism? As Fred Roche saw it, the problem was a kind of designers' double vision: 'If you said to a talented architect, "I want you to design 100 rented houses," one half of his brain would come into operation. If you said to the same guy for the same site, "Design me 100 private houses," the other half of his brain would come into operation.

'We used to haggle about this for hours in the corporation and we used to say, "Look fellas, they are the same people, they have got the same aspirations."' At the root of the haggling lay a knot of deeply entrenched professional values. 'We were trying to push a culture change,' Roche added, 'but there was a lot of opposition.'[9]

In the 1970s the board itself took a close interest in architecture, landscape architecture, exhibition design and graphics. Design was one of the means by which the corporation pursued quality. It was, therefore, characteristic that when the members saw Fullers Slade in 1971 they noted that 'the design team should be congratulated on ... a very fine piece of planning and design'.[10]

Twenty years later, with the benefit of experience, the borough council's chief executive saw the same place in a different light. 'Fullers Slade is a beautiful-looking estate. It's got roses. It *looks* really, really nice. It was, of course, unlivable. People had no privacy – and the corporation recognised that eventually and did things about it.'[11]

If the board members failed to detect the shortcomings of Fullers Slade, they were very shrewd in their assessment of other schemes. They were, for instance, instantly suspicious of Norman Foster's design for 569 houses at Beanhill. Difficult ground had led to a choice of Llewellyn's 'Quickbuild' system 'with virtually flat aluminium roofs clad with ESSEM, profiled-aluminium panels'. Members were told that 'a lucid plan of quiet suburban simplicity had been achieved – dominated by existing strong hedgerows and new landscaping'.

Members nevertheless 'had reservations about the roofs and cladding and wished to see examples'. It was agreed that visits should be made but, as Foster's Beanhill scheme was built as designed, it may be assumed that the technocrats overcame the objections of the laymen. Not many years later, the corporation, following a court case, was awarded damages against the architects on grounds of rain penetration. Later still, Beanhill's flat roofs were replaced by pitched ones.[12]

Meanwhile change was slowly overtaking the design of the corporation's housing. The master plan had called for variety and choice. Netherfield, Coffee Hall, even Fullers Slade did not give it. As the *Architects' Journal* observed in a review of Neath Hill, a reaction was bound to set in against the 'appalling regimentation and image of the worker's paradise'.[13]

This reaction began very early on, although it was some time before its effects became widespread. Signs of it can be seen at Great Linford and Eaglestone as well as Neath Hill. Not only did the appearance of the corporation's houses begin to change, but experiments were made as well, mixing different kinds of tenure.

Great Linford was the first grid-square to reflect a new approach. The planners proposed and the board agreed to its being divided up into over twenty sites. To give 'variety' it was proposed that every site be allocated to a different architect but, to give 'coherence', every architect was to be made responsible for designing houses to let and for sale.[14]

Fred Roche recalled later that this social engineering was done 'in the face of tremendous opposition from the surveying profession. Martin Richardson did a rented scheme in Great Linford. Immediately adjacent was a private housing scheme ... That was sacrilege in the early seventies.'[15]

Today Great Linford is an attractive village set 'in an aspic of green space' in the biggest square in the city. The Ouzel valley with its spacious linear park runs past it. Houses at France Furlong and Cottisford Crescent were designed by Richard MacCormac; Campion was done by Stephen Gardiner (architecture correspondent of *The Observer*); while Hazelwood is the work of Peter Moss.[16] It is as pretty a place as anywhere in the city. Derek Walker, with his well-trained eye, set up an office in Great Linford's old rectory when he left the corporation in 1976.

Eaglestone, which was designed by Ralph Erskine for Bovis Homes, illustrates a different aspect of the reaction. *New City 1975* called Eaglestone 'a jumble of houses, not unlike a small fishing village, with intricate patterns of courtyards, narrow alleys, and little terraces clustered on the side of a hill'. A Mr and Mrs Scott were quoted saying: 'We swore we'd never have a terraced house,' but they had been persuaded to change their minds by the individuality of Erskine's short rows.

Two civic designers from Oxford Polytechnic visited Eaglestone and wrote: 'The architect seems to have created houses which, when personalised with ornaments on window sills, net curtains tied back at the sides, and potted plants on the doorsteps, look

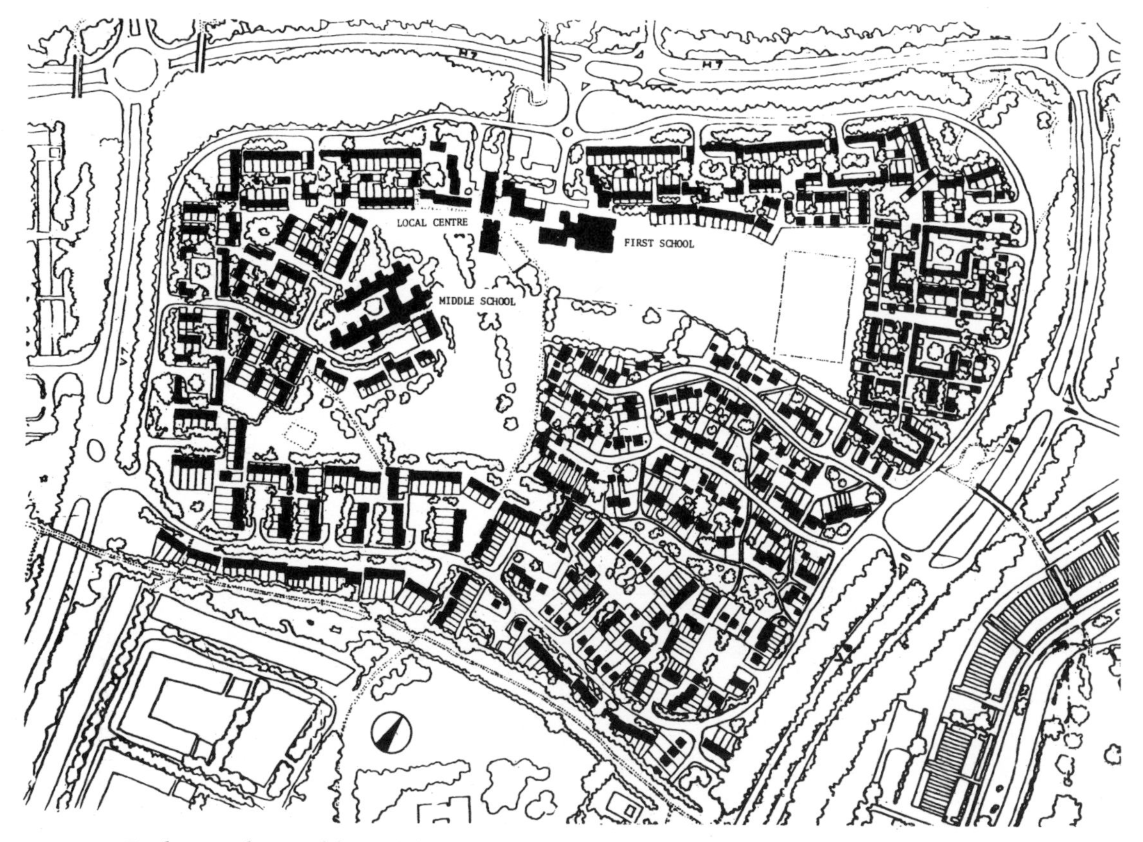

Eaglestone designed by Ralph Erskine with the jumbled layout of an old fishing village.

better and better.'[17] Personalised houses! Potted plants on the doorsteps! Horror of horrors! Bauhaus architects never tolerated that. Had not Mies van der Rohe insisted that all the occupants of some of his Chicago apartments have the same curtains – lest variety distract from the purity of his design?

Wayland Tunley, a corporation architect who designed Neath Hill in 1974, likewise aimed for a village effect even when working on a square containing 800 houses. He arranged Neath Hill in mews around village greens and, for the local centre, designed a clock tower with gables that are Anglo-Japanese. The Oxford Polytechnic reviewers saw in Neath Hill evidence of the resurgence of a 'townscape' movement in housing layouts. *New City 1975* said: 'There is very little here which couldn't have been built one hundred and fifty years ago.'[18]

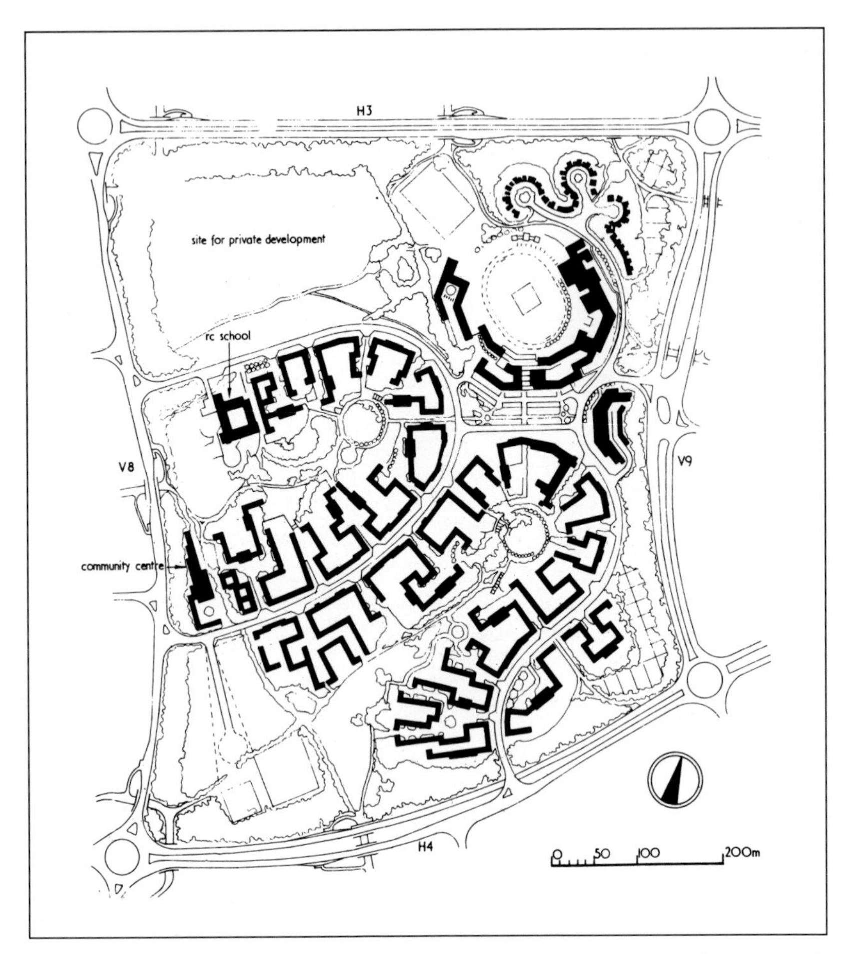

Neath Hill designed by Wayland Tunley as mews looped around parks and gardens.

The origins in this shift in design philosophy seem to have been both internal and external. Board members were one internal force for change. Another was Fred Roche. 'Derek [Walker] was a brilliant designer and a brilliant publicist but he knew very little about large scale housing and I had spent virtually the whole of my career in it,' he said. However, when Roche became general manager he decided not to interfere in Walker's work. 'I did not have a great deal of sympathy with what he was doing and I said so. But having done so, I backed him.' The two worked together for over five years, but Roche eventually decided 'enough is enough'. Walker went back to private practice.

A totally different influence on design was feedback from tenants. A 1974 study for the corporation by Gerald Hoinville of Social and Community Research was the first source of insights. It took the form of a two-way exchange of information. The tenants on five different estates were questioned about their houses, but were also told about the ins and outs of designing them. The same residents were then invited to join discussion evenings. Further insights were gathered through detailed questionnaires completed at these meetings and at sessions with families in their own houses.

A desire for privacy, a preference for kitchens big enough to eat in, a rejection of flats by families with children (and a wish for houses with decent gardens), concern about neighbours' noise in narrow terrace houses, and a longing for lots of indoor and outdoor storage space – all these points emerged from the study. But according to Rowan Mactaggart, the results did not suggest that one estate was better than another; 'nor did they suggest that an average housing solution, which could be the lowest common denominator with available resources, would make families happier'. Instead, they underlined the value of variety – while also giving the thumbs down to such extremes as the allocation of land to parks at the expense of private gardens.[19]

The external sources of a changed approach to design are much harder to pin down. Architecture as a profession was in a state of turmoil in the period when Milton Keynes was getting under way. Public dislike of tower blocks was already strong when Ronan Point collapsed in East Ham in 1968. Architectural arrogance was held, rightly or wrongly, to be substantially to blame. Britain was changing too. The people of the 1960s were less deferential than their parents had been. They were harder to bulldoze than earlier generations. Architects were part of this evolution. They too wanted change.

Camillo Sitte had, of course, been instrumental in bringing about a similar transformation in design in Vienna almost a hundred years before. Writing of his time in a way that seems oddly up to date, he lamented: 'It is only in our mathematical century that the ... enlarging and laying out of cities has become an almost purely technical process.' What appealed to him were the 'sublime and graceful things' to be found in the old cities of Europe where 'magnificent town views, monuments and public squares, beautiful vistas all parade before our musing eye'.

Sitte had schooled his eye in the picturesque as a tourist in Italy and France. Holidays in Spain and Greece must, likewise, have played some part in the changes that architecture underwent at Milton Keynes. How otherwise may one explain the replacement of 'Bauhaus-regimentation' by 'fishing-village romantic'?[20]

11

IMAGE

London first learnt about Milton Keynes through an exhibition at the Design Centre in the Haymarket in 1972. The theme was green and the showmanship was stunning. Derek Walker, who was responsible, recalls: 'We used Astroturf to create the impression of a green field. Malcolm Fowler ... painted idyllic country scenes with blue skies. It was lyrical and actually very like Milton Keynes. There were life-sized sheep in the entrance and the centrepiece was a huge model of Central Milton Keynes.'[1]

Helmut Jacoby's image of an unrealised project for a water garden running down the hill from the city centre towards the River Ouzel.

This was the beginning of a design publicity blitzkrieg that carried the name of Milton Keynes to architects, town planners and landscape architects at the far ends of the earth. As Jeff Bishop observed a few years later: 'It is remarkable how many people know at least the name "Milton Keynes" ... It is not inconceivable to imagine striking up a conversation with a New Zealander at a conference in Canada and finding Milton Keynes emerging into the exchange.'[2]

For three years, starting in 1973, *Architectural Design*, then Britain's most avant-garde design magazine, was commissioned to devote entire issues to Milton Keynes. The first two were all about aesthetics and were written entirely by Derek Walker's staff. The third was devoted to building the city and contained 'A plain man's guide to Milton Keynes without the glossy covers'. It was written by David Crewe, editor of the *Milton Keynes Gazette* and later the corporation's information director. Crewe described the 'mud, sweat and tears' of Milton Keynes life, said that buses were a thorny problem and advised potential residents to think about buying cars. The articles also conveyed the excitement of a great adventure. There were pictures of fibreglass modules, inflatable playgrounds and projects (sadly never built) for a water carpet and cone and a glass bridge in the city park. The graphics were beautiful.[3]

Domus, an Italian journal directed by Gio Ponti, architect of the Pirelli Building in Milan, published in 1973 and 1974 major articles on 'la "grande" nuova cita ... il piu grandioso progetto della storia inglese'.[4] Seductive drawings by Helmut Jacoby and Andrew Mahaddie showed the future city and its citizens; new buildings were illustrated by John Donat – one of Britain's leading architectural photographers; other pictures showed models built by Walker's hand-picked craftsmen ('the group was second to none in the country – only Norman Foster was in the same class'); all conveyed a feel of ethereal modernity. It was image-building of the highest quality and it spread round the world. New-town architecture in Britain had not been so celebrated since the days when Geoffrey Copcutt designed Cumbernauld's city centre in the form of a megastructure – but that had been a much smaller show.

Corporate publicity began to emerge from Wavendon Tower at about the same time. It was aimed at Westminster, Fleet Street, potential investors and, above all, at inadequately housed Londoners. Edition one of *New City*, the corporation's own brochure, was characteristically go-ahead: 'Milton Keynes is conceived as a city of the future – to stand the test of time,' it said, but was also careful to show the city's medieval churches, old pubs and quiet canalside walks. Elsie Reynolds of Mauleverer Road, Brixton, her son and daughter-in-law Tony and Geraldine and their son Jason were the subject of a photo-story. Black and white images, some dramatically overexposed, showed the family's tin bath hanging on a nail in Brixton. A colour photo showed young Jason in his new Fullers Slade

living room looking across an unmade garden to the parkland beyond.

The text recounted how the young couple had looked fruitlessly for two years for a place of their own and how, in the end, Shelter told Tony about opportunities in building work at Milton Keynes. Elsie was sad to see them go. The couple were not sure about moving out of London. The writer makes clear that Tony and Geraldine's new beginning was also the tearful end of a close-knit Brixton family.

Edition two of *New City* aimed likewise at being realistic – 'Milton Keynes ... offers, in the early days, mud in the hallways, a foot in the door and big bills in the letterbox' – while still conveying a strong impression of opportunity at work, school and play. The cover shows an environmentally friendly highway skirting a tree while the layout and photography inside are modelled on high-quality magazines. Not for Milton Keynes the staid commercial brochures of other new-town corporations. *New City 1975* opens with a picture of a family moving in to a new house. The shot is grainy. In the foreground, leaning against a wall, stands a woman looking as sexy as Marlene Dietrich in *The Blue Angel.*[5] Corporate publicity as arty as this sometimes backfired. Frank Henshaw, who was later to succeed Fred Roche as general manager, recalled one purple and black brochure aimed at industrialists. So funereal was it that the commercial staff could never bring themselves to use it.

If the image of Milton Keynes in the early 1970s was created out of nothing by the drawings of architects and graphic artists, it began to be given reality by the great glass shopping building and, in the 1980s, by exhibitions such as 'Homeworld' and 'EnergyWorld'. The exhibitions had a dual function. They drew visitors to the city and led to Press and television coverage. The role of image-maker was meanwhile passing to media experts from whose fertile minds flowed a lively and memorable series of television spots and billboard posters.

Homeworld was the corporation's first exercise in promoting house sales and most of the country's best-known builders took part in it. The exhibition, by giving the builders a shop window for their latest designs, helped to sell Milton Keynes as a place to live. Keith Revill contrasted its consumer-oriented design philosophy with that of 'monolithic schemes such as Netherfield which were not rich enough in choice'. Homeworld ushered in a new era of variety and choice in housing. The corporation's role as a builder shrank to providing sheltered housing for elderly people, homes for the disabled and experiments in energy conservation.

Energy conservation first began to concern the corporation after the oil price increases

LEFT: Homeworld was a corporation-inspired 'Ideal Home' show. Its objectives were to persuade house-builders to innovate, create a wider choice of housing for sale and attract people to Milton Keynes.

Queens Court in the shopping building – an image worked up from the architects' drawings by Helmut Jacoby.

of 1973. The economics of the West suffered a heavy blow. Inflation became traumatic and the long-term effects were far-reaching. An International Energy Agency was set up in Paris. The gas-guzzling US motor industry began a decade of 'downsizing'. And conservation of fuel entered into the calculations of every major user.

Milton Keynes, based as it was on the assumption that there were limitless supplies of fuel, suddenly seemed to be at risk. Yet hidden in the action of the oil-producing states was a bonus. The corporation, uncertainly at first but then with more conviction, began to play a national role in energy conservation. Starting with an assessment of how the city might be endangered by rising energy costs, the corporation moved on to gather publicity from its innovative 'green' houses and, in the 1980s, to assist in the definition of national energy efficiency standards. It was a role to which Henry Chilver, with his deep interest in science and engineering, was ideally suited when he became chairman.

The corporation first sought to establish to what extent the city was at risk in a report called 'The plan for Milton Keynes: flexibility 1975', on which Richard Llewelyn-Davies and Dr Peter Chapman of the Open University Energy Research Unit collaborated. The authors reached three main conclusions: the plan had sufficient flexibility to cope with changes such as the increased cost of energy; an increase in population density was needed for the city to accommodate 250,000 people; and the evolution of public transport would probably result in greater travel along some corridors which could be supported by raising development densities.

Jock Campbell called a seminar to debate these issues and invited those present to consider 'whether in the light of economic changes brought about by the energy crisis, a policy of higher densities centred on public transport routes and local facilities should be adopted'.

The members were sceptical about the conclusions in 'Flexibility 1975' and reluctant to accept the officers' arguments that housing densities should be increased. The minutes indicate that Ray Bellchambers was particularly forthright. 'He was amazed by the paper's prediction that cars would be the first thing that people would give up in the face of economic pressure. The car had widened the horizons of the lower wage groups enormously.'

Peter Chapman went out on a limb. 'The current economic difficulties were not just a hiccup in the former economic growth trend,' he prophesied. They were 'a fundamental change in the economic situation ... His personal view was that in no way could technological advance cope with the continuous increase in energy demand forecast for the next forty to fifty years; and as oil deposits were limited a world shortage must be expected by the year 2000.'

With the benefit of hindsight it is clear that Chapman was wrong and Bellchambers

right. Traffic growth did blip down a little in the early 1970s and again after the 1978 price increase but it was soon rocketing up again as car owners decided that driving was one of the last things they were prepared to give up. Meanwhile the skills of the automotive engineers were bringing steady improvements in the fuel efficiency of cars even though during the 1980s the price of oil fell back to pre-1973 levels.[6]

Housing design began to be influenced by the pursuit of energy efficiency during the same period. The foundations were laid in 1976 when the corporation set up an energy consultative unit and again formed a link with the Open University. From this collaboration flowed insulation kits, low-energy and solar-energy houses and a series of solar houses at Pennyland and Great Linford. By the beginning of the 1980s the corporation estimated that eight of its energy-saving projects were saving £200,000 a year in fuel bills.[7]

In 1982 the unit conceived the idea of an 'energy-conserving park' which led in time to a 300-acre site at Knowlhill and Shenley Lodge. Frank Henshaw regarded the park as one of the major innovations of the 1980s. It was also a product of the corporate style he introduced into the executive. Everybody was behind it.[8] 'EnergyWorld' – an exhibition of fifty-one energy-efficient houses – followed in 1986. The show was for Milton Keynes what the Wissenschaft Werkbund was for the Bauhaus architects. It generated widespread coverage in the media and attracted huge numbers of visitors. One of them was Margaret Thatcher whom Henry Chilver invited to the exhibition while it was being devoted to promoting energy efficiency in business.[9]

Writing about EnergyWorld, *The Times* said: 'The exhibition showed that energy-efficient houses did not have to be built underground or have vast solar panels, though that helps. Most looked "ordinary", and were made energy-efficient by simple means that added little to the building cost.' The houses showed that fuel bills could be cut by about one third.[10] Some of the ideas shown were simplicity itself. In one house hot water consumption was cut by installing a small bath and sprinkler taps.

By 1990 Milton Keynes had a national reputation for leadership in energy management. Thermal efficiency standards such as the Milton Keynes Energy Cost Index had been defined and a national centre set up to promote awareness of efficient energy use. Nowhere in Britain was there such a concentration of 'green' houses. Five thousand of them, mostly south-facing, were equipped with underfloor and roof insulation, double glazing and high-efficiency boilers. About 600 of these, which were in the energy park, were rated seven on a one-to-ten thermal efficiency index devised by the National Energy Foundation (NEF). This rating was one point ahead of the standard set for the country as a whole by the 1990

LEFT: Milton Keynes' earliest imagery was generated by architecture and design. From 1985 onwards, television and poster campaigns featured children with balloons and other lifestyle images.

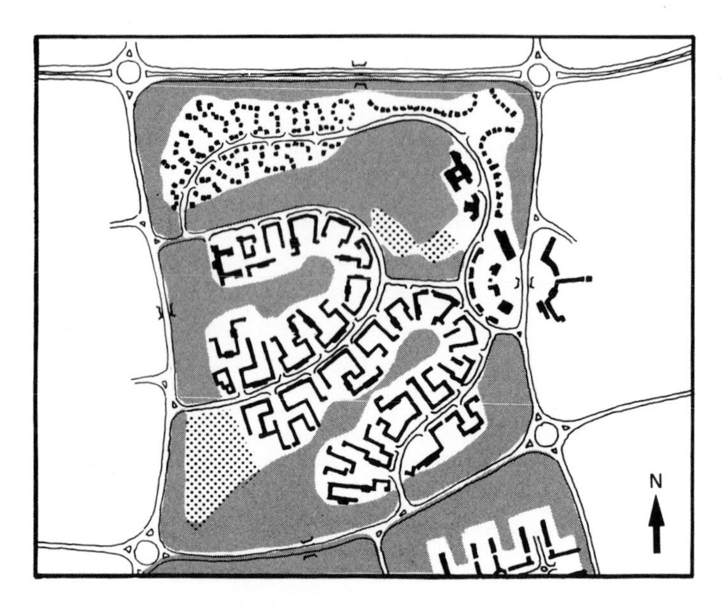

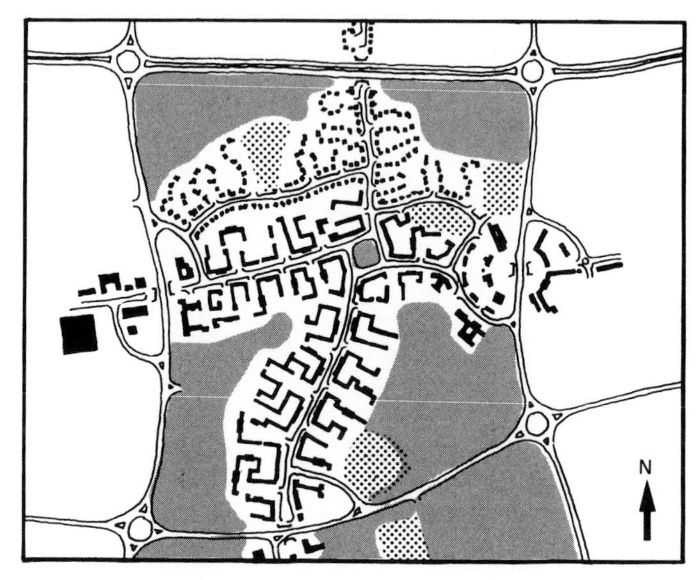

In 1979 the energy unit redesigned Neath Hill to show how fuel consumption might have been minimised. Several changes were suggested: houses should be faced southwards and given space to catch the sun; routes should be defined for buses (and hot water pipes from a local power station) and higher density houses built close to them; cycle- and footways should be modified to make them more attractive; allotments should be provided close to houses.

National Building Regulations. Subsequent houses in the energy park were expected to be rated eight.

Building quoted Richard Amos, design manager for Bovis Homes, as saying that 'the extra £2,000 incurred on a three- and four-bedroomed house demonstrated that energy efficiency was not out of the reach of most people'. And Bovis were aiming to go well beyond eight on the NEF index.[11]

Henry Chilver viewed the city in the 1980s as a place to which people were drawn by the promise of opportunity. 'People came with very real expectations – which were fulfilled – that you could, almost by dint of personal and family enterprise, get involved in a city of enormously high quality. The environment was excellent. There were opportunities for starting up afresh. Your children went to new schools. The streets were clean and wide open.'

The corollary of this was that the city was increasingly given its shape by agents other than the corporation. Speaking of the board, Chilver said: 'We concentrate very much on principles. We provide a clearly defined role for the executive. I believe we have made it as simple as we can for the executives to operate and get moving fast. I suspect that in the seventies where buildings were concerned the board might even have decided which colour of bricks to use. Nowadays we listen to members' criticisms of the schemes being put up, let the schemes go through and say these are the features we will be looking for next time ... We don't hold up the progress of executive action.'

Using the city centre as an example, Chilver added: 'We've got an enormous variety of architecture now ... and that's been achieved by not letting the board meddle in the initial details put to them. We've encouraged variety. A board cannot work effectively if it's going to deal with all the minutiae. What it has to check is whether the minutiae are within the framework of its policies.'[12]

While changes of this kind were going on in the way that Milton Keynes was designed and shaped, the consumer's view of the city was changing too. 'It used to be a music hall joke – a place where you sent your mother-in-law,' Bill Benyon, the MP for Milton Keynes, observed during the recession of the early 1990s. 'It has changed a bit now. There is a very, very strong undercurrent of envy. They [other MPs] can't quite understand why we have done so well.'[13]

Erroll Ray, whose recollections of the city went back to its earliest days, noticed something else. 'A few years ago, if you said to somebody living here, "Where do you come from?", they would answer "Liverpool", "Leeds" or "London". There was nothing to identify with. I think that is changing. Nowadays if you meet somebody on holiday from the city, he will say he comes from Milton Keynes.'[14] The city was growing up. No longer just a name, some clever graphics and an easy butt for jokes about concrete cows, it was becoming a place to which its citizens belonged.

12

HOUSES FOR RENT

Building a new town is about jobs and homes, but development corporations do not create the jobs. They attract employers by building houses – and Milton Keynes was going to build them as no new town had ever done before. During the very month that Walter Ismay was named the corporation's managing director, East Kilbride, Scotland's first new town, announced that it had built 1,486 houses over the preceding year. It took East Kilbride twenty years to work up to this new-town record. Milton Keynes was, within a few years, going to build houses at almost twice that rate.

It took some time to get going. An earlier start might have been possible had Whitehall commissioned the master plan. As it was, 1968 was taken up with planning, 1969 with planning and buying sites (at about £1,000 an acre) and it was only in 1970 that decisions began to be made about building the first houses. Up until then the huge, grey estate being built by the Greater London Council (GLC) on the outskirts of Bletchley at Water Eaton was widely thought to be the beginning of the new city. It had been announced on the day that Ismay's name was made public.

Water Eaton's 2,000 houses symbolised Bletchley's determination to go on growing and, new town or no new town, to use its partnership with the GLC to push towards a population of 40,000 people by 1981. It took nearly four years to build the vast estate and it was, for that plucky, go-ahead railway junction, a sad swan-song.

In March 1971 Jock Campbell was able to report to the Minister that the corporation had 453 homes under construction and that builders of houses for sale had signed contracts to build 543 more. Negotiations for a further 455 privately financed houses were 'at a very

LEFT: The repetition of porticos on Victorian terraces reinterpreted at Netherfield in the form of projecting fins.

advanced stage'.[1] Houses were, at long last, on the way and even seemed to be on target for the Minister's fifty-fifty split between public and private finance.

A year later Campbell was able to report that 1,477 houses had been started, that contracts for 3,500 would be signed within six months and that no fewer than 6,000 more dwellings were at an advanced stage of design.[2] The Roche–Walker machine was rolling. But all was not well. The lowest tender for Bradville, one of the corporation's very first schemes, came in at fifteen per cent over the government's cost limit, the notorious 'yardstick'. Two years later Whitehall agreed to a special seven per cent tolerance for Milton Keynes but still the architects complained that their task was nearly impossible.[3]

Government regulation by 'cost yardsticks' was to dog the corporation throughout the 1970s. It affected the design, production and management of corporation-built houses. Together with Britain's roller-coaster economy it turned house-building at Milton Keynes into a task of the most testing kind.

Yardsticks were introduced in 1967. Two years earlier Harold Wilson's Government, as its contribution to the money that local authorities borrowed to build houses, had started paying councils the difference between four per cent and the prevailing rate of interest. (Interest was then 6.25 per cent.) It was the first major change in housing subsidies since the 1920s and perhaps because of this Whitehall made a nonsense and failed to put any limit on what a house might cost. The effect was to give a blank cheque to housing authorities, which were not only in the midst of the hugely expensive tower-block era, but also under pressure to build to the higher space standards urged in *Homes for Today and Tomorrow* – the 1961 Parker Morris report.

The Government stopped the rot by making a version of the Parker Morris standards obligatory and setting down the maximum costs it would subsidise. This took the form of an index, 'the yardsticks', variable from place to place depending on local building costs, and from site to site depending on housing density.

According to Patrick Dunleavy the yardsticks were intended not only to encourage efficient design and production but also 'to discourage local authorities from building unnecessarily expensive houses, especially high-rise housing'.[4] Milton Keynes discovered something else. They were designed to discourage as well the eight- or ten-to-the-acre houses to which the corporation was committed.

It was an issue to which the board returned repeatedly as the architects, seemingly ground between the upper and nether millstones of Parker Morris space standards and financial yardsticks, were forced to simplify their designs and push up densities. As the board saw it, the result was barrack-like terraces instead of cottages with roses round the door.

Jock Campbell left the Minister in no doubt about the problems he was facing. 'Ever increasing building costs, combined with the limitations and constraints of the housing cost yardstick system have made the production of houses for rent difficult and frustrating,' he reported in March 1972. The following year he described house-building as 'one of the most intractable problems of the past 12 months'.[5]

In June 1973 the board was told that the gap between building costs and yardstick allowances would, over a period of three years, endanger the whole of the first seven years' housing programme. There 'never had been a period of greater constraint; and because of the sheer size of the programme … the inadequacy of current standards would be magnified'. The houses being designed for the six squares surrounding the future city centre were particularly at risk.

It was agreed to approach the Government through the annual report, by high-level meetings, by writing to Paul Channon, the Housing and Construction Minister, and by writing 'even possibly to senior ministers'.[6]

The oil price increases of 1973 which led to the miners' strike and Edward Heath's ill-judged 'Who rules Britain?' election of 1974 were at the centre of the corporation's difficulties. Public housing was already in a state of transformation as a result of changes introduced by the Conservatives after 1970. Subsidies tied to buildings were abolished by the 1972 Housing Finance Act and replaced by 'fair rents' and rent allowances related to the incomes of tenants. Councils also had their power to subsidise rents from the rates limited and became subject to a mechanism designed to eliminate deficits in their housing revenue accounts. Behind these changes and a commitment to raise rents in line with inflation, was the aim of the Conservatives to encourage tenants to buy their houses.

On his return to power in 1974, Harold Wilson stood all this on its head. While construction costs (and therefore subsidy costs) soared, Labour struggled to speed up public house-building and to switch improvement grants from the terraced houses of the gentry to older council estates. At Milton Keynes, shortages of building materials (due to the three-day week induced by the miners' strike) delayed completions and financial constraints caused 'an erosion of housing standards'. Corners were cut to keep up output. 'In some cases, footpaths, fencing, gates and landscaping have had to be sacrificed for the sake of the actual building,' Campbell told the Minister.[7]

By 1976 the country had exhausted its foreign currency reserves in trying to defend the pound. The Government, virtually bankrupt, obtained a loan from the International Monetary Fund (IMF) only on the condition that public spending was severely cut. In many ways it was the beginning of the end for the welfare state.

Derek Walker and Frank Henshaw (chief architect and chief quantity surveyor respectively) set down the agony of it all in a paper entitled *The Housing Dilemma*. 'We face a crisis in housing which most of us working on the subject … view with profound pessimism. It's not just that we can't build enough – it's about the quality of those we can build.'

The ruthless limits of the yardstick frustrated the introduction of variety and quality in large schemes. They forced down ceiling heights, killed off balconies and bay windows and 'led to an architecture of cosmetics where colour and ultimately blanket landscape form a camouflage ... It seems sad to reduce housing design to an assemblage of inadequate shells in pleasant and variable landscaped spaces.'

Industrialised building was another problem. Most of the systems were 'ugly ducklings' although a glimmer of hope lay in factory-made houses with timber frames. They, at least in theory, offered some latitude to the designer. Furthermore, the yardsticks were supposed to permit 'special architectural treatment or special materials' although Whitehall rarely allowed such additions. As for the supposed discretion of housing authorities to go above basic standards, it had become 'meaningless'. The frustration felt by these two able officials at working an impossible system is almost palpable. The yardsticks were a huge costly bureaucracy which the country 'with its continuing housing need, can ill afford'.[8]

For the board members a related and vexing issue was housing density. The members wanted to see the Milton Keynes promised in the master plan – a place of cottages with roses round the door. What they feared they were getting was a camp of barrack-like terraces. (This was the period which saw Netherfield, Coffee Hall and Beanhill.) Ralph Verney was particularly sensitive to this issue. In the summer of 1972 the minutes report him questioning 'the use of so much terrace housing on low-density layouts'. Yardstick terrace housing had, he thought, 'destroyed much of the environment'. With incomes rising, it should surely be possible to spend more money and press the Department of the Environment to adjust the yardsticks accordingly.

Derek Walker replied that it was very difficult to design semi-detached houses within the yardsticks and that, furthermore, 'with terrace housing a much better total environment could be produced'. To his architect's eye the 'whole was greater than the

Houses for rent at Heelands designed for the development corporation by MacCormac Jamieson in 1979. The houses with their distinctive towers formed part of the final surge of public housing.

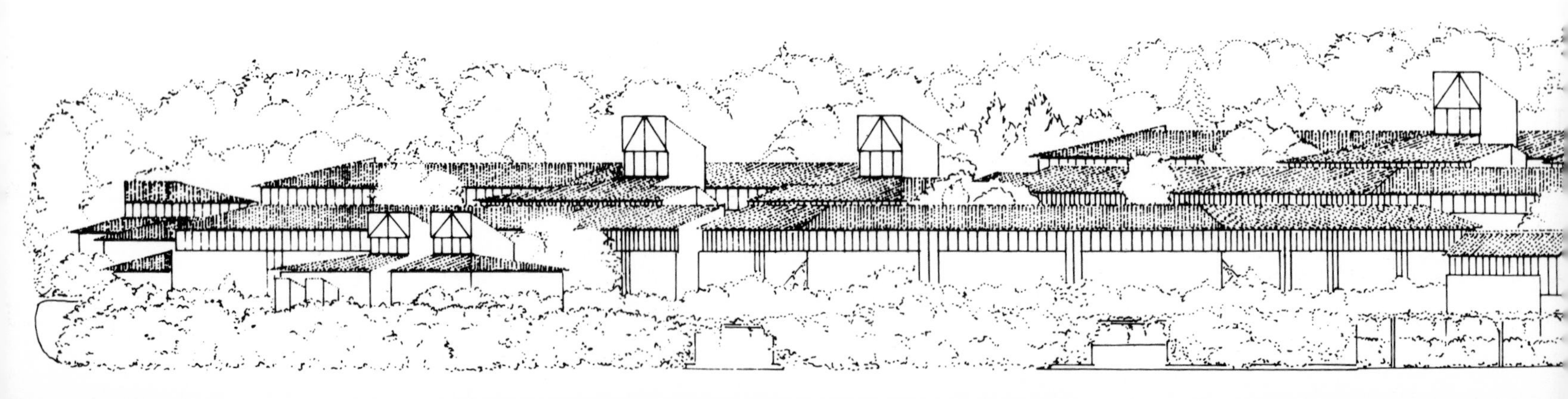

parts' and with a terrace 'the proportions were much pleasanter to look at than with semi-detached [houses]'.[9]

Looking back on this period Jock Campbell wondered whether the architects were being entirely straight about what they could and could not do. 'The problems of the yardstick always made it possible for the architects to say they could not afford to do it in the proper way,' he observed. 'I never really believed that – but it was very difficult to challenge.'[10]

Meanwhile, Fred Roche's efforts to persuade Whitehall to agree to higher standards were paying off. The Ministry had already agreed to houses of higher quality being built in central Milton Keynes and the architects were hard at work designing town houses for Fishermead, Springfield and other squares adjacent to the central area. Further moves in this direction were taken in July 1974 when the board decided to seek Ministry agreement to a ten per cent allowance for large numbers of 'higher standard' houses and a fifteen per cent allowance for a smaller number of 'standard 2' houses.

All the higher quality houses were to be assessed on a fair-rent and not a cost-rent basis, thereby giving the corporation freedom to assign expensive houses to low-income tenants and so pursue social balance in all parts of the city. Roche foresaw problems if the fair-rent legislation were repealed but considered that the right policy was 'to build to as high a quality as was feasible and to rely on inflation to overtake the rents as historically it had always done'.[11]

But the lean years were not over. In 1975 a circular from the Department of the Environment banned the provision of garages and carports and even reduced the extent of the hard standings that could be provided for cars. The corporation cursed the Department for its obliviousness to lead times, decided to press for concessions and 'to ignore the instruction in all schemes on which designing had already begun'.[12]

Yet by 1976, although the Treasury was by then beholden to the IMF, the corporation's push for higher standards and for architectural variety was showing. 'The opening up of new areas and the addition of higher-standard housing has, during the past year, created a much wider choice of house types and sizes for new tenants,' Jock Campbell reported to the Minister.[13]

The storms of the mid-1970s were abating and Milton Keynes was a vast construction

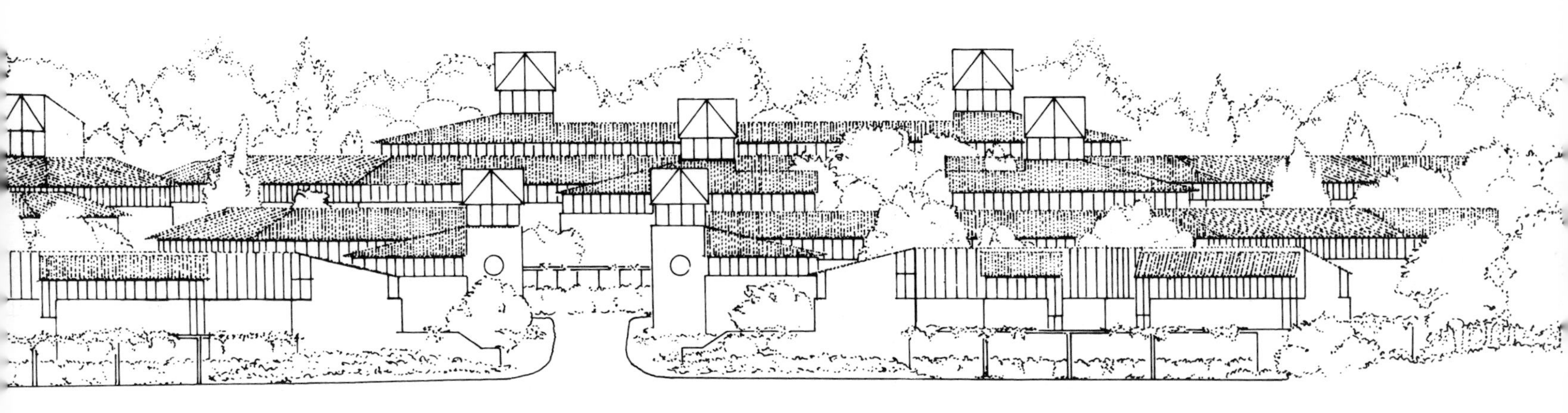

site. Gone were the days when firms like Hinkins and Frewin had to bus bricklayers in from Oxford. Six thousand building workers were employed on the new city and Llewellyn Construction were turning out timber-framed houses which did not resemble air-raid bunkers. Prefabrication was coming of age.

Prototypes of timber-house technology had arrived over a decade earlier when the country was still in the heavy embrace of concrete high-risers. The Canadian government was looking for ways to sell more timber and Richard Crossman was shown what they had to offer. He was impressed. The houses were 'just as safe in terms of fire damage as brick houses, infinitely warmer in terms of insulation and about the same price even with imported Canadian timber'. They had, however, 'been made to look as much like English council houses as possible, which destroys their whole colonial attraction'. Crossman was objecting to their brick casings.[14]

A decade later such prejudices were irrelevant. Brick and tile were by then the height of fashion; the adaptability of timber offered the architects useful freedom and, in places like Milton Keynes, public housing was moving away from 'good design' and beginning to lose its municipal image.

In 1976, the year of the New Towns Amendment Act, the output of public-sector houses reached its peak and the corporation began to consider handing over its stock to the borough council. John Silkin's strictures about local authorities playing a bigger role in new towns made such a move obligatory. But when the two bodies discussed the matter, it became clear that the borough was deeply worried by the prospect. The council was concerned, Jock Campbell told the board, that 'when the corporation began to hand over their houses, probably in the mid-eighties, they would be handing over house designs, rent policies, and management systems, which with the best will in the world, might land the borough in acute difficulties'. The borough, therefore, proposed an evolutionary process leading to a common housing policy.

Campbell had made clear to the liaison committee that the corporation had a job to do and could not accept divided responsibilities but, with that proviso, the more consultation the better. A joint working group was accordingly set up and in due course Frank Atter became its chairman.[15]

'The most intractable problem, to which the borough would have to find the solution,

TOP RIGHT: Fishermead, like all the groups of houses close to the city centre, was built as a series of terraces and squares rather like Edinburgh's eighteenth-century new town. Helmut Jacoby drew this perspective when Fishermead's main street was still unbuilt.

BOTTOM RIGHT: Terrace houses around a square at Fishermead: most of the flat roofs were later given a pitch.

36
40

was the widening gap between the rents charged by the corporation and the council,' Atter reported a year later. The high cost (and therefore rents) of the borough's expensive new houses were cross-subsidised by its stock of older houses, the costs of which had been amortised by time and inflation. The borough could also channel money from the rates into housing management. But when it took over the corporation's stock of newish houses the effect on rents of its stock of older houses would become insignificant. Unless the DoE could be persuaded to help, rents would rise inevitably and steeply.[16]

Margaret Thatcher's arrival at Downing Street in 1979 changed the rules and tested to the hilt the corporation's resourcefulness in the face of new conditions. Between 1974 and 1982 the number of new houses for rent built annually by the corporation only once fell below 2,000. When the ready supply of Treasury money that made this possible was chopped by the Conservatives, the corporation turned to houses for shared ownership (regarded by the Government as 'in the spirit of home ownership'). When even those funds were withdrawn the corporation sought to build affordable homes by setting up a housing association and providing it with private money.

The corporation had no choice but to promote housing for sale. As Henry Chilver, who became chairman in 1983, put it, 'Development corporations have to exploit the climate in which they operate ... [and] the environment we came in on was one in which there was a general movement politically against public housing in cities.'

Complaining that Milton Keynes would be ruined by this change would have been fruitless. It would have been 'bashing your head against a brick wall. It is not that we discouraged public housing,' Chilver added. 'We would have liked some – particularly sheltered housing [in order] to improve the variety there.'[17]

The election of the Conservatives in 1979 coincided with further efforts to transfer houses to the borough council under the provisions of Labour's 1976 Act. Within months of Mrs Thatcher's election, the two authorities decided that the borough should become involved 'as soon as practicable in the actual management of corporation housing'. They agreed to make 1 April 1982 a target date for transfer and to approach the Environment Secretary for the necessary authority. They decided too that, except for certain types of specialist housing, the corporation should still be 'the sole agency for public sector house building in the city'.

The atmosphere was positive. The officers who had designed the management agency plan were commended for their excellent work and Luing Cowley, leader of the borough council, called it 'a good attempt to provide a means of solving the main problems

LEFT: *Fullers Slade, an architectural showpiece dating from the early 1970s. The houses had single sloped roofs, criss-cross cedar cladding and tiny gardens.*

experienced by other new towns in transferring housing'.[18]

In 1982 the borough began to administer the corporation's houses under a management agreement, and most people assumed that, in due course, ownership would be transferred too. 'Until recently it was government policy that [new-town] houses went to the local housing authority,' Michael Murray, the chief executive of the borough council, said later. 'It was always the plan here.'[19]

Meanwhile, although public house-building petered out, the huge stock built up by the corporation during the 1970s stood it in good stead. As Bill Benyon later observed, until the mid-1980s 'we were still housing young couples on their wedding day. They gave notice that they would be getting married and there was the house waiting for them.'[20]

It was too good to last. The drying up of the supply of new houses to rent coupled with the sale of those that existed to their occupants ('particularly the best stuff,' Fred Roche observed)[21] led eventually to a shortage of modestly priced accommodation. By 1986, although forty-two per cent of the houses in the city were still rented (the average for other English new towns was forty-seven per cent), applicants for lettings were running at 3,000 a year. Yet the housing authorities could only lay their hands on about 1,200 vacancies. Milton Keynes began, for the first time, to know homelessness.

One of the few avenues open to the corporation to increase the supply of lettings was to persuade tenants to become owner-occupiers elsewhere. In the early 1980s such transfers were assisted by Treasury finance for shared ownership but by the middle of the decade even this source of public funds dried up. Surveys showed that thirty to forty per cent of tenants might be able to afford mortgages but, as the board noted, 'the dilemma was how to get people to move on'.[22]

It was at this point that government policy started to drive a wedge between the corporation and the borough council. The cause was John Silkin's 1976 New Towns Amendment Act. Conservative ministers began to realise that it promised to perpetuate the role of local authorities as landlords. The Government's objective was otherwise. It was, the board heard, 'to diversify the ownership and management of public sector housing and to give tenants more say in the running of their estates'. The DoE, therefore, told the corporation not to transfer its houses to the council but to find a variety of future owners for them.[23]

The issue came to a head when the borough, disregarding a request from the corporation, undertook a survey 'directed at obtaining views on tenants' co-operatives'. This caused an explosion. The board considered that 'the survey did not give a broad enough view of the options that would be available' and, after the borough failed to agree to follow its directions, decided to take back the management of its houses.[24] Michael Murray observed that the grounds given by the corporation for this change were 'specious'. The government was talking about holding ballots among tenants and 'we had sent a leaflet to all our tenants and all the corporation tenants about the future of the housing stock. We said we were the best people in the world to manage it.'[25] Frank Henshaw emphasised that the dispute was about authority, not about the quality of housing management. The corporation would never have employed agents unwilling to heed its wishes.

Erroll Ray, clerk of the old Bletchley council and first chief executive of the borough council, reckoned 'there was always a germ of dispute' between the corporation and the borough. The germ had been kept from spreading in the 1970s by circumstances and by Jock Campbell. 'He was courteous and he was tough,' but he knew about the divisions in other new towns and 'he would try and give [Milton Keynes] a new sort of emphasis and to a very large extent I think he did ... I can't recall any occasion on which we were unable to arrive at a sensible conclusion or compromise. He was very good from that point of view.'[26]

Conditions in the 1980s and early 1990s could not have been more different. Political attitudes became more acutely defined. The personalities and politics of the corporation's chairmen changed and the political complexion of Milton Keynes Borough Council changed too. Having been Conservative from 1976 to 1984, it was hung until May 1990 and then went Labour.

Senior councillors became increasingly critical of the corporation. 'It has been very frustrating watching a group of unelected people spending our money,' Kevin Wilson, the Labour leader told the *Milton Keynes Gazette* in 1990. Sam Crooks, the Liberal Democrat leader, went further and characterised Henry Chilver as a dictator. 'He appears to have continually carried out his policies without any kind of consultation unless it is absolutely required,' he said. 'I am told there is only one person on the board who will stand up to him and that is no way to run this city.'[27]

People needing houses to rent were amongst the sufferers of these more ideologically charged times. No one saw that more clearly than Bill Benyon, the city's Conservative MP. 'We did very well out of the Thatcher years – with one notable exception – low-cost housing for rent and purchase. The government didn't, and still doesn't, realise how important it is to prime the pump.' To enable people to move into the city 'you have got initially to have low-cost housing for rent and purchase. That is still the main thing that is going wrong.'[28]

Henry Chilver, characteristically, saw solutions emerging from the private sector. 'I think that will be the major revolution in Britain as we break down the problem of housing – particularly as we get involved in the EEC,' he said. Continental countries were likely to be a source of ideas and finance. 'We shall shortly have mortgages from European banks coming into Milton Keynes.'[29]

13

Central Milton Keynes

Most towns grow outwards. The first buildings appear by a bridge or a landing and eventually they become the centre of a city. Milton Keynes was different. It grew inwards from the fringes of Bletchley and the northern towns towards what was, for many years, a vast building site. During this period the city was little more than a ribbon of housing estates, factories and, of course, the Open University. There was, as Gertrude Stein observed of Los Angeles, 'no there, there'.

The coming into use of the first buildings in Central Milton Keynes completed the ribbon. Fred Roche told the board at its 1977 seminar that he saw it as the beginning of a new era. 'The opening of CMK would create a different image, which the corporation must be quick to exploit during the next ten years.' It was time to start building hotels and other community facilities as well as houses. The age of predominantly public finance would give way to one in which private funds would play an increasing role in shaping the new city.[1]

Creating CMK was for the corporation a task second only in importance to the master plan. The centre would have to cater for people on foot in the motor age and be the symbolic heart of the city. It would begin too to provide a wider range of jobs for women; and, with its brand-new railway station, would become the focus of the city's bus services. Gradually it would become a great regional centre for offices.

The plan that was eventually adopted was bold, brave and un-English. Its rectangularity is without precedent in other English new towns and has few parallels in city centres elsewhere. It was also radically different from the city centre envisaged by the master planners. They designed CMK as a rambling place arranged around pedestrian squares and malls and topped off by eye-catching (and no doubt wind-blasting) towers. They also

Left: The Point, the first place of entertainment built in the city centre: bars, a bingo hall, a night-club and a multi-screen cinema are all topped off in red neon.

Central Milton Keynes looking westwards from above the M1: the master planners showed towers of offices being used to create the feel of a big city.

attempted to distance cars from people by pushing parking to the fringes of the centre. In all this there was a strong resemblance to the centre of a never-built new town proposed by the London County Council for Hook in Hampshire.

Hook was high-fashion 1960s town planning and of it Robert Maxwell (the architect, not the tycoon) wrote: 'The pedestrian scale introduces a kind of touristic aesthetic, the qualities enjoyed by architects on holiday, the guilt-free harmony of architecture without architects.'[2] The master plan version of CMK was similar.

Derek Walker's team had a vision that enabled them to forget all about their holidays. They started by looking at the consequences of gathering all the buildings into one square but, in the end, to provide room for cars, decided to disperse them across three and a half squares. But how were the cars to circulate? The planners decided on broad boulevards flanked by parking and then by footways – classic city streets expanded to provide room for the age of the Ford Sierra. The result is three long boulevards that run across the centre from one end to the other. Beside them are planted 6,500 London planes. Station Square, at one end of the boulevards, is a 'Trafalgar Square' surrounded on three sides by office buildings. Early drawings of it show a spire or obelisk at the foot of Midsummer Boulevard – a yet-to-be-built Milton Keynes variant on Nelson's column. At the other end of the boulevards is a park with a belvedere offering long views to the east.

In contradistinction to the city plan, the layout of the centre and its adjoining residential squares is a celebration of the right angle. It is very formal, very continental. It could be the work of Wren. Robert Maxwell called it 'astonishing in its purity of form'. It seemed to him barely possible that such 'geometrical rigour' could be built in Britain where new towns were conceived as 'neo-medieval enclaves of picturesque variety, offering closure of views ... and meandering streets'.[2]

The planners of the city centre drew attention to something else. 'It is ironic,' they noted, 'that some of the urban forms previously designed for the aggrandisement of princes are now very suitable for accommodating and lessening the impact of the motor vehicle.'

Yet providing elegantly for cars was not their overriding concern. By the early 1970s central London may have been a mess of traffic but it was also a stubble of egotistical office towers. The towers, with the exception of London Wall, formed no pattern. Their locations were not the fruit of design. They were the chance offerings of the property market. The *tabula rasa* of Bradwell Common offered the possibility of something different. The plan would be a framework to ensure that the city centre as a whole was greater than the parts contributed to it by individual architects.

The planners aimed to provide 'some of those urban delights, space, greenery, the opportunity for peace and quiet, and the absence of paternalistic or authoritarian gestures which [quoting from the master plan] "will enable the people of Milton Keynes to

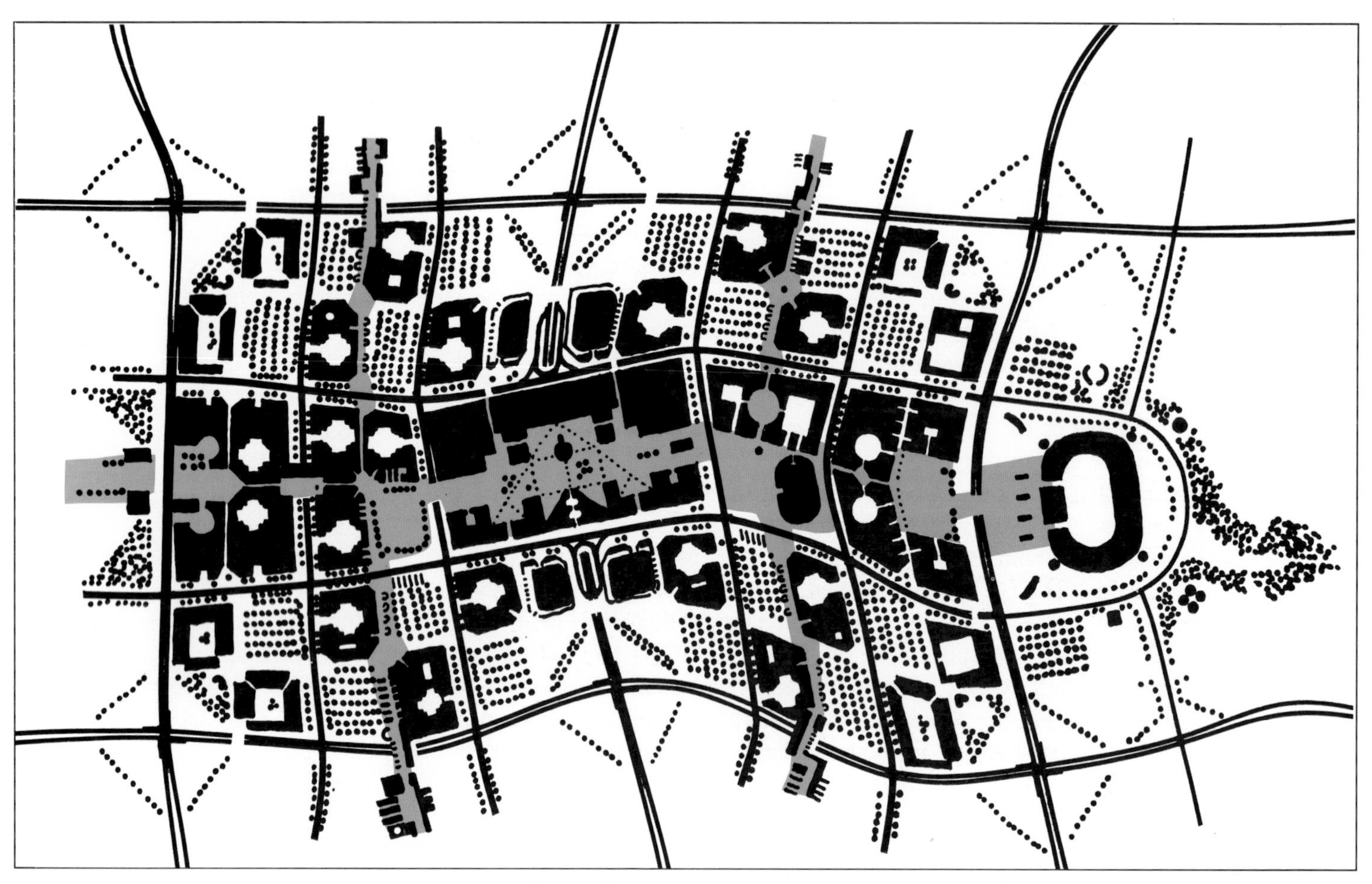

Central Milton Keynes arranged around a pedestrian mall – from the master plan. The dotted areas were intended as parks.

experience and contribute to a richness of environment free from the constraints often imposed by the very technologies with which man intended to liberate himself"'.

Fred Roche first reported about the design of CMK in October 1972. (A team of professionals led by Stuart Mosscrop had already been beavering away on the plan for twelve months.) Roche told the members that it would be an investment of £60m and should be 'judged against the seven goals which it set out to achieve – diversity, viability, flexibility, identity, accessibility, safety and interaction'.

The quality of flexibility was intended, above all, to cope with the ups and downs of the property market. It was for this reason that CMK was not designed as a 'megastructure' or battleship-like building as at Cumbernauld and Runcorn. On the contrary, it was laid out as a surveyor might have suggested, and indeed Mervyn and Paul Orchard Lisle of Healey and Baker, the leading London retail property surveyors, were present at that October 1972 meeting.

Yet CMK was not just a property developer's dream. In presenting it to the board, Derek Walker said: 'Great emphasis would be placed on the quality of the road system and tree planting. The movement of people and traffic in superb surroundings would be of more importance to the quality of Milton Keynes than the elevations of the buildings, which might even include some vulgarity.'

Walker described how other cities had been studied to find spaces that would 'be both manageable and human in scale'. Grosvenor Square had been chosen 'as the right size' for the main subdivisions of the city centre. Ease of parking for visitors would be reconciled with the good appearance of the streets by sinking all the car spaces slightly below the level of the boulevards and by surrounding them with bushes. This promised to avoid both 'the expense of multi-storey parks' and the ugliness of asphalt deserts. Spaces for 6,500 cars would be within five minutes' walk of the main shops with 9,000 spaces within seven minutes. Walkways would link all parts of CMK and be ramped under the boulevards.

The scale of the city centre was hard to grasp. It was huge. Members were told that it would cover 162 hectares or an area equivalent to those parts of London's West End bounded by Oxford Street and Piccadilly, Park Lane and St Martin's Lane.

Richard Llewelyn-Davies showed no regrets at the vanquishing of his design. He was thrilled by the new thinking and commended it as 'a very exciting break-away from the established approach'. The proposals would be 'a landmark in city centre planning'. Ralph Verney was less enthusiastic. With Fred Pooley's monorail city apparently still in mind, he questioned whether motor cars would 'still be playing a dominant role by the time the city was built'. He thought that by then the railway station and public transport would be more important.

It was wishful thinking. CMK was going to be a drive-in centre. Buses would circulate the boulevards (a sixteen-passenger, electrically operated vehicle was under test in Leeds) and the 'central road reservations would permit other forms of transport' but studies by Sainsbury's suggested that seven out of ten shoppers would arrive by car. The plan was agreed, and congratulations were minuted to those who had worked so hard to design and present it.[3]

If the shopping building was the corporation's first priority in the city centre, getting British Rail to commit itself to a new railway station was almost as important. These two

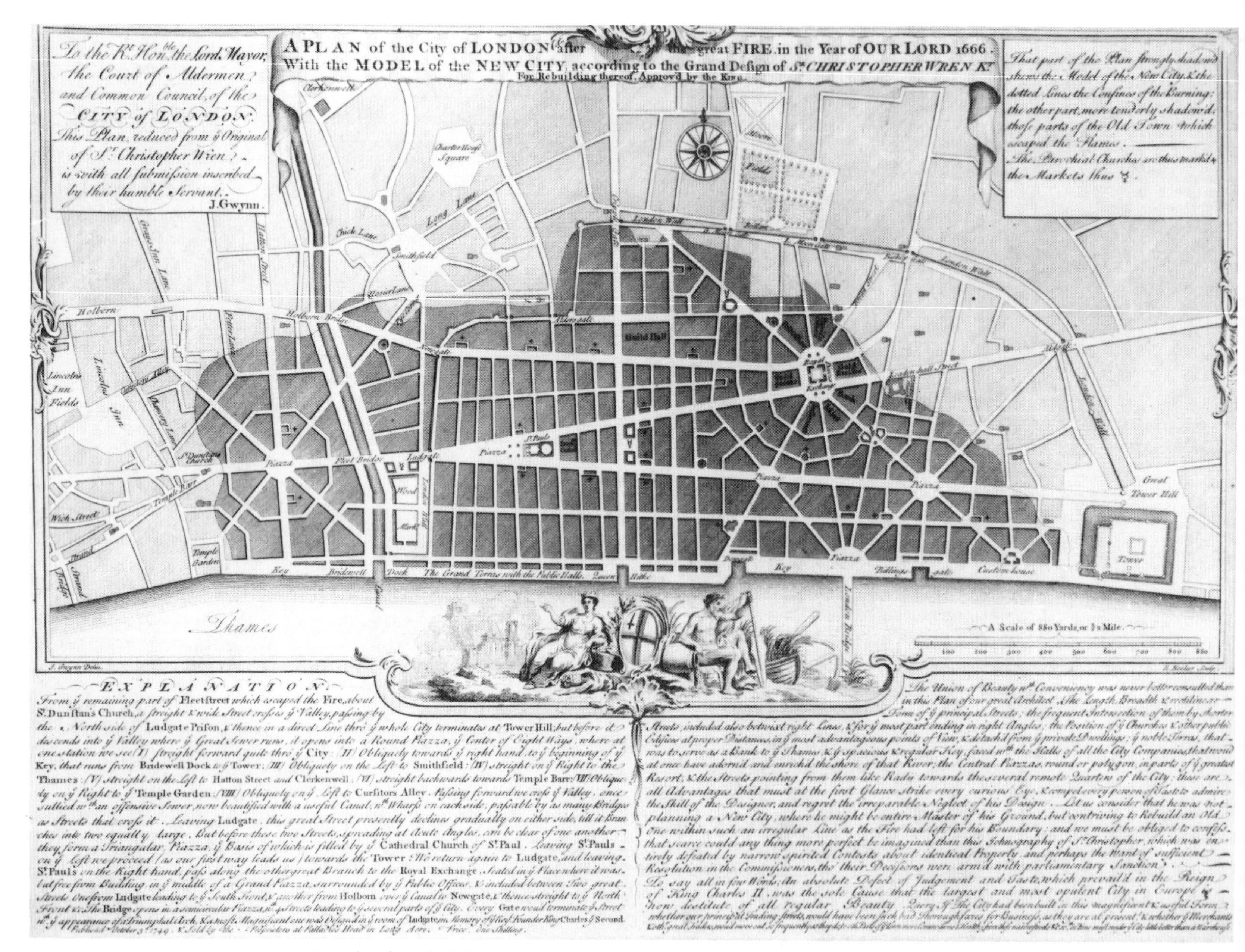

Wren's 1666 plan for rebuilding London that would have led to a grid of streets from Ludgate Circus eastwards across much of the City.

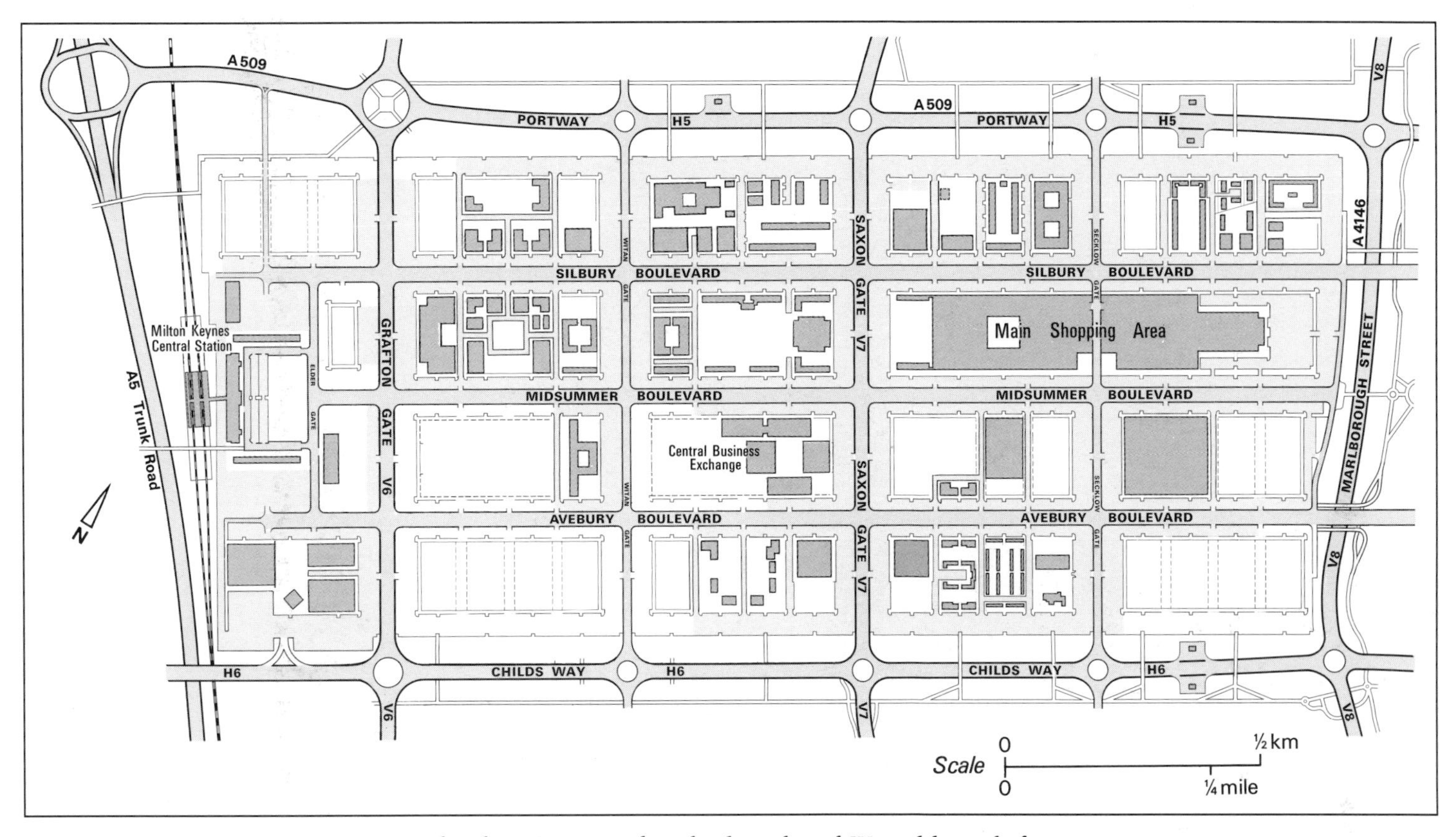

Central Milton Keynes with its boulevards and Wren-like grid of streets.

projects lay at either end of the design. Once both were secured all subsequent development, apart from the city park planned to overlook the Ouzel valley, could be fitted into the gap between.

The board first saw an outline design for the new railway station in 1975. Rectangular office blocks with graph-paper façades were set around three sides of a broad square. Behind them lay parking spaces for 1,000 cars and beneath were to be shops, ticket offices and a restaurant. The board heard that 'agreement had been reached with British Rail on the content of the station but not yet on the financial apportionment'.[4]

It took a long time to get that apportionment. To start with, British Rail's investment programme suffered from the roller-coaster economic conditions of the 1970s. Doubts about the city's population then provided BR with an additional reason for being cautious.

The corporation became impatient. Getting BR to commit itself was, Frank Henshaw told the board during the summer of 1977, a vital step. 'The station was the key to opening up the western end and establishing CMK as a major employment centre.'[5]

It took the corporation a further year of persistent hard work to get the quarry into the net. Central Milton Keynes was to be the first station to be opened on the London–Glasgow main line since the turn of the century. Jock Campbell called BR's decision 'very welcome' though 'it was sad that the media had taken so little notice of it'.[6]

Even at this stage things moved at the pace of a snail rather than an InterCity 125. Stuart Mosscrop showed the board a revised design for the station square late in 1979. He promised a building offering 'clear views of its clean rectangular profile from the west and south' and cladding that would be 'sleek, self-cleaning and significant at 100 m.p.h.'[7] The station was opened formally by the Prince of Wales in May 1982. The offices next to it were completed three years later. Central Milton Keynes was under way.

The history of the 'city club' had a different ending. In 1973, in response to a corporation brief for a modest set of family leisure facilities, Raymond and Ronald Foulk of Ultramarina Ltd approached the corporation with a proposal for an enormous 'pleasure centre'. Its main features were an indoor stadium seating 65,000 spectators and 'an indoor park of six acres at several levels in which would be set a great range of cultural, recreational and sports facilities'. To be profitable it would need to attract at least 40,000 people a week.

The board was told that the city club would combine the characteristics of 'Disneyland, Tivoli Gardens, Soho and the Houston Astrodome'. Members were not overawed by this profusion of images and feared that the club would be cheap and nasty. Raymond Foulk countered with the suggestion that it 'might turn the key which would create pride in the city'. The board agreed to look into the proposal more deeply.[8]

When the city club came back to the board, the idea of a unified 'fun palace' had been abandoned. Further study had suggested that so big a building would make crowd control almost impossible. The scheme was, therefore, broken down into more manageable parts and amongst the additions were a 'Japanese water garden', a swimming pool and a wave pool.

Derek Walker did his best to convince members that the club would have the widest possible appeal yet not become 'a gigantic fun fair'. Fred Roche supported him. He said that the club promised 'items which residents could not otherwise get'. Moving to a higher plane he added that the executive was concerned 'to give the city a soul – to create a national

Right: Station Square, the main urban open space, lies at the west end of the city centre. The railway station is part of the central office block.

Jacoby
74

PREVIOUS SPREAD: Helmut Jacoby's rendering of the central concourse in the never-built city club.

identity for the city of which the citizens would feel proud – as the cathedral had done for Coventry'.

The scepticism of the board was deafening. Members even questioned the city club's name. Derek Walker, no doubt correctly, suggested that a fun palace might appeal more to ordinary people than to the board members and it was agreed to hold a seminar at which to give the proposal further study.[9]

Executives from Wembley, Tivoli and Madison Square Garden all attended the seminar. David Griffiths, the manager of Wembley ('the largest leisure complex in Europe,' so he said), was very positive about the Milton Keynes 'city club and stadium', as it was by then called. It was the only scheme he had seen which offered any competition to Wembley. Alvin Grant from New York described how the Madison Square Garden arena, with 470 performances a year, was the busiest in the world, while Hans Thiesen from Copenhagen explained that Tivoli, now in the midst of the city, had once been on the edge of it. Tivoli was based on 'a few simple principles – flower gardens and trees and coloured lights, music and places to eat ... No matter what your mood there was something for everyone.'

Margaret Durbridge and Ray Bellchambers were, by this time, convinced about the desirability of the idea although Bellchambers pointed out, somewhat elliptically, that 'high standards must come before high profits and without leading to high prices'. Ralph Verney was less abstract. He had never visited Tivoli but feared that vulgarity and quietness were incompatible; he disliked the prospect of an Olympic swimming pool in a 'plastic environment'; and he was unconvinced that the scheme could be privately financed. However, he accepted that studies of the project should go forward – which they did.[10]

The city club and stadium did not survive further scrutiny. The project was killed by the economic and political changes of the mid-1970s – but not before the architects, perspective artists and model-makers had sketched out what it might have been like. Would it have been all tinsel and trash as some members feared? Would it – and this was another concern – have become as shabby as the fun-fair in Battersea Park? Both questions are impossible to answer. All that can be said is that the architecture was anything but flighty. The huge stadium would have been covered by a lacy but rectangular space frame of the utmost severity. The contents of the main club building, discos, cafés, pools and cinemas, were likewise set out as strictly as the squares on a chess board. As with Central Milton Keynes as a whole, the basis of the city club was a rigorous grid.

By 1977 the board was again pursuing the idea of building a stadium and 'the possibility of attracting the Commonwealth Games was being investigated'. The aim 'was to keep revenue costs to a minimum' and the architects, therefore, produced an elegant, circus-shaped arena without a roof. Contact was made with the licensing authorities for speedways and for greyhound racing and in July Jock Campbell saw Dennis Howell, the Minister for Sport, to press him about the Games. Again all was in vain: the Government decided to support a rival proposal from Edinburgh.[11]

'Never give up' was one of the corporation's most deeply ingrained instincts. In 1983, when Luton Town Football Club had to give up its ground to make way for a new road, Milton Keynes set about wooing it. Luton needed a new stadium by the beginning of the 1984/5 football season. The board agreed that a simplified version of the ill-fated city club should be worked up.

A prospectus, sent out in 1984, attracted proposals from promoters of a 20,000-seat stadium with leisure and retail attachments and an 18,000-seater. Both backers assumed that the corporation would guarantee rent for the stadium and contribute to its capital cost.[12]

After protracted negotiations it became clear that the Department of the Environment would not contribute a penny and that the promoters could not make the finances of the scheme stand unaided. In July 1990 Bob Hill, the commerce director, reported a 'funding gap' to the board. He added that Mowlem Spectacor, the remaining backer, was 'still enthusiastic' but his sanguine air failed to dispel a feeling that the project was doomed.[13]

Long-established city centres are complex webs of interrelated activities. People may be drawn to them in their greatest numbers to work or shop but it is the rich mix of such services as pubs, clubs, dentists, travel agents, discos, cinemas, museums, betting shops, antique dealers and restaurants that distinguish them from the centres of smaller towns. Bob Hill recalled that in the 1970s Central Milton Keynes was void of all such attractions. About all it offered was parks.

Amongst the first modest signs of enrichment were a garden centre and a restaurant, the Beefeater, but, as the corporation's periodic household surveys made clear, cinemas, night-clubs and discos were wanted too and, thanks to skaters like Jayne Torvill and Christopher Dean, 'an ice rink was always at the top of people's wants list'. Armed with these insights the corporation, by now in its market-oriented 1980s phase, sought developers willing to invest in costly city centre leisure developments.

It was not easy. Cinema promoters, only too aware that audiences had been dropping for ten years, were moving down-market to bingo – hardly the image the corporation was seeking to create. The problem was solved by persuading AMC, an American firm, to invest in the first ten-screen cinema in Britain. According to Bob Hill, the result exceeded everyone's expectations. 'Within a year of opening it was achieving more bums on seats than any AMC cinema in the world. It established the market for multi-screens in the UK.' It also gave Central Milton Keynes a landmark – an orange neon pyramid – and its first hint of bright lights.[14]

The Point, as the cinema complex was called, was followed by the Leisure Plaza with its skating rink and night-club – a classic example of packaging. Skating rinks are not money-spinners. The corporation, therefore, put together a 'menu' of various leisure and shopping possibilities from which promoters could select an investment meal to suit their tastes. It worked. By the end of the 1980s not only did the city centre contain a Sainsbury's Homebase and an Argos store but an ice rink was no longer on the residents' wants list. Milton Keynes gained a night-club too.

14

'SHOPPING AS IT SHOULD BE'

Indoor shopping centres were still new in Britain when the Milton Keynes designers began work on what they decided to call 'the shopping building'. Brent Cross was not due to open until 1976 and it was necessary to go to the United States to see large drive-in centres in full swing. And even there it is unlikely that one could have been found in a field that was destined to become the middle of a city.

Forty miles away in Peterborough, where another late-1960s new town was under construction, Keith Maplestone chose to give his shopping centre the atmosphere of an Aladdin's cave. Shoppers outside would not be able to see in, but once there, they would find themselves in a huge tent-like space with sunlight streaming through the roof. The outcome was widely admired, but Peterborough was a medieval town and its new shops could afford to be inward looking. They were beside a fine old square and a stone's throw from a huge Norman cathedral.[1]

Faced by diametrically opposite conditions at Milton Keynes, the architects began by examining inward-looking designs but, after days of debate, decided to put the shops in a crystal palace serviced at first-floor level. This arrangement made it possible to get rid of ugly, ground-floor service bays and led to a building surrounded by windows and crossed by high, glazed galleries.

Stuart Mosscrop, the team leader, wanted these galleries to be clothed in transparency, filled with trees and sparkling with reflections. Terence Conran of Habitat, a rising star of designer retailing in the early 1970s, was impressed. He thought that 'many a developer's dream works on the assumption that the prison block exterior leads to wonderland inside; a seedy night-club to you and me ... The shopping places I have liked seemed to be airy places, just covered streets.'

Conran also had a piece of advice. 'What a shopping centre should be, to succeed, is a place to which you would happily drive fifteen or twenty miles. You have to have price

incentive, which is the biggest motive.' But the shopping centre also needs to be 'the only place the public know [where] they can get a specialist product, whether it is a rare book, a vintage wine, or a customised "beach buggy"'. He, therefore, urged the Milton Keynes estates surveyors to analyse the specialised retailers in the city's catchment area and 'court them with the same thoroughness you would give to John Lewis, Marks & Spencer and Sainsbury's'.[2]

The crystal palace and what was to become Lloyd's Court, an adjacent square of offices, were ready to go out to tender in 1974. The bids were judged to be 'very favourable' but the country was in a state of turmoil. Edward Heath's Government had just been toppled in a general election, and Harold Wilson's 'new government had not yet decided whether to continue the policy of accepting substantial private investment' in new towns.

Jock Campbell wrote to Anthony Crosland, the new Environment Secretary, urging an early decision and stressing that the town's housing programme would be held up if the corporation could not get on with providing amenities. Meanwhile inflation was at work and Healey and Baker were warning that the profitability of the shopping building could be at risk.

Campbell, Evelyn de Rothschild, the deputy chairman, and Fred Roche coolly recommended the board 'to accept these favourable tenders (subject to DoE and Treasury approval) recognising the risks but also that the housing programme must have these supporting facilities'. The necessary approvals were received, a contract was awarded to Laings and CMK was under way.[3]

Gradually the shopping centre came together. By the summer of 1975 John Lewis had been signed up although W H Smith, Boots and Marks & Spencer were still prevaricating. But the national economy was in terrible shape and in 1976 there was a hiccup. Retailers were being slow to invest and it was decided to postpone the opening of the shopping building until the summer of 1978. It was agreed to tell the Press nothing unless forced to and then to stress that while Phase I was being deferred, Phase II would be brought forward.[4]

By the summer of 1977 Laings were handing over shop units, Waitrose had agreed to come in, and it was decided to open in September 1978. Discussions were also under way about a covered market of a hundred stalls.[5] In the end the opening of the shopping building was influenced by John Lewis. They decided to open in September 1979 and many of the smaller shops did the same. They wanted to begin with as big a bang as possible.[6]

Landing Marks & Spencer was harder than getting John Lewis. M&S had never opened a shop in the first phase of a new-town shopping centre and did not intend to change their

LEFT: *Glazed colonnades and courtyards give the shopping building an air of lightness and openness.*

ways. Fred Roche told the board in 1978 that 'it was hoped they would make a decision in 1980'. In the meantime the corporation was free to put up hoardings saying 'reserved for Marks & Spencer'.[7] It was better than nothing.

Jim Callaghan's Labour Government had fallen and Margaret Thatcher was in her first term when the big bang occurred. Further financial cuts were in the wind and the new towns, like other quangos, had become an endangered species. Nevertheless, the new Prime Minister welcomed the opportunity to perform the opening ceremony. The occasion, as befitted the greatest of the corporation's works, was a huge affair. Lunch was arranged in marquees for a thousand people while the building itself was packed. Light poured through the glass walls and bounced off the honey-coloured travertine floor as Mrs Thatcher toured the shops and bought some oranges.

If Jock Campbell had important things on his mind, so did the trades unions representing, among others, the corporation's staff. They were worried by the new Government's union-bashing statements and wanted to demonstrate their feelings in front of the Prime Minister. Campbell, by contrast, wanted his guest to have a quiet visit during which she could absorb the impressive achievements of the corporation. He needed to ensure the survival of the still emerging city and he wanted the Prime Minister to know that Milton Keynes had been waiting an unconscionable time for a hospital.

Needless to say, Campbell got his way (Downing Street said later that 'it had been the best organised prime minister's visit they had known') and, equally unsurprisingly, the Prime Minister got things moving. She told Gerard Vaughan, her Health Minister, about the problem at the new city and he in turn cut through red tape. The health authority let a contract for the first phase of a district general hospital shortly after: work on it was programmed to begin in June 1980.

The trades union representatives probably thought that they too had got their way but, as Campbell observed later, 'the continuous shouting of the demonstrators during all the

BELOW: The shopping building from the south with City Square at the west end, Queens Court in the middle and John Lewis's store at the east end.

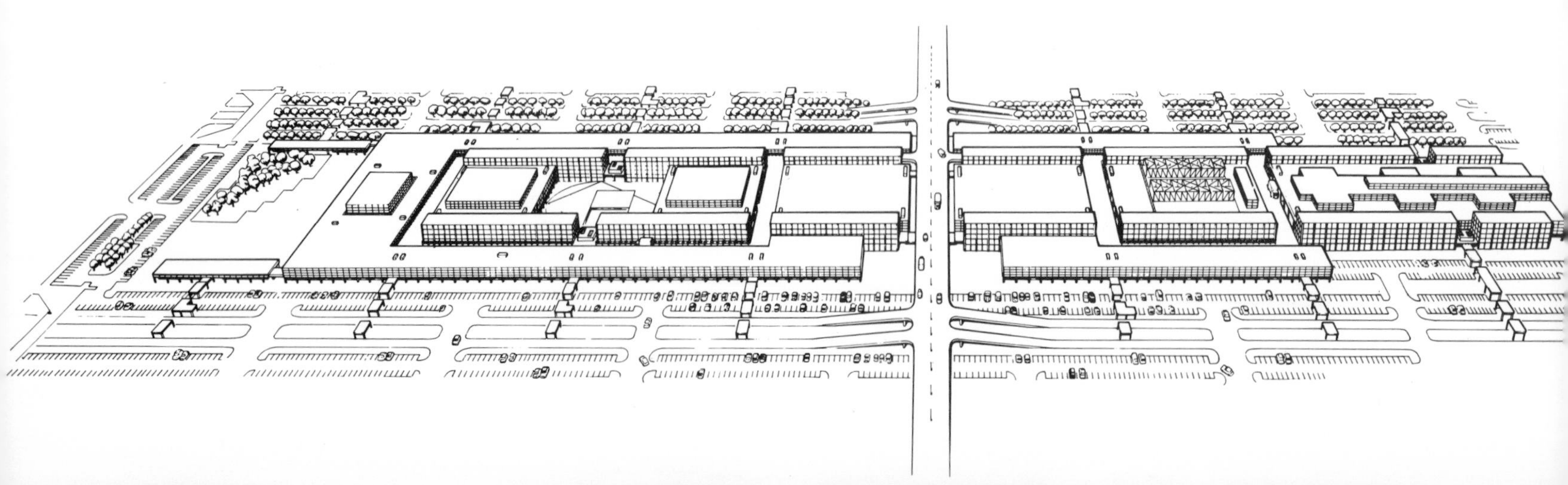

speeches was grist to the [Prime Minister's] mill. The discourtesy of their behaviour and her resolution and courage in getting her speech across, loud and clear, had been most impressive, and had attracted even more support and sympathy than might otherwise have been expected.' It was left to Fred Roche to tell the staff unions that the continued work of the corporation depended on the support of the Government and investors 'and that all this had been jeopardised by the disgraceful episode in Middleton Hall'.[8]

The day of 25 September 1979, when the shopping building was formally opened, was thus twice over a red-letter one in the history of Milton Keynes. As Campbell wrote in his thirteenth annual report: the building 'is not only a great commercial success, but, equally important, has provided a unifying feature for the city'. Milton Keynes had acquired a heart and secured a long-needed hospital at the same time.

'I was absolutely wrong about the centre,' Campbell said later. Temperamentally a decentraliser, he wanted the city, for traffic reasons, to have three centres. 'Then what I thought was going to be a white elephant ... began to take shape under Roche and Derek Walker. I admit ... I was against it ... When it was opened at half cock on 9 August, I took my whole family there and I gave them each £10 to spend because I thought no one would come at all. I was wrong, of course. It was the most enormous success right from the beginning.'[9]

Modern retailers are highly professional in the way they go about their business and making shopping fun rather than a chore is one of their topmost goals. A lively programme of events was accordingly set in motion by the corporation and the shopping building's management company. (Horace Cutler, who was knighted in the 1979 birthday honours, was the board's representative on the management company and its chairman.) Indoor happenings ranged from organ competitions to exhibitions of paintings and cartoons. Outdoors there were vintage car runs and Guy Fawkes fireworks. It all helped to pull the customers in and by November 1979 the new building was attracting about 170,000 adults a week – half of them on Saturdays.[10]

It was only a beginning. Consultants retained by the corporation before the opening had unleashed a television and press advertising campaign aimed at attracting a weekly flood of 250,000 shoppers from as far afield as Cheltenham, Birmingham, Cambridge and north London. Research showed that shoppers were looking for a variety of shops, free parking, easy access, somewhere to eat and sit, and something for their children. All this was covered in a campaign the catchphrases of which were 'Shopping as it should be' and 'You've never seen anything like it'.[11]

A November 1979 survey, in addition to counting gross numbers, gave the first detailed picture of the magnetism of Central Milton Keynes. Over half of the visitors questioned came from within the borough, but of the remainder few came from outlying towns such

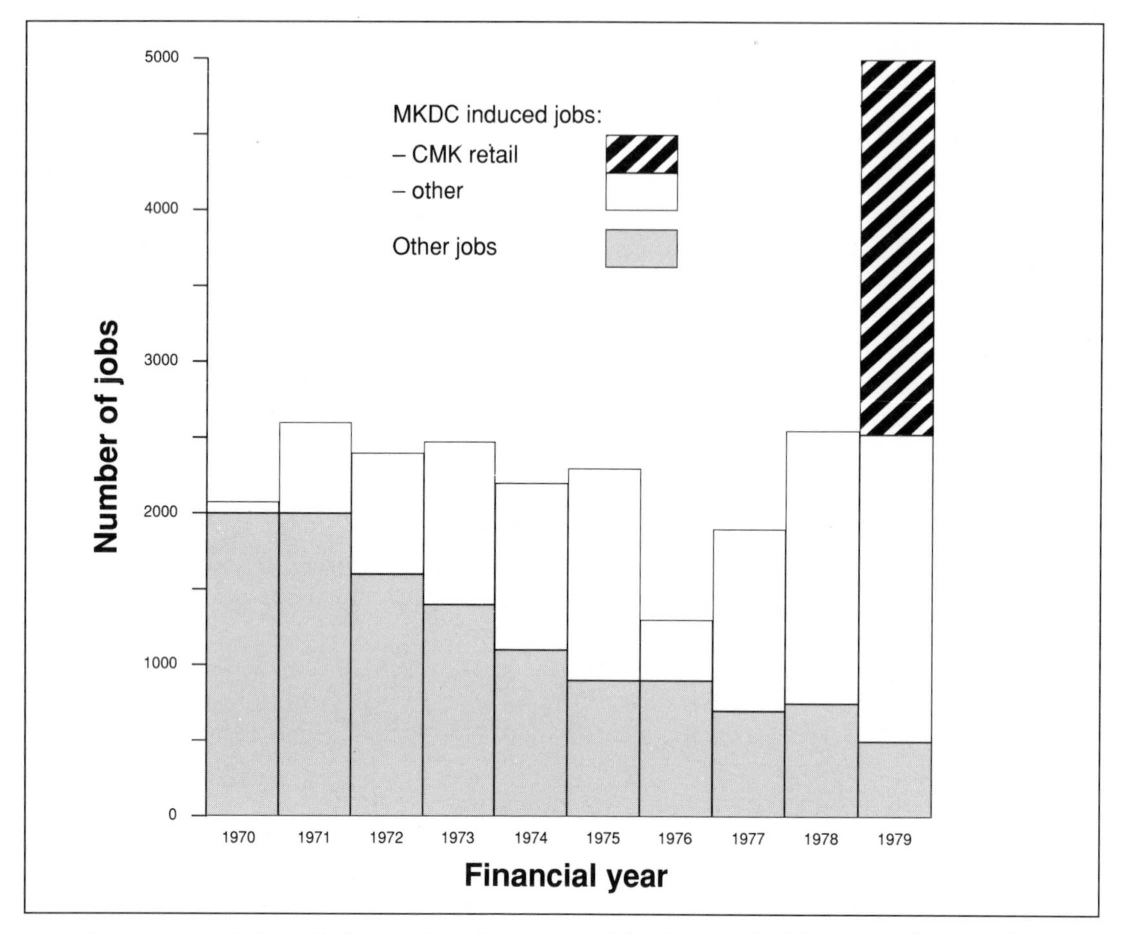

Employment growth 1970–79 showing how the opening of the shopping building created a huge demand for jobs.

as Northampton and Luton. They came instead, travelling for up to an hour, from the rural districts in between. As seven out of ten of those counted came by car, it is not surprising that easy parking was an important draw. But parties of shopping trippers arrived too. They came from as far away as Carlisle and resorts on the south coast.[12] Milton Keynes was on the map.

Shortly after the opening of the shopping building the board found itself having to grapple with draughts. Winter winds, which blow coldly across the exposed eminence of Central Milton Keynes, were whistling through the open entrances of the galleries and upsetting shoppers and shopkeepers alike. Doors had been considered but the architects had been against them and the Buckinghamshire County Fire Officer, mindful of the way that people had been trapped in an Isle of Man leisure centre, had gone one better and vetoed them.

After Zales and other shopkeepers close to the entrances started to erect baffles against the icy blasts, the fire officer was persuaded to agree to doors that could be opened automatically by electronic smoke sniffers. It may seem in retrospect to have been a minor issue but the saga of the doors, which at one stage threatened to cost £2.2m, and necessitated the seeking of further finance from the Post Office Staff Superannuation Fund, occupied the board for months.[13]

Many technical problems had to be solved and the chosen design approved by the Building Research Establishment before doors could be ordered. It all took time. Meanwhile criticism was hurled at the corporation and Horace Cutler told the board that a decision was 'imperative'. It was a time of frustration only partly offset by the receipt by the shopping building of a design award from the Royal Institute of British Architects.[14]

All the parties involved took until March 1981 to agree that ordinary doors would be safe but no sooner had they done so than the board was told of a risk of gas explosions. Mains ran underneath the marble malls and, should one leak, gas might build up inside the building. Keith Revill, who, on the departure of the officers who went to Conran Roche, became building director, explained that tests were being carried out and models made but 'the gas board had very stringent regulations'. If the underfloor gas mains proved to be unacceptable they would have to be rerouted over the roofs of the shopping building.

Was too much pressure being put on the gas board and fire authority, Roger Parker-Jervis asked? Might it cause them to act against their better judgement? 'He was acutely anxious that the board should not be seen to have taken a needless risk with people's lives.' Jock Campbell agreed and proposed that, whatever the technical decision, the board should ask the two bodies involved to certify that they were 'entirely satisfied with what was being done'.

Changing from automatic to manual doors did at least bring down the cost of the project, including gas main rerouting, from £2m to £1.7m but some members feared that it might make the spanking-new building look old-fashioned. They were, however, overlooking the unreliability and heavy maintenance burden of forty sets of power-operated doors. 'Brent Cross and Wood Green were having considerable trouble with them,' Keith Revill explained.[15]

By the time bids for the work were received, the gas board had still not decided whether its mains would have to be rerouted but, following representations on behalf of disabled shoppers, it was agreed that some of the doors be power-operated. Meanwhile fears that doors would damage their trade were beginning to be voiced by some shopkeepers.[16]

A month later, with a decision on the gas mains still outstanding, Horace Cutler said that, subject to the outcome of a meeting with the gas board, he was 'prepared to write to them in the strongest terms'. But he had other news. At a recent meeting of the shopping management company, 'extreme concern' had been voiced about defects in the ventilation units.[17]

In July the board heard that work on installing the doors was under way and that 'the gas board had written to the corporation to confirm that they had no objection to the proposals'. Satisfaction about the gas decision was offset by a report on the air handling units. Defects had been found and reconditioning them was unlikely to cost less than £750,000. There was little consolation in Keith Revill's observation that the installation of the doors was likely to have had little effect on the life of the air units.[18]

The saga of the doors finally disappeared from the minutes only at the end of 1981. By then legal redress was being considered against the suppliers of the air units, the management company was turning its attention to cutting energy costs and the board was noting the receipt of an award from the Royal Association for Disability and Rehabilitation. Stuart Mosscrop, by then working for Conran Roche, and Keith Revill received it on behalf of the corporation from the Duke of Gloucester.[19]

The doors transformed conditions inside the building and by November 1981 the crystal palace was attracting 214,000 shoppers a week – an increase of over one-third in two years. About half the visitors came from outside the city but, wherever they came from, they liked what they found. Proof of it lay in the tinkle at the cash tills and the keenness of other traders to join those already there.[20]

Two major shopping innovations – superstores and retail warehouses – swept through Britain in the 1980s. The shopping building initially contained two supermarkets, Waitrose and Bishops (later Budgens), but they were small fry by the standards of the 120,000 sq ft monsters of the Thatcher decade. Firms like Tesco (which had earlier failed to get into the centre), Sainsbury's, Asda and Carrefour all began to knock on the corporation's door.

Firms selling carpets, bottom-of-the-market furniture and do-it-yourself goods called as well. All needed space for display and free parking – neither of which could be found in traditional high streets. The answer was 'retail barns' – cheap, garish, corrugated sheds dropped down in industrial areas preferably next to main roads.

As the master plan gave no guidance on how to cope with either of these innovations, the board debated what to do about them. Where should a superstore be located? Should it be steered into Central Milton Keynes where it would be widely accessible but compete fiercely with its smaller brethren? Or should it go out to a district centre in the eastern or western flank of the city where it would be less accessible for bus-borne shoppers?

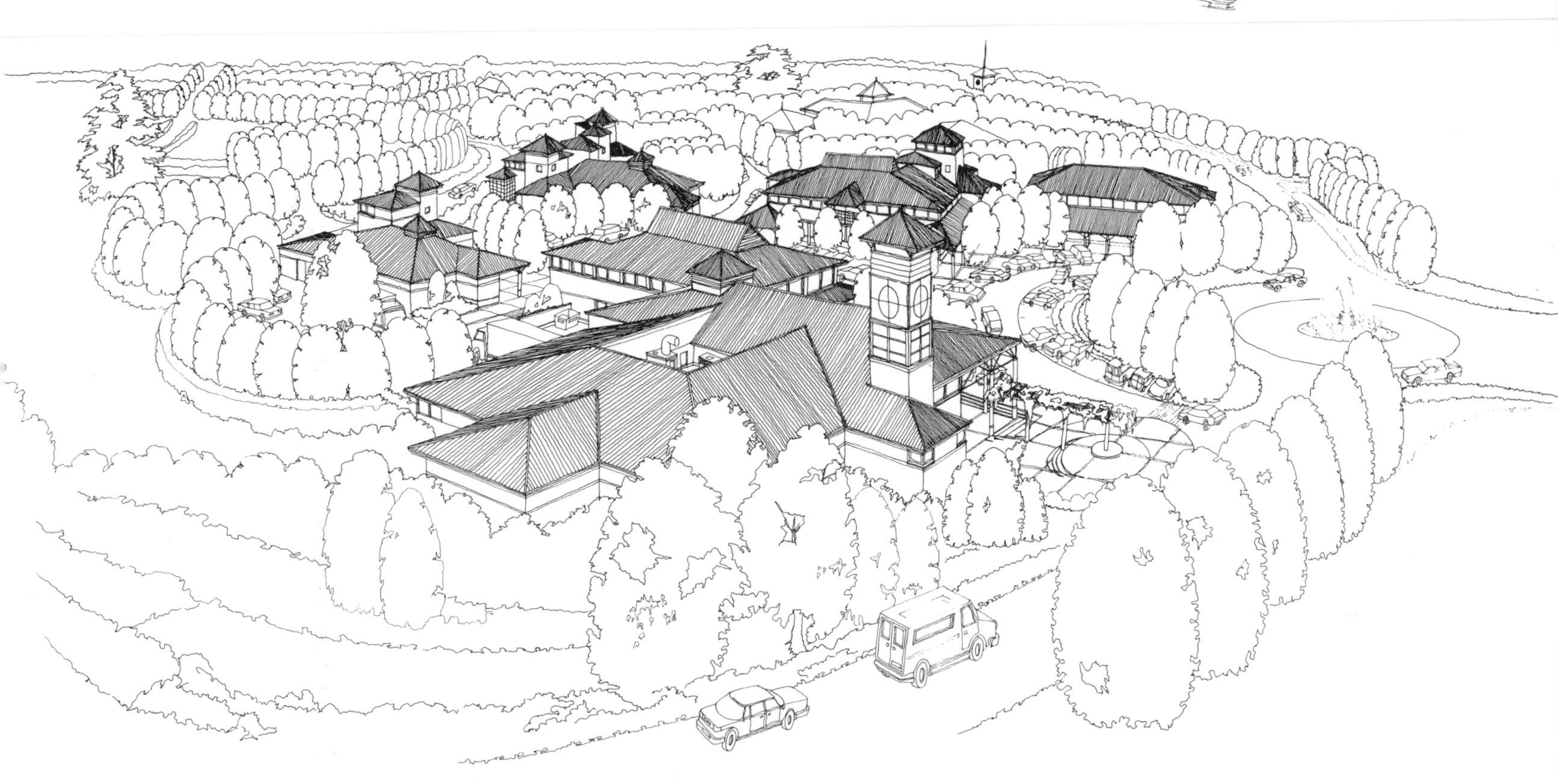

Shenley Church End's local centre was completed in 1991. With several shops, a supermarket, three showrooms, three offices and twenty flats, it is amongst the largest in the city. Its clock tower, reminiscent of Neath Hill, is visible from Watling Street.

The executive produced a 'city retailing strategy' which, in a major departure from the master plan, proposed postponing the creation of large district centres in order to boost the city-centre shops while they were in their infancy. It followed that the city centre was the best place for a superstore. The strategy also proposed that, in consultation with the borough, sites be found for retail barns.

Members were worried about the damage a superstore might do to the city's existing shops but Allen Duff, commercial director, reminded them how population growth would create additional purchasing power and argued that existing tenants were in the same position as those in any other high street when faced by competition. 'The corporation had no legal commitment to consider their interests, but perhaps some moral obligation. It would certainly be common sense not to endanger existing tenancies.'

Jock Campbell added that existing traders 'could have no power of veto over further development' and reminded his colleagues about Tesco. The firm's 'very keen bid to be included in the shopping building had been turned down'. The corporation had, he

GREEN LINE

suggested, 'an element of commitment' to them. (Campbell himself had written in 1977 saying that, subject to agreement on details, Tesco 'would be given the first opportunity to take space in the second phase'.)[21]

It took eighteen months to turn the strategy into action. The planners needed to be sure that a superstore would not damage the city's existing retailers. Complex calculations were involved. It was necessary to estimate – given that the city's population was growing and that incomes were rising – where people would spend their money. After much deliberation Healey and Baker, the corporation's consultants, advised that a city-centre superstore could be authorised to be in use by 1986 'without serious risk to the viability of other retailing in the city'.[22]

A year later the strategy was ready to go out to consultation but Jock Campbell was worried. The corporation 'found itself between the upper and nether millstones,' he said. 'On the one hand was the need to reinforce the success of those who had invested in Milton Keynes; on the other the duty to ensure that the shopping and prices were right for the residents.' He was certain that a food superstore was right but he was uneasy about its being in the city centre.

Allen Duff had no such doubts. It was not 'a prerequisite for hypermarkets to be out-of-town. In older towns planning problems invariably dictated this, but not in Milton Keynes. It was essential to put shops in the city centre to support the regional nature of the retailing business already there.' John Darby, chief estates manager for the Norwich Union whom Michael Heseltine had appointed to the board the previous year, was equally businesslike. 'Food retailing competition in the city centre would be good and the corporation should not be too sensitive to existing tenants' views,' he said.[23]

The upshot of this debate was the 'food centre', described by Frank Henshaw as one of 'two new concepts introduced into Milton Keynes in the 1980s'. (The other was the energy park.) The food centre, which was to be across the road from all the other shops, contained in a single large building space for two supermarkets and multi-storey parking. The aim was to provide 'competition and choice for the food shopper'. This flew in the face of conventional retailing wisdom which was that 'people don't combine their comparison and convenience shopping trips'. 'We said, they have never been given the chance,' Henshaw noted.[24]

The board made great efforts to accommodate Tesco in the food centre but began early in 1985 to lose patience and decided that if agreement were not reached by May they 'would take the food-store opportunity to the market'.[25]

Not only was no agreement reached but Tesco decided, to the board's astonishment, that

LEFT: Central Milton Keynes, a late twentieth-century city centre with plenty of room for cars.

'they were only prepared to develop an "out-of-town" store in Milton Keynes'. The board had no option but to seek bids from other firms. The highest was put in by Sainsbury's who added an assurance that, if successful, they would not shut their store in Bletchley. It took over two years to get the food centre built but it was finally opened in March 1988. From then on shoppers were able to buy a shirt or a silk dress at Dickins and Jones, walk across the road, and buy their food from Waitrose or Sainsbury's.[26]

Tesco, meanwhile, persisted with their own ideas and bid successfully for a site at Kingston district centre not far from the M1. There they were able to have a huge store surrounded by parking. A gym, a table-tennis centre, community buildings, a craft workshop and a charity shop were included in this 'retail and leisure development'. Work began on the Tesco site in March 1991 with completion due early in 1992.[27]

15

Waiting for the Bus

Milton Keynes was born in the midst of an intense debate about the relative merits of cities designed around monorails and motor cars. After much agonising the board chose to build a dispersed garden city designed for easy driving. If they thought by so doing that they had got transport under control, they could not have been more wrong. The shortcomings of the city's buses were to preoccupy them for over a decade.

A fairy godmother then arrived in the guise of deregulation. Services in the city were taken over by a private company and darting minibuses soon replaced lumbering double-deckers on many of the city's roads. Ironically, this was roughly the kind of public transport service envisaged by the master planners fifteen years before.

In the decade up to 1973, the year of the first oil price shock, king car was everywhere in the ascendant, and public transport everywhere in decline. Most people thought they were living through something as unstoppable as the conquest of the stage-coach by the railway. The Transport Act 1968 made it possible to pay subsidies to transit operators but it did nothing to stop public transport from becoming less and less used for urban travel. The corporation struggled to give buses a more important role but found it difficult to isolate Milton Keynes from economic changes taking place in the world at large.

Not surprisingly, bus services appeared early on as an item on the board's agenda. 'Four years on ...', the corporation's 1973 survey of 1,453 households, identified six key problems. One was 'the inadequate level of public transport'.[1] Nine months later the board received a quarterly progress report in which public transport (along with the lack of a hospital and the shortage of local authority funds) was noted as a problem of 'particular concern'.[2]

By the mid-1970s Jock Campbell was seriously worried about the inadequacy of the bus service and the corporation was even discussing the possibility of setting up its own bus company. Furthermore, the 1973 oil crisis had caused people to start asking questions about

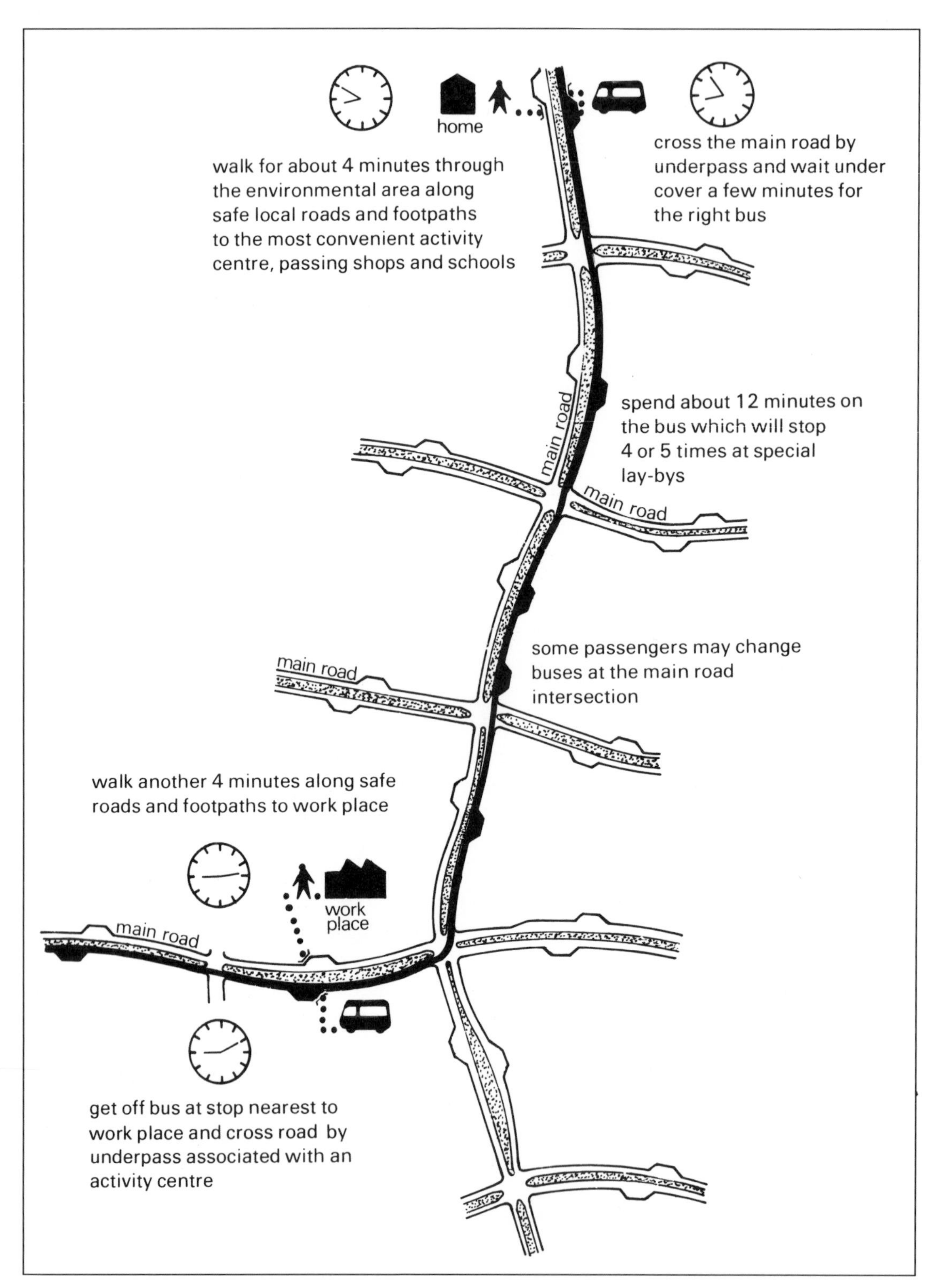
home
cross the main road by underpass and wait under cover a few minutes for the right bus
walk for about 4 minutes through the environmental area along safe local roads and footpaths to the most convenient activity centre, passing shops and schools
main road
spend about 12 minutes on the bus which will stop 4 or 5 times at special lay-bys
main road
main road
some passengers may change buses at the main road intersection
walk another 4 minutes along safe roads and footpaths to work place
work place
main road
get off bus at stop nearest to work place and cross road by underpass associated with an activity centre

A typical journey to work by bus – as envisaged by the master planners.

the future of the car. Campbell, therefore, raised the issue of public transport at a board seminar in 1976. Characteristically, he drove to the heart of the matter. 'The city's public transport was abysmally bad,' the minutes report him saying.

Campbell went on to ask whether it was the fault of the plan. Critics of the city argued, he said, that its diffuse structure forced people into dependency on cars, that those without them were marooned and that the corporation should have foreseen such problems. 'It was, therefore, fair to ask with the private car and public transport now in trouble (due to rising fuel prices), whether the corporation ought to have changed the plan to get higher densities, and to get people living closer to each other and to other facilities.'

Richard Llewelyn-Davies, who had earlier enthused about the experience of seeing the city taking shape as planned 'with speed and success', faced up boldly to the chairman's bowling. Increasing densities 'to the limits of what might have been socially acceptable or desirable' would not have had a significant effect on transport. The grid lent itself to fast bus services and gave the right kind of walking distance to bus stops.

David Jamieson, the corporation's director of infrastructure, added that 'where it had been possible to institute bus services of the kind envisaged in the plan, they were being highly successful – fast, low-cost, popular and with satisfactory financial performance'. A good suburban service was being provided in many areas and he got surprisingly few complaints about the buses at user group meetings. He 'did not feel the service was as bad as it was made out to be'. Ray Bellchambers observed that the villages had a much better service with the city than they had had before without it.[3]

That the shortcomings of the bus service stemmed from the master plan was given credence by, more than anyone else, Stephen Potter at the Open University. In lectures, monographs and submissions to parliamentary committees (some of them written with Ray Thomas), he bashed away at what he saw as the shortcomings of a suburban city based on a grid of roads.

People would only use public transport if their houses, jobs and shops were clustered around it – as Arthur Ling had arranged at Runcorn new town and as Fred Pooley had proposed for North Bucks. Milton Keynes, with its dispersed activities and low residential densities, was the wrong design.

One of Potter's strengths was his knowledge of the technical appendices to the plan. These were not policy documents, but they provided the plan with its intellectual foundations. Any inconsistency between the two was, therefore, useful ammunition for a critic of the plan. Potter thought he had found one. 'Although the published plans refer to a high quality public transport service with a two-and-a-half- to five-minute frequency,' he wrote, the appendix said that 'in the light of the selected land use plan, the provision of a competitive form of public transport does not make practical sense.'

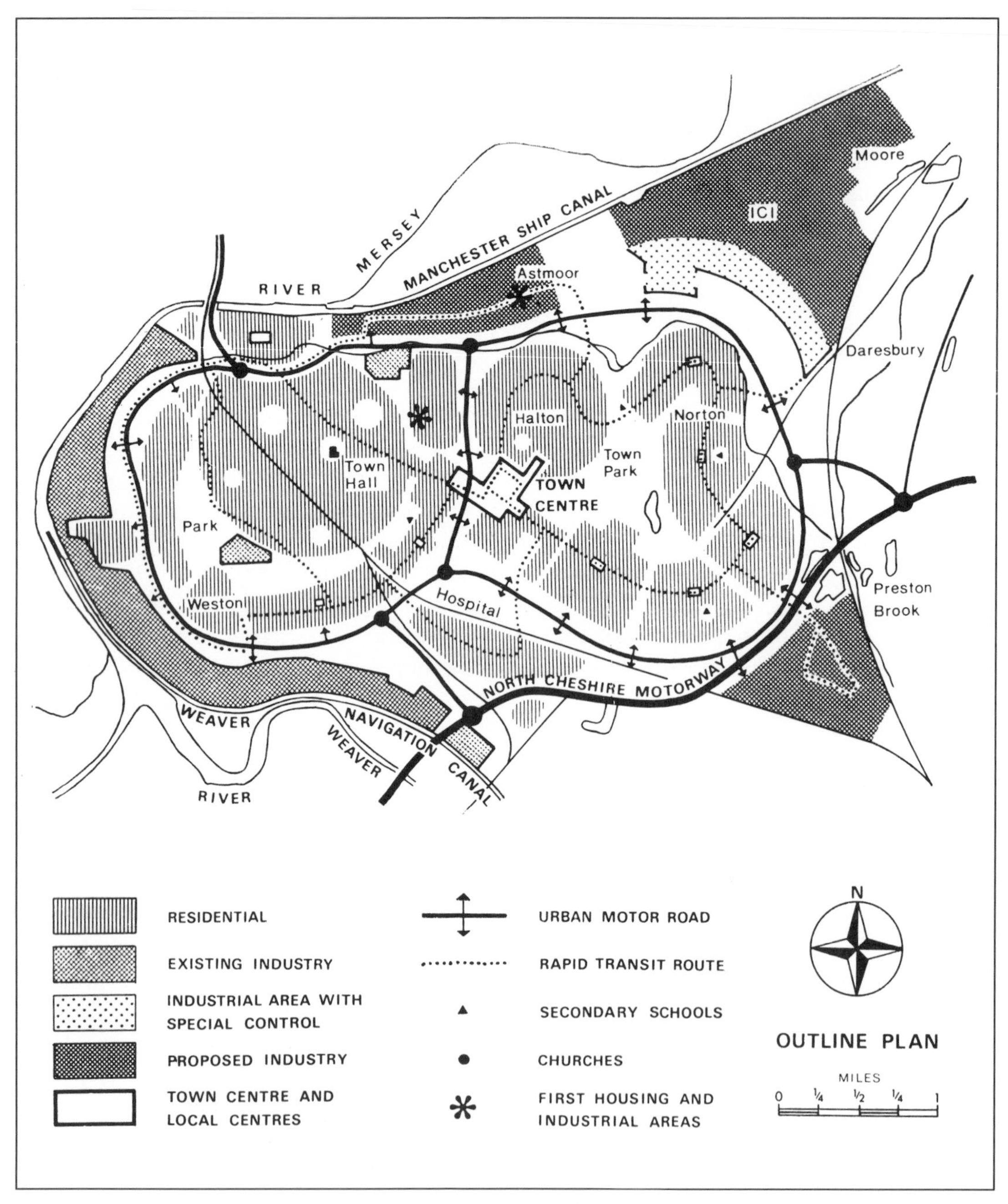

A new town with development arranged around a busway (it was at first to be a monorail): Runcorn in Cheshire.

However, this was not really as damaging as Potter implied. The board recognised that its goal of freedom of choice would not be met by cars and a minimum bus service. As had been acknowledged when the interim plan was debated, public transport in Milton Keynes would need subsidy.

Potter's other contention was that the Milton Keynes plan was wasteful of transport resources. Over £100m had been spent on a network of main roads, the dispersed land-use pattern meant that motorists were obliged to make heavy use of them, and in 1980, when the population had reached 90,000, 'a subsidy of £735,000 per annum was required to maintain a thirty-minute frequency of Milton Keynes' fifteen bus routes'.

In Runcorn, by comparison, the roads were of 'ample capacity with no restrictions on car use' while the buses, which ran every five to seven-and-a-half minutes on a congestion-free 'busway', required little or no subsidy.

Potter's conclusion was that the state (he was writing about 'state intervention') 'far from encouraging economic prosperity' was forcing more resources than necessary into public and private transport, and in so doing was reducing the country's economic prosperity.[4]

Academics, like the rest of us, have a point of view. Potter's perspective was that of a Fabian socialist sympathetic to Ebenezer Howard's belief in land reform and the redistribution of wealth. The plight of those who waited in the pouring rain for unpunctual United Counties' buses was part of his experience; he believed the corporation had been negligent in not foreseeing such problems; and he wanted action – *now*.

The master planners had taken a longer view and they were not collectivists. Jock Campbell, though a socialist, was more humanist than collectivist, but waiting in the rain for a bus was not part of his everyday life. Furthermore, the planners were convinced that as people's incomes increased they would use them to buy space – indoors and outdoors. From this they deduced that the future of Milton Keynes lay with the house and garden rather than with the flat and balcony. It followed that the city should be designed for a future in which more and more people had access to cars. Public transport had to be fitted into this concept. Whatever the strengths of this viewpoint for the future of the city, it had, until bus deregulation in 1985, great weaknesses as a plan for public transport.

The corporation's earliest response to these problems was, as the master plan proposed, to support conventional bus services along the main roads and experiment with 'dial-a-ride' or radio-dispatched minibuses within the squares. Dial-a-ride, an American development, involved a marriage of electronic and automotive engineering, a union at the root of the majority of late twentieth-century road transport innovations. Potential travellers could hail a bus anywhere they saw one or phone an office and give details of the trip they wished to make. A dispatcher then passed the request to the driver of an appropriate minibus. For the passenger the technology turned the humble omnibus into a shared taxi.

A 'demand-responsive bus system' was first put forward by a corporation public transport working party in October 1973. Woughton in the south of the city was chosen for a trial and, because few corporation tenants had telephones, special dial-a-ride phones were installed in Woughton's streets. The estimated cost of this service over a full year was £59,000. Fares were expected to bring in only £8,500.[5]

Dial-a-ride was justified on the grounds that, although it would cost more than a 'minimal acceptable' conventional service, it would cost '*substantially* less than a stage carriage system implemented to give as near as possible a similar level of service'. It was also expected to attract more riders.[6]

It did not take the corporation long to discover that it was promoting this innovation with one hand tied behind its back. The United Counties Omnibus Company, a subsidiary of the National Bus Company, was the problem. United Counties was country-bus minded. Restrictive practices gave it the flexibility of a ramrod and, worst of all, its two depots at Bletchley and Stony Stratford, which shared responsibility for providing Milton Keynes with its services, were on terms that made Rangers and Celtic seem paragons of harmony.

A special dial-a-ride unit (by now called Dial-a-Bus) was accordingly set up, not with the local operator, but with the National Bus Company in London. It was a pyrrhic victory. United Counties not only gained responsibility for the unit's administration and maintenance but, being a high-cost operation, they paid the minibus drivers big-bus wages plus a supplement for operating a radio. The board made one last stand. United Counties 'must not ... handle complaints'.[7]

United Counties was again causing the board unease in the following year. Confronted, no doubt, by rising costs the bus company threatened, unless it received additional subsidies, to withdraw all its conventional bus services from the existing towns. The county agreed to add £35,000 to the sum it was already paying and the corporation provisionally agreed to an additional £30,000, but the borough council declined 'to put £35,000 into what it regarded as a bottomless pit'. This provoked a crisis. The board urged haste in drawing up contingency plans for an emergency service financed partly out of parking charges. They had long expected a showdown with United Counties but knew that the existing operator had first to fail for an alternative to be viable.[8]

The Woughton Dial-a-Bus was part of what the borough saw as a bottomless pit. Whitehall authorised an experiment to begin in March 1975 but a year later fares were covering only a quarter of its running costs. This compared with nearly two-thirds for the most successful scheduled services.[9] It was impossible to keep up this kind of expenditure.

'What killed the small buses was economics,' Wayne Perdue later recalled. (He was head

RIGHT: An experimental Dial-a-Bus passing the Barge Inn at Woolstone.

Barge Inn
Charrington
WOUGHTON DIAL A BUS
MILTON KEYNES
67 8811
HBD 167N

of the corporation's transport unit from 1979 to 1986.) 'It was not politically acceptable that fares on the small buses should be higher than on the big ones' – even though their operating costs were greater. The service was a valuable learning experience for the planners but it was 'too extreme'. Long deviations to reach front doors led to scenic and convoluted routes which inconvenienced other passengers.[10]

In 1977 transit was made the subject of a searching review. The existing system was examined and considered in the light of the way travel would change as Central Milton Keynes began to grow. A key conclusion concerned demand-responsive minibuses. Costly though they were to run, they met a need for shorter trips even though the main-road buses were performing better and better as the grid-squares filled up and provided them with continuous sources of demand. The board members were, therefore, offered a choice between main-road buses only, and a mix of main-road buses and local minibuses driven in the off-peak by drivers not needed on the big buses.

After debate it was agreed to discuss the latter option with the local authorities and United Counties (the company had survived the subsidy battle of 1975) and then approach the Department of the Environment. Opposition by the unions was anticipated. Driving buses of different sizes at different times of day was not something drivers were expected to welcome. Cost was likely to be another problem. Roger Parker-Jervis suggested that one solution might be to privatise the local buses. He seemed to have in mind that taxi firms might run minibuses or that some kind of lower-cost, non-union service might be possible. Philip Oxley, a consultant from the nearby Cranfield Centre for Transport Studies, feared the idea would create more problems than it would solve.[11]

Public transport remained a problem throughout the decade; 'unreliability ... as regards routes and ... timekeeping continued to hinder the delivery of a quality service'. It certainly made a nonsense of attempts to co-ordinate cross-town and local buses. The board did what it could. New main roads were built without space being reserved beside them for a future tracked transport system. This enabled local centres to be pushed nearer to the roads, helped reduce the isolation of bus stops and made walking distances to them seem shorter.

Surveys, meanwhile, began to show that Milton Keynes was indeed becoming the drive-in city envisaged by the master planners. Residents were making as many trips as their opposite numbers in comparable towns 'but more by foot and by bicycle' and fewer by bus. Don Ritson advised the board that the unreliability of the buses or 'perhaps the convenience of the footpath system' might explain this, but there was also evidence of higher than average car ownership. 'Nearly eight in ten of rental households as against the national average of four in ten' owned cars, he said.

The corporation's transport unit and United Counties were, however, at long last beginning to produce results. Plans were made for a new central depot to replace the old warring satellites. New buses were bought, inspectors were given radios and off-peak travellers were attracted with cheap 'shopabout' and 'buzzabout' tickets. The overall aim was to have a half-hourly service within 500 metres of all new houses.

The corporation also looked to see if the order in which the city was being developed could be adjusted to favour the buses. A modest discovery was that 'too many lengths of bus route ... carried no development on either side'. More important was the prospect that when Central Milton Keynes became a major shopping centre, the whole pattern of movement in the city would change.

Jock Campbell remained uneasy. 'In his view, one of the great failures so far of Milton Keynes was in mobility. He was particularly concerned about what was being done to enable the young to visit leisure centres and other amenities.' Their ease of movement was vital to the future of the city and the avoidance of vandalism. He said: 'teenagers should be able to reach leisure facilities in the evenings, or just to visit each other'.

The dilemma facing the board was set out by Fred Roche. There were advantages in grouping activities, as had been done with the two leisure centres at Bletchley and Stantonbury. 'On the other hand there was now a movement ... to regard smaller as better and to disperse public facilities whenever possible to ease the problems of mobility.'[12]

And there, on the eve of the opening of Central Milton Keynes, the vexed issue of decentralisation versus public transport lay.

As it turned out, it took a combination of two events – the coming on stream of Central Milton Keynes and the deregulation of public transport – to transform the city's bus services. The first led to the introduction of radial services akin to those found in other towns – even if they ran along the grid roads. The second, set in motion by the Transport Act 1985, took place in Milton Keynes on 26 October 1986.

'Deregulation has resulted in a radically new route network, based on a series of commercial high-frequency minibus routes operating mainly on local roads within grid-squares,' the executive was told in April 1987. 'These "street shuttle" routes make up about two-thirds of the new network ... the remainder being mainly services operated on contract to Buckinghamshire County Council. The new route network is more comprehensive than the old one it replaced.'

Despite initial unreliability and bunching, the new shuttles proved to be 'markedly more popular than the old big bus system'. However, 'a particular difficulty is that street-shuttle vehicles do not easily accept bulky luggage and pushchairs'.[13]

Wayne Perdue summarised the old bus services as 'high-cost, low fares, high subsidy, low frequency, low reliability and low patronage'. The Thatcher Government's belief in competition created 'a radically different situation ... from what we had before'.

4
BLETCHLEY
MILTON KEYNES CITY BUS
E72 MVV
G3

Deregulation 'slashed the costs of the bus industry overnight'. Even the prospect of competition 'made bus operators take the risk of going for a minibus solution'.

For passengers the street shuttles meant shorter walking distances, shorter waiting times and relatively lower fares. For Milton Keynes City Bus Company (which replaced United Counties in a management buy-out) the new services attracted thirty to forty per cent more riders. For the corporation and the local authorities the shuttles meant subsidy costs 'an order of magnitude lower' in 1990 (about seventy-five per cent in real terms) than a decade before. More efficient management, more revenue, cheaper vehicles and lower driver wages all contributed to this saving.[14]

Little evidence of this revolution appeared in the board minutes in the 1980s. Under Henry Chilver's chairmanship, public transport matters were delegated to the executive. Furthermore, the chairmanship of the Public Transport Policy Liaison Committee (embracing the corporation, the county and the borough), which Campbell had held in the 1970s, was passed to the county council and its business ceased to be reported to the board.

Frank Henshaw confirmed that, for the executive, the 1980s saw two key transport developments: recognition that both public transport and cars needed to run through the squares because 'that was where the people were'; and, thanks to bus deregulation, the advent of minibuses. The two were complementary because, with the coming of minibuses, it became possible for the first time to move public transport off the main roads and into the streets within the squares.

By the end of the 1980s there was no doubt that the street shuttles were a success. Ian Alston, the corporation's transport co-ordinator, judged that they gave the city a bus service that was 'as good as in many areas but in more difficult operating circumstances'. One problem was the city's suburban density. Another was its lack of a spider's web road pattern. 'This makes it more difficult to identify the routes on which to put the buses,' Alston said. Nevertheless the 1988 household survey showed increases in both patronage and popularity.[15]

Meanwhile, Stephen Potter's argument about transport investment in the city being a waste of national resources began to look increasingly shaky. 'I don't believe Milton Keynes is capital intensive in road terms,' Wayne Perdue said. Big savings came from the lack of flyovers on the main roads. 'You can almost correlate the costs of roads with their structures.'[16]

Potter's argument also failed to take into account the savings that flowed from uncongested roads. In Milton Keynes, unlike other cities, there was no congestion to

Left: Following deregulation, a fleet of small shuttle buses appeared on the streets of Milton Keynes.

increase the running costs of buses, cars, lorries and emergency vehicles. 'Most planners say "thou shalt not use thy car",' observed Alston. They did not have to in Milton Keynes. Vehicles could go everywhere freely. This, he argued, needed to be taken into account before claiming that the city was a burden on the nation.[17]

The absence of congestion also had energy implications. This emerged from a study commissioned in 1990 by John Walker, the deputy general manager. He wanted to be able to answer questions about the allegedly wasteful drive-in city.

Wayne Perdue, who did the analysis, came to the counter-intuitive conclusion that 'Milton Keynes is better in energy terms than other urban areas of a comparable size. The city's good aspects outweigh the bad.' The absence of congestion led to vehicle speeds that gave, per mile, high fuel-efficiency and low exhaust emissions, while the city's dispersed land-use pattern (including its drive-in city centre) kept down the length of trips.

Perdue discovered that traditional cities with their clogged streets exhibited the opposite characteristics. Longer trip distances and slow-speed, stop-start travel sent them 'through the roof on fuel consumption and output of pollutants'. Was he confident in the output of the study? 'I think,' he said, 'that in broad terms it is robust.'[18]

16

A Grand Suburban Design

Milton Keynes is suburban. It is a city of trees. Its uniqueness is that it is also a grand design. No comparable claim can be made for Solihull or Bromley. Such suburbs and, for instance, the swathe of post-1960 estates that stretches from Reading to Aldershot are, at best, described as semiorganic. At worst they are sprawl. Milton Keynes, by comparison, fits Lynch's ideal of 'an environment which is not simply well organised, but poetic and symbolic as well'.[1] Like Bath or Belgravia, Milton Keynes has a structure that is bold, recognisable and coherent. Its elements include the main roads, the places they enclose, the linear parks and the central area.

Milton Keynes also has a microstructure. It is largely confined to the squares and to links between them. The need for this secondary structure was initially little recognised but, when the time came to build up the flanks of the city, district plans were drawn up to ensure that adjacent squares, instead of being designed in isolation, were knitted together.

As Milton Keynes got under way, the engineers, the city's master *tricoteurs*, assembled strand after strand of the great fishnet of city roads. By the end of the decade a strip of them, with Central Milton Keynes in its midst, stretched between Bletchley and the northern towns. This was the 'crescent'. Local drivers found the roads within the crescent to be simple and memorable and that for many trips there was a choice of routes. According to Jeff Bishop of the School for Advanced Urban Studies, the residents took to the road pattern like ducks to water.[2]

Nevertheless it is part of the folklore of the London intelligentsia that Milton Keynes is a maze. Stories about its impenetrability are repeated *ad nauseam* and it is a measure of the city's infamy that a Christmas card on sale in 1990 depicted the three wise men in front of a Milton Keynes road sign. One was saying to the others, 'I am sure I saw a star somewhere.'

Milton Keynes *is* different from other cities. You do not give directions to someone by saying 'Keep straight on until you come to the Marquis of Granby, then go left at the second traffic signal, turn right and go on until you get to the Odeon cinema.' The main roads of Milton Keynes run through bands of lawns, shrubs and trees that are up to one hundred metres wide. They are parkways and have the gradients and curvatures specified by the Department of Transport for rural roads. The buildings of the city are often invisible from them.

According to Opher and Bird, two Oxford Polytechnic urban designers, all this hinders strangers and residents alike from finding their way. 'The undifferentiated nature of the grid system means that all roads feel much the same,' they wrote in 1981. (Clearly *they* got lost.) 'At the city scale, there is little sense of "major" and "minor" roads; nor is the motorist aware of approaching the centre.'[3]

Why do outsiders judge Milton Keynes to be a maze? Jeff Bishop hazarded a guess. The lost sheep seemed 'to be predominantly visiting architects and planners who come with a preconceived idea of what clues and landmarks a city should offer ... and are then confused when such landmarks are not apparent'. They want to see buildings and are confused by the trees.[4]

A more humdrum explanation may be that traffic on the grid roads bowls along at 40 m.p.h. or more and hardly seems to slow down at the roundabouts. Strangers, therefore, have little time in which to consider where they are and where they are going.

By the mid-1970s the navigation question was being raised by the board. Was Milton Keynes developing 'a sufficiently strong urban identity and sense of place', members asked? Richard Llewelyn-Davies thought the question premature though he too observed that planting was beginning to prevent motorists from getting views of the city. The roads were tending to become 'divisive, screened tunnels ... This was not what the planners had in mind.'

Campbell agreed that travelling on some city roads was like 'driving underground', but Fred Roche cautioned against over-reacting to the work of the landscape architects. The problem called for a change of degree rather than of principle. The members then discussed using towers and spires as landmarks and to add identity. The idea was welcomed but, presumably with its cost in mind, the board decided to 'let some suitable suggestion emerge' rather than commission something from the architects.[5]

Three years later, after confirming its policy to limit houses to three storeys and city-centre commercial buildings to six storeys, the board was again worrying about the city's lack of urban character and agreed to study 'the feasibility of promoting slender landmark structures ... in strategic locations'. Again nothing came of it, but bolder planting was later on introduced at roundabouts and in 1989 they were given names.[6]

RIGHT: The Grand Union Canal, once a freight highway, now carries holidaymakers on narrow boats through the city's Ouzel valley.

A 1980 impression of how the main roads might look in 1995.

At the board's 1977 seminar Llewelyn-Davies raised a different aspect of the same problem. He 'thought that the embankments made along certain grid roads in response to the Wilson report on noise had been overdone. He hoped the planners would get back to producing a more urban effect.'[7] The urban designers responded with a revised treatment of the local centre for Neath Hill and Pennyland. The shops, pub and a commercial site were located 'specifically to face the road' (Overstreet) which sailed above them. However, this meant omitting the ten-metre strip normally left for a possible future fixed-track transit system. Fred Roche reminded members that this roadside reservation 'was a requirement imposed ... by Bucks County ... which the board had not thought necessary but had accepted in order to secure approval of the plan'.

As Fred Pooley had by this time left the county to become controller of planning and architect to the Greater London Council, Roche proposed that an effort be made to get agreement to lift the requirement. He thought that Bucks would 'no longer feel strongly' about it.[8]

A subsequent meeting between officers of the corporation, the county and the borough concluded that 'provided road capacity was planned for high car usage, any substantial decrease in car usage would leave space on the roads for trams or trolley buses'. The roadside reservations were therefore abandoned. There would be, Roche said, important benefits. Buildings could be built closer to the roads thereby giving the city a more urban quality. Valuable land could be freed for development and main-road buses promised to become more attractive thanks to a shortening in walking distances to and from stops.

Nevertheless, memories of Pooley's monorail lingered on in the minds of some members. Roger Parker-Jervis speculated that 'a system of transport completely incompatible with roads might have to be developed at some time in the future'. Horace Cutler, by then leader of the Greater London Council, suggested that the original reason for the reservations ought to be looked at again. It was, but no justification could be found for them and the board later approved a recommendation 'that fixed track reservations were no longer required'.[9]

Arguments in favour of a more urban treatment of the main roads led, by 1979, to the restoration of the approach outlined in the master plan. The board was told that main-road reservations 'had generally been reduced to between sixty and eighty metres ... local centres would be designed closer to the grid roads, and a landmark policy to aid navigation was being formulated'. Changes were even being considered to the shaping and planting of main-road verges.[10]

The 'urban character' issue reflected, at least to some extent, a profound difference of opinion. Was Milton Keynes to be *urbs in rure* or *rus in urbe*? What, in other words, was to be the role of nature in the new city? The question was made all the more tantalising by the slowness of nature to reveal herself. Take, for instance, the trees beside the main roads. One day they would billow outwards and upwards in the most spectacular way. Derek Walker was deeply enthusiastic about such a prospect. 'The grid roads could be the most enjoyable part of the city – our Venice canals, our Paris boulevards, our London squares,' he wrote.[11]

But if the architects were happy to see the work of the engineers vanish into the trees, it did not follow that they felt the same about their own buildings. Derek Walker, for instance, was seen by Neil Higson, the corporation's chief landscape architect from 1976 to 1988, as 'the Busby Berkeley of architecture'. He did 'some splendid things for the city'. He had 'a bold enough vision to go for some majestic urban design aims (it would be juvenile not to credit these things) but he was barely capable of responding to landscape. All the early designs,' Higson added, 'dominated nature.' Those who produced them 'believed architecture was ... omnipotent and landscape architects were fuzz-producers around the edges'.

Although work on the parkways and on providing a green setting for the city's new houses began in 1970, a central landscape unit was not set up until 1976. Neil Higson (with whom Fred Roche had worked at Runcorn), having been 'dragged kicking and screaming

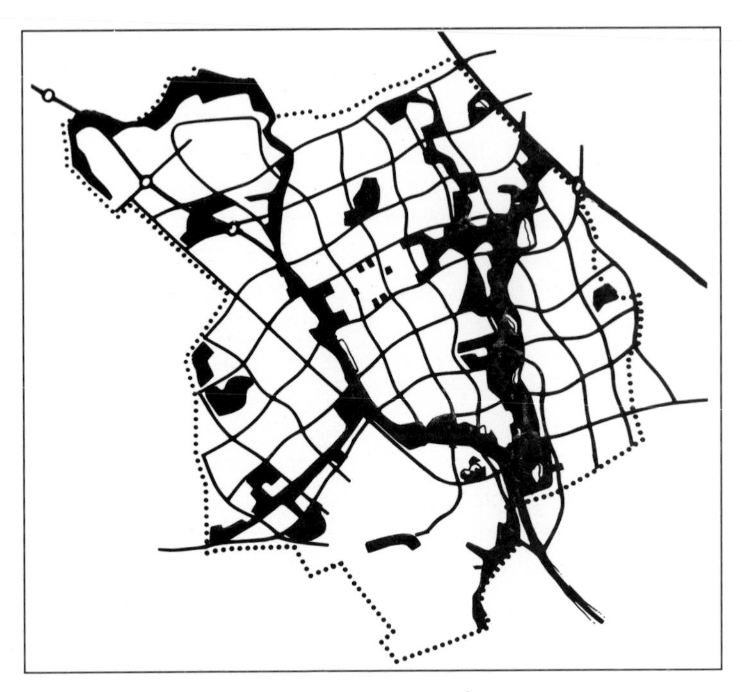

The city's linear parks.

by Fred's firm hand', was its first head. Higson had at once to decide whether or not to carry on with what was already being done. His experience was that 'changing direction is always incredibly wasteful' so, with one or two exceptions, he decided to build on the existing policies. One departure affected the city centre where it was decided to plant boulevards of London planes crossed by avenues of smaller species. Another was to put much greater reliance than before on fast-growing poplars and willows. 'We kept the rest,' Higson observed.

The northwards-flowing Ouzel and Loughton Brook valleys and the Ouse valley itself, all of which were identified as parks in the master plan, provided the landscape architects with their greatest challenges. When Higson arrived North Buckinghamshire seemed to him to be 'a forgotten corner' of England. 'The old A5 had been a generator of life whereas the M1 swept through and bypassed the place.' A lot of farms were struggling and the Ouzel valley, which was to become the greatest of the three parks, was subject to flooding. 'It was valuable for grazing but often in an ungrazable state,' he remembered. Disease had ravaged the once-great elms. The villages of Woughton and Woolstone were 'not in good heart. The whole area was slightly down-at-heel.'

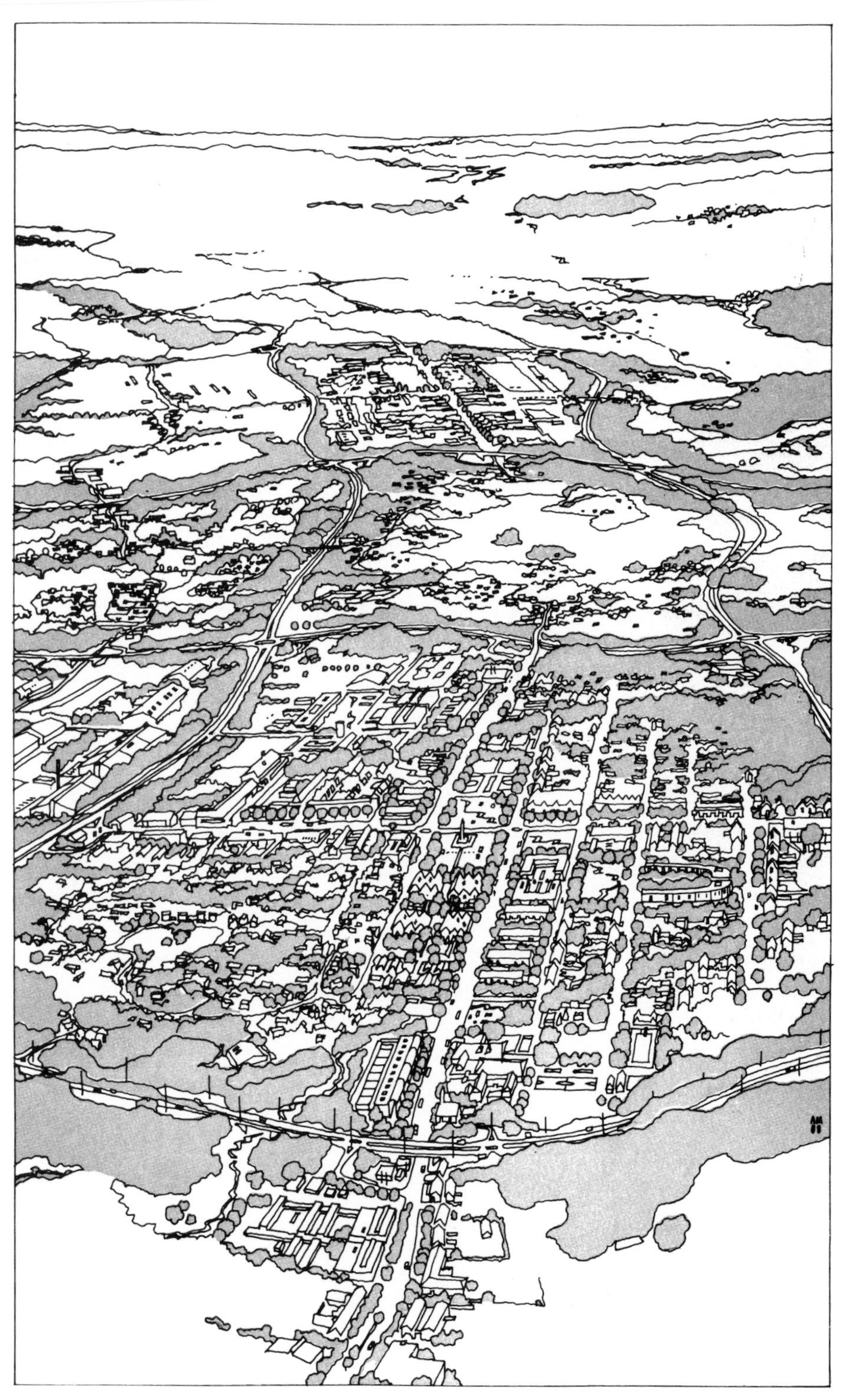

Milton Keynes as portrayed by the 'City structure' report: a quilt of secluded but connected villages.

Bit by bit, one of the grandest city parks in Britain began to take shape in the Ouzel valley. An avenue of Lombardy poplars was planted along the contour-following Grand Union canal. Lakes were created to enable rain to be released into the Ouzel without flooding it. Yet, as Higson recalled, nobody had any real notion how to develop the park as a whole. They all knew it would be too expensive to treat 1,650 hectares as a Royal Park (they were concerned with an area nearly a third larger than Richmond and over ten times the size of Hyde Park) but no one had any idea what to do instead.

Higson and his colleagues filled this conceptual vacuum by drawing on the experience of national parks. They divided the Ouzel valley into 'strings, beads and settings'. The strings are well-maintained routes, be they for walking, bicycling or riding; the beads are sports centres, lakeside cafes and other activity areas; the settings, which form the bulk of the park, are self-managed land-uses such as woods, riding paddocks, a golf course and a farm for handicapped children. There is also a nature reserve which, although prompted by the presence of the rare redshank, is now also inhabited by sand martins and kingfishers. There is even an island for harvest mice.

The clarity of Higson's concept turned what might otherwise have been a formless straggle into a park that attracts people from all over the south Midlands. There is lots to do and lots to see. The visitors picnic, ride, water-ski and go boating. They wander around the Japanese peace pagoda, explore the labyrinth and stroll onto the Willen promontory. Like the park of a great eighteenth-century house, the Ouzel valley is largely man-made but looks natural.[12]

Elsewhere the landscape architects made major and still growing contributions to the appearance of every corner of the city. The early housing layouts called only for 'street trees and grass with little shrub planting'. However, as Bauhaus designs gave way to fishing-village romantic, so the landscape architects started to influence layouts and 'the way houses sit in the landscape'. Things changed again in the 1980s as houses for sale replaced houses to let. Developers were required to contribute to a city-wide budget that enabled the landscape architects to concentrate their planting where its effect would be most dramatic. Residents could then 'introduce their own identity' outside their front doors.[13]

By this time landscape design was becoming a very powerful force. In aiming to dramatise the natural features of the site, Higson and his colleagues were also contriving to 'de-dramatise architecture'. At Great Holm, for instance, they planted trees 'on high land to break the mass of roofs and the dominant housing-estate image'. If the trees took time to overtop the houses, it was because the architects had put 'their more majestic buildings on the ridge'. Higson was philosophical about that. 'We'll beat them in the long run,' he observed with the quiet confidence of a man who has nature on his side.[14]

By the late 1970s the executive began to consider building on the flanks of the city and,

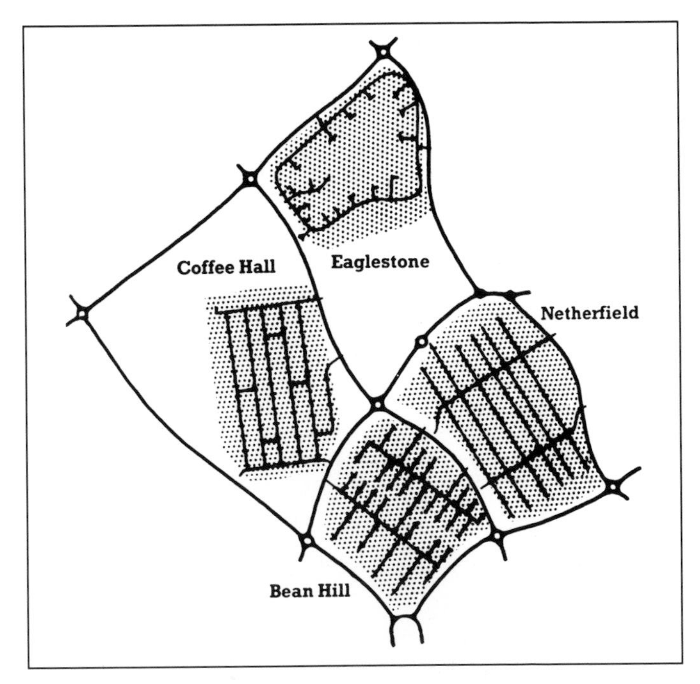

Early self-contained housing squares.

at the same time, to scrutinise what had been achieved in the crescent. It soon became clear that the city's microstructure suffered from a variety of defects. The squares were too self-contained. With one or two exceptions, local centres were not acting as links between them. And the state of the cycle- and footways left much to be desired. Fred Roche was brutal in his condemnation of the way in which walking and cycling had been neglected. 'The corporation should have put as much emphasis on these in the early days as on grid roads,' he told the board. They had fallen into the trap of 'treating cyclists and pedestrians as second class citizens'.[15]

Work was soon put in hand to remedy this situation but, as Opher and Bird noted, catering adequately for 'unprotected' road users in suburban conditions was difficult. 'Walking and cycling along one of the pedestrian routes is undoubtedly safe and free from the dangers of motor vehicles.' However, the routes were seldom thronged and at night, with even fewer people around, could be lonely and frightening. This probably explained why it was 'not uncommon to see people, including women with prams, appearing over the tops of the mounds beside the grid roads, to walk by the edge of what is effectively a rural motorway'.[16]

The corporation dealt with these issues in reports on the city's structure, on the redways (the cycleway system) and in a series of district plans starting with the Watling Valley and moving on in the 1980s to the city's eastern and western flanks. The problem, as defined in a report, 'City structure', stemmed from the master plan. It set out the grid of main roads but made only limited proposals for any 'finer grain structure'. People could walk between adjacent squares but if they wanted to drive they had to cross fast-moving streams of main-road traffic. (It should, however, be remembered that the master planners envisaged main roads with traffic signals and 30 m.p.h. driving, not roundabouts and 40 to 50 m.p.h. driving.)

The authors of 'City structure' accordingly recommended putting local shops, pubs and primary schools back beside the city roads as had been proposed in the master plan. They made a case for a new type of road ('main local routes') suitable for pedestrians, cyclists, and motorists; they proposed to emphasise these roads within the squares by lining them with buildings; and, to increase the connectedness of the city, they proposed to run the local roads from square to square by way of the activity centres. The report also proposed that local parks should be located in the corners of squares so that houses and other buildings could be clustered in a village in the midst of them.

Don Perkins, team leader on the north-east district plan (which was a test-bed for these principles), stressed their contribution to 'getting away from suburbia' towards a new kind of city that is differentiated and connected. Adjacent squares were prevented from sprawling into one another by the parkways and the local parks, but the new local roads and redways linked them into a continuous city. The quality of the connections was all-important. They enabled people to live in both a village and a city.[17]

Designing roads that ran from square to square without attracting speeding drivers who would create dangers for pedestrians and cyclists gave the planners one of their biggest headaches. A first attempt to resolve this problem was made in north-east Milton Keynes where a continuous local road (which was also a redway) runs the length of the district. This connected adjacent squares but attracted unwanted traffic because drivers failed to find their way on to the main roads. Furthermore, the underpasses were brutish structures and unneighbourly for the nearby activity centres.

East Milton Keynes saw the planners take their thinking a step forward. They continued to run local roads from square to square but designed them to make it harder for drivers to stay on them. They also reduced the height of the main-road underpasses. This ensured that lorries did not use them and led to bridgeworks that were less daunting for the

Left: Milton Keynes has the most extensive network of cycle routes and footpaths – called redways – of any city in Britain.

adjacent shops, pubs and schools. This was the state of thinking at the end of 1987.

Thinking about the design of the redways, 'Britain's largest urban footway/cycleway network', evolved within the context of the work on city structure. The redways got their name by chance. Don Perkins was hunting for a characterful name for them when his secretary typed 'redway' for 'pedway'. Perkins knew instantly that his search was over.

According to a 1980 handbook, the redways are mostly separate rights of way but 'sometimes join village streets or follow country lanes which are lightly used by motor traffic'. The planners envisaged that 'as many as eight out of every ten secondary school children ... will go to school on a redway' and argued that this would free the roads from cars during peak hours – 'often a cause of congestion in conventional cities'.[18]

There was, however, room for improvement. The city structure report found that redways were 'often too isolated to be used safely at night' (they were not adequately overlooked) and too circuitous for cyclists making longer trips. The corporation responded by routing subsequent redways close to buildings and roads and by creating more direct main routes.[19]

The plan for west Milton Keynes, which was published in 1989, showed a further stage in the corporation's design thinking. West Milton Keynes is a series of undulating ridges sprinkled with oak, ash and field maple. It is half the size of an inner London borough such as Islington and will eventually be the home of about 20,000 people. Woodhill prison (tinted lilac for 'employment' in the district plan) lies in one corner but far more noticeable are the redways which, looking like healthy blood vessels, run, often beside the main roads, direct from square to square. In some places they share low underpasses with equestrian routes. In others they share full-height ones with local motor traffic.

The decision to revert to full-height underpasses was not taken lightly. The lower ones had worked well enough for cyclists and cars but there had been a tendency for lorries to get stuck at them. This had in turn obliged the corporation to provide obtrusive turning circles. However, as so often in the complex field of urban design, solving one problem creates others. The main roads in west Milton Keynes, with their full-height underpasses, were going to be more difficult to tuck neatly into the landscape.[20]

Something impossible to incorporate neatly into the landscape was a line of 132kV electricity cables and pylons that ran across the west flank. Corporation board members saw the pylons as an unacceptable part of a modern city almost from the day they were erected and efforts to have the cables buried were first made by Walter Ismay and Ernest Pye in the late 1960s. However, burial would have cost £400,000 (then felt to be an astronomical sum) and the executive grudgingly agreed to nothing being done until action was necessitated by the spread of the city westwards. Time passed. The generating board was replaced by the East Midlands Electricity Board (EMEB) but Frank Henshaw and John

Napleton, the infrastructure director, continued to press for burial. As the town's development crept westwards, health hazards from power lines became a national concern and with wind-up day approaching, John Harris, chairman of EMEB, at last agreed with the corporation to split the cost of cable burial. In January 1991, a 22-year saga was ended and Henshaw had the satisfaction of seeing the clutter of cables give way to open sky over the west flank. The cost to the corporation was a mere £5 million.[21]

At Milton Keynes, as in older cities, the passage of time brought changes in layout. In Frank Henshaw's view, the 'ultimate expression' of this development in thinking can be found in the plan for the west flank. In it the self-contained squares of the early days and the limited-headroom connections of the east flank – 'more popular with the designers than the executive' – gave way to unconstrained linking roads 'planned to be unattractive to all but local journeys' but uncluttered with turning circles. After many trials the corporation had found a balance between the competing concepts of the secluded village and the interconnected city.

'Suburb' was a word of abuse amongst London's charmed circle of 'architects' architects' in the days when Milton Keynes was getting under way – and it still is. As Bishop put it, urban is good, rural is good but suburban, 'being incoherent, neither one thing or the other, undifferentiated', is bad. Architects, therefore, tended to be enthusiastic about working on city sites but felt uneasy about suburban ones. Suburban environments were, Bishop suggested, symbols of individual rather than collective aspirations. They were certainly not worker housing. Therefore they could not be 'good design'.[22]

Yet, thanks to the master plan, Milton Keynes was a suburb with a difference. Shortly after his arrival, Derek Walker climbed up the Brickhills just to the south of the city and saw what was to a Yorkshireman, 'the most boring, bloody site' in the country. It varied in height by no more than 200 feet and its best trees were 'rampant with Dutch Elm Disease'. Walker told Roche and Campbell later, 'I'd like to see the city greener than the surrounding countryside.'[23]

The board's commitment to landscape architecture promises that, fifty years hence, Milton Keynes will be home to perhaps 250,000 people and a green oasis in North Bucks. It will, in Neil Higson's phrase, be 'a totally new form of urbanism'. Milton Keynes is a place for suburban living where the whole is greater than the parts. It is a city.

GB
5736 NC

17

THREATENED BY INNER CITIES

The summer of 1976 was long and hot and laid waste 200,000 of the corporation's carefully planted shrubs and trees.[1] But as summer heat turned to autumn dust, and as the landscape architects counted their losses, the drought took a political turn. On 17 September in Manchester Peter Shore, the Environment Secretary, made public what had hitherto been largely confined to the corridors of power. He spoke of 'directing the country's resources towards inner-city areas and about reappraising the role of the new towns'.[2]

Shore, as MP for Hackney and Poplar, had begun to mull over the implications of inner-city deprivation while in opposition during the Heath administration. He recalled later that, although the Labour party had not formulated an inner-city policy, 'I had come myself personally to the conclusion that we needed a radical departure in policy to give a new priority to the inner cities and to reject the view that you can just allow them gradually to empty leaving behind a legacy of problems.'

He got his chance when Jim Callaghan made him Environment Secretary. Callaghan had already decided to shave transport off the mammoth DoE but at Shore's behest he also made an addition – the Home Office's urban programme, a mechanism for pouring oil on racial conflict.[3]

Thus, by the time he gave his Manchester speech, Shore was well positioned to bring about a radical departure in policy and it is not surprising that the new towns interpreted his remarks as their death knell. Campbell, in his role as chairman of all the new-town chairmen, wrote at once to the Secretary of State and followed up with a visit on 18 October.[4]

LEFT: *London in the 1960s: a street in Battersea.*

When Shore was told by Campbell that he had caused a collapse in confidence at the new towns he 'replied amiably that he had not realised that his speech, which was directed at the problems of inner-city areas, would have such drastic repercussions for new towns'. He had, he added, done his best in a later speech to redress the balance. He would try to reach decisions by Christmas. He 'thought that the "majority of new towns would be unaffected"'..

Campbell interpreted this as meaning that Milton Keynes was unlikely to be harmed. Not only did he believe that they could convince Shore that new towns and inner areas were complementary but 'Milton Keynes had got too far to be significantly affected by public expenditure cuts', and 'people would continue to need houses'.[5]

Peter Shore may have spoken in Manchester but changes taking place in London, and particularly in overcrowded, old-fashioned, Victorian London, were at the root of the matter. Migration from the metropolis was running at a high rate. The Registrar-General's projections showed a reduction in the rate of population growth in the south east. And public expenditure was increasingly constrained. The upshot was mounting pressure on the Labour-controlled Greater London Council to change its legendary generosity towards new and expanding towns. (Bletchley was only one of many objects of the GLC's benevolence.)

Changes in London's population are, of course, the result of huge flows of migration in and out. But what counts is the net result, and in the 1970s this amounted to an outflow of nearly 100,000 people a year. Over two decades the capital was therefore thought likely to lose over one and a half million residents.

A particularly worrying aspect of the outflow was the departure of so many middle-income families from inner London. No fewer than 200,000 skilled workers left between 1961 and 1974. The explosive implications of this were vividly portrayed by Graeme Shankland in one of a series of inner area studies commissioned from consultants by the Home Office. Shankland and his team examined Lambeth and threw light on who was leaving and who was staying behind. 'Our survey showed that between a quarter and a third of households, mostly with children, would move [from inner London] if they could. But the less skilled and the less affluent among them, the very people who most need to move to new jobs, have little chance of doing so. These families are thus caught in what we call the "housing trap". The choices available to them are owner-occupied houses, which they cannot buy, and public housing, to which they are denied access.' Shankland added, in words that brought the new towns first comfort and then pain, 'We do not believe that further dispersal will impoverish London: a less congested London would be cheaper to run.' But he added that the new towns – by which he meant Milton Keynes, Northampton and Peterborough – were too far from London to help the poorest families.

Although the new towns challenged Shankland's views about their inability to help the inner urban poor, London's predicament was that the home counties were booming. Not only were electronics and other completely new industries being born there, but some existing London firms, fleeing high costs, were moving out to join them. Between 1961 and 1974, when manufacturing jobs in the south east increased by twenty-one per cent, the number in London fell by no fewer than 489,000.

Fundamental shifts were taking place in the nature and the geography of manufacturing industry. Research done for the corporation by Lee Shostak, an American-born planner, showed that two-thirds of the industrial jobs lost by London just disappeared. The replacement of the old, labour-intensive, up-river docks by the container port at Tilbury was typical of this phenomenon. Tony Judge, a GLC Labour councillor, explained to the board how other jobs vanished. Many London firms were, he said, 'inefficient and overmanned, and ... when they moved they only took a proportion of their workforce'.

The new towns were not major players in this process. Shostak calculated that fewer than one-fifth of the jobs that moved out had ended up in the new towns and only 1,095 went to Milton Keynes. He added that 'much of London's unemployment was due to the mismatching of skills to jobs'. Jobs in services were increasing; those in manufacturing, which had been below fifty per cent for many years, were declining. 'The holding up of migration would not change the problem. The Greater London Council needed to look at ways of making London more attractive.'

The GLC, with its Labour constituency, found it impossible to adopt such a perspective. The councillors saw their objective, Tony Judge explained, as 'trying to tackle this problem of retaining industry in London, but were hampered by the shortage of land, the shortage of skilled labour, and the enormous cost to firms of operating in London'. The GLC, therefore, welcomed the action of the new towns in taking a high proportion of problem households, wanted it to continue but also wanted the towns 'to look elsewhere than London for their employment base, and to stop all action to attract industry away from London'.

Alan Ashton, the corporation's commercial director, said that 'government policy was in direct conflict with the GLC's views'. The corporation was 'directed to look to London for its employment'. IDCs for firms from abroad (industrial development certificates were permits designed by the Department of Trade to try to steer footloose industrial firms to the north) were, with a few exceptions, not obtainable.[6]

Notwithstanding the housing programme cuts, the uncertainty created by Peter Shore's speech and rising interest rates, Fred Roche reported that, 'Overall the picture was of body blows so far successfully withstood, but there was not much margin left. A cautious lack of pessimism was justified.'[7] Four weeks later Jock Campbell, representing the new-town chairmen, was summoned to Whitehall by Peter Shore to be told that, with a national economic crisis looming, the cabinet had cut the number of houses the new towns could build in 1977 from 10,000 to 5,000. The decision was part of Denis Healey's minibudget of 15 December. Campbell and his new-town colleagues could only protest against a *fait accompli*.

Milton Keynes' housing starts in 1977 fell from 2,874 to 1,489. Campbell told the board that this cut 'coupled with the uncertainty about the city's ultimate target, was the first severe setback' to threaten their work. If it was not possible to expand housing output again in 1978 the target catchment of 100,000 people for the city-centre shops would not be met and the corporation's staff would face compulsory redundancies. Yet other new towns fared even worse. Warrington's starts were cut to 618. Northampton and Runcorn got none.

Members interpreted this latest disaster in a variety of ways. Horace Cutler was gloomy. He thought it presaged a switch of finance to inner areas and an end of new towns. Roger Parker-Jervis drew upon the recent *Strategy for the South East* which strongly supported Milton Keynes. He thought that 'the main issue for the government was whether it could afford the new city'. Derk Pelly, vice-chairman of Barclays International and later deputy chairman of the main bank, looked for solutions. Big builders might, he suggested, be offered attractive deals to finance and build houses for sale. It was one way to keep going. Campbell was, as usual, equally positive. Drawing on his experience of Whitehall and Westminster he observed that officials still supported new towns in general and Milton Keynes in particular and there was no evidence that Peter Shore, though preoccupied with inner cities, 'was positively hostile to new towns'.[8]

Campbell's judgement seems to have been well-founded. 'I did not in any way want to destroy [the new towns],' Shore later recalled. 'I liked them too much for that and liked the people who were running them. They had energy and enterprise – all the things which were lacking in the inner cities.' He had gained some of these impressions from living in Harlow in the late 1950s. 'But it seemed to me,' he added, 'that we had reached a point where the ebbing away from the great conurbations had gone far enough.'[9]

The real enemy of the new towns was the parlous state of the economy. It was this that made the winter of 1976/7 such a dispiriting time. Not only did the DoE try to cut Milton Keynes' 1977 housing starts to below even the paltry number decided in December, but the new towns had no success in obtaining 'flexibility' – freedom to go on building houses and cut expenditure elsewhere. The only consolation was a promise of more starts in 1978. Meanwhile Peter Shore, steadfast in his commitment to the inner cities, sent confidential requests to the chairmen of the six newest towns to consider the implications of cutting short their development programmes. Jock Campbell was given three possible population targets: 150,000, 200,000 and 250,000.

When the details of Shore's request leaked, Campbell was pleased. He thought Milton

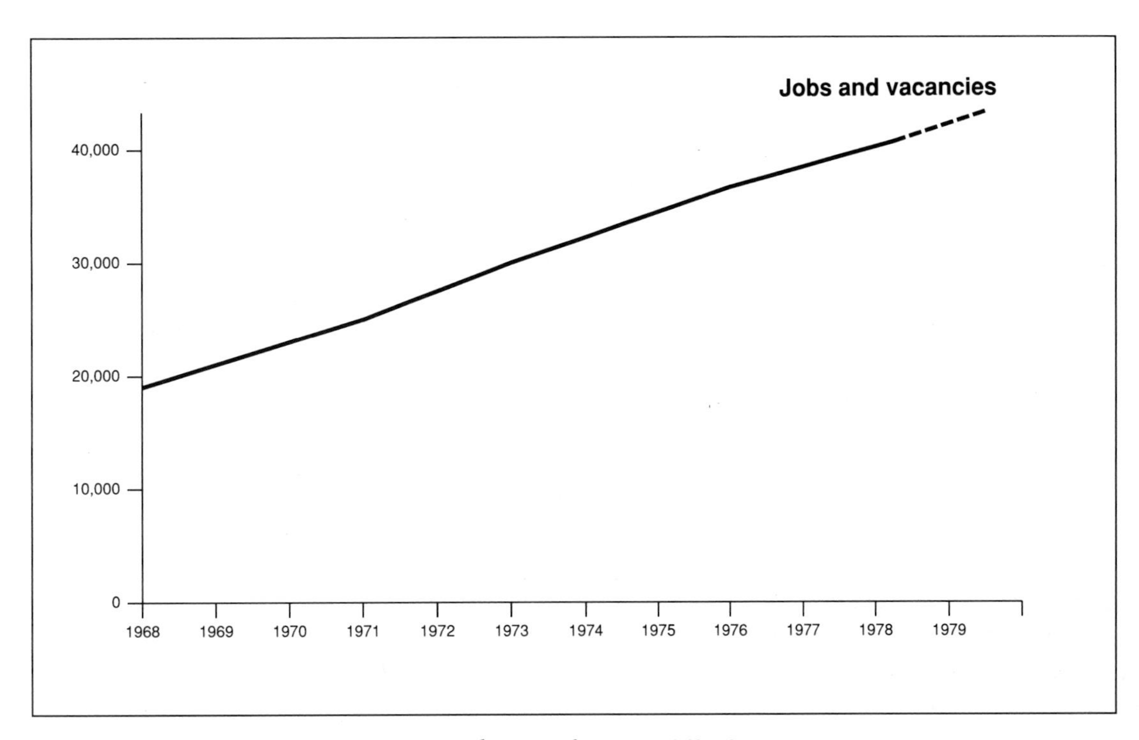

Growth in employment 1968–78.

Keynes would benefit 'as its battles could now be fought in the open. There were strong arguments in favour of proceeding with the city and there would be strong support from the local authorities and elsewhere.'[10]

On 10 March Peter Shore entered the lion's den – he visited Milton Keynes. The board members decided to be tough. A few days earlier they had resolved that they were 'not prepared to contemplate any target lower than 200,000' and they told Campbell they did not want him to negotiate any figure below 250,000 without first discussing it with them.[11]

In due course an iron-clad case was put by the corporation to the Secretary of State. The report said that Milton Keynes was making a contribution not just to housing stress in London but to national economic growth. It was a huge project with its own momentum and years would be needed to slow it down sufficiently to divert meaningful resources elsewhere. Furthermore, many people and firms had made commitments to the city in the belief that the Government would support it. Were the corporation to modify the population target it would 'be seen to have issued a false prospectus for the new city and will, therefore, fail to honour its obligations'.

An *aide-mémoire* prepared for Campbell before the meeting pressed home the housing argument. 'There can be little dispute about the very high level of unsatisfied housing demand which exists in London at the moment.' Numerous agencies testified to long housing waiting lists and increasing homelessness. 'Any presumption that Milton Keynes is not necessary to meet long term needs must be based on the belief that families with below average incomes will be able to find housing which meets their aspirations in London or in existing towns in the region ... There is no indication that these beliefs are valid.'

Another briefing note discussed reductions in capital expenditure. Shore had not himself raised the subject but the executive wanted Campbell to be prepared for it if he did. They believed that, given the all-important 'statement of complete support from the government for industrial growth', it would be more fruitful to consider 'reductions in the amount of public expenditure in Milton Keynes than abstract discussions of population targets'.

It was thought that cuts of ten to twenty per cent in Treasury support could be handled without damaging the standard or pace of development. Given freedom to sell assets and reinvest the proceeds (roll-over financing), to borrow short-term in the market, and to build houses to let unconstrained by cost yardsticks or Parker-Morris standards, even greater reductions could be managed. It would be 'possible to consider reductions of ... 20 to 40 per cent in the amount of public sector capital required each year ... after 1980'.[12]

Shore announced his preliminary conclusions about Milton Keynes a month later. Forced growth would be allowed to continue up to a population of 150,000 in the mid-1980s. Thereafter, natural growth would be permitted to upwards of 180,000 by the late 1980s with the possibility of continuing to 200,000.

The National Farmers Union was delighted and began to press for 'de-designation'. The local authorities – the borough plus the three counties of Buckinghamshire, Bedfordshire and Hertfordshire – took a contrary view. They all wanted to keep the old target of 250,000. Londoners added a complexity to the equation by electing a Conservative GLC led by none other than Milton Keynes' very own Horace Cutler. As Fred Roche remarked, the GLC's policy might change.[13]

'Seven years on', the second of the corporation's periodic surveys of the attitudes of city residents, was delivered by Gerald Hoinville's firm during the board's negotiations with Peter Shore. The surveys disclosed that six out of ten new households were coming from London and that, of these, four out of five were in housing need. This contribution to reducing housing stress in the capital was an impressive achievement but the board was disquieted by the discovery that incomes in Milton Keynes were lower than in London and other parts of the south east. They were worried, too, by the results of the 'satisfaction' survey. It showed, not surprisingly, that residents were divided in their views but also that the proportion who were 'a bit disappointed' had increased since 1973.[14]

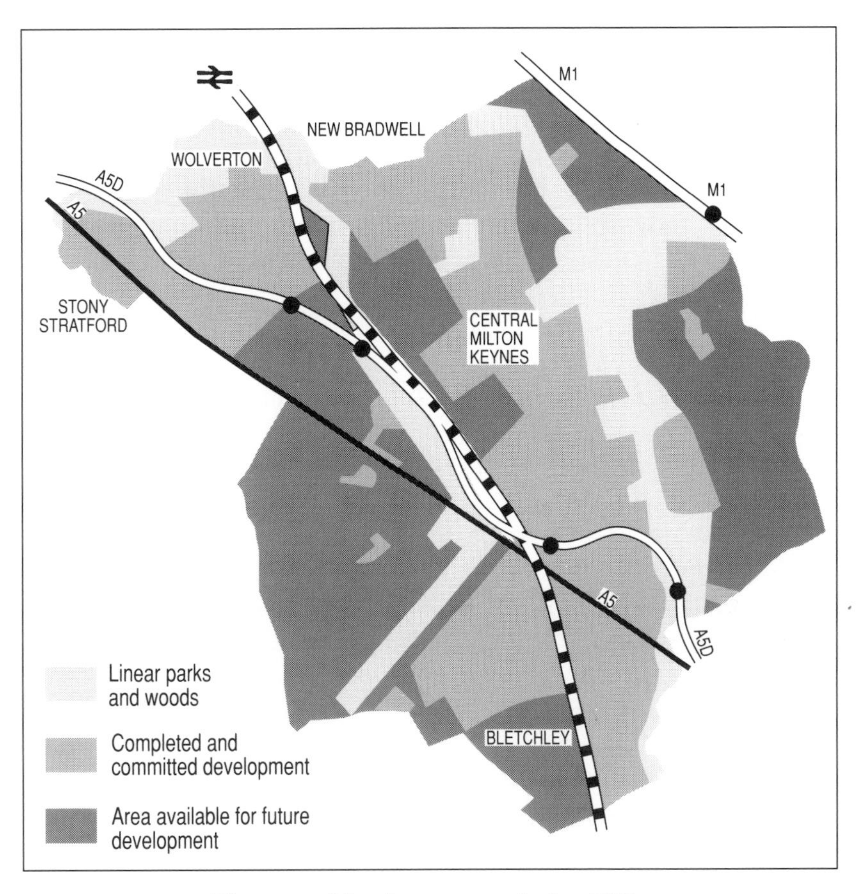

The stage of development reached in 1978.

Those	very pleased	20 per cent
	quite pleased	50 " "
	a bit disappointed	25 " "
	wanting to go back	5 " "

Explanations could be found for both these unwelcome results. Not only was the city attracting low-income households but many of the women in them, who had been working in London, were starting to have families and unable to work. This cut their incomes. As for disappointment, it could be attributed to a fall in living standards that was afflicting the country as a whole.

Campbell was, nevertheless, worried that the Press might use the survey results to defame the city. He even suggested that the board might like to delay their publication. Members did have their concerns. Tony Judge feared that the city might be becoming a low-income area. If it did, it 'would endanger the city's economic stability and indeed militate against home ownership'. But most of the board thought they should publish and be damned. As Derk Pelly said, the report 'was immensely impressive'. The corporation 'deserved a firm vote of confidence. Social engineering was extremely difficult, but Milton Keynes was a real success.'[15]

None of the representations made by the counties about keeping Milton Keynes as a growth area had any effect on Peter Shore. He had political reasons for winding down the new towns and in July he duly confirmed that the city's induced growth should not exceed 150,000.[16]

With uncertainty put to one side, the corporation got on with its job. The planners revised the implementation programme for 1978–85 which had been drafted under the old conditions. Their new scenario, aimed at an eventual population of 200,000, showed growth initially channelled into the crescent linking Bletchley with the northern towns and then into new areas associated with it. After that, development would shift into three places on the flanks of the city – next to the M1 in the north east, beside Watling Street in the Loughton Valley, and in the vicinity of the Open University. Beyond that, uncertainties about the shape of the employment market and about the region's future road pattern made it necessary to keep development options open.[17]

The corporation also began to address itself to new objectives. The review set in motion by Peter Shore had led to emphasis being put 'on the city's function as a centre to reflect the national policy of employment generation'. Milton Keynes had already been party to the generation of 22,000 jobs, many of them in firms with no previous existence. 'The new city has and is achieving the fastest rate of job creation and investment in urban development in the United Kingdom,' the corporation said in a note to John Stevenson, chief executive of the county council. As such 'it is meeting the national and regional objective which it has been set'.

Despite this sparkling performance, a South Bucks wit, concerned about the alleged cost of the city to the ratepayers, coined the label 'Millstone Keynes'. John Stevenson accordingly produced the relevant figures. These showed that the county's contribution, over a decade, had been £16 million. The county's offsetting income from rates was not given but it is typical that the corporation had just arranged with the DoE for a £250,000

RIGHT: Few actions of the corporation attracted more notice than the unveiling at Bancroft of Liz Leyh's concrete cows, a present to the city from the corporation's first artist-in-residence.

contribution, under 'undue burden' rules, to the cost of stocking the new county library in the city centre.

Capital cost of Milton Keynes at 31 March 1978

Milton Keynes Dev. Corp.	£ 216m	40	per cent
Bucks County Council	16	3	
Other public agencies*	164	30	
Private investors	143	27	
TOTAL	539	100	

* Milton Keynes Borough Council, gas, electricity and water authorities, etc.

No doubt the baser kind of party politics played a part in these incidents but to some extent even the Conservative majority at Aylesbury was penetrated by anti-new-town feeling. The councillors were beginning to worry that, with so much rented housing being built, they might soon be faced by a low-skilled, unbalanced and therefore Labour-voting city. Buckinghamshire was, it has to be remembered, a very Conservative county.

Not long afterwards the cost of the city was debated at a meeting of the liaison committee of the two bodies. Campbell reported that the county was concerned 'not only with the ratepayers' interests, but also with the taxpayers''. They wanted to satisfy themselves that 'the money going to build Milton Keynes was justified' before they would put in services. It provided Campbell with just the opening he needed. He told the council, in the politest possible way, to mind its own business.[18]

The second part of 1978 saw the Labour Government's pre-election boom pushing up building prices and creating shortages of skilled labour for construction. The corporation found that builders were losing interest in contracts and in the last three months of the year managed to get only 296 houses under way. Private builders, also going slow, started a mere 106.[19]

Scenting the impending death of the Government, Campbell and Roche began peering into the future. 'I took the executive to Broadway for the weekend and asked two of my colleagues to write a paper,' Roche recalled. The essay was called 'Here comes Maggie!': its authors were Lee Shostak, recently appointed planning director, and David Crewe, information director. The aim of the paper, which was very free in style, was to identify new policy directions for submission later on to the board. 'We spent a weekend debating it,' Roche said. 'I don't think it ever went to the board. It was very political. Some was tongue in cheek – but the conclusions became board policy.'[20]

The deliberations of the Broadway think-tank enabled the corporation to start switching its efforts into home ownership and other Conservative policies before Mrs Thatcher was elected. There was, however, a possibility that a Tory government would want to rid itself of development corporations altogether. Campbell kept a close watch on Westminster and, in particular, on Hugh Rossi MP, opposition spokesman on new towns. One speech gave him grounds for optimism. Rossi's remarks had, he told the board, 'done much to dispel doubts about the future of Milton Keynes if there were a change of government'.[21]

18

THATCHER-EFFECT

No sooner had the newly elected Conservative Government taken office than it ordered a five per cent cut in the corporation's budget. Margaret Thatcher was intent on one of the strictest efficiency drives the country had ever seen. She was determined to give Britain new economic foundations based on private enterprise, individual responsibility and minimum government intervention. The power of the trades unions would be curbed. The roar of the British lion would be heard again. The corporation totted up the effect of the cuts and found they would remove one-eighth of its house-building programme, a slice from the roads programme (down from £11.5m to £10.8m) and £1m from its £12.17m 'other local expenditure' budget.

Fred Roche reported that the effect of the cuts 'would not be too drastic' and that the executive was already working on a list of assets that could be 'rolled over' to provide an alternative source of funds. Frank Henshaw predicted that, given the prevailing climate of high interest rates and public expenditure cuts, conditions affecting the building industry were about to change again. Campbell thought that much would turn on the forthcoming visits of Margaret Thatcher and Michael Heseltine, her Environment Secretary. He hoped they 'would recognise that this was an expanding area and allow the funds needed'.[1]

Michael Heseltine's first step was to change the ground rules of new-town financing. He called in the chairmen and told them he was cutting £100m from their current £390m budget but added: 'The cut could ... be made good if £100m of new towns' assets could be sold.' He also warned them that further asset sales would be required of them the following year.

Jock Campbell's conclusion was that Milton Keynes and Telford (in Shropshire) were

LEFT: Over the years the corporation commissioned or bought a wide variety of pieces of modern sculpture: High Flyer by Philomena Davis is in Queens Court.

FASTEST GROWING AREAS			
1971–81		1981–89	
DISTRICTS	JOBS	DISTRICTS	JOBS
1 Aberdeen	48,505	**1 Milton Keynes**	**30,500**
2 Milton Keynes	**27,481**	2 Leeds	20,300
3 Reading	26,025	3 Tower Hamlets	19,600
4 Inverness	22,607	4 Aberdeen	18,800
5 Cambridge	20,512	5 Northampton	18,500
6 Southampton	20,050	6 The Wrekin	17,500
7 Northampton	19,086	7 Kirklees	15,600
8 Cheltenham	18,452	8 Thamesdown	15,400
9 Aldershot & Farnborough	17,741	9 Cambridge	14,600
10 Bournemouth	17,125	10 Crawley	14,200

Milton Keynes was second in Britain for job growth between 1971 and 1981: in the following decade it moved into the lead.

likely to be less affected than places such as Peterborough and Northampton which, because they were established cities, could be relieved of their new-town status more easily. He therefore wrote to Heseltine accepting the new policies and suggesting that they 'could be achieved without destroying the third-generation new towns if the proposed cuts and future financing could come from the earlier new towns and from the commission'. (The Commission for the New Towns was set up under the New Towns Act 1959 to take over the assets of mature new towns.)

Campbell went on to argue that no justification could be found for running down Milton Keynes. 'The city was generating badly-needed investment and employment, and was a fruitful object of public investment as against public expenditure.' Allowing himself a rare flight into hyperbole, he added: 'It was one of the few British success stories since the war.'[2]

Gradually the outlines of the new Thatcherite era came into focus. After the cuts came the quango hunt. Intent on 'rolling back the frontiers of the state', ministers began to lay indiscriminately into the country's rich collection of quasi non-governmental organisations. This included, amongst others, the Trustees of the British Museum, The Royal Commission on the Exhibition of 1851 and the Coypu Strategy Group – but also new-town corporations.

Fearing for their jobs, the new-towns staff suffered a collapse of morale. John Stanley and Geoffrey Finsberg, respectively Minister of State and Parliamentary Secretary in the Department of the Environment, then did a high-speed U-turn. They let it be known that their kill-quango noises had not been intended for new towns. At a meeting with the chairmen Campbell then heard them make 'some very explicit and encouraging, and indeed remarkable, statements about new towns'. The Government, acknowledging that new towns were useful, was prepared to treat them individually and was interested in their potential for extending private ownership. It would even increase their borrowing powers.

All this, Campbell told the board, combined with the prospect of development corporations being set up in the London and Liverpool docks, 'gave a focus for encouragement which had not been there before'. But times were changing. 'The corporation would need to plan and execute its future programme with great care and the best possible use of available resources.' It was clear that money was going to be much tighter.[3]

Turning the warm-hearted, motherly, public-service-oriented Milton Keynes of the 1970s into a slim-jim, self-financing, property investment machine designed to suit the commercial disciplines of the 1980s was a huge task. Sir John Garlick, the DoE's permanent secretary, started to set things in motion in December. His instructions were to cut public expenditure and to do so quickly. One solution was to sell assets. But as Milton Keynes was still a young place, there had been little time for the value of its factories and offices to grow. Meanwhile, huge sums had been invested in drains, roads and trees. Keeping a balance between the corporation's debts, accumulated during years of high interest rates, and its assets, therefore promised to be tricky.

Garlick was told that 'the corporation was at present solvent with assets valued at £580m and a debt of £350m. But with construction costs increasing faster than property values, and the accumulation of high interest rates on sixty-year loans, the corporation could get into a position of never being able to settle its debts, particularly if it had to sell its assets prematurely.'

The corporation asked for three remedies: interest-free loans on projects until they began to make profits; flexible borrowing powers; and grants for all non-remunerative expenditure. Garlick was sympathetic but firm. He understood about the immaturity of the city's assets and thought that selling those in Bletchley might provide a solution. And flexible borrowing powers were on the way in the Local Government and Land Bill. Campbell concluded that the corporation was 'pushing at an open door'.[4]

Finance was to preoccupy the corporation throughout the 1980s. Michael Heseltine may have set in motion a 180-degree turn in the way development corporations operated, but the supertanker of state took a long time to respond to his heave on the tiller. It was not, for instance, until the summer of 1987 that the Department of the Environment authorised the roll-over of investments – and then only with heavy restrictions.[5]

Conditions were particularly difficult in the opening years of the decade. The board found itself gripped between the jaws of a powerful vice. On the one hand, the cost of development rose while the value of property stagnated, thereby creating the worst possible conditions in which to have to sell assets. On the other, budgets were cut and made subject to 'cash limits' instead of being, as in the sloppy 1970s, indexed to rise with inflation. Whitehall's day-to-day control over the corporation increased too. The growing number of projects financed by grant-in-aid became subject to ever more detailed scrutiny.

All hopes of Milton Keynes following the example of the earlier new towns and becoming 'profitable' flew out of the window. The problem was a system of financing long since rendered inappropriate by rigidity and high interest rates. Every annual report since 1978 had urged its replacement. The financial policy committee, led by Evelyn de Rothschild, had played a leading role in devising a new system, and the Treasury and the DoE were finally considering one. Meanwhile, long-term projections based on the 1981 management accounts indicated 'no prospect of eventual revenue surplus'.

The board became downcast. Horace Cutler said 'the corporation could not carry on under existing methods of financing; nor could any other third generation new town'. Jock Campbell added that no business could be run 'in the way in which the corporation was financed. Nor would it cream off immature assets to balance the books.' However, they had to bend to Heseltine's will. In 1980 they sold assets worth £9m and in 1981 sold £11m more.[6]

Cuts in public spending and the switch to houses for sale obliged the corporation to rethink the timing and ordering of the physical development of the city. More sites were going to be needed. Lee Shostak told the board that to achieve 1,000 sales a year it would be necessary to have at least 3,000 houses under contract.

The new directions imposed by Thatcherism were first set out in the corporation's implementation strategy for 1980–6. Fred Roche put it to the board with a scheme for building 2,000 houses a year. It included proposals to provide a wide range of opportunities for developers; a low-cost, starter-home programme; and a pilot scheme for equity sharing. Roche proposed too that the corporation ask the Treasury for permission to buy from developers starter-homes they could not sell; and that they try to get authority to start more than an annual 538 houses to rent, although there was 'no great hope' of doing so.

'Maintaining the housing programme at 2,000 a year,' Roche said, 'would not be easy and would require ingenuity and flexibility; it might just be possible provided interest rates came down.' The members then put their minds to ways of ensuring they hit their target,

RIGHT: One of the many attractive private housing developments of the 1980s.

WATER
WEAVER I

and Tony Judge suggested that as the era for short waiting lists was over 'tenants should be offered financial inducements to move into sale housing'. Campbell observed that the output of rented houses could be boosted by making use of housing associations.

A silver lining to the clouds on the horizon was provided by employment which 'was enjoying a high degree of buoyancy. Enquiries and commitments were running at a higher level than for several years and it looked as if the target of 3,500 jobs a year would be achieved over the next two years.' Six weeks later, enquiries for commercial and office properties were higher than for ten years and 'much firmer'.

Little of this appeared in the local Press. The papers were deeply suspicious of the Thatcherite revolution and as the output of houses shrank and the threat of unemployment grew, the corporation was increasingly seen as an ogre. The minutes reflect the board's despair. Evelyn de Rothschild wished that the media would give the good news more publicity. Ray Bellchambers thought they themselves should spend money to broadcast it. The 'very poor local press ... should be overcome by full page advertisements telling the public what was really going on with a view to boosting local morale,' he said.[7]

Throughout 1980, as the board waited for Heseltine to decide their fate, the Government chopped away at Parker-Morris house standards and other pillars of what it saw as inflexible socialist bureaucracy. Meanwhile, jobs increased faster than houses and Campbell had to acknowledge that 'any imbalance would be taken up by more people commuting in from surrounding towns in which unemployment was growing'. The corporation, once in a position to fine-tune the development of its bailiwick, was gradually being obliged to take a more relaxed, pragmatic view of the growth of Milton Keynes.

Two junior ministers toured the city and became 'enthusiastic' about it and then in October, Michael Heseltine himself arrived. 'Much would turn on that visit,' Campbell forecast.[8]

Heseltine was in a dilemma over the newest new towns. They generated employment which was a plus but they also competed for a diminishing flow of Treasury funds. Campbell surmised that, in these circumstances, the Secretary of State 'would look for ways of developing the third generation [towns] more from private finance, rather than pronounce on targets and dissolution dates'.[9]

Heseltine duly came and went. Campbell thought he was impressed by what he saw, although privately he had kept 'harping on his shortage of resources generally, and on his need to find funds for inner cities ... He had kept on talking about "packaging" as a major job for the corporation – that is preparing opportunities for private investment and development.' He also wanted to see the corporation cut its staff.

At a meeting with John Stanley, the Housing Minister, the new towns heard that the Government had accepted two of the financing proposals urged by the working group

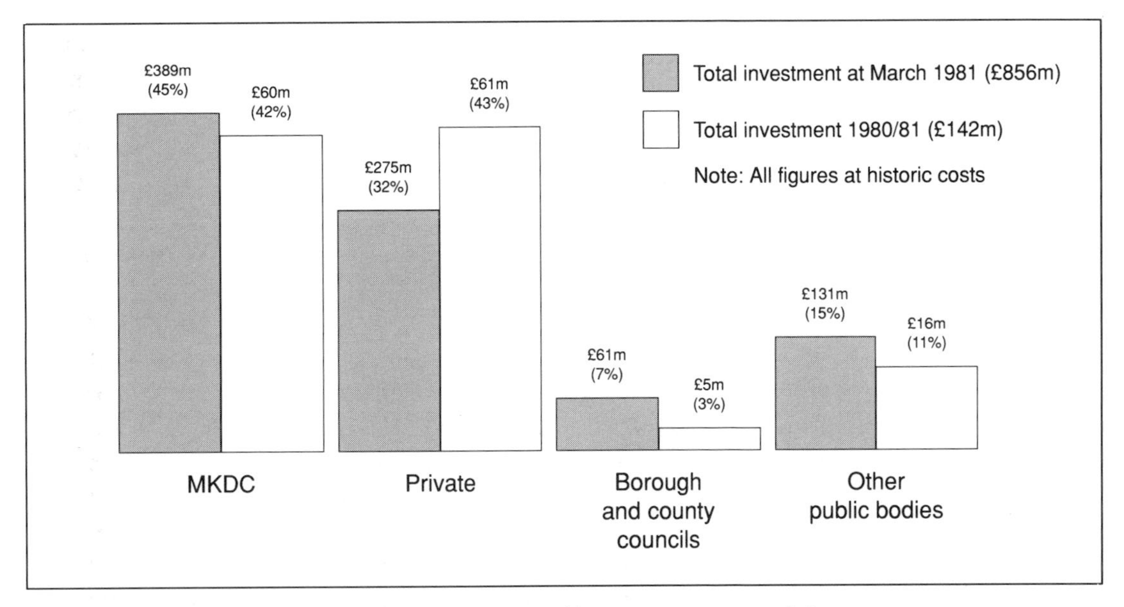

Investment in Milton Keynes up to 1980/1: public investment exceeded private investment.

chaired by Evelyn de Rothschild. Roads, parks and 'undue burden' payments to local authorities were, in future, to be substantially grant-aided. And, where an asset had a short life, corporations would be given freedom to borrow for periods shorter than sixty years.[10] The mounting deficit of the last of the new towns was finally being dealt with. In the end £1,688m had to be written off. Milton Keynes' share was £510m; a further £410m remained on the corporation's books.[11]

John Stanley also made clear that the era of rented public housing was over. He wanted 'the emphasis in new towns to be overwhelmingly on schemes which provided the opportunity either for outright ownership or for shared ownership ... The numbers of rented houses built would remain low.'[12]

The future of the new-town development corporations was announced by Heseltine in Parliament in February 1981. Northampton and Central Lancashire were to be wound up in 1984 and 1985. Milton Keynes, Peterborough, Telford and Warrington were to go at the end of the decade. Jock Campbell welcomed the ending of uncertainty and hoped that the Government would support the balanced growth of 'one of the most rapid, exciting and successful urban developments ever to be carried out in this country'.[13]

The task of continuing the build-up of Milton Keynes fell to Frank Henshaw. Like Fred Roche, whom he succeeded in November 1980, Henshaw had spent a significant part of his career with Coventry City Council in the 1950s. He arrived in Milton Keynes via Runcorn new town and the city council at Sheffield. Jock Campbell called him 'a consolidator', but his task involved far more than building on the achievements of his predecessor. The rules of the new-town game were changing and Henshaw had to redesign the corporation so that it could play them.

One of his most far-reaching changes was to introduce a corporate style into the working of the executive and the board. Detailed and regularly updated strategies became the main means by which policy was defined and modified. The strategies enabled the executive to ask the board 'do you want more of the same, do you think we are doing too much of anything or too little ... or have missed out a whole section?' Henshaw said later. He also introduced something akin to collective responsibility to the executive management committee.

This was a major shift from the free-booting style of the 1970s when individual directors committed large amounts of resources to pet projects. Some of these ideas, such as the city club and a water organ (the biggest in Europe), were based on superb drawings but were totally impractical. Of the city club Henshaw said, 'It was a good idea but the timing was terrible.' In the 1980s comparable ideas were tested by the executive before being worked up. 'We have been more conscious of putting our resources in support of corporate ... and not individual objectives,' Henshaw observed.

One result of this change in style was that board meetings became less discursive, the minutes were shorter, and seminars were abandoned altogether. By 1983, when Henry Chilver replaced Jock Campbell as chairman, the minutes ceased to name members who contributed to boardroom debates. An air of business efficiency replaced one of paternalism.

Henshaw indicated that the switch was not achieved without sweat. 'Things were much more difficult to achieve in the eighties. In the seventies we could rely on quite large amounts of government funding.' In the 1980s, except for infrastructure and other aids to development, Treasury support dropped away. 'We have had to be far more entrepreneurial and find a far greater variety of ways of getting things done ... and often ways of getting the more difficult things done ... Life is more complex.'[14]

The corporation's 'extremely commercial' style was warmly approved by Bill Benyon, MP for Milton Keynes. 'It is the first time that a statutory body has ever been ... driven by commercial incentives,' he noted.[15]

By 1981, the board was faced with the problem of high unemployment spreading its unremitting gloom across the country. The babies of the early 1960s boom who had, indirectly, led to the foundation of Milton Keynes had grown up and were pouring into the labour market at a time when international recession had been provoked by a second outburst of greed on the part of the oil producing countries. Milton Keynes did not escape the consequences. Indeed, in 1982 Chiltern Radio (whether out of malice or ignorance is unclear) dubbed the city an unemployment 'black spot' and reported that 16.6 per cent of its labour force was out of work. The station's error was to relate current unemployment figures to an out-of-date population figure. David Lee, board member and borough councillor, feared 'that such inaccurate reporting might frighten away business and investment'. Campbell, characteristically, invited Chiltern's programme controller to lunch.[16]

Confidence in Milton Keynes, nevertheless, remained remarkably strong. Near the end of 1981 the board was told that ninety-three private housing schemes covering 5,592 dwellings were in the pipeline while Allen Duff, commercial director, reported that the Abbey National was only one of several firms negotiating for sites on which to build themselves offices. And even though the city saw 2,500 jobs disappear in 1981 and 1982 (including a considerable number from the corporation itself), employment actually grew by 200. Few places in the country could equal such a performance. Jock Campbell heard John Stanley refer to Milton Keynes as 'the flagship' of the new towns.[17]

Part of the secret of the corporation's success was a marketing campaign of such unprecedented power that a shocked John Stanley asked about its cost at a meeting with the new-town chairmen. Campbell said that the 1982/3 figure was £1.5m. It may have looked high, he told the board later, but 'it had emerged that new towns were not all using the same basis for calculation'. As in so many ways Milton Keynes acted bigger and bolder than the rest. The London Docklands Development Corporation, which began its aggressive 'Why move to the middle of nowhere, when you can move to the middle of London?' campaign in 1982, was the corporation's only rival.[18]

The LDDC's anti-new-town propaganda (summed up by a picture of a scarecrow in a field) was met by Milton Keynes with 'Your company could be the next to go – to Milton Keynes' and with a series of posters – 'Bumper to bumper in Milton Keynes', 'Inner city rot', 'Concrete jungle' and 'The East End'. All pictured the new city as a rural idyll while the words described London's shame.

In April 1983 Sir Henry Chilver joined the corporation and took over as chairman. Lord Campbell's wife was seriously ill and he was unable to be present at what would have been his last board meeting. In his absence Rothschild read out a message in which Campbell paid tribute to Chilver's 'enormous administrative experience and his wealth of contacts with Westminster, with Whitehall, with finance and with industry'. His colleagues on the board he described as 'strong and widely experienced' but he reserved his warmest praise for the general manager and his staff. 'I have never worked,' he said, 'with a more professional and devoted body of men and women.'

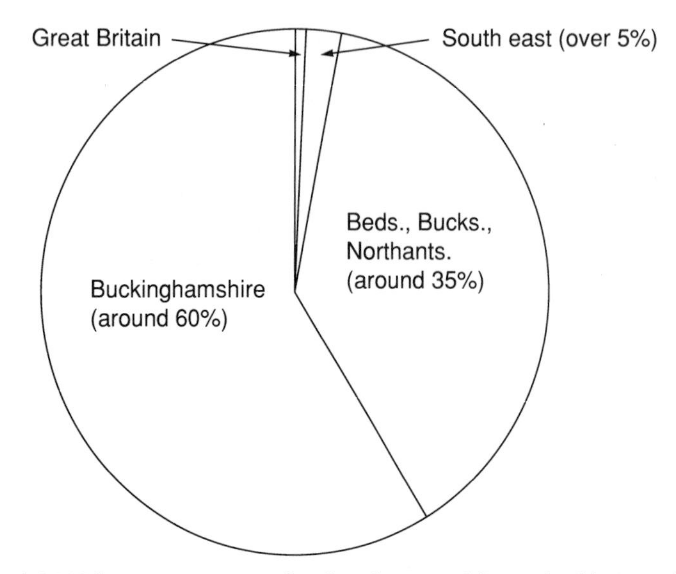

Milton Keynes contributed 2,500 houses per year to local and national house-building in the early 1980s.

Horace Cutler, one of two surviving founder members of the board, in turn acknowledged Campbell's 'sure-footed conduct of the board's business and his great talent for assimilating into the board's affairs people from all walks of life – from bankers to politicians, and from building society directors to sociologists. He had been particularly adept in his relations with the Press.' Frank Henshaw added: 'No chairman could have put more of himself into the task. He had set and demanded high standards, rejecting the mediocre and trivial.'[19]

At the time Campbell handed over his chairman's baton to Chilver the corporation had witnessed the generation of 34,000 jobs and the building of 32,000 houses. Over five per cent of all the houses going up in south-east England were by then under construction in Milton Keynes. Jock Campbell had achieved something that is given to few individuals. He had taken a village and left it a city.

19

A Regional Office Centre

In the 1960s, when he was MP for Buckingham, Robert Maxwell had foreseen that Milton Keynes would be an important office centre. The city's first realisation of this vision was Lloyds Court in Avebury Boulevard. It is named after the bank which helped finance it and whose handsome bronze horse (by Elisabeth Frink) seems to be trying to walk away from it. In 1977, the year after Lloyds Court was completed, work began on new civic offices for the borough council. Central Milton Keynes was then still a blasted heath and Erroll Ray, former chief executive of the council, remembers that the idea of moving there from Bletchley met opposition. The cost of a site was one problem. Councillors said, 'land is cheaper on the outskirts ... but they eventually came to the right decision. No one is in doubt now.'[1]

In 1979, when the Queen visited the shopping building and opened the civic offices, Silbury Boulevard was taking shape and the board agreed to an office-building programme. The aim was to slot 150,000 sq ft a year between the shops and the station. Fred Roche saw this as vital. With the completion of the shopping building there was a danger of 'an anticlimax not just in the corporation and the city, but also in investment,' he told the board in 1980. The 1980s required a 'major target ... which would reflect the dynamism and spirit of the city'.

Milton Keynes had, despite the ups and downs of the 1970s, already 'established itself as one of the major growth points' for industry and private housing, and was on the way to becoming a regional shopping centre. 'It had yet to make its name as an important centre of office development. It was important to do so,' Roche went on, 'because with manufacturing industry becoming increasingly capital intensive, job opportunities for the rising generation would have to be provided increasingly in service industry.'

Hot competition from Docklands (with its enterprise zone), Watford and other well-established office centres meant that 'Milton Keynes would have to produce something

special'. It was well-placed to do so. With its steadily improving communications the city centre was 'one of the ripest pieces of development land in Europe'.

The concept put to the board by Stuart Mosscrop was for a mixed development combining offices designed for the most modern communications, a hotel, shops and recreation facilities. It was to be called the Central Business Exchange (CBX). Fred Roche proposed that up to £100,000 be spent on consultants retained to define these projects more precisely and two board members declared interests in some of the proposed studies.[2]

In November 1980, Roche told the board that 'Milton Keynes had always aimed to create quality products ... and they had created their own demand'. Witness the shopping building and advance factories. He maintained that 'this was the secret of building a city; the project which was being recommended ... would create its own demand rather than respond to the statistics of supply and demand'. The alternative of 'piecemeal speculative development ... would not compete effectively in the situation of over-supply predicted for the 1980s'.

Only one major change was made to the original CBX plan. The consultants had found that the full scheme was too big for institutional investors to swallow in one mouthful. They therefore proposed a first phase costing £30m at 1980 prices. This included a 250-bed hotel, 400,000 sq ft of offices, shops, a health club and a telecommunications centre. (The entire project contained three times the office floorspace, another hotel, an ice rink, a conference hall and an 18,000-seat sports arena. This compared with the 4 million sq ft of offices envisaged for Central Milton Keynes in the master plan.)

Stuart Mosscrop presented sketches of the exchange showing office buildings on either side of a long, glazed courtyard. Galleries overlooking the courtyard provided access to spaces divisible into offices of various sizes. Two towers of light – 'columns clad in mirror glass ... aligned on the cardinal points and the summer solstice' – stood outside. Mosscrop added that these spires, which contained lifts giving a sky-ride, 'would need to be funded by some generous foundation'.

Investors took to the business exchange with alacrity. Of the fourteen approached by the corporation, ten expressed interest. It seemed reasonable to expect that a start could be made in 1982 with completion two years later. Fred Roche, though not wishing to minimise the difficulties, said he thought the corporation 'had an opportunity to build one of the most exciting pieces of development in Europe'.

By this time, Frank Henshaw had taken over as general manager and Jock Campbell, after congratulating Roche and Mosscrop for 'their imaginative leadership', went on to voice worries about the ability of the corporation to carry the project forward. Fred Roche's

Left: Campbell Park, which is adjacent to the city centre, gives views across the Ouzel valley to Bedfordshire.

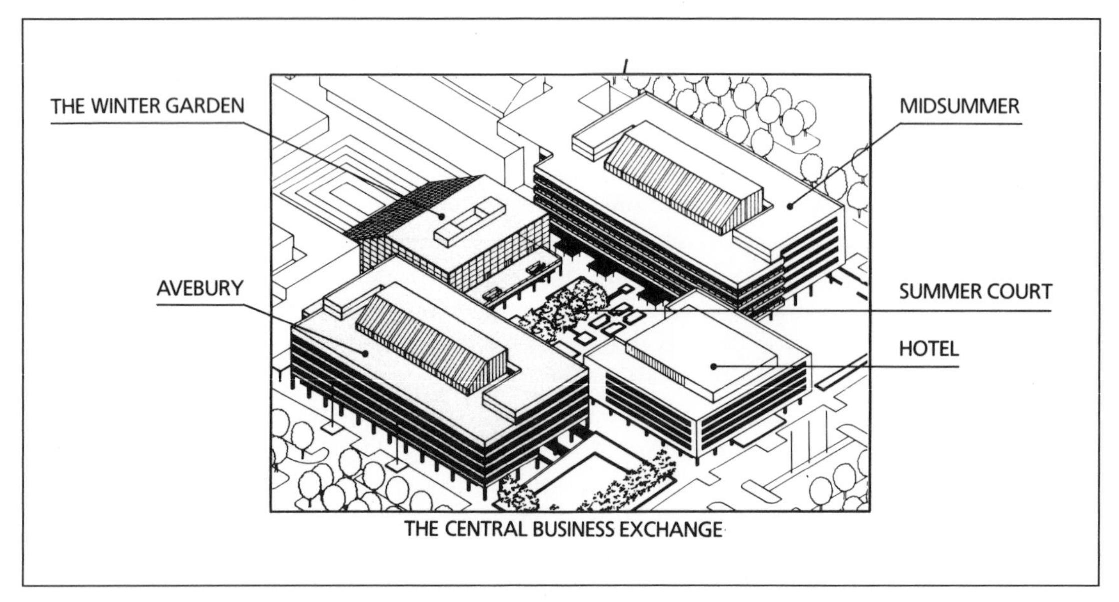

Stage one of the Central Business Exchange consisted of two office buildings, a hotel and a glazed winter garden overlooked by cafés and a health club.

departure was going to leave a huge hole in the executive. (He took with him, among others, Stuart Mosscrop, Nigel Lane and Lee Shostak.) Campbell said it was no reflection on the ability of the officers remaining behind, but Frank Henshaw, the new general manager, was bound to have to review the relationship between his staff resources and 'the demands of existing programmes and of an exciting but formidable new project'.[3]

Fred Roche, who had hoped to take the CBX project with him, left because he saw opportunities in private development. 'I went into the public sector in the fifties because I thought that was where the big things were going to happen and they did. I was lucky. By the end of the seventies I was convinced that public authorities were going to become enabling authorities' and that 'the fun ... was going to be in the private sector – and it was. Now [in the 1990s] there is no fun anywhere,' he added.

'Jock and I talked about his retirement ... and we sort of came to a deal on these things,' Roche said. He also told Terence Conran that he was restless and thinking of going private. Conran said, 'Come on, I'll back you. Let's do it.' The temptation was too great and Roche decided to join Conran. Leaving was 'a great wrench but I could never have done the job Frank has done'.

Roche's departure was, he acknowledged, 'disruptive to the corporation' and particularly upsetting for Campbell 'because the relationship between Jock and myself was very close. We were politically sympathetic.' Being blamed for luring away other members of the staff was, furthermore, 'very understandable. I accept that ... but it wasn't totally the story because I think they were restless, they were considering their careers.'[4]

Jock Campbell was equally frank about Roche's departure. 'I was very angry. He almost did a Saddam on me,' he commented. 'He was a wonderful general manager ... but he was fairly difficult to deal with. Fred cut corners and was a sort of commando ... and didn't always come clean with the board or anybody else. He was a very tough cookie.'[5]

The problems with the Central Business Exchange turned out to be even greater than Campbell had foreseen. They coincided with external pressures created by Geoffrey Howe's determined effort to crush inflation. Investors became more cautious and the promoters of the hotel began to prevaricate. Richard Seifert, their architect (and the designer of Centrepoint, the crinkly office shaft at the bottom of London's Tottenham Court Road), was unable to produce a scheme that fitted the company's limited budget. By 1982 the cost of the project had risen to £52m at current prices, investors were demanding higher yields from property, and Whitehall was becoming increasingly Thatcherite. The DoE wanted to know the extent of public money in the project and how much the corporation would be 'sharing in the development risk by way of guarantees'.[6]

Despite these setbacks, Allen Duff, the commercial director, and his staff succeeded by the end of the year in winning financial support from the Shell Pension Fund and agreement in principle from the Housing Minister. The need for air conditioning throughout the building was debated at length by the board. Members favoured it and thought international clients would demand it but Frank Henshaw explained that 'this ... had been discussed with potential investors ... and all had felt that, noise and pollution being largely absent in Milton Keynes, it was unnecessary'.

Keith Revill, who had been appointed building director and taken charge of the project, went into the design in detail. Much work had been done on the winter garden and, when it came to planting, advice would be taken from Kew. His main concern was how to cope if Shell asked for fundamental changes. 'Against a background of reducing staff resources ... this could cause considerable difficulties,' he said. The rundown of the corporation set in motion by Michael Heseltine was beginning to bite.[7]

Getting commitment from a hotel group proved more difficult than dealing with Shell. When negotiations with the first hoteliers collapsed, the corporation turned to Trust House Forte but once again ran into problems. The group began to trim its proposal in order to cut costs. Keith Revill told the board that the 'implications for the Central Business Exchange of the delay and modified plans were considerable'. A hunt began for yet another hotel company.[8]

The prospect of competition prompted Rocco Forte to write saying he wished to proceed with a 164-bed hotel with an atrium, conference suites and health club. Meanwhile, the corporation was in touch with Ramada who were working on a 200-bed design. Both companies were aware that the corporation would sign with whichever was first with acceptable proposals.[9]

Plans from Ramada were considered by the board in August. They were 'more ambitious' than Forte's and members preferred them but were disappointed by the skimpy financial details. Meanwhile, Forte's was promising to begin building before the end of the year and to be open by spring 1986. This was later than the completion date for the first CBX offices and members were keen to get moving. They agreed to offer exclusive negotiations to Rocco Forte. The Post House Hotel, Central Milton Keynes (later renamed the Forte Crest), was duly opened in October 1986.[10]

The first CBX offices were completed the same year and by its end half had been leased to Argos Distributors as their headquarters. Three months later, in the corporation's twentieth annual report, Henry Chilver was able to tell the Environment Secretary that over three-quarters of the space had been let. Rank Xerox and Midland Bank were other tenants. Plans were immediately laid for a second phase of the CBX which was completed in January 1991.[11]

Gradually, other elements of a complex, many-faceted city centre began to fall into place. The county library on Silbury Boulevard was followed by a building for the Institute of Chartered Accountants and then others for the police and the courts. During the 1980s the look of the centre began to change too. The board's decision to sell freeholds led to smaller buildings and to greater diversity in design. The accountants, for instance, clad their building in white marble. Other building owners went neo-Georgian. It was not what the planners had envisaged, but it did not matter. The diversity was given order by the street pattern.

'The vistas of Central Milton Keynes are changing rapidly as many new buildings appear,' Chilver wrote in the corporation's twenty-third report. 'The quality for which the city is noted is particularly evident here and the city centre is home to many well-known professional firms. The fiftieth office building is now under construction.' Milton Keynes was moving up into the same league as Croydon, Reading and Southampton – the principal office centres in the south east outside central London.[12]

Amongst the city centre's qualities were its ample supply of open-air car parking and its easily understood road pattern. However, no city centre in the world is without some

RIGHT: The Central Business Exchange, one of the corporation's major works, contains offices, a hotel, a health club and a winter garden.

CINZANO

parking problems and the corporation and the borough were obliged to introduce time limits in some places as early as 1980.[13]

It was clear that in the longer term the county would have to adopt all the car parks as public highways. This alone would enable disabled persons parking, taxi ranks, yellow lines, traffic wardens and the full panoply of traffic regulations to be unleashed on (depending on your point of view) wilful or long-suffering motorists. However, this idea was initially kept under wraps because it was important, when launching the shops, for parking to be free. Nevertheless by 1982 the need for tighter control was becoming a necessity and the board agreed to transfer 6,000 bays to the county on the understanding that, unless otherwise decided, charges would not be introduced before 1990.[14]

As the 1990s dawned it became clear that firmer control was going to be needed. Paula Burnett, in a review of the city centre in the *Estates Times*, paid tribute to the corporation for phasing its disposal of sites and noted that Ternion Court, with its 'sub-classical façades in white stone' and rear courtyards, was reminiscent of 'some of the posher addresses in London'. But she had clearly had trouble finding a place for her car. 'Pressure for parking around the shopping building is intense, particularly at lunch-time,' she wrote, adding that the relationship between parking space around buildings and car-borne staff was mismatched and likely to become a major headache. An indication of concern was 'the chorus of developers and agents calling for management of the city's parking, as opposed to the current free-for-all'. Another symptom of problems was the prominence being given by letting agents to reserved parking. Acknowledging the existence of 10,000 spaces and the eventual prospect of 31,000, she added ominously 'demand in a city designed for the car seems to be endless'.[15]

The board had already considered parking earlier in the year. Given that 'flexibility exists to raise the total parking provision in Central Milton Keynes to 45,000 spaces', supply was not seen as a problem. The issues were location and management. Already office developers were being made responsible for one-third of the needs of their buildings and British Rail was being pushed to do something about the pile-up of commuters' cars around the station where demand had reached 1,700 slots by 1988 and might rise to 3,000 or even more. One multi-storey had been built. A second was needed.

But what should be done about city-centre parking management in general? Control had 'to a large extent' (some said totally) lapsed since the county had taken it over. A solution was seen in a parking places order covering the 20,000 bays likely to remain in the public realm. It would be administered by the county and parkers would pay to cover the cost of enforcing it.[16]

With its end looming, the board strove to put the future of parking on a firm basis. Early in 1991 John Walker told members that, out of a planned total of 31,300 bays, 'some

23,100 would (by March 1992) have been completed or committed'. In the longer term, briefs for developers on the one hand, and parking standards set out in the local plan on the other, promised to ensure that both the Commission for the New Towns and the borough council would carry on the policies of the corporation. As for effective parking management, prospects in the vicinity of the station would not be good until the county introduced a scheme in August 1991.[17]

As the branches of the plane trees along CMK's three green boulevards began to reach out towards one another, the board turned its attention towards the city park and, on the retirement of their first chairman, named it Campbell Park. A plaque paying tribute to him stands beneath a tall yew hedge. The inscription is the same as the one in St Paul's commemorating Sir Christopher Wren: '*Si monumentum requiris, circumspice*' (If you seek a monument, look about you).

Churchgoers in Milton Keynes may, according to *The Times*, see a different connection between Wren and the city. The octagonal dome of Christ the Cornerstone, Britain's first cathedral-sized, ecumenical church, was lifted into place in December 1990 and its lantern was put on top not long after. Keith Revill, by then the managing director of Planning Design Development (a business venture formed by the corporation's architects and planners), recalled Jock Campbell's ringing him up and asking, 'How much does a church

Christ the Cornerstone, an ecumenical church, designed by Planning Design Development.

cost, Keith?' Campbell, having agreed to be a fund-raiser, needed to know what to raise. Revill helped and when the time came his firm received the commission to design the building.[18]

Planning Design Development decided on a neo-classical design and the funds available enabled them to provide a dome that is about half the size of that on St Paul's. Hugh Cross, who took up his post as ecumenical moderator (equivalent to a bishop) during the same month, told *The Times*: 'The church will not be called a cathedral, but it will be that sort of place ... It is a splendid building and very exciting.'[19]

Frank Henshaw, who watched the dome, cupola and cross of Christ the Cornerstone rising higher and higher day by day from the window of his office in Saxon Court, was particularly pleased. He understood better than most the problems of financing a new city during the 1980s and that this place of worship was achieved without the kind of budget available to medieval cathedral builders. Indeed, it was yet another example of packaging: two adjacent blocks of offices were helping to pay for it. Yet there it was, a year before the corporation was wound up. 'When you go out to the western extremity of the city and look back,' Henshaw said, 'it really stands out.'[20] And so it does. Milton Keynes had acquired a landmark and one that was spiritual as well as physical.

20

Boom Years

Henry Chilver's appointment to Milton Keynes was organised by Jock Campbell. The Department of the Environment, learning of Campbell's plans to retire, began to put forward names, but Campbell thought them 'not suitable'. He, therefore, paid a visit to Cranfield Institute of Technology where Chilver, as vice-chancellor, had steered the college further towards self-financing than any other institution of higher education in the country. Campbell persuaded him to let his name be put forward to the Secretary of State.

'I knew he'd been a success at Cranfield. I knew he'd got in an enormous amount of private development money and we were beginning to want private money too,' Campbell said later. 'I knew he'd be good at that.' Yet the two men could not have been further apart in politics or in personality.[1] Just how far was brought out by the *Independent* in an interview with Chilver in his capacity as chairman of the Universities Funding Council, a post which he accepted in 1988. The Government was counting on this brilliant, purposeful and self-styled 'radical Tory' to bring a breath of Cranfield-like modernity to the old-fashioned parts of the university system. His appointment sent a shiver of anxiety through the entire apparatus of higher education. (Chilver was, as the *Times Educational Supplement* observed in another article, 'the *bête noire* of the educational establishment' on account of his declaration that 'higher education should be available to those prepared to show their commitment by paying for it'.)[2]

'All our thought processes and values are totally different,' Campbell later acknowledged. 'I wanted a cross-section of people, coloured families, minority groups, one-parent families, unemployed families ... and a good deal of public money.' How would he have coped with Thatcherism? 'I would certainly have resigned. I couldn't have gone on. Chilver has done the job much better than I could in this climate. He has done it extremely well.'[3]

Carol Kennedy, who interviewed Henry Chilver for the Institute of Directors in 1988, found him dapper and soft-spoken, a man conveying 'a sense of highly focused mental and physical energy'. She quoted a development corporation colleague saying of him: 'He questions things relentlessly. He is very clear about his philosophy and he can be ruthless about muddled or woolly thinking. He is intellectually very vigorous, academically extremely bright, but also worldly-wise and politically very shrewd.' Yet all who interviewed this courteous man agreed that he did not give much away. He was inscrutable.[4]

In a small way, the wheel of Chilver's remarkable career came full circle when he took over from Campbell. A Fellow of the Royal Society skilled in engineering research but also in administration and business; a man welcome at Downing Street, knighted by a Labour government and ennobled by a Conservative one; a man for whom intellectual challenge was itself enough of a pastime to replace leisure pursuits – Henry Chilver had been one of Richard Llewelyn-Davies' colleagues at University College during the period when Milton Keynes was being designed. He took part in debates about it and recalled the expertise of Llewelyn-Davies 'in getting out of you what your ideas were'.[5]

'What is your general policy on new towns?' Chilver asked Tom King, the Environment Secretary, shortly after his appointment. He was told that he was not in charge of a winding-down process – 'the policy was to complete the new towns'.[6] This tied in with Chilver's own view that the foundations of the city had already been laid. 'When I was appointed all the major decisions had been made. Jock took the lion's share of them.' Yet it was equally clear to him that there was still much to be done and that because 'the economics changed ... and the political scene changed', new ways were going to have to be found to do it.

There was, indeed, much to be done. At the time of Chilver's appointment half of the city's land was still undeveloped and half of its main roads remained to be built. In the city centre there was nearly three times as much land devoted to rough grazing as to buildings. The prospects were decidedly good. The city was not locked into an industrial past. It was already attracting electronics and office firms and, with an economic upturn on the way, was likely to be able to attract more. It was reasonable to expect that it would be possible to go on seeing an annual increase in jobs of 3,500.

The scope for house-building looked even rosier. In a paper prepared for the county in 1984 as it reviewed its structure plan up to the year 2001, John Walker, the planning director, reported: 'Many counties were finding it difficult to identify sufficient land to cater for their housing needs in the 1990s, but Milton Keynes provided a clear opportunity for employment and development into the 1990s; a planned programme of house-building had every chance of achieving 2,500 completions a year.'[7]

The common-room of Milton Keynes prison, the first 'new-generation' prison to be built by the Home Office.

Chilver was well-suited to the task of realising these opportunities. As the *Independent* noted of Cranfield Institute of Technology, of which he was vice-chancellor from 1970 to 1989, 'A very high proportion of its income comes from industry and commerce: in 1988 only fourteen per cent of its £56.2m came from government grant. A further £9m was earned by Cranfield's twenty-plus wholly-owned research companies.'[8]

Milton Keynes would have to move in the same direction. This meant marketing. 'There was increasing awareness of Milton Keynes,' Chilver recalled, 'and I encouraged Frank and his colleagues to get on ... and be really innovative in how they presented the city to the world. We were drawing in companies from overseas ... as well as people from less than 100 miles away.' It was an 'extremely complex constituency to try and communicate with'.[9]

The corporation under Chilver's leadership did, indeed, attract private investment and, as the country's economy improved, so a diverse array of developments appeared. These included private health clinics and a private hospital, an English prep school and a boarding school for the children of Japanese families based in Europe. Central Milton Keynes saw the completion of a winter garden, a Trust House Forte hotel and 'The Point' – a welcome touch of vulgar neon jazziness. Down at Peartree Bridge people who liked 'messin' about in boats' began to congregate at a canal marina.

Many other changes took place too. On the employment front emphasis shifted from factories to offices and even to 'campus' office sites outside the centre. Housing went up-market. In the corporation's 1984–91 implementation strategy John Walker observed that: 'Since 1982, much greater emphasis has been placed on higher-price housing, including

SABRE
S&S DONNELLY
MILTON KEYNES

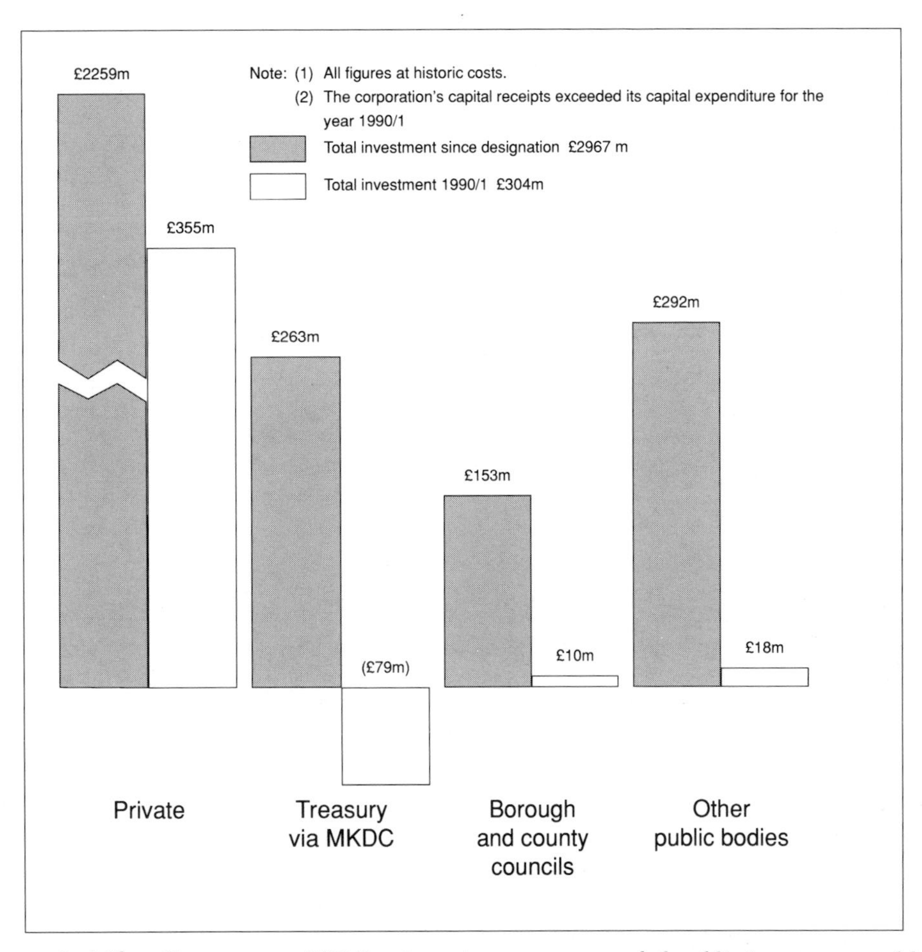

Investment in Milton Keynes up to 1990/1: private investment exceeded public investment and by this time the corporation was no longer borrowing from the Exchequer. Indeed, it was repaying the loans of earlier years.

dwellings of individual character. A reduction in density has resulted from this change and has been taken into account in the development proposals of the strategy.'[10]

Public investment continued as well. Milton Keynes' persistent growth necessitated it. Additions to the city included premises for keeping the peace, upholding the law and

LEFT: One of a series of posters depicting for Londoners the problems of living in Milton Keynes. It carried the caption 'Bumper to bumper in Milton Keynes'.

punishing the wicked. The police, the county courts and the magistrates located themselves in the city centre, while over by Shenley Wood the Home Office bought forty acres for an innovative 560-place prison. According to the *Independent* this 'new generation' prison was destined to have more in common with a university than a Victorian penitentiary. The inmates would spend 'the bulk of their days in open-plan accommodation' where they would eat and have access to education and recreation. The paper added that the prison might be run by a private company.[11]

In 1985 the corporation's future was again put under review (this time the Environment Secretary was Patrick Jenkin) and the planners considered how the city might look by 1989, the Government's provisional wind-up date, or 1995, the terminal year advocated by the corporation. The six-year gap between the two dates underscored a profound difference of opinion. At Westminster, Milton Keynes was seen as an undesirable leakage of public expenditure to be stemmed as quickly as possible. Within the corporation, the city was seen as a project that was barely half finished. New jobs may have been appearing at a rate of over 4,000 a year and private builders may have been completing 1,500 houses 'at a time of rapidly reducing public expenditure and staff resources', but, as the board told Jenkin, the land available promised to enable this pace of development to continue into the late 1990s.

Furthermore, despite all the progress that had been made, the city still lacked many of the useful odds and ends of urban life that go on in back streets where rents are low and imagination can flourish. 'Companies and people seldom move to Milton Keynes simply for its entertainment, health care, educational or public transport facilities – or, indeed, for the depth of its business infrastructure,' a review of corporate priorities noted in 1986. The corporation's high aspirations made it necessary to do something about these shortcomings, although, this being the 1980s, its role would be 'catalytic and supportive'. Given that the staff had been reduced by forty per cent over five years, there was little alternative.[12]

Throughout the late 1980s the corporation worked steadily away at being a catalyst – Michael Heseltine had called it 'packaging' – while still keeping an eye on quality. Developers could, for instance, be made responsible for designing and building the drains and roads needed by their buildings. This reduced corporation expenditure on engineers and architects and avoided public investment, but it did carry risks. In the board's view 'selling semi-serviced land to developers would, for several reasons, be tantamount to accepting second best and be likely to reduce the momentum and quality of development'.[13]

Confirmation that 1992 would be the corporation's wind-up date came at a time (December 1986) when the house-builders were beginning to think big. They were forming consortia with the object of erecting houses not in hundreds but thousands. With the

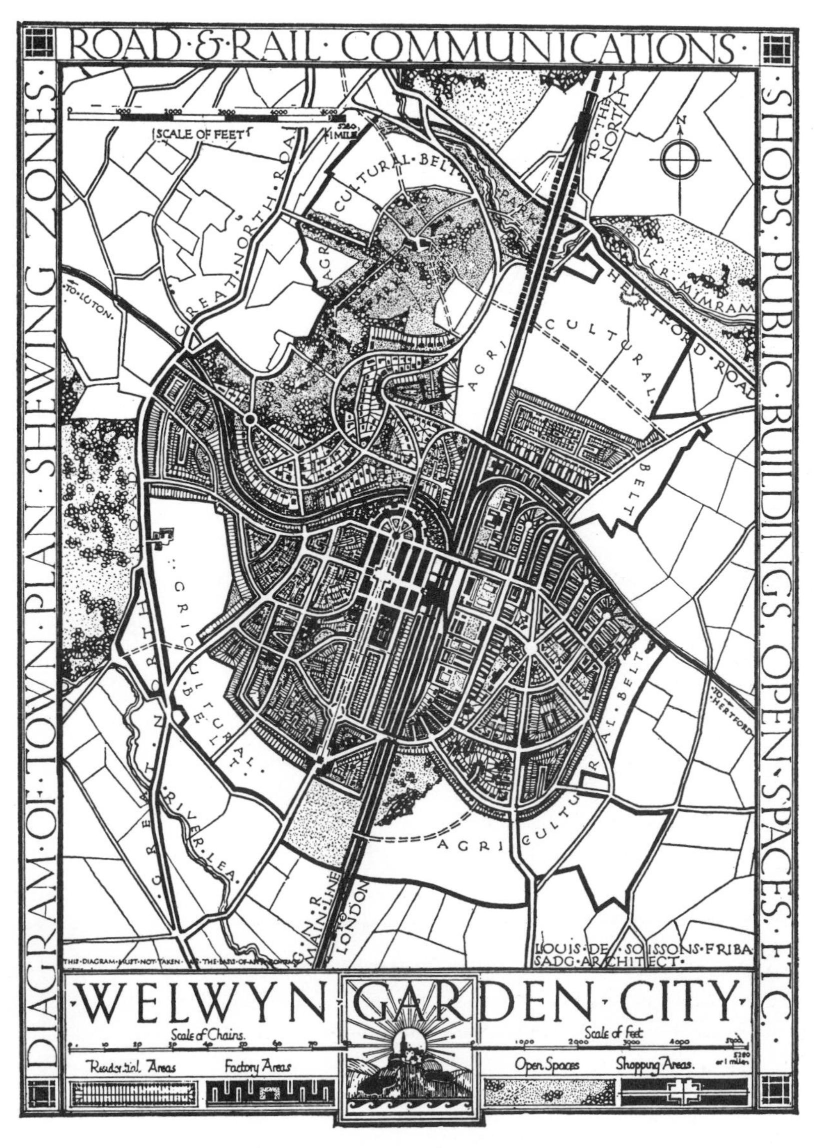

Louis de Soissons' 1921 plan of Welwyn Garden City: the axial layout of the centre and the curving residential roads were design ideas that re-emerged in the 'private new towns' of the 1980s.

corporation looking for ways to meet its 1992 deadline, it was bound to take an interest in these new agencies. There was, furthermore, one firm, Consortium Developments, which had links with Conran Roche – the firm which Fred Roche had helped found when he left the corporation in 1980. Here, surely, was a way of getting the best of both worlds – private development and high-quality design.

Consortium Developments was a characteristic creation of the mid-1980s. London and its surrounding counties were once again bursting at the seams, but the Government had largely withdrawn from trying to plan the development of the region. Nicholas Ridley, the fourth and most radical of Mrs Thatcher's environment secretaries, therefore let it be known that he would look favourably on private new towns. Who better to pick up the gauntlet than the country's biggest house-builders combined with leading firms of land-use planners? Consortium Developments started by designing a 'small new country town' for a site at Tillingham Hall in Essex. However, in David Lock's words, they made the mistake of stirring the 'never-sleeping giant of green belt' and the Secretary of State found it impossible to acquiesce to the development.

Proposals for other sites, none of them on green-belt land, followed. The developers took options on them and applied for permissions to develop knowing that, if successful, the resulting gain in land values would pay for the unprofitable aspects of the schemes.

Lord Northfield, chairman of Consortium Developments (and of Shropshire's Telford new town from 1975 to 1987), wrote in 1988: 'Of course there is little new in this idea. In Britain we have led the work in building new towns. But what Consortium Developments have as much been concerned with, since the termination of the government's own new-town programme and the quite proper shift of emphasis towards the inner cities, is to ensure that this simple, practical and well-tried approach should remain firmly on the regional planning agenda.'[14]

The Town and Country Planning Association, for years the lobby for public-sector new towns and long-time scourge of developers, was in favour. 'There can be no objection in principle to "private" new towns ... the new town movement has its roots in the individual enterprise of Ebenezer Howard,' said an editorial in its journal.[15]

But the cult of enterprise and individualism showed up too in attitudes towards development. The acronym NIMBY (Not In My Back Yard) was coined and if there was anything that NIMBYs hated it was new small country towns. One by one Consortium Developments had its schemes shot from under it as environment secretaries shied away from schemes that, whatever their virtues, meant electoral death. In turning down Foxley Wood, Chris Patten said, 'I am not rejecting the concept of new settlements. New towns and

Left: Offices of the late 1980s in the emerging business district of the city centre.

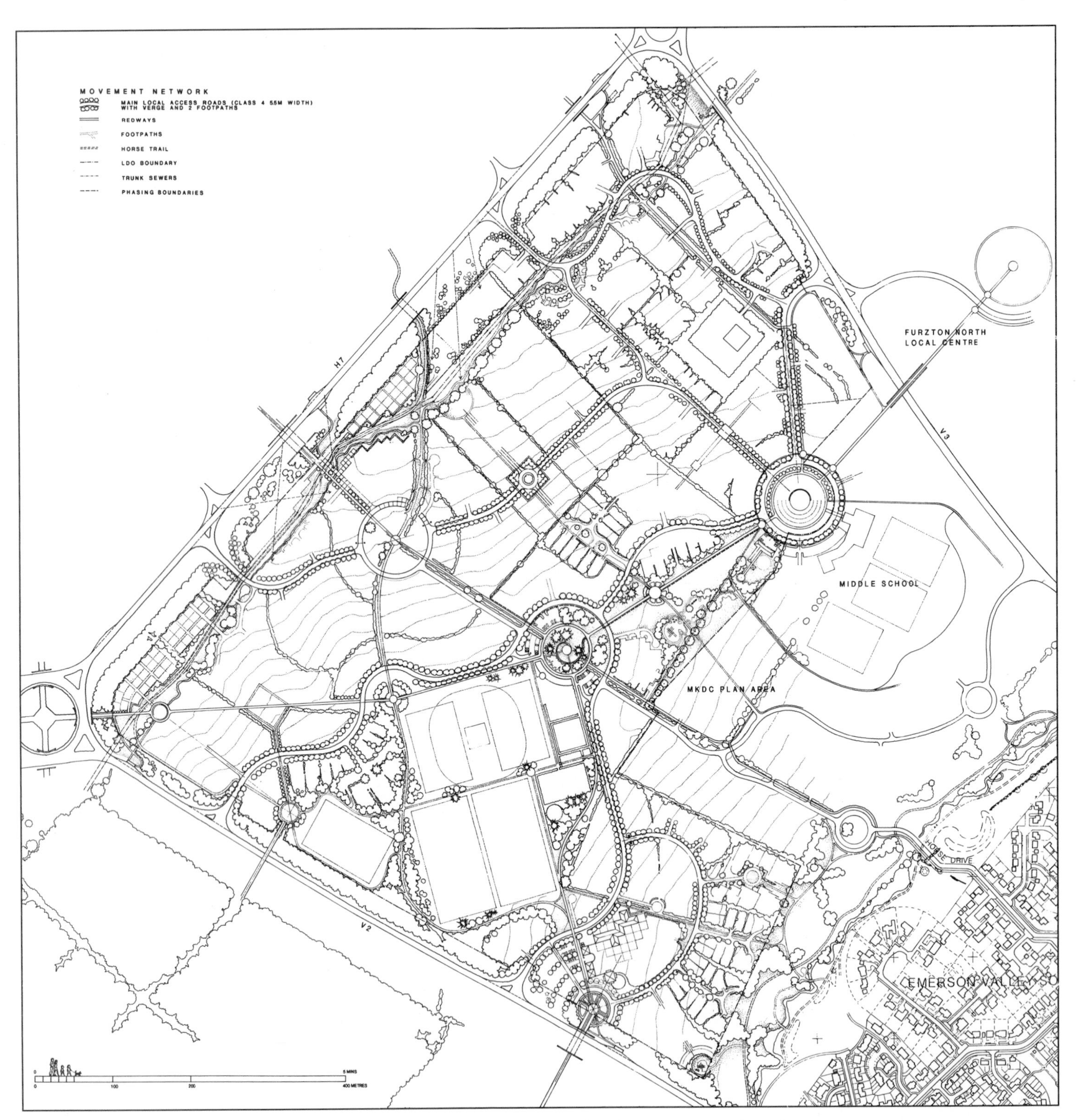

Conran Roche's plan for Emerson Valley North, based on curving roads and circuses.

villages may have a role to play in accommodating future housing.' But 'the planning authorities in consultation with the people of Hampshire are best placed to choose how and where future housing in the county should be accommodated'.[16]

Milton Keynes had none of these problems. Buckinghamshire and Bedfordshire were behind it, and within it were square kilometres of farmland for which the Environment Secretary would automatically grant development rights.

Large development opportunities (LDOs) were, Frank Henshaw told the board in 1987, a means of testing the ability of developers to make a good job of schemes which included roads, parks and local shopping centres. They were not an entirely new idea. Eaglestone had been the result of an agreement with Bovis in 1973, although it had been terminated when the developers failed to deliver the required shops and meeting rooms. Another precedent was Two Mile Ash. It was taken on in the late 1970s by Whelmar, Barratt, Broseley and Wimpey on the basis of an outline plan, but it too had brought problems and alerted the corporation to the importance of getting agreement on details. By 1983, when agreement was reached with Whelmar Homes to build Bancroft Park and Blue Bridge, such an approach was followed. The company provided a park, a club and a shop and the corporation was satisfied by the development's overall standard.

Despite this track record, the members were unconvinced by the case for large development opportunities. Felicity Freeman doubted whether the communal facilities would be adequate. Roger Parker-Jervis, concerned at the possibility of an economic downturn, feared lest the corporation might have to repurchase land at a loss. Board members in general confirmed their preference for the devil they knew and were 'somewhat reluctant to change a successful formula'. They thought that land should be released in a controlled way and that negotiation as well as tendering should continue to be used in the disposal of housing land.[17]

A fuller report on LDOs was, nevertheless, put to the board a few months later. It suggested that a scheme of about 100 acres would fit the corporation's objectives and test whether it would increase the pace and variety of house-building. It would also test the ability of developers 'to undertake comprehensive development of this scale ... while paying a satisfactory price for the land and achieving an acceptable pace and quality of development'. Emerson Valley North was identified as a suitable location for an experiment.[18]

The Emerson Valley North LDO was posted to potential developers during the summer of 1988, on the eve of a downturn in the housing market. Nevertheless, the corporation received two 'outstanding' designs which enabled it to accept the highest financial bid. This was from the Milton Keynes Housing Group which included Abbey National Homes, Coventry Churches Housing Association and two private house-builders. Their 150-acre scheme was for 1,161 houses and flats designed by Conran Roche. A clause in the agreement enabled the housing group to defer payment for part of the site until the low-cost homes to be built on it had been sold.[19]

Once again, as at Beanhill and Netherfield, a square was being designed all of a piece. John Billingham, director of design and development, was confident that the outcome would 'meet the standards which the corporation has consistently achieved for years'.

Shared-ownership and low-price homes were amongst those scheduled for an early start at Emerson Valley. They followed winding, tree-lined roads leading to circuses like those Louis de Soissons had designed at Welwyn Garden City in the 1920s. Here and there, the roads crossed horse trails. Consortium Developments did not bid for Emerson Valley but the winning scheme was very similar to the small new country towns which had aroused the ire of the home-county NIMBYs.[20]

The corporation's 1989 implementation strategy signalled that Emerson Valley would be only the first of many large housing developments. The Government had agreed to the corporation aiming 'substantially to secure the laying out and development of Milton Keynes and its city centre'. Agreement had been reached too, Frank Henshaw reported, to switching funds from roads and sewers to main roads. Thus, hitherto inaccessible squares could be opened up, enabling 'the corporation to finish its work in a way that would not have been possible under the old plan'. Furthermore, consortia of developers were putting forward schemes for 'complete communities and the corporation had the opportunity to harness this resource'.

Packaging was coming into its own and promised to secure the development of most of the city by 1992. Private investment from 1989 to 1992 was likely to rise from an earlier forecast of £850m to £1,660m. Public investment was likely to be £350m to £360m.

Wilfred Rooke, the county chairman, welcomed this increase in opportunities for private investors and pledged his council's support for it. The only difficulty he could see was money. The board also discussed how the quality of development might be maintained after the corporation had been wound up. John Walker said that legal agreements with developers would help, although some control over the detailed design of housing would be lost. Joe Oblein reflected the board's view that: 'The selection of developers with good track records would be of paramount importance.'

The financial year 1987/8 was an incredible one for Milton Keynes. The 1988 employers' survey showed a net growth of more than 8,000 jobs. (The corporation's target was 3,500.) Developers were falling over one another to get their hands on sites. In 1989 the corporation approved its first privately financed business park at Caldecotte and a record number of office buildings was going up in the city centre. Opportunities for active recreation were increased too. The financing of an ice rink and a ten-pin bowling alley was packaged up with developments by Argos and Sainsbury's. Car-racing fanatics were catered for too. In 1990 the James Hunt Racing Centre opened at Rooksley. It was a mini-Silverstone where, for £7.50 (plus a fiver for an annual licence) drivers could chicane in computer-controlled safety.[21]

Given this mounting concentration of activity, Milton Keynes was casting its influence over an ever wider area. Henry Chilver had begun to notice it in the 1970s when he had lived ten miles from the city. 'What I suddenly realised was that the villages were becoming rich ... The citizens [of Milton Keynes] had no idea of the impact they were having. You suddenly found that the villages were very proud of the city.' Milton Keynes was becoming 'a massive centre of regional development', even though this was not widely realised. 'I think this regional development effect should have been spotted earlier,' Chilver added. Then 'it could have influenced the design of roads and railways'.[22]

Late in 1988, the economic boom began to slow down. The housing market was affected first. Retailing followed soon. Yet the corporation was still selling commercial assets as fast as it could – its target for 1989/90 was raised from £93m to £127m in the course of the year to compensate for shortfalls in receipts from housing.

The board pondered the implications of the downturn and concluded that 'housing land was the most vulnerable and was heavily dependent on getting large development opportunities under way'. It was also concerned about its successor, the Commission for the New Towns. It wanted the CNT to follow in its footsteps and pursue high standards, but was uneasy that money might be put before quality in the sale of the city's assets.[23]

21

'Home Sweet Home'

The Government's instructions to the corporation were to ensure that at least half the houses in the new city were privately financed and owner-occupied. This was a new departure.[1] The earlier new towns had been glorified council estates. 'They were developed,' Derek Walker observed, 'as cloth-capped places.' The Government's aim was to give Milton Keynes and its sister towns a more conventional social structure.[2]

It looked initially as if banishing the cloth-cap image from Milton Keynes might not be too difficult. Nathaniel Lichfield's work for the master plan team – based on assumptions about the way in which incomes and house prices would rise – suggested that in the early years only about one-third of new residents would be able to afford to buy houses. However, incomes and prices moved more favourably than Lichfield assumed and by 1971 Jock Campbell was able to report to Peter Walker, Edward Heath's Environment Minister, that: 'Perhaps the most encouraging aspect of the development of Milton Keynes so far has been the clear evidence that people want to own their own homes ... and that developers want to build here.' Campbell went on to say that contracts with developers to build a thousand houses had been signed or were very close to being signed.[3] The pipeline also contained over a thousand houses to rent.

As it turned out, events conspired against those who wanted to own their homes. In a speech to the corporation staff in 1972, in which he also referred to the lack of accommodation for building workers and the need for caravans 'provided always that the sites are in some other local authority's back garden', Campbell lamented the difficulty of keeping 'the cost of houses for sale within what buyers can be expected to pay'.[4]

Some claimed that the grip of Derek Walker's development control staff over the house-builders was another hindrance. In 1973 the board heard of complaints from would-be developers that the corporation's 'design control ... was too inflexible and arrogant and that builders were being forced to build houses which were not commercially successful, thus slowing down sales and output'. The criticisms came from the Royal Institute of British Architects, Whitehall and the building societies.

Derek Walker did not mince his words when justifying his strictness in development control to the board. 'The god of total commercialism had taken control in almost all aspects of living,' he told members. 'Most of our cities were disgusting because of this attitude of *laissez-faire*, and the reluctance of the community to agitate consistently for planning and design for quality. Those responsible for development were walking away from the problem of stating categorical standards; they included some architects who seemed incapable of, or uninterested in, producing work of an acceptable standard.' Milton Keynes offered a chance 'not to lie down and let the world walk over one', but to set worthwhile standards.

Fred Roche backed Walker vigorously. Developers were slowing up for reasons other than development control, he said. 'Some builders had indeed been frightened off, but others had welcomed control.' The corporation's system was to indicate to builders which architects met its standards. 'It was easier to exercise control by choosing architects in whom the corporation had confidence and to let them get on with the job, rather than argue over drawings,' Roche said. No doubt this infuriated those architects in whom the corporation did not have confidence.

The board, as resolute as Roche, decided that upsetting a few architects was unavoidable if Milton Keynes was to be the incomparable city they all wanted. Horace Cutler 'confirmed the commercial motivation and lack of social conscience of most developers. London, for instance, was littered with architectural pollution ... He gave Mr Walker's team his wholehearted backing.' Other members did too, though one mentioned the need for humility.[5] The word is unlikely to have left much impression on Derek Walker. The realisation of a grand design is not for the lily-livered. It calls for heroic self-confidence – something bound to resemble ruthless arrogance to those not in sympathy with it.

Other events conspiring against home ownership included high interest rates, the low incomes of many incoming households, and periodic government clamp-downs on selling to tenants. The board struggled against these constraints as best it could. In 1975 it put 'even more emphasis' on its policy 'that every house should be saleable'. Yet it was simultaneously agreeing to 'accommodate a greater proportion of unskilled people to achieve a balanced population'.[6]

Was the provision of rented houses for London's poor in conflict with attracting investment in houses for sale? What about the policy for blurring differences between different forms of tenure and different levels of income? Did these deter investors in private houses?

Richard Llewelyn-Davies undoubtedly thought so. The corporation ought, he told the board's 1977 seminar, 'to do more to persuade professionals and managers to live in the city. Many appeared to be living deliberately outside.'

He went on to describe how Washington new town (County Durham), of which he had also been the master planner, 'had been very successful in setting aside a tract along the River Wear for the well-to-do to build their own houses on large plots'. Campbell was clearly uneasy about the whole idea. He knew the city 'must become more responsive to home ownership and private-sector finance' but 'a "nobs' hill" must be avoided'. Furthermore, with attractive village houses outside the city, but within easy reach for managers, he feared 'it was going to be a struggle to attract developers into the city and to get sufficient private housing schemes going'.

The chairman's worries about class distinctions being given physical expression were not shared by the board. Fred Roche, with the full weight of the executive behind him, likewise made clear that a change in direction was essential. 'The corporation could be criticised for not exploiting private housing to the full and for not putting enough resources into it,' he said. 'A private housing group was now being formed to undo the damage which had been done.' The group would, amongst other things, find sites suitable for executive housing and so 'improve the image of the city for management'.

He went on: 'This was not a change of policy into creating a "nobs' hill", but rather a change of emphasis.' He then described 'the wonderful opportunities presented by the linear park for campus office development, high-technology industry and executive housing'. Packaged and marketed with Central Milton Keynes, this new development would give the city's image the boost it needed.[7]

A few months later, when the board organised a seminar for city industrialists, the issue came up again. The members present heard that few senior and middle managers lived in Milton Keynes because of the lack of suitable housing and 'the policy of juxtaposing sale and rental housing'.

When this problem was reviewed at a subsequent board meeting, Roger Parker-Jervis observed that the housing requirements of middle management 'were in conflict with the social goals of the new city'. Furthermore, the growing number of applications to build houses for sale in nearby villages 'appeared to be a fairly substantial criticism of corporation policy, and would, if approved, deprive the city of potential customers'.[8]

By 1978 Fred Roche, sensing that a Conservative government was likely to be elected, was urging the corporation to put increasing emphasis on houses for sale. The recently

RIGHT: Corporation-designed flats, with an Italianate feeling, built at Bradwell Common in the early 1980s.

Bradwell Common
Boulevard

formed private housing unit (led by Brian Brookman and Bob Clarke) was briefed to step up the tempo of building for sale and the sale of houses to tenants. (Restrictions on sales to tenants were loosened by the Labour Government in the late 1970s.) But Roche deduced, too, that limits would be put on building houses to let and that other ways would have to be found to provide for households with modest incomes.

The executive had been thinking about this problem for some time. The key seemed to lie in selling houses to people bit by bit or, in other words, sharing the equity between the buyer and the seller. Alan Ashton first discussed this idea with housing officials in Whitehall in 1976, and in 1978 the DoE approved a scheme whereby the corporation could sell houses to tenants on a drip-feed principle. This 'equity-sharing' scheme enabled tenants to take out mortgages for between thirty and seventy per cent of their houses and to pay rent on the balance. As their incomes increased so they could buy progressively larger shares of their homes.[9]

Following Margaret Thatcher's 1979 election victory, John Stanley, the new Housing Minister, took warmly to equity sharing, by then called by the cosier name of shared ownership. It was a great success in Milton Keynes. When the corporation announced the part-sale of attractive homes being designed by Keith Revill and his team, buyers hoping to secure them would camp outside the housing offices. Private house-builders then took up the idea and 100 households a year began to be nominated and supported by the corporation as shared owners.

Not surprisingly, housing was something the Prime Minister talked to Jock Campbell about when she opened the shopping building in September 1979. Mrs Thatcher told him she was concerned 'about the need for young people to be able to buy their houses', and was surprised that this was being hindered by rising prices. Campbell suggested that the way forward lay in 'an adequate programme of rental houses which young couples could then buy when they could afford to do so' – but only part of that was to be. The Conservatives backed the right for council and corporation tenants to buy, but first cut back and then phased out the building of houses for rent.[10]

By 1980 Campbell sensed that there was no going back to public housing and that it was 'extremely important that Milton Keynes should make a success of shared ownership – important for incoming employees, for relations with the government and for the future of the city'.[11] The corporation's share of such deals was for several years financed by the Treasury, but in 1984 the Government cancelled this arrangement and the corporation had to seek private funds to replace what had been supplied by taxpayers. A successful partnership was eventually established with the Halifax.

The corporation had to be fleet-footed to cope with changes of this kind, Frank Henshaw recalled later. In this case, one of its actions was to set up the Milton Keynes

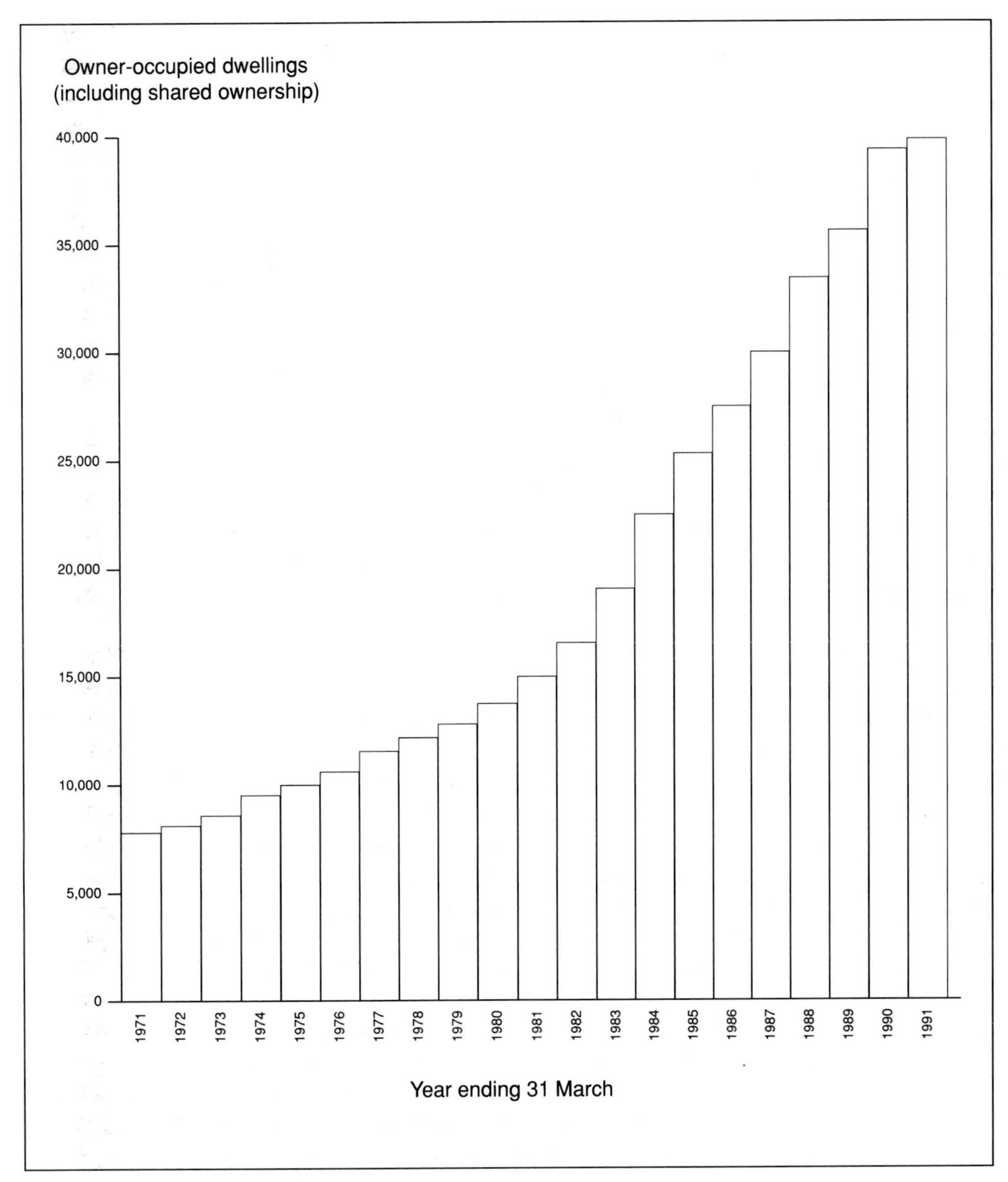

Owner-occupation grew only slowly in the 1970s: in the 1980s it soared.

One of a group of thirteen spacious houses designed by MacCormac Jamieson Pritchard and built at Great Linford by Greenwood Homes. The scheme, called The Pavilions, was the result of a competition in 1981.

Housing Association. Not only was MKHA able to take advantage of the finance made available by the Halifax and keep the shared-ownership programme going, but its existence helped to attract other housing associations to the city.[12]

Starter-homes were another way of widening the housing market. They led to higher densities, which worried the board, and they were not popular with the builders when the market for housing was buoyant (they were less profitable than more expensive homes), but substantial numbers were built. Such houses contributed to social balance. 'Not only is a reasonable proportion of private-developer housing needed at lower price levels,' John Walker told the board in 1984, but a shared-ownership programme of 500 houses a year was needed too. Only by these means and by building for elderly, disabled and single people could such balance be achieved.[13]

At the beginning of the 1980s more public than private housing was being built. By the end of the decade, the reverse was true. Three main causes for the change-over may be detected: the corporation's private-housing initiatives; the efforts of private builders; and the effect of the Government's 'right-to-buy' legislation on tenants.

By the mid-1980s more than eight out of ten of the houses being built in the city were for sale – some at prices as high as £150,000 – and residents, like others all over the country, were trading upwards. However, 'sale housing for the elderly had not proved as attractive as had been expected'.[14]

By 1987, the corporation's review of housing disclosed that developers were building houses to sell at over £300,000 and that 'the prices of new houses in Milton Keynes had risen by ninety-eight per cent' between 1981 and 1986 compared with fifty-eight per cent nationally. This signalled a significant change in the Milton Keynes housing market. Whereas in 1981 houses in the city were cheap relative to many other parts of the south east, by 1986 they were cheaper only than those at locations closer to London. Rising incomes in the city had contributed to this change, although first-time buyers were suffering. Between 1983 and 1986 the proportion of new homes bought by first-timers fell from over a half to a quarter.

Nevertheless, John Walker, planning director, argued that such events should not automatically be construed as bad. 'Despite the difficulties caused by rising house prices, they are in many ways a positive sign of the increasing attractiveness of Milton Keynes as a place to live.'[15]

The city was moving up-market. Its new-town, cloth-cap image was all but lost. It was taking on the housing market characteristics to be expected from its superb location. Buyers were even discovering that it had its share of houses such as might appear in *Country Life*. The remains of one, a cause of endless distress to the corporation, stand in the original village of Milton Keynes. It is a hall house with a central room that rises from ground to roof via a criss-cross of timber crucks, trusses and a king post. In the Middle Ages an open fire would have flickered and smouldered in the midst of the hall and Paul Woodfield, in a guide to the city's historic buildings, writes: 'The whole roof is smoke-blackened, including the thatch battens.'

No. 22 Broughton Road is probably the oldest house in Milton Keynes and perhaps the manor of a branch of the Cahaines family. As the name Milton Keynes is a linguistic marriage of the Saxon place name 'Middle Tun' (later 'Middleton') and the family name Cahaines (or de Cahaignes), the house is not without its importance in the history of the new city.[16]

In 1991 No. 22 was placed on English Heritage's 'buildings-in-danger' list following the owner's unsuccessful attempt to finance its modernisation. Frank Henshaw was not optimistic about its survival even though, as Paul Woodfield observed, 'no really significant building has been lost since 1973'. This was, he added, 'no mean accomplishment' in the circumstances of building a city.

If, as Milton Keynes moved up-market, the board ceased to worry about the creation of 'nobs' hills', it was not because members forgot about the poor and concerned themselves solely with those who were upwardly mobile. On the contrary, Henry Chilver and his colleagues found themselves grappling again and again, though often unsuccessfully, with the housing problems of those on modest incomes. Private rented accommodation, shared mortgages for older properties and other ideas were explored. The corporation also urged employers to hire unemployed local people in preference to bringing in outsiders and generally worried away at the emergence of a housing waiting list.

Throughout this period Frank Henshaw repeatedly urged his colleagues in the executive to look for market-based solutions to the housing problems that faced them. He was convinced that 'only by showing what the market would and would not do' did the corporation have any hope of persuading Whitehall officials of the need for public finance for housing. The good sense of this approach was revealed by *Housing – The Government's Proposals*, a white paper of September 1987 (Cmnd 214). It set out 'opportunities for the private sector to provide housing at "affordable" levels' and 'acknowledges the role of public funding in supporting this kind of provision'.[17] And, thanks to Henshaw's leadership, it set out a philosophy that was by then already well established at Milton Keynes.

At a subsequent meeting the board heard that the corporation could expect the equivalent of £24m a year to support a programme of about 1,000 houses aimed at people with annual incomes ranging from £7,000 to £15,000. Support might take two forms. One, involving grants towards land or other costs, was aimed at reducing the money that house-builders had to borrow. The other, which had been advocated by Michael Heseltine at the beginning of the decade, was 'packaging' – combining expensive and low-cost houses so that the one helped to pay for the other. As the Department of the Environment was known to prefer the latter, the corporation decided to try and package at least half its social housing programme.[18]

Browns Wood, a 1990 development by Westbury Homes and Milton Keynes Housing Association, illustrated packaging in action. The corporation set the process in motion by selling a site to Westbury for a sum that took account of the low price of the houses when sold by the developer to MKHA. It was arranged that the corporation (or its successor) would recover the investment as and when the houses were sold and as the owners of them increased their share in the equity.

Large development opportunities were, of course, an example of similar principles applied on a scale that included roads, sewers and local centres as well as houses. The financial effect was, however, roughly the same. The proceeds of sites sold by the corporation were less than they would have been had no encumbrances been placed on developers – but the Treasury was saved from having to pay for the infrastructure.

For Henry Chilver, for whom 'providing quality homes' and 'getting the balance right' were key maxims, 1987/8 was the corporation's 'most successful year so far'. In his report to the Environment Secretary he noted that private builders completed 1,694 houses, shared-ownership buyers reached a total of 3,585 (of whom about one in ten had gone on to buy their freeholds) while another 832 corporation-owned houses had been bought by their occupants. Twelve months later Chilver reported 'another remarkable year' but noted that the housing market had finished the year 'in quieter fashion'.[19]

During the summer of 1989 the corporation worked away preparing more large development opportunities. If contracts could be signed for a number of packages similar to Emerson Valley North it would be a reasonable guarantee that the city would be completed in the spirit of the master plan. Yet suddenly this last and most spectacular of the corporation's private-housing initiatives was at risk. Bids were invited for Grange Farm with 1,300 homes, but only one was received and it put too low a value on the land. It was decided to remarket the scheme at an appropriate time.[20] Two other development opportunities, Tattenhoe with about 1,400 dwellings and Monkston with 1,300, were also put out to tender in 1990. Tattenhoe came in first. A bid from a consortium led by Countryside Homes and designed as 'an elegant and leafy residential park', though not the highest in price, best met the corporation's brief. It was agreed to accept it and to 'investigate the scope for increasing the ... consortium's land offer'. Six months later, after

One of an estate of houses at Old Farm Park built for Milton Keynes Housing Association for shared ownership. The architects were Planning Design Development.

much haggling, Countryside submitted a revised offer which the corporation found unacceptable. Negotiations were then opened with another consortium.[21]

As dissolution day approached, it became necessary to revise the completion targets set in the 1980s. The market for house sales was sluggish and the price of housing land was half what it had been at its peak in 1988. However, towards the end of 1990 small sites were still being sold and interest in the larger ones began to resurface. Were developers building up land banks? It was a possibility against which the board took precautions. Claw-back clauses were inserted into sales contracts to enable idle land to be repurchased by the corporation (or the new-towns commission).[22] The board was determined that no one should be able to control the land market and block the future development of the city.

LEFT: Milton Keynes 'Tudor': one of several such houses built by Bovis at Woolstone in the mid-1980s.

22

JOBS

It is an old adage in property development that success is dependent on three iron laws – location, location and location. If an investment is in the right place it will succeed, if not, watch out! The position of Milton Keynes, half-way between London and Birmingham, and half-way too between the brain boxes of Oxford and Cambridge, was unequalled in Britain in the second half of the twentieth century. The city had space in which to grow, a modern infrastructure and good external lines of communication (though work was needed on an east–west route). It was even within the European megalopolis that stretches, with only two major gaps, from south Lancashire (or perhaps even Glasgow) to Milan and Turin.[1]

Jock Campbell alluded to this in the annual report he sent to Environment Secretary Peter Walker in 1971. The city had, he said 'unparalleled advantages' which were bringing about 'a relatively high level of industrial development and commercial interest'. There was, however, a problem. Maintaining and realising this interest depended on 'the continuing availability of Industrial Development Certificates and Office Development Permits'.

IDCs and ODPs were parts of the apparatus by which Whitehall operated the quasi-command economy of post-1945 Britain and which Margaret Thatcher swept into the waste basket of history in 1979. The controls were applied with varying degrees of strictness at various times – Labour governments tended to be tougher than Conservative ones. Their purpose was to give Whitehall power to say where new or mobile companies above specified sizes could establish themselves.

From the very beginning, the London new towns created a dilemma for Whitehall. They could only succeed in reducing overcrowding in London and on its commuter routes if they were 'self-contained' – places where there was a balance between workers and jobs. Some firms had, therefore, to be allowed to set up in the new towns even though the fundamental role of IDCs and ODPs was to steer them northwards to offset unemployment caused by the decline of coal, cotton and shipbuilding.

Battling for permits, therefore, became a familiar occupation for Milton Keynes. It became a particularly difficult one in the recession that followed the 1973/4 increase in oil prices. During this period the board became seriously worried that the jobs needed to match their bold house-building aims would not materialise. (Until Peter Shore and the inner-cities issue intervened, the corporation aimed at building 4,000 houses in 1976/7.)

Fred Roche set out the corporation's concerns in a letter to the Department of the Environment in May 1975. He enclosed a copy of an earlier letter to the Department of Industry. The corporation had evidently heard that getting permits was going to become tougher – no doubt as a result of Harold Wilson taking over from Edward Heath at 10 Downing Street.

Roche stressed how important it was not to lose the 'momentum and confidence which has slowly been built up at Milton Keynes'. He went on to outline: the corporation's plan for a 'major recruiting campaign on employment, oriented both nationally and towards Europe'; the scale of the city's housing programme; and the need for manufacturing jobs which would produce 'the side benefit of female labour' needed for the vast shopping centre by then going up in Central Milton Keynes.

After asking for an assurance that the DoE would support this development, Roche indulged in a bit of Whitehall tail-twisting. The absence of such an assurance would, he wrote, 'be tantamount to an instruction to the board not only to stop the development of the city but, indeed, to unravel the immensely complicated and inter-related investments which are already under construction'.

The board had little reason to expect that this would happen. The Secretary of State for Industry had, a few years earlier, said to Campbell: 'We recognise your problems: we shall be difficult – but we shall not be stupid.' It was because of this attitude and 'the support of successive Ministers and governments and you yourselves in the Department' that Milton Keynes was the success it was, Roche said. 'What would stop it, and indeed probably discredit one of the most exciting projects in Europe, would be the withdrawal of the understanding and support for IDCs and ODPs which you have given us in the past.'[2]

The reply, when it came, was not encouraging. New towns in non-assisted areas (such as the south east) were said to have second priority. The department could offer 'no hope at all of persuading anyone in today's economic and political climate to put them on a par with assisted areas'. There was 'not enough mobile industry to go round'.[3]

The minutes tell of other difficulties. On one occasion at least Bletchley, quick to take offence at the rejection of a proposed development, accused the corporation of ignoring 'the

views of the elected representatives of the people'. The board informed the council that the limits being put on development had been agreed by all parties in 1970, and they had been designed to ensure that Bletchley did not become a shopping ghost town when Central Milton Keynes opened its doors.[4]

Keeping London happy occupied the corporation too. Following the new city's presence at a business exhibition at Olympia, Horace Cutler and Tony Judge (both GLC councillors) reminded the board about 'the GLC's concern about the rapid decline of industry in London'. (The closure of the up-river London docks had recently become an issue.) They wondered whether the corporation's '"vigorous campaign" to attract industry from London might be resented, particularly at a time when the hard-sell campaign by development areas for the same purpose was having some impact'.

Bearing in mind that one function of Milton Keynes was 'to help in solving London's appalling housing problems', Jock Campbell thought they 'should not pass a self-denying ordinance against attracting industry from London'. But they ought, if possible, to avoid offending the GLC's susceptibilities.[5]

Milton Keynes was, in fact, less dependent on firms moving from London than might be thought. By 1978, when the board held a seminar with industrialists, 23,000 new jobs had been created, although only one in five was in an incoming firm. Another fifth had grown up in firms already in the city, while the remainder were in construction or services. Building the new city and servicing its new residents were thus, at this stage, the pre-eminent sources of new jobs in Milton Keynes.

The best way for the corporation to offset the negative effect of IDCs and ODPs was marketing and in 1977 the board decided to be more aggressive. Activities of various kinds were stepped up, including advertising in newspapers and magazines, attending exhibitions, the appointment of commercial property agents, keeping in touch with local firms, and public relations.

Increasing resources also began to be devoted to market research. This enabled potential investors to be located, targeted, contacted, the contact followed up and, where appropriate, pressed home by means of a helicopter trip over the city.[6] Market research also disclosed a 'negative perception of Milton Keynes among key target audiences'. Most potential residents – managers, skilled manual workers and office workers – were found to share such views. It was reckoned to be 'largely influenced by hostile feelings about new towns generally, but still a potential handicap for Milton Keynes'.[7]

Negative image or not, 1978 was a highly successful year. Allen Duff, commercial

LEFT: The Aurora at Rooksley, a late-1980s building designed to bring together production and administration.

director, reported in June that the letting of factories built speculatively by the corporation was being 'tremendously successful'. A month later the board congratulated David Crewe, information director, when told that 40,000 people had visited a second Milton Keynes exhibition arranged by him and his staff at the Design Centre in London. In September the *New York Journal of Commerce* ran a story headed 'UK's newest new town successful in attracting US investment'. (The piece was about the opening in Milton Keynes by National Can Company of Chicago of a £12m, automated plant next door to Coca-Cola.) And in December, following a 'significant increase in inquiries for ... office accommodation', Fred Roche reported that General Motors had decided to move their European headquarters from Hendon to Milton Keynes, bringing in 250 jobs.[8]

All this coincided with a new phase in the board's employment strategy and in the city's development. Office jobs had hitherto been negligible in Milton Keynes – indeed by mid-1978 only three large office buildings had been completed. But with the opening of the shopping building in sight, Milton Keynes was about to acquire a city centre which, within a decade, would become the city's dominant concentration of jobs. This also promised to provide something that the marketing men, who were considering a move into radio and television, felt the city still lacked – an image.

Soon the board began receiving reports about the corporation's marketing activities in the United States and Germany. Firms making plastics, pharmaceuticals, soft drinks and electronics were the initial targets. Going after soft-drink firms was questioned by Evelyn de Rothschild. He feared they would only bring warehousing and distribution jobs, thereby contributing to a trend away from productive and towards service industries.

Instead, he advocated going for firms working in optics and instrumentation. He also wanted to see them targeting the Japanese 'who were very interested in Britain as a springboard into Europe'. (Sansetsu, the first Japanese firm to settle in Milton Keynes, had arrived in 1978.) He acknowledged that 'a "silicon valley" might not be feasible but a regional reputation for particular kinds of industries would bring enormous benefits'. Fred Roche later confirmed that the Luton–Milton Keynes corridor did, indeed, contain a high proportion of science-based industry. The executive was aware of it and was associated in a region-wide bid, that included Plessey at Towcester, for the government-sponsored INMOS printed-circuit plant. 'Tremendous support was being given, particularly as there was a concentration of [microelectronic] firms in ... Stevenage, Hatfield and Harlow, which were in Milton Keynes' catchment area.' (INMOS was, in the end, a fish that got away. It went to South Wales.)[9]

Within a year, the board was being asked to concur with the corporation's first sally into Japan. Members questioned 'the costs of the intended visit ... and the hidden costs of follow-up' and even Rothschild had lost his earlier enthusiasm for the Japanese. They

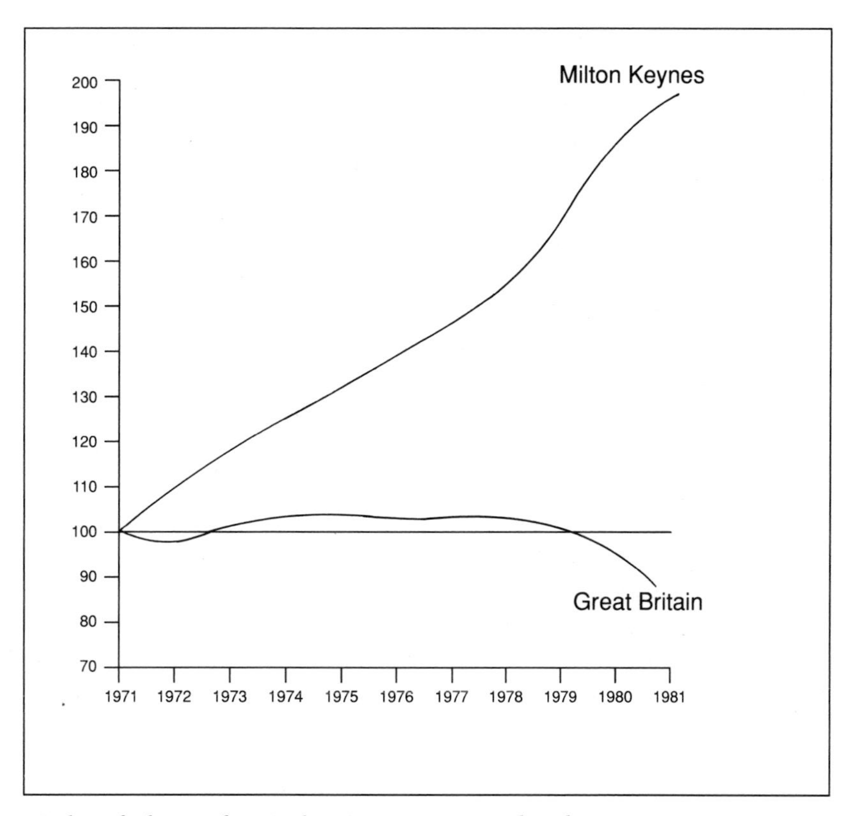

Index of job growth at Milton Keynes compared with Great Britain 1971–81.

'might easily establish assembly lines which put British firms elsewhere out of business'. This could have political repercussions. It was agreed to defer the oriental trip until the board had considered a further report.[10]

As the corporation succeeded in attracting firms, so it became clear that they tended to be capital rather than labour intensive. This had several implications. It slowed up the rate at which Londoners could be brought to the new town. It made it necessary to devote more land to industry than had been foreseen and it called for greater efforts to attract a given number of jobs. Yet, as Campbell said: 'It would be folly to try to fly in the face of this trend and to seek to attract labour-intensive industries.' The logical thing was for the city to become capital intensive, to do it as efficiently as possible and thus 'be better able to accept its fair share of the disadvantaged'.[11]

The early 1980s saw the corporation finally cast its bread upon the waters in Japan. The

economy was in recession and 13,000 commuters were flowing in to take advantage of the jobs that had been created in the city. About £80,000 had already been spent on overseas marketing in the previous three years, most of it in the United States, and Lee Shostak said 'the USA was still the largest source of foreign investment in Britain, and would continue to be so. There was plenty more to come.' The board were told that 'introductions and personal contact' had produced 'encouraging results' in the United States and were asked to agree a 1981/2 budget of £35,000. They were also asked to approve a start with 'marketing by personal approach ... in Japan at a cost in 1981–2 of £17,000 plus staff time'.[12]

This last decision had far-reaching effects. Through the efforts of commercial directors Allen Duff and then Bob Hill, not only had two Japanese companies (Sansetsu and Noritake) become thirty-two, but Milton Keynes had gained the Gyosei boarding school and the corporation had appointed a Japanese liaison officer. The city had come a long way since Akira Hayakawa, Sansetsu's managing director and a karate expert, had given the corporation staff their first, hard-to-come-by understanding of Japanese business and customs.

As the effect of Mrs Thatcher's economic stringency began to bite, firms large and small were forced to reorganise or close. General Motors left and then Scot Meats closed with a loss of 1,000 jobs. The city's confidence was hit and the corporation began to back initiatives designed to give school-leavers jobs or work experience. Early in 1981 Peter Waterman told the board to expect 1,100 young people to be on the dole later that year. Shortly afterwards he reported that he was allocating one of his officers to work almost full-time with employers, statutory services and voluntary organisations in order to create 955 additional places in the Youth Opportunities Programme.[13]

The seriousness of the jobless trend was shown by the corporation's employment development strategy for 1981. The executive distinguished it from other board papers by marking it 'strictly confidential'. Ever since 1975, the city's unemployment rate had been above that of south-east England although it had zigzagged around the rate for the east Midlands. Now it was persistently worse than the east Midlands level, shooting upwards through the ten per cent barrier and heading towards the average for Great Britain.

Happily, there was a brighter side. There was a high turnover in and out of jobs and few people were on the dole for long. Furthermore, the unemployed were relatively young and therefore likely to be able to adapt to new industries as and when training for them was available. The corporation put its head down and set a target of 3,500 new jobs a year. This was well above anything that had been achieved before, except in the *annus mirabilis* of 1979 when, as a result of the opening of the shopping centre, 2,500 jobs were created in retailing.[14]

RIGHT: Milton Keynes is home to many Japanese companies and the Gyosei School at Willen Park.

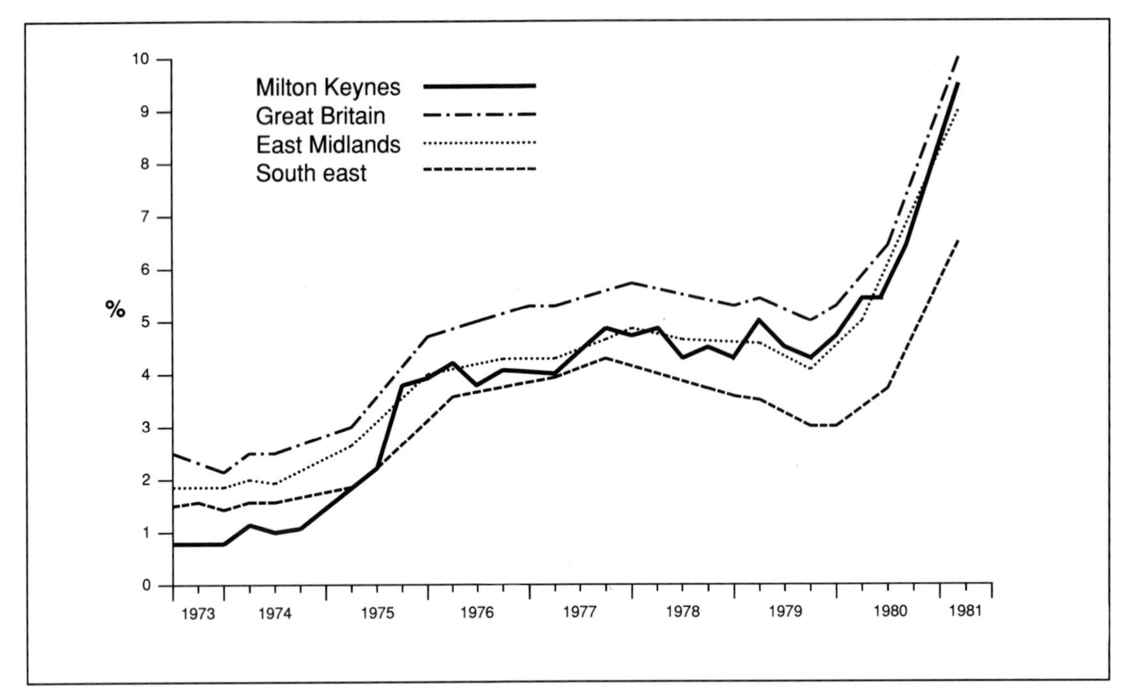

The percentage of the workforce unemployed 1973-81: by 1981 the rate in Milton Keynes was exceeding that for the east Midlands.

Bob Hill and his colleagues put all their effort into hitting the corporation's target and, by 1985, had driven the unemployment rate in Milton Keynes below that for the east Midlands. Four years later, with advice from John Darby and Tony Solomons on the institutional property market, they had got it below the rate for the south east. Yet, no sooner had that point been reached than firms again began shedding labour as the industrialised world plunged once more into recession. The fall in the dollar, the unification of the two Germanies and Bonn's shift from being a lender to a borrower, a credit squeeze at home, and finally the war with Iraq – all proved too much for the over-borrowed British economy.

What is surprising, given such a zigzagging economy, is how doggedly the corporation forged ahead. The board minutes tell not of hands being wrung but of problems being solved. Typical of this grit in the face of a seemingly insoluble problem was the pursuit of a heliport. A site for one was found in an industrial area at Pineham and agreed with the local authorities in 1981 but, following a public inquiry and strenuous local objections, the inspector recommended its rejection and his judgement was upheld by the Secretary of

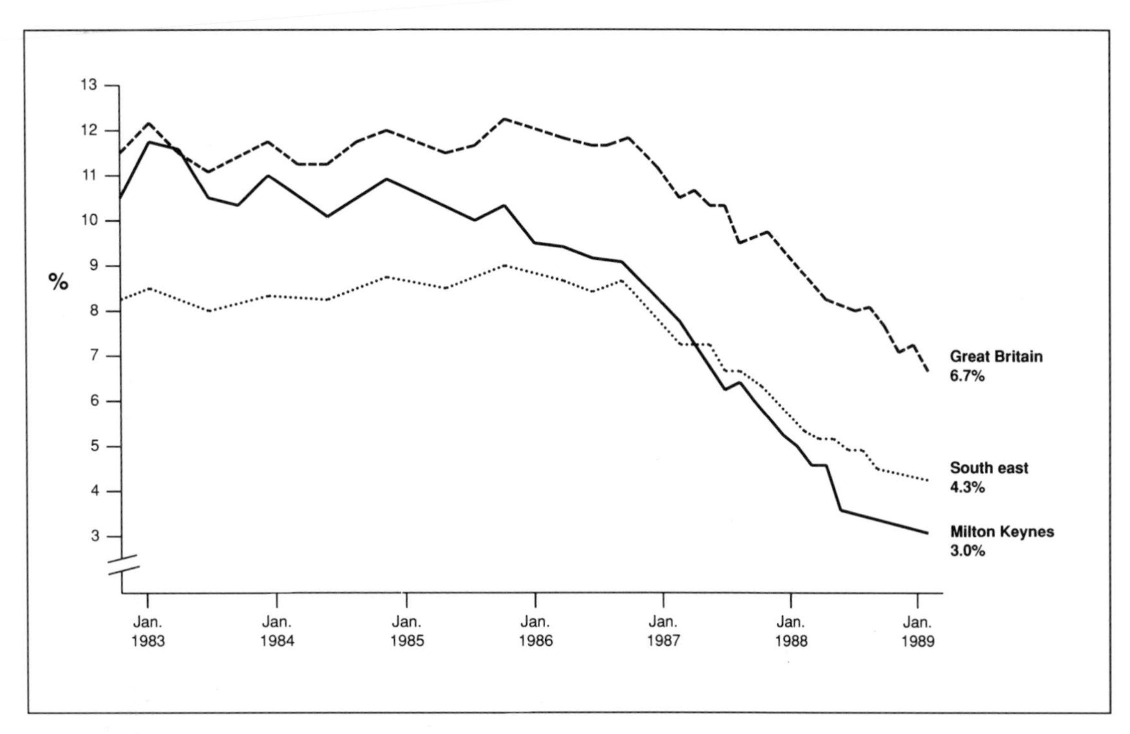

The percentage of the workforce unemployed 1983–89: by 1987 the rate for Milton Keynes was below that for the south east.

State. The objections were on grounds of noise and unproven need.

The corporation remained convinced that 'a heliport, particularly one with a regular link to Heathrow, would be in the best interests of the growth and prosperity of the city'. Companies were making increasing use of helicopters and, in the absence of a proper heliport, 'a greater number of company and air taxi helicopters would fly direct to employment sites, thus creating an environmental nuisance for adjacent residential areas. Without a heliport such traffic would be virtually impossible to control.'

Contrary to the executive's earlier expectations, consultation made clear that an open site at Kingston near the M1 was preferred to Pineham. 'An environmental impact study had shown,' John Walker told the board, 'that the effects [on nearby farmland] would be negligible.' Noise nuisance would also be 'substantially less' than at Pineham. The board agreed to the new site.[15]

It was not to be. The aim of having the heliport in operation before adjacent sites at Kingston were developed was frustrated. In 1989, after eight years of striving, the heliport

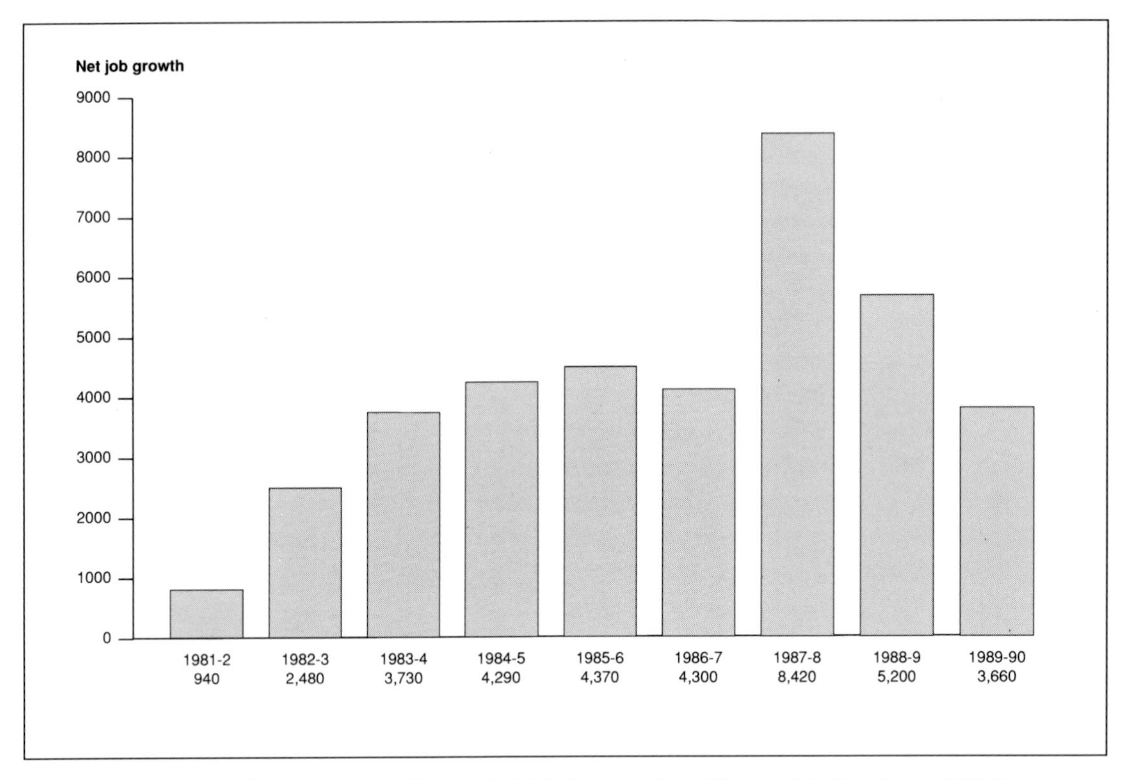

Net job growth between 1981/2 and 1989/90 showing the addition of 8,420 jobs in 1987/8.

proposal was abandoned. The board decided to try to secure helicopter services by other means.[16]

Henry Chilver regarded job generation as the key to the city's overall success and wanted Milton Keynes to be a place where firms could invest and develop in confidence. The arrival of such household names as Abbey National, British Telecom, Mercedes-Benz, Mercury and TSB make clear that the city did not fall short of his expectations.

The late 1980s were, in particular, amazing years for job creation. Chilver called them 'greater than anything we have known'. In May 1989, John Walker reported that: 'For the fifth year in succession annual net employment growth had exceeded 4,000.' In 1987/8 the increase in jobs was an astonishing 8,240 – half of them provided by newly arriving employers. The dole queues shrank. At the same meeting, the board heard that unemployment was down to three per cent – slightly over two-thirds the rate for the south east. It was agreed to increase the annual job creation target to 4,000.[17]

Abbey National was a star performer. The building society first considered locating its headquarters at Milton Keynes in the early 1970s when Stanley Morton, its chairman, was a board member. Action followed in the mid-1980s. The society turned itself into a bank, became too big for its headquarters at the Sherlock Holmes end of Baker Street, and moved its administration to Milton Keynes. By 1990 the Abbey occupied a 22-acre campus at Shenley Wood and was planning to extend its city-centre building in Grafton Gate. As *The Financial Times* observed, 'Milton Keynes appears to have worked for the Abbey National.' With an investment in the city passing £47m it may also be said that Abbey National worked for Milton Keynes.

Other stars in the city's firmament were overseas firms and higher education. The corporation's 1990 employment survey threw light on the city's broad base of international firms. It showed that the employers of Milton Keynes' 80,000 workers included no fewer than 246 foreign companies.[18]

Higher education was important in Milton Keynes almost from day one, thanks to the Open University. But the OU, although it was the city's greatest employer, was a national institution. Henry Chilver, former London University professor and vice-chancellor of Cranfield University of Technology, observed that higher education for the city itself seemed, as a result, to have been 'overlooked'. Under his leadership the corporation, therefore, sought to put this right. 'We have been trying to remedy that by introducing the concept of a higher education campus,' Chilver said.[19]

It was a successful endeavour. In 1991, The Polytechnic – Milton Keynes, an offshoot of Leicester Poly, welcomed its first 400 students, a number expected to grow to 3,500 within five years. The poly's campus was at Kents Hill next door to the Open University, and the two institutions planned to collaborate over several courses, including a new master of science degree by individual study designed to enable students to base much of their work on their employers' business.

Peter Thewlis, Hewlett Packard Professor of Computing Science and the man in charge of the venture, was aiming to work closely with employers in business and the public sector. 'We hope those links will be one of the strengths of the new polytechnic,' he said.[20]

This educational presence was further strengthened by BT's 1990 decision to establish a national training centre next door to the polytechnic. The management college was due to be in operation three years later, by which time a staff of 500 would be organising courses for the huge telecommunications company's senior commercial and technical staff.

The board, meanwhile, was seeking commitments from other investors to develop still vacant commercial sites and thus ensure the continued growth of the city. Bob Hill advised the board that, even though the corporation preferred to have offices built for owner-occupiers, it might be necessary to accept developments that were speculative. And although industrial investment flagged, Henry Chilver saw grounds for optimism. 'I don't think the recession has hit Milton Keynes as badly as other parts of the country,' he said in February 1991. Perhaps the continuous influx of people explained the difference. As for 'completing the city' – that was not one of his objectives. 'What you want to do is give such momentum that evolution doesn't stop. You then allow other forces to come in to continue the evolution ... You must leave enough for them to have their impact on the long-term future of the city.'[21]

23

REALITY

It takes a long time to build a city. The job is never-ending. As soon as something is completed, something else needs building or replacing. Only cities like Pompeii are finished and only then because they are finished off.

Milton Keynes, set in motion in 1967, was never going to be complete by the time the development corporation was wound up. A year before the final day, it was not even a real city. It had not been granted a royal charter – though for a place heading for equality with Plymouth and Southampton that was clearly only a matter of time. But if Milton Keynes was not going to be finished for several millennia, it was no longer just a series of images – the fishnet road plan, the Jacoby 'Central Milton Keynes in 1990' drawing, the boy with the balloon – it was, like other cities, both image and reality.

How was the city seen in the 1980s? David Crewe told the board in 1982 that perceptions of it had undergone substantial changes since the 1970s. 'The Milton Keynes image was now both lucid and diverse' but still 'encumbered by negative perceptions of earlier new towns, of the "planned city" and of earlier housing schemes.' Something needed to be done. The board agreed to an 'image audit' and to a long-term public relations policy designed to promote Milton Keynes as 'the first major city going north from London' and as 'a thriving pleasant city in which many varied lifestyles could be satisfied'.[1]

The image audit took over a year to complete and revealed mostly what was already known. It found, amongst other things, that executives were strongly aware of Milton Keynes as a business location and that there was an 'unwillingness among social classes A and B [managing directors and surgeons to bank managers and GPs] to consider living in a new town'.[2]

Subsequent newspaper and magazine articles tended to sustain the results of the audit. 'Milton Keynes' businesses growing furiously,' the *Japan Times* reported two years later, adding that the greatest concentration of Japanese companies in Britain outside London

was to be found in the new city.[3] *Harpers & Queen*, bible of the Knightsbridge set, sank its snobbish fangs into Milton Keynes for being 'unbearably new and depressingly desolate' and for being everything that Margaret Thatcher admired – progressive, positive and optimistic.[4]

Margaret Thatcher herself was, meanwhile, acquiring a real taste for the city. Invited to open a business week, she visited the houses of the EnergyWorld exhibition and looked at the conservatories attached to many of them and said longingly: 'I wish we could have one at 10 Downing Street, but we can't. It is built the wrong way round and the Foreign Office would stop the sun coming in.' She went on to praise the development corporation for its initiative and express the hope that energy-efficient houses would not be 'limited to this remarkable site' but would spread throughout the country.[5]

This was one of the occasions on which the Prime Minister acquired what Bill Benyon called her 'extraordinary impression of Milton Keynes'. She thought the city 'was totally populated by entrepreneurs. We kept on showing her businesses that had been started with one man and which had moved about four times and were employing sixty … and it was what she wanted to see.'[6] A tongue-in-cheek cynic to whom I reported this tale added: 'And went bust two years later'. Witticisms aside, Milton Keynes was a dynamo of job-creation. 'It is a private-enterprise town. People have done very well. Unemployment is relatively low,' Benyon observed. It was also a town not like others.

'The thing I notice when I go elsewhere, particularly to more established places, is how volatile people are. Here [in Milton Keynes] they are apolitical. They are classless. They are the new Britain.' Benyon recalled how different it was when he arrived in North Bucks in the late 1960s. 'Labour did not talk to Tory.' It was old-time politics. 'Lady Markham always told me she was spat on in New Bradwell.' And, in apology for the spitter, he added: 'They were low paid; their houses were not good.'

A similar bitterness pervaded local government. 'It was a pretty scratchy area. People were … bloody minded … There were about five different local councils all fighting their corner.'

With the coming of the new town the place had become 'far more united'. Those on the extreme left had moderated their views. 'They sense they stand or fall by the commercial success of this place.' The same thing had happened on the Tory side. 'We've had right-wing attempts to bring back grammar schools but … they have not carried people with them. There has been a coming together. Politics in the party sense don't impinge a great deal.'

LEFT: The Peace Pagoda, built by Japanese Buddhists at Willen Lake, was completed in 1980. It was the first of its kind in the western hemisphere.

Nevertheless, Benyon admitted that, at one point, he had misjudged his classless constituents. He had backed the idea of bringing in Luton Town football club – until people 'started shouting that they didn't want a first-division football team … with all the hooligans and the rest of it'.

Perhaps Milton Keynes was not so much classless as middle class. And if so, wasn't that a danger? 'Someone once said it was a middle-class ghetto,' Benyon replied. 'There was nobody who would deliver the mail or clean the streets. That is not true, but it has got an element of truth in it.'[7]

What did the future hold for these new Britons? By the late 1980s it was becoming clear that there was no prospect of 250,000 of them living within the boundaries decided upon by Tony Greenwood in 1967. Household sizes had been falling for years and promised to continue their downward path. Married couples were having fewer children, young people were living on their own rather than with their parents, divorce was creating small households and people were also living longer and often on their own.

The plan for Milton Keynes had, however, suggested that ultimately the city might contain 78,000 to 80,000 dwellings. This number of dwellings was still expected, but with a fall in the size of households living in them, the city would become less populous. 'It would be preferable in future,' the board was advised, 'to refer to the population capacity as "about 210,000 subject to future demographic trends and the patterns of development".'

The board was assured that this need not bode ill for the city's economy. 'There were now 850,000 people living within thirty minutes' driving time of Central Milton Keynes', and city firms benefited every time one of them arrived to spend money on business or pleasure. Indeed, it no longer made sense to relate economic growth to population. Long-term forecasts for Europe suggested that while the economy would grow at about three per cent a year, the population would decline. 'Individuals were becoming better off.' It was likely that the same would be the case in Milton Keynes.[8]

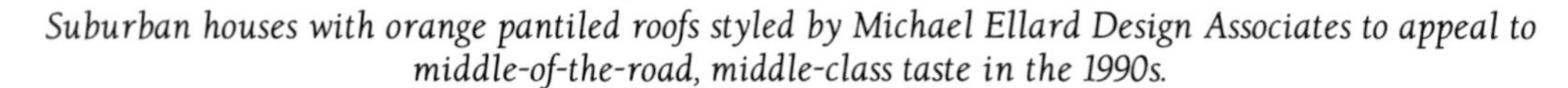

Suburban houses with orange pantiled roofs styled by Michael Ellard Design Associates to appeal to middle-of-the-road, middle-class taste in the 1990s.

Population decline was, however, not in prospect for Milton Keynes. SERPLAN, the south-east planning think-tank, made this clear in a survey of the region. The planners acknowledged the economic diversity surrounding the city, described the M40 as a movement rather than a development corridor, declined to identify sites for further new towns ('it was not SERPLAN's role'), and noted that 'no part of Hampshire should now be regarded as having a regional growth role, leaving Milton Keynes as the only remaining regional growth centre'.

All the counties in the south east had turned into NIMBYs. It was understandable. The bottom right-hand corner of Britain is, of all the large urban regions in Europe, the most heavily peopled. About 20 million bodies occupy the territory bounded by Northampton, Southampton, Dover and Peterborough. Consciously or unconsciously, these people seem to know that they are living in an anthill and want development to go elsewhere.

Milton Keynes was not so much an exception as a little island of 'yes' in a sea of 'no'. But not perhaps for long. The corporation, in its comments to SERPLAN on the future of the region, said 'it should not be assumed that further expansion of the city was appropriate or desirable'. Careful study should precede any step towards further expansion.[9] Was development-minded Milton Keynes succumbing to the siren song of nimbyism? Frank Henshaw said this was anything but the case. The corporation's concern was to put down a marker against *haphazard* future growth.

A more pressing aspect of the future was the date on which the corporation would be wound up. That end was first mooted by Michael Heseltine in 1981 but he spoke only of the late 1980s. The subject became urgent when Patrick Jenkin visited the city in January 1985 and said he had come to discuss 'how long the corporation should remain in being'. This unleashed a flurry of activity. The board took the view that 'the city and its investors would be the main victims of a decision to terminate the corporation's life in 1989/90' and that any pressure on the Government to change that date should come 'from the community'. The community sprang into action.[10]

The county and the borough speedily concluded that a wind-up in 1989 was

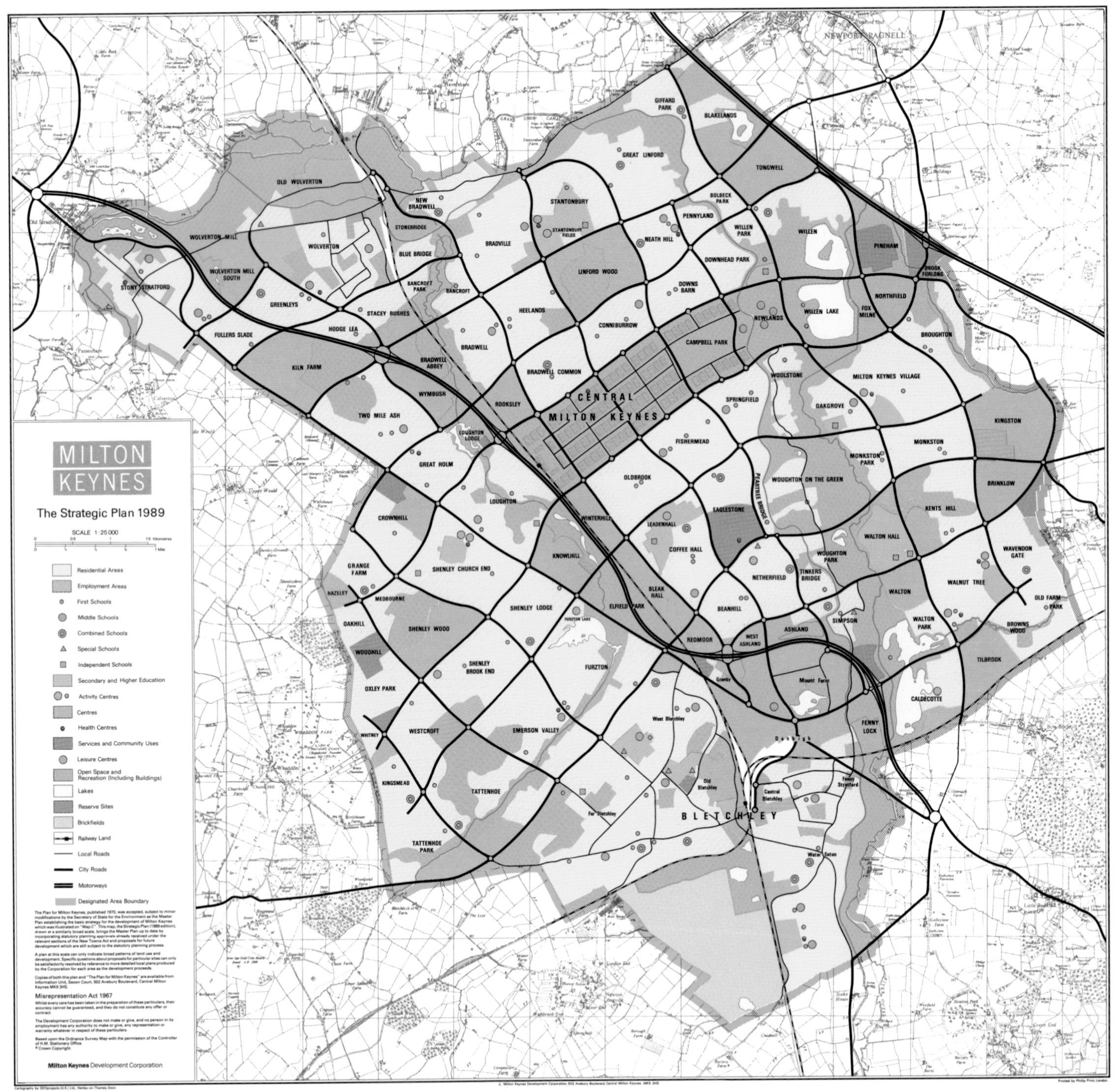

The corporation's strategic plan showing the city's full development as envisaged in 1989.

'impractical', while over 1,000 firms and individuals wrote to the Minister to protest. Business leaders as varied as the Abbey National's Sir Campbell Adamson and Axel Zaiser of Isringhausen, a German-owned seating manufacturer, picked up their pens. Some of the letters were justifiably peevish. Harry Legg of John Lewis left the Minister in no doubt that earlier government decisions to arrest the growth of the city had short-changed his department store of customers and that premature winding up of the corporation would be the last straw.

Residents expressed their views too. The Daniel Sullivans of Oldbrook wrote, saying 'We both believe that you have done a wonderful job in building the new city.' Frank Henshaw forwarded the letter to the Minister. It was clear that the corporation had its supporters.

As this community support was gathering power, Henry Chilver told Patrick Jenkin that 'the longer-term success of Milton Keynes would be put at grave risk' by the corporation's premature closure. The corporation should be allowed to continue until the mid-1990s. Henshaw drafted an accompanying note setting out in twenty-eight points the case for continuation. Amongst the most telling was that forty per cent of the city and fifty per cent of the city centre would remain undeveloped in 1989. So huge was Milton Keynes that even by 1989 the corporation would face a task equal to that taken on by Stevenage development corporation when it was set up.

The note dealt with investment and house-building as well. If allowed to continue into the 1990s, the corporation promised to attract a further £2,000m of private funds with 'relatively low levels of public investment'. And given 'land shortage elsewhere in the south east' the city's contribution to private house-building was 'particularly important'.[11]

By the autumn of 1985, Kenneth Baker had taken over the environment portfolio from Patrick Jenkin and Chilver wrote again, this time 'in strict confidence'. He wanted to raise issues not sufficiently considered in earlier discussions with ministers. Sustained private house-building was needed to achieve 'a more balanced social structure' (Baker's finely tuned political mind will have understood that to mean more Tory voters). The development of the city centre (by then judged to be only thirty per cent complete) needed to be carried on in an 'unbroken' way. And the corporation needed to explain its revolutionary plans for privatising its staff.[12]

The Government's decision was not made until summer 1986, when Lord Elton announced that the target date for winding up the corporation was 1 April 1992. He added that in the meantime the corporation should go flat out for growth, concentrating on the central area and the still rural flanks.[13] If a decision on the wind-up target removed uncertainty, it did not create plain sailing for the corporation. Corporate planning was interrupted, and in April 1987 John Walker reported to the board that the previous year's plan was still 'with the Minister' and not formally agreed.[14]

A few months later, the board was told that although good progress was being made with development and with launching certain groups of the staff into 'business ventures' (corporationese for private firms), Milton Keynes was suffering from 'a disappointing lack of commitment by the DoE'. An increasing amount of a shrinking staff's time was being spent in protracted and frustrating discussions with Whitehall. The result was 'delays in settling corporation plans and budgets and in dealing with development proposals'.[15]

Things were no better in 1988. The board heard that 'delays in taking decisions on funding were eating massively into the time available ... to complete' the city. The Department did not even seem to understand the basis of development. The corporation was told by the Secretary of State that it should '*plan for* the substantial completion of Milton Keynes and its city centre by 1992'. This was 'not at all helpful'. The corporation's task was '*to secure* the substantial completion' of the city and it aimed to do this by drawing up plans, getting permission for them and, where possible, signing contracts with developers. This involved far more than planning.[16]

If negotiations with Whitehall were tedious and time-consuming, the transformation of half the salaried staff (those whose work gave them potential to set up as consultants) into business ventures went ahead apace. Henry Chilver described it as successful, innovative and unique. It demonstrated 'the logical evolution of the staff of a [public-sector] body with a limited period to complete its work'.

The starting point, Chilver said, was decisions by staff who knew their jobs were due to go, to set up on their own. The corporation then hired them for the rest of its period of existence knowing that they would not lose interest in the problems being dealt with. It had been a success. Computer services left and, as a result of obtaining work for other clients, grew from seventeen to sixty. The architects and quantity surveyors grew from seventy to 110 until, like everyone, they were hit by the recession. There were no precedents for this form of privatisation, and 'the field is full of traps where you can be in danger of being maligned' for giving preference to a particular firm. 'You opened the door to somebody coming in and saying this is a carve-up,' Chilver observed.

The key was finding ways to test the business ventures against other potential contractors. 'It was a very interesting field and we piloted our way through it,' Chilver said. 'We had some very wise counsel from the board,' Henshaw added.[17]

Relations between the corporation and the borough were always cordial during the 1970s. Jock Campbell bent over backwards to have them that way. 'I spent a lot [of time] on relations with local politicians of all parties,' he later recalled. 'I always realised they were going to inherit Milton Keynes and we had got to work with them. I realised there was a tendency for them to take the credit for everything that went well and to blame us for everything that went badly, which I thought was fair enough ... We always turned the other cheek. I could never quarrel – which Chilver has done – with the local authorities.' But Campbell was equipped for this role as few men in public life. 'Being a member of the Labour party, I knew a lot of their politicians, but also ... I knew a lot of Tory politicians because I had been at school with them. In a way, I was in both camps.'[18]

Relations grew stormier in the 1980s. An issue quite as contentious as the ownership of the corporation's houses was the future of its community assets – a huge array of non-commercial institutions and properties – all of which had to be found new owners. The destiny of these assets, which included the city's immense parks, was set out in a 'will'. The borough councillors, like the children of a wealthy family, had expectations of receiving a rich inheritance. Mrs Thatcher, whose local government model was Wandsworth, thought otherwise. 'Government policy now favours wider diversity in the ownership and management of community-related assets', John Napleton, infrastructure and engineering director, told the board. To the borough council, which came under Labour control in 1990, it seemed as if Tory Westminster were depriving it of its rights. The result was a deep rift between the council and the board.

The corporation planned to divide its community assets into six parts. It aimed to sell some to its tenants and to package the rest with rent-producing industrial and commercial properties to make them self-financing. The main roads (but not their contiguous parks) plus all buildings for adult education, welfare and social services would go to the county. Play areas, parks department depots and open spaces associated with housing, incidental open spaces and local and district recreation facilities would go to the borough. And meeting halls and allotments would go, where possible, to parish councils.

This left some of the biggest jewels in the corporation's crown to go to independent trusts. Trusts, the board was advised, 'should be considered for the linear parks, including the city road landscaping, and the property which is used by the voluntary bodies and which it is beyond their means to purchase outright'. It would be important to ensure that the trusts were not dominated by 'single interest groups ... that they remain politically independent and that they are capable of responding flexibly to changing demands from the local community and voluntary bodies'.

As the executive beavered away at the problem, the shape of the future guardians of Milton Keynes' unique assets gradually began to emerge. It was decided that an ideal trustee would be someone who lived or worked in the city or was an officer of a local charity in addition to having professional, technical or business skills; that the trustees would employ staff; and that, in the event of a trust failing, the Charity Commissioners would be responsible for finding another body to take over. The borough was not involved. The board saw no need to concur with the council's belief that 'as the "trustee of last resort" in the district it was the practical body to control residual freeholds'.[19]

LEFT: *The dome of the Church of Christ the Cornerstone before being hoisted into place in 1990.*

When the corporation put this scheme to the DoE, it won approval for the idea of a Milton Keynes parks trust with annual operating costs estimated at £1.8m in 1987. The objectives of the trust would be to conserve the city's parks and provide for education and recreation.

The borough councillors were deeply unhappy at being, as they saw it, victims of unwarranted discrimination. Had not another development corporation, a mere forty miles away at Peterborough, seen fit to make the local council the freeholder of 660 hectares of Nene Park? Milton Keynes Borough Council requested a judicial review of the plan for a parks trust in the High Court. The application was heard, but failed.

Michael Murray, the council's chief executive, explained their case. The corporation's plan was flawed. There was no guarantee that a Milton Keynes parks trust would do what was required of it. No comparison could be made with London's royal parks because the maintenance of them was a statutory duty. 'A trust has no such responsibility. A trust can go out of existence. That is our most genuine long-term concern. No trust in this country has existed on any scale for more than 100 years,' he added more with verve than veracity.*

Underlying the council's criticism of the corporation for 'short-term thinking' was the indignity of being without powers of compulsory purchase and, therefore, never 'in a position to own any of the land in its own town'. Aylesbury and Milton Keynes spent about the same, Murray explained, 'but our net budgets are £10m apart because they have £100m of assets which produce a ten per cent income. Our asset base is very limited. Trust lands would put that right.'[21]

Henry Chilver's concerns were more philosophical. The parks in Milton Keynes were, more than anything else, symbols of the green city. His aim was to ensure that those symbols 'are preserved for all time for all people and cannot be tampered with too easily (of course, they can be by Act of Parliament) by any sort of local attitudes'. How did one design an institution to achieve that end? 'It's got to have an absolutely clear aim of protecting those amenities for all time.' An independent trust was chosen as the institution best designed to serve that end.

The board was not intent on excluding particular bodies. It wanted to assemble a mix of

---

* Smith's Charity received bequests from the will of Henry Smith in 1627 'for the use of the poore captives being slaves under the Turkish pirate' and 'for the use and relief' of the poor in general. Three hundred and fifty years and an Act of Parliament later, the charity, which owns land in South Kensington in London, had an income (1990) from investments and property of £11m and was still going strong.[22]

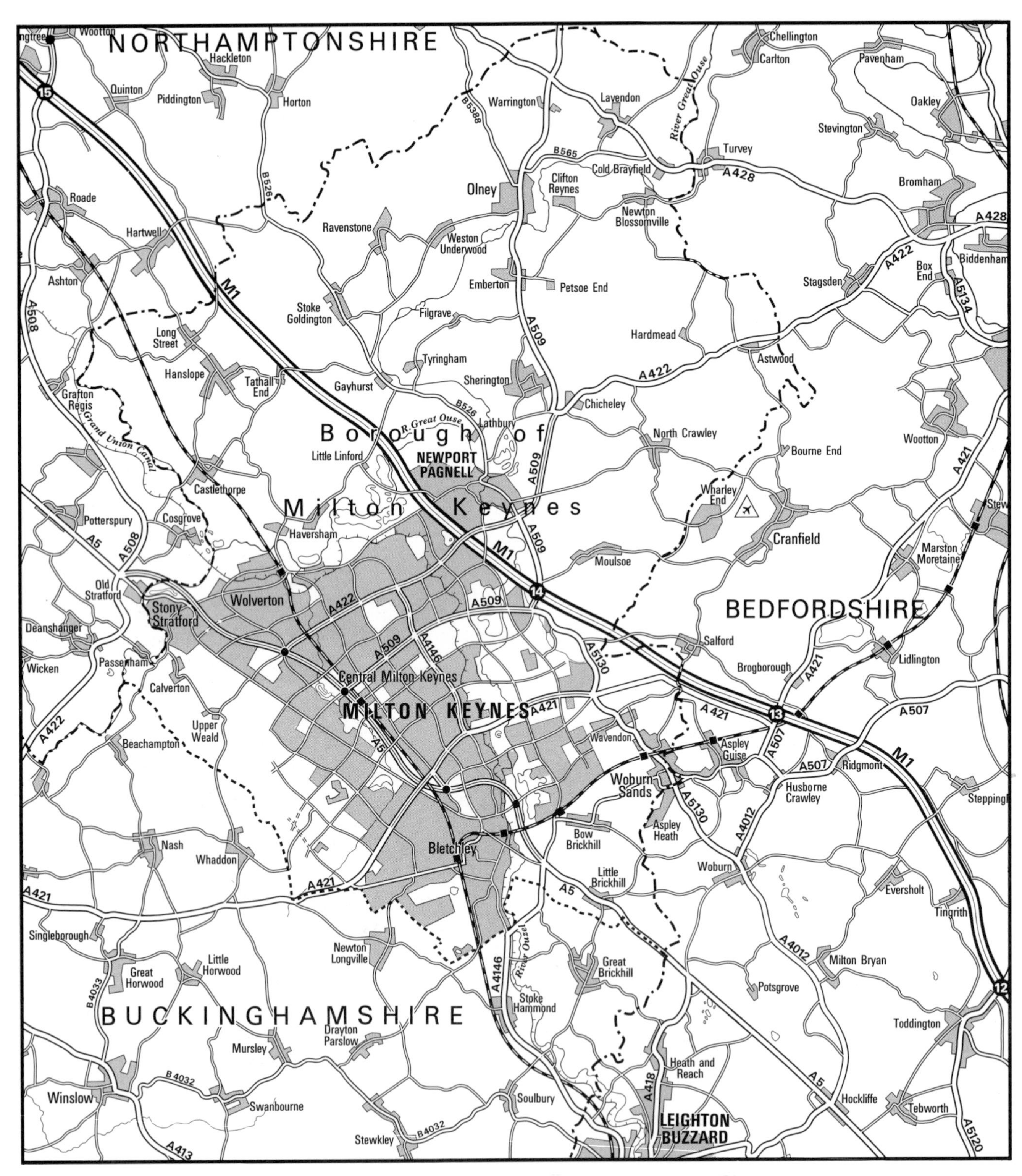

The boundaries of the borough of Milton Keynes which enclose an area of city and countryside amounting to 76,678 acres (119.8 sq miles).

interests, all determined to protect the city's parks. Such a role was not necessarily suited to local government. It was too far-reaching and too wide-ranging, Chilver said.[23]

The scientist's cool, analytical approach to conserving the city's green mantle was viewed with deep suspicion at the council offices. 'Henry Chilver is very pro-government and anti-local government,' Michael Murray remarked. 'Some of the senior officers share that view. They have no confidence in the borough council. I think that is largely based on arrogance. They can do it. Nobody else can.'[24]

Relations between the two bodies were never so strained as they became over the parks trust but, as Frank Henshaw was quick to point out, the officers continued to work together. He was always able to pick up the phone to speak to his opposite number at the council house. Michael Murray thought likewise. 'I don't want to appear over-critical of the corporation. The borough council is probably the only organisation which has the strength and the purpose to regularly criticise the corporation. We've tended to be less in their pocket than anybody else. Having said all that, our view of them is one of admiration, and appreciation of what we have got out of them. Speaking personally,' Murray added, 'I am extremely proud to be the chief executive of a town as good as this.'[25]

In 1990 the wind-up issue came up again when the Government began a final round of consultations on the 1992 target. As the board considered its final years, Frank Henshaw reminded members that the market had long been recognised as crucial in determining the pace of the city's development. And so it had turned out to be. With the market in a depressed state the executive estimated that uncommitted sites amounted to 2,000 acres, or one-quarter of the developable city.

Henshaw counselled that, rather than go for a postponement of the wind-up date, the corporation should stress the importance of continuity in the quality of development. The high standards which had always been pursued should not be allowed to sink.[26] He was aware that if they were to argue for deferment, they would open themselves to accusations of self-interest and so devalue their case for upholding quality.

The county and the borough were like-minded. They drafted a 'long list of assurances' which they wanted Chris Patten, the Environment Secretary, to give them. The county was nervous lest the Commission for the New Towns allow the still unbuilt flanks of the city to be built on the cheap. 'I do not think it is generally appreciated that the population of each of these two flanks will be equivalent to ... towns such as Amersham, Buckingham, Chesham and Marlow,' Henry Powell-Shedden, the Bucks policy and resources chairman, said. 'We want a seamless city, which is our shorthand way of stressing the importance of retaining the same overall high standards when developing the rest of the city,' he added.[27]

In March 1991 the Government announced that the 1992 target would stay. The county failed to get the extension it wanted but got the reassurances it desired about quality. Tim

Yeo, junior Housing Minister, said in a parliamentary answer 'It is important that Milton Keynes be brought to completion to the high standards established by the development corporation, and that inward investment and promotion of the city continue.'[28]

Frank Henshaw had never believed that the corporation would have its life extended for the three or more years necessary to be meaningful, and was relieved not to be involved in a wasteful short stay of execution. Meanwhile, a change of great portent for Milton Keynes took place at the Commission for the New Towns. CNT, its work in the earlier new towns over, reorganised itself in order to prepare to take over the remaining assets of Milton Keynes and Telford. In the course of this reorganisation John Walker, Henshaw's deputy, was appointed general manager.

It was a good omen. CNT's expertise lay in selling completed developments and turning over the proceeds to the Treasury. A very different set of skills was needed if Milton Keynes was to be the seamless city that the corporation and the local authorities wanted. The CNT, requested by Tim Yeo 'to pay special attention to balanced development ... at Milton Keynes', and with John Walker on its staff, promised to be able to provide them.

24

THE NEXT THOUSAND YEARS

The idea of building new cities, instead of tacking additions onto existing ones, has been around for a long time. Its modern origins seem to lie in the awfulness of urban living in the first half of the nineteenth century, a period that saw many pioneering efforts to break away from foul environments. One of the first writers to refer specifically to new cities, rather than towns, was T. J. Maslen. Queen Victoria was 24 when he wrote:

> It may startle some political economists to talk of commencing the building of *new cities* ... planned as cities from their first foundation, and not mere small towns or villages ... A time will arrive when something of this sort must be done ... England cannot escape from the alternative of new city building.[1]

The concept underlying Milton Keynes is thus over 150 years old. Furthermore, Milton Keynes is by far the most extensive exemplar of Maslen's thinking ever attempted in Britain and, looked at from the point of view of cautious, conservative, even reactionary 1991, it seems hardly believable that the decision to set it in motion was taken. No government today would attempt to urbanise thirty-four square miles of rural England. Not only have inner cities become the focus of urban public investment, but regional planning is little practised and building in open country arouses passionate opposition.

The decision to build Milton Keynes, like decisions to build the M25 and the Channel Tunnel, or to revive London's Docklands, has had far-reaching results. The city will span the next thousand years, just as its precedessor, the Saxon settlement of Middle Tun, spanned the last thousand. It will continue to change the map of southern England.

This prospect has been brought about by Milton Keynes Development Corporation which, in little over two decades, has, among other things, enabled the creation of 83,000 jobs, the construction of 44,000 houses and the planting of some 14 million trees and shrubs.

There are many outstanding features to this short history, but it is impossible not to start with the master plan. Jock Campbell made a brilliant decision in choosing Richard Llewelyn-Davies. 'What can be done in the design of towns to make change and growth easy, and to minimise disruptions when they occur?' Llewelyn-Davies asked a year before he started working on Milton Keynes.[2] The answer is there on the ground in North Bucks. Both the consultants' plan for the city as a whole, and the plan for the city centre designed by the corporation staff, are towering peaks in the evolution of thinking about town design in Britain. Their secret is their loose fit. This provides room for change. Milton Keynes today has room for cars and, unlike most other places, it is a pleasure to drive in. Tomorrow, people may be riding electric bicycles or sitting in computer-guided buggies on electronic highways – or both. Either way, Milton Keynes will be found to have the space to cope with these changes.

The determination of the board, after months of agonising debate, to create a city that would accommodate cars showed courage and steadiness. Then, as now, the arguments to base the new city on public transport were insistent and persuasive. Had they been accepted they would have undoubtedly given Milton Keynes better public transport, but at a cost of turning it into a glorified council estate.

A question repeatedly asked about Milton Keynes is whether the corporation was faithful to the plan. People also ask whether Milton Keynes is a success. Part of an answer to the question about the plan may be found in a document issued by the county and borough councils during consultation on the corporation's wind-up date. It contains a comparison between the master planners' 1970 forecast of land use and the situation in 1990.

The comparison makes clear that several major shifts in the use of land have taken place. In particular, industry and parks occupy more space than forecast, while houses occupy less. There are various reasons for these changes. The amount of land allocated to industry had to be increased because of the popularity of Milton Keynes with firms setting up huge, single-storey distribution centres filled with goods and managed by small staffs driving forklift trucks. This kind of firm employs fewer workers per acre than a manufacturing company and, as a result, additional land had to be allocated to industry if it was to create enough jobs.

The *increase* in the amount of space allocated to parks, by far the most striking change between forecast and reality, is because verges along the main roads are wider than planned and because all the old villages are set in parks. Milton Keynes was always going to be green but the corporation has made it nearly twice as green as was originally intended.

More surprising is that less space was allocated to houses than foreseen in the plan. This reduction was associated with houses being built at 23 to every acre of residential land compared with the planners' 21.5. A fall in the size of households (which meant that, for a given number of houses, fewer people were accommodated) also occurred. The 'revision downwards' of the city's eventual population from 250,000 to 210,000 closely reflected these changes.

Land-uses in Milton Keynes 1970 and 1990[3]

	1970 Master Plan		1990 MKDC	
	acres	%	acres	%
Housing (gross area)	11,614	53.0	9,118	42.0
Open space	2,866	13.0	4,867	22.0
Roads and railways	2,471	11.3	3,089	14.0
Industry, shops and offices	1,977	9.0	3,015	14.0
Reserve land	733	4.0	not available	
Social/education	733	4.0	1,174 (Social/education and Centres/health combined)	5.0
Centres/health	642	3.0		
Brickfields	593	2.7	680	3.0

None of this means that the corporation failed to implement the plan. How could it be so, given that Richard Llewelyn-Davies set out to provide a flexible framework? Changes took place and the plan accommodated them. But is the city a success? The question seems simple but is really meaningless. Is London a success? Is Berlin a success? How successful are Milton Keynes' main contemporaries, the Blackwater valley towns of Farnham, Aldershot, Farnborough and Camberley? They too saw a furious pace of development in the 1970s and 1980s but, not having a development corporation, their growth was more haphazard and, almost certainly, without comparable investment in infrastructure. Students of planning could usefully examine this question.

In the meantime, it is possible only to note that those who live in Milton Keynes are proud of it; and that there are enough people buying houses, or investing in the place in other ways, to make it the most dynamic spot in Britain.

It is unfashionable to admire the spare, angular architecture of the late 1960s. The cool, austere, international style is as disliked now as repetitive Georgian terraces were in the

nineteenth century. Yet Milton Keynes has some outstanding work of that period – the shopping building and Station Square with their graph-paper façades and, in housing, the magnificent and underrated Netherfield. If those great terraces of worker housing survive the next twenty-five years, it is a fair bet that they will become a conservation area. These and other aspects of architecture and design reflect the corporation's persistent drive to rise above the ordinary.

The achievements of the 1980s are of a different kind. The most remarkable was the rejection of 1970s thinking and the conversion of the corporation from a 'nationalised industry' into an agency for enabling private investment. The figures for 1990/1 speak for themselves. The corporation's capital receipts were £146m; its expenditure was £67m and it transferred £79m to the Treasury. Private investment totalled £355m.[4]

Henry Chilver, a Thatcherite at heart, was the ideal person to oversee this change. He had already turned Cranfield into a largely self-financing institution of higher learning before he took on the Milton Keynes chairmanship. Frank Henshaw had the more taxing job of ensuring that this complex task was executed. He had to respond to the challenge set by Michael Heseltine and Henry Chilver and persuade an old public-service dog to perform new private-enterprise tricks. Out went asking Whitehall for money to build houses for rent and directly financed amenities; in came shared-ownership houses financed by building societies and the packaging of such unlikely partners as a church with offices or a night-club with a DIY shop.

Bringing about such changes in thinking in a public-service bureaucracy was tantamount to bringing about a cultural revolution, and neither the difficulties encountered nor Henshaw's role in surmounting them should be underestimated. Henshaw's management style was never flashy. He was, as one of his colleagues observed, someone who 'hides his charisma', but he piloted the corporation into completely new waters.

The early new towns were seen as being umbilically linked to a mother city but also 'self-contained'. No one was expected to commute to or from them. The coming of popular car-ownership changed all that and, as the perceptive Richard Llewelyn-Davies observed in the late 1960s, 'the links connecting the [new] town with other centres in the regional complex become important, formative elements in the plan'.[5]

Some of these road and rail links exist, or are in the pipeline, and they need to be. Already 19,600 commuters leave Milton Keynes every weekday while another 25,000 come in. Major events at the Milton Keynes Bowl, fun and games at Willen Lake and the shops in the city centre likewise attract people from all over the region. As the future population of

LEFT: A quiet corner in Milton Keynes.

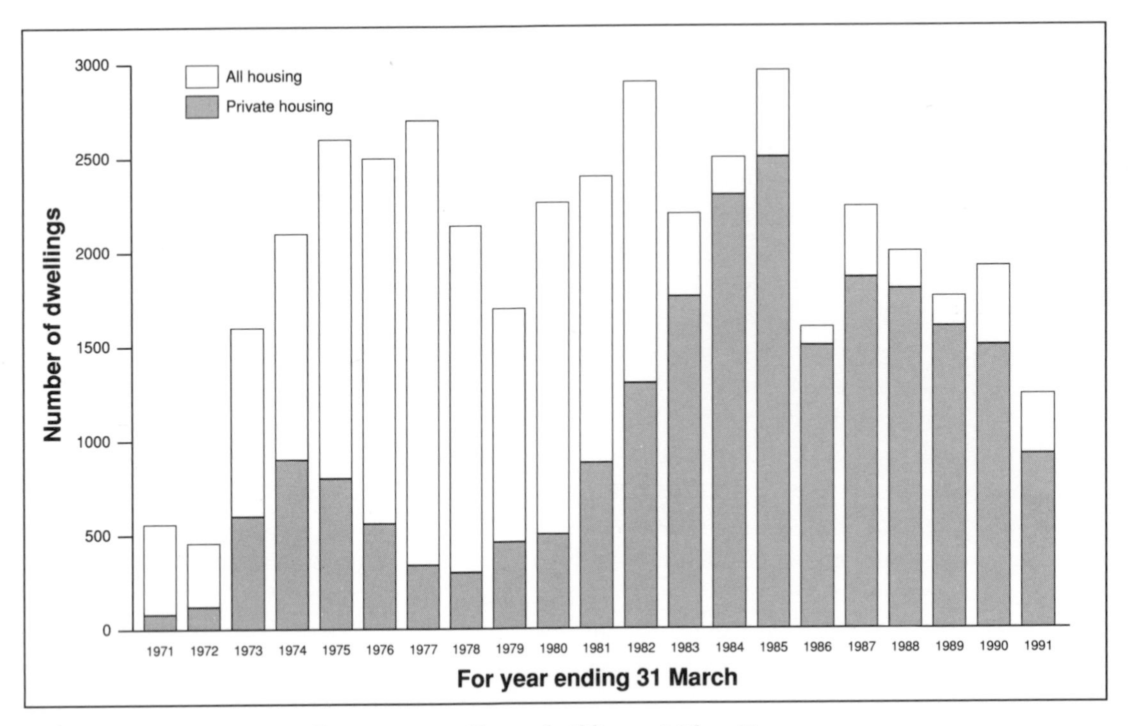

Twenty years of house-building at Milton Keynes.

the city moves up from its 1990 total of 148,000 towards 200,000 (and that of the more extensive borough of Milton Keynes from 181,000 to 250,000) the volume of such flows will increase.

Coping with this interaction is not going to be the responsibility of the corporation or even the new towns commission. They will, by then, be no more than the stuff of history. Nor is the problem confined to Milton Keynes. A loose-knit urban constellation is growing up that stretches from the Solent to the Wash by way of Basingstoke, Newbury, Oxford, Northampton and Peterborough. This Milky Way of towns and cities is the fastest-growing part of southern England. Milton Keynes is in the midst of it, is one of the very few places where growth is welcome and is the only one where the long-term future has been considered.

As the Milton Keynes Development Corporation is wound up, it is time to take stock. The city's birth was the result of a government review of the future shape of the south east – then, as now, by far the most populous great urban region in Europe. Economic and social conditions have, in the intervening decades, undergone major changes. Prosperity has

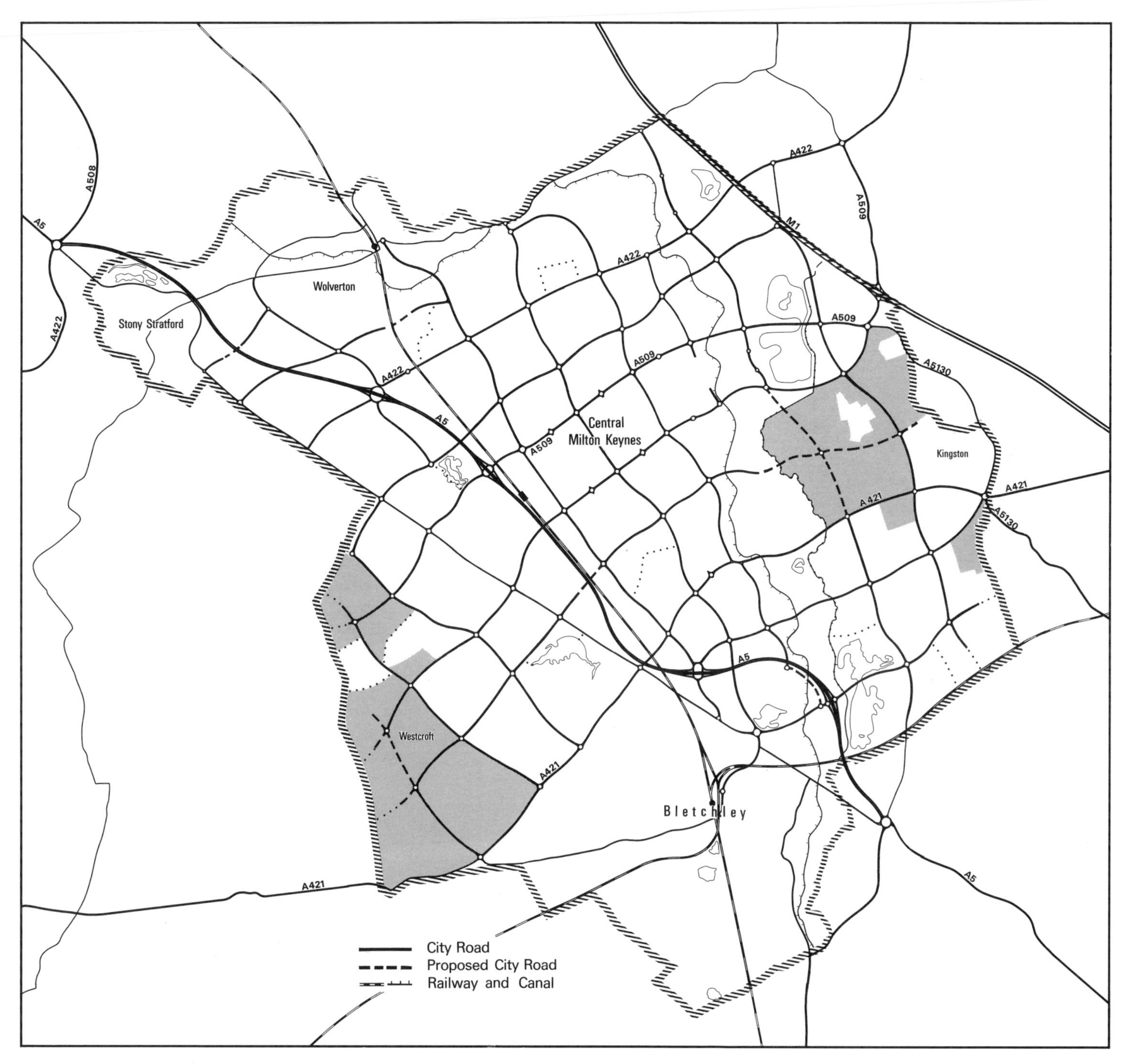

Major areas remaining for development at summer 1991. Additional areas for development remained in Central Milton Keynes.

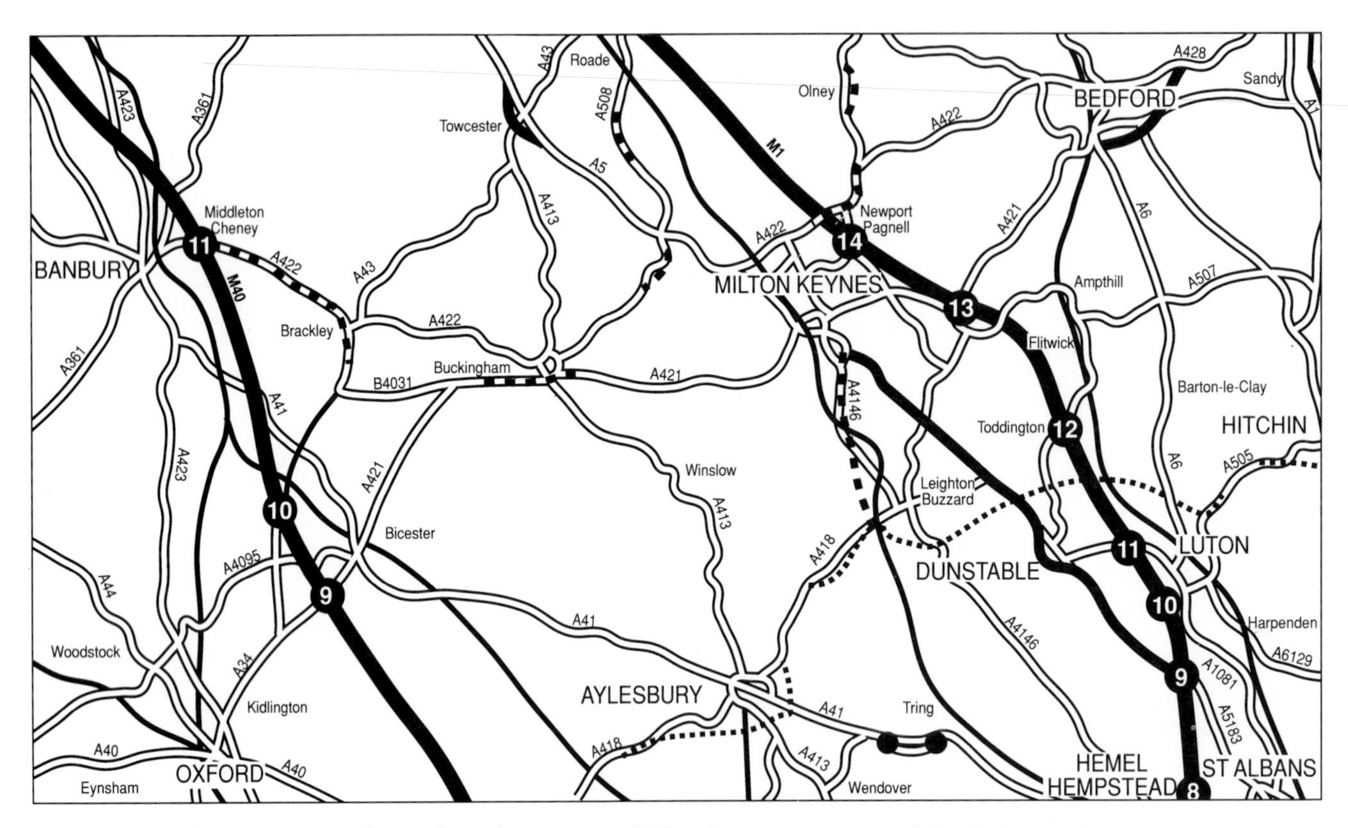

Improvements to the roads in the vicinity of Milton Keynes programmed for the 1990s. The route bypassing Aylesbury, Leighton Buzzard, Luton and Hitchin will lead to Stansted Airport and is part of the London super-orbital. It is being built by the Department of Transport.

increased, home-ownership has expanded and continental Europe has come to play a greater part in British affairs. Yet one thing remains constant: southern England is a vital economic resource. The people who live in it and the skills they deploy make a major contribution to the country's well-being. Growth and change in the towns, cities, airports, railways and roads are too important to be left to happenstance.

John Major's government has begun to acknowledge this. Ministers have identified the Thames estuary as London's growth corridor, looking east towards Europe, and agreed to route the new Channel Tunnel railway through it. Yet much development will take place on London's other sides. Where will it go? It is time to ask again the recurrent question: how and where are the people going to live?

Appendix 1

MILTON KEYNES AT 31 MARCH 1991

POPULATION	*1967*		*1991*
Designated area	40,000		148,800
MK borough	60,000	(est)	183,300

JOBS	*1967*		*1991*
Designated area	18,350		84,100
MK borough	21,350	(est)	96,200

UNEMPLOYMENT INCLUDING SCHOOL-LEAVERS	*1991*
MK travel to work area	5.5%
South east	6.2%
East Midlands	6.9%
Great Britain	7.4%

COMMERCIAL FLOORSPACE	*Completed in 1990/91*		*Total*	
Factories and warehouses	122,599	sq.m	1,844,452	sq.m
Offices	41,701	sq.m	356,602	sq.m
Shopping (local)	220	sq.m	100,156	sq.m
Shopping (Central Milton Keynes)	-		116,987	sq.m
Floorspace totals	164,520	sq.m	2,418,197	sq.m

HOUSES	*Completed in 1990/91*	*Total*
Owner-occupied (including shared ownership)	957	(69%) 39,327
Private and housing association rent	284	(5%) 3,092
Public rent	0	(26%) 14,953
Total	1,241	57,372

SCHOOLS, ROADS ETC.	*Completed in 1990/91*	*Total*
Schools	0	83
Pupil places	0	30,379
Health centres	1	11
City roads	6.90 kms	108.63 kms
Redways	11 kms	228 kms

CAPITAL EXPENDITURE	*In 1990/91*	*Total*
Private	£ 355 m	£ 2,259 m
Milton Keynes Development Corporation (net)	£ (79) m	£ 263 m
Other public agencies	£ 28 m	£ 445 m
Total	£ 304 m	£ 2,967 m

EXPENDITURE UNDER MKDC CONTROL	*In 1990/91*
Expenditure	£ 67 m
Capital receipts	£ 146 m
Net contribution to Treasury	£ (79) m

Appendix 2

MILTON KEYNES DEVELOPMENT CORPORATION–THE BOARD

		Meetings attended (to 31.3.91)
CHAIRMEN		
Lord Campbell of Eskan	1967-83	169
Lord Chilver, FRS	1983-	81
DEPUTY CHAIRMEN		
Walter Ismay, FIMechE	1967-71	40
Sir Evelyn de Rothschild	1971-84	72
John Darby, FRICS (appointed to board 1981)	1985-	101
MEMBERS		
Raymond Bellchambers, OBE§	1967-84	172
James Cassidy†	1967-75	71
Sir Horace Cutler, OBE, DL¥	1967-86	181
Margaret Durbridge, OBE, JP*	1967-77	107
Alexander Meikle, CBE, CA	1967-68	7
The Baroness Serota, JP	1967-68	6
Sir Ralph Verney, Bt, KBE, JP, DL*	1967-75	73
Sir Stanley Morton, FCIS	1968-75	63
Professor Roy Parker	1968-71	25
Peter Willcock	1971-75	35
Frank Atter, JP, DL¶*	1975-91	163
Tony Judge¥	1975-80	42
Roger Parker-Jervis, DL*	1975-	129

		Meetings attended (to 31.3.91)
Derk Pelly	1976-85	59
Joan Christodoulou	1978-82	41
Luing Cowley, JP¶	1978-	114
Eric Barratt, FCA*	1980-85	43
David Lee¶*	1980-	96
Felicity Freeman	1982-	81
Malcolm Brighton, FIS	1984-	62
Joseph Oblein, FCIB	1985-	45
Anthony Solomons, FCA	1985-	35
Wilfred Rooke, DL*	1986-	49
Raymond Waite	1987-	35
Gillian Miscampbell, OBE*	1990-	12

Members who served on the following local authorities while on the board are marked thus:

* Buckinghamshire County Council
¶ Milton Keynes Borough Council
† Bletchley Urban District Council
§ Newport Pagnell Rural District Council
¥ Greater London Council

Appendix 3

Milton Keynes Development Corporation Executive

Chief Executives

Walter Ismay, BSc(Eng), CEng, FIMechE
Managing Director 1967–71
Fred Roche, DipArch, RIBA
General Manager 1971–80
Frank Henshaw, FRICS
General Manager 1980–

Chief Officers

Ben Affleck, FIH, MRSH
Chief Housing Officer 1970–71
Chief Social Development & Housing Officer 1971–74
Housing Director 1974–80
Alan Ashton, FRICS
Chief Estates Officer 1968–74
Commerce Director 1974–76
Director of Commerce & Finance 1976–77
Bill Berrett, RIBA
Planning Director 1974–75
John Billingham, MArch(Penn), DipTP, RIBA, MRTPI
Director of Design & Development 1988–
Bill Clewett, FCCA
Finance Director 1986–87
Finance & Administration Director 1987–

David Crewe
- Information Director 1978–81
- Property Management & Information Director 1981–83

Allen Duff, FRICS
- Commerce Director 1977–83

Ted Hardy, CEng, MICE, MIHT
- Infrastructure Director 1980–87

Peter Hawkes, MA(Hons) (Eng)
- Planning Director 1987–88

Frank Henshaw, FRICS
- Chief Quantity Surveyor 1973–74
- Executive Director, North Milton Keynes 1974–76
- Project Director, Central Area 1976
- Assistant General Manager 1976–78
- Deputy General Manager 1978–80

Bob Hill, BSc, FRICS
- Commerce Director 1983–

Chris Hopkinson, LLB, LAMRTPI
- Chief Legal Officer 1971–74
- Administration Director & Solicitor 1974–87

David Jamieson, CEng, MICE, AMIMunE, AMInstHE
- Executive Director, Infrastructure 1974–77

John Jew, FCIS, IPFA
- Chief Finance Officer 1973–74
- Finance Director 1974–76

Nigel Lane, DipArch, RIBA
- Executive Director, North Milton Keynes 1976–80

Dudley Leaker, RIBA
- Executive Director, South Milton Keynes 1975–78

Stuart Mosscrop, AA(Dipl), RIBA
- Executive Director, Central Milton Keynes 1976–78
- Executive Director, Central & South Milton Keynes 1978–80

John Napleton, CEng, FICE ....
- Property Management Director 1983–87
- Infrastructure & Engineering Director 1987–

Norman Owen, FIHM
- Housing Director 1981

Ernest Pye, MEng, DipTP, CEng, FICE, FIMunE,FRTPI, FIHE
- Chief Engineer 1967–74
- Assistant General Manager 1974–84

Keith Revill, RIBA	
Building Director	1980-87
Don Ritson, DipArch(Manch), RIBA, DipTP(Manch), MRTPI	
Executive Director, South Milton Keynes	1974-75
Director of Planning, Social Development & Information	1975-78
Assistant General Manager	1978-85
Fred Roche, DipArch, RIBA	
Director of Design & Production	1970-71
Mike Roberts, IPFA, FCCA	
Finance Director	1977-86
Lee Shostak, BA	
Planning Director	1978-80
John Sullivan, MTech, BSc(Econ), FIH	
Housing and Community Buildings Director	1989-
Derek Walker, DipArch, RIBA	
Chief Architect & Planning Officer	1970-74
Executive Director, Central Milton Keynes	1974-76
John Walker, BSc, DipTP	
Planning Director	1981-87
Deputy General Manager	1987-
Peter Waterman, MA	
Social Development Director	1978-88
Kenneth Wren, FIMTA, FRVA	
Chief Finance Officer	1968-70
Chief Administrative & Finance Officer	1970-72
Chief Finance Officer	1972-73

Appendix 4

SOURCES

PREFACE

1. Frederic J. Osborn and Arnold Whittick, *New Towns: Their Origins, Achievements and Progress*, Leonard Hill, 1977, p. 78.

2. J. B. Cullingworth, *Environmental Planning 1939–1969*, vol. 3, *New Towns Policy*, HMSO, London, 1979, p. 25.

3. Kathleen Raine, *Golgonooza City of Imagination*, Golgonooza Press, Ipswich, 1991, pp. 1–39, 100–20.

4. Françoise Choay, *The Modern City: Planning in the 19th Century*, Studio Vista, London, undated.

5. Italo Calvino, *Invisible Cities* (trans. William Weaver), Pan Books, London, 1979.

CHAPTER ONE

1. Meeting with John Palmer, former assistant secretary, Ministry of Housing and Local Government, 8 February 1991.

2. 'Bletchley, Wolverton in new town site', *Bletchley District Gazette*, 14 January 1966.

3. Quoted by Anthony Howard in *Crossman - The Pursuit of Power*, Jonathan Cape, London, 1990, p. 267.

4. Letter from Alun Sylvester-Evans to Terence Bendixson, 18 February 1991.

5. Opinion: 'Cause and effect', *Wolverton Express*, 21 January 1966.

6. 'A definite "no" to new town', *Wolverton Express*, 11 February 1966.

7. 'Minister in N Bucks', *Wolverton Express*, 18 March 1966.

8. Richard Crossman, *Diaries of a Cabinet Minister*, vol. 1, Hamish Hamilton and Jonathan Cape, London, 1975, p. 470, entry for 3 March 1966.

9. 'Crossman's concessions', *Wolverton Express*, 15 April 1966.

10. 'Villagers prepare for new town inquiry', *Wolverton Express*, 29 April 1966.

11. 'New town: The first salvoes', *Wolverton Express*, 8 July 1966.

12. Alun Sylvester-Evans, 'Milton Keynes as seen from the Ministry'. A note accompanying a letter to Terence Bendixson, 18 February 1991

13. 'Towns put forward as "multi-centres", *Wolverton Express*, 15 July 1966.

14. 'Master plan in 18 months', *Wolverton Express*, 15 July 1966.

15. Ministry of Housing and Local Government, 'Report of the inquiry into the draft of the North Buckinghamshire New Town (Designation) Order 196-,' London, January 1967.

16. Ministry of Housing and Local Government Ref. NT/256/53/23, 'New Towns Act 1965 draft North

Buckinghamshire New Town (Designation Order) 196-,' London, 11 January 1967.

17. 'We deplore land loss but will pull together', *North Bucks Times*, 18 January 1967.

18. Lord Campbell questioned this account. 'I had,' he said, 'a very close relationship with Dick [Crossman] ... I used to see a lot of Dick and I was very fond of him and Anne ... Certainly Tony Greenwood announced the name [Milton Keynes] but I'm pretty sure it was thought of ... by Dick – and Dick certainly claimed it. He used to say it combined poetic vision and economic realism.' Interview with Lord Campbell, Nettlebed, 23 February 1991. MK/TB tape 4. The final sentence in this quotation was added by Lord Campbell after seeing a draft of the chapter.

19. J. B. Cullingworth, *Environmental Planning 1939–1969*, vol. 3, *New Towns Policy*, HMSO, London, 1979, pp. 278–9.

CHAPTER TWO

1. Frank Markham, *History of Milton Keynes and District*, vol. 1, White Crescent Press, Luton, 1973, p. 11.

2. ibid, vol. 1, pp. 311 and 324; vol. 2, p.77.

3. Francis E. Hyde, *Wolverton: A Short History of its Economic and Social Development*, A. J. Emerton, Wolverton, 1945, p. 40.

4. P. L. Mortimer, 'Urban development in North Buckinghamshire 1930–1970', M.Phil. thesis, Open University, 1984, p. 45.

5. David Starkie, *The Motorway Age: Road and Traffic Policies in Postwar Britain*, Pergamon Press, Oxford, 1982, pp. 1–6.

6. Frank Markham, *History of Milton Keynes and District*, vol. 2, White Crescent Press, Luton, 1975, p. 305.

7. P. L. Mortimer, 'Urban development in North Buckinghamshire 1930–1970', M.Phil. thesis, Open University, 1984, pp. 81–2.

8. Fred Pooley, *North Bucks New City*, Departments of Architecture and Planning, Buckinghamshire County Council, Aylesbury, 1966, p. 3.

CHAPTER THREE

1. *The South East Study 1961–1981*, HMSO, London, 1964, pp. 24, 51–7, 71–4.

2. George Cyriax, 'The £400m Bletchley new city – Buchanan into practice?', *The Financial Times*, 3 April 1964.

3. 'New city at Bletchley', *Wolverton Express*, 20 March 1964.

4. 'Plan to turn Bletchley into £195m "new city"', *The Financial Times*, 1 September 1964.

5. 'A giant "yes" to the super city', *Chronicle & Echo*, 2 September 1964.

6. 'MP advises all councils: Make your plans now', *Bletchley Gazette*, 4 December 1964.

7. Richard Crossman, *The Diaries of a Cabinet Minister*, vol. 1, Hamish Hamilton and Jonathan Cape, London, 1975, p. 147, entry for 3 February 1965.

8. 'New town coming: Britain's biggest, but no decision on site', *Wolverton Express*, 5 February 1965.

9. 'County Council leaves new town to a corporation: Unable to take risk', *Wolverton Express*, 28 May 1965.

10. 'Bletchley – political powder keg', *Evening News and Star*, 3 December 1965.

CHAPTER FOUR

1. 'Towns as part of city?', *Wolverton Express*, 10 December 1965.

2. Richard Crossman, *The Diaries of a Cabinet Minister*, vol. 2, Hamish Hamilton and Jonathan Cape, London, 1976, p. 733, entry for March 1968.

3. Interview with Lord Campbell at Nettlebed, 23 February 1991. MK/TB tape 4.

4. 'N Bucks future in their hands', *Chronicle & Echo*, 24 April 1967.

5. 'Chairman's prefatory remarks', 'Compensation to tenant farmers' and 'Planning consultants', MKDC, Board minutes 2, 17 and 20, 15 June 1967.

6. 'Hopes for close link with new town', *Chronicle & Echo*, 5 July 1967.

7. 'Milton Keynes: Brief for master plan', MKDC, 20 June 1967.

8. Nicholas Taylor, 'Big city plan job for Labour peer', *The Sunday Times*, 24 September 1967.

9. Meeting with Walter Bor at the Reform Club, London, 3 December 1990.

10. Interview with Lord Campbell, 23 February 1991.

11. Nicholas Taylor, 'Big city plan job for Labour peer'.

12. Interview with Lord Campbell, 23 February 1991.

13. Richard Crossman, *The Diaries of a Cabinet Minister*, vol. 1, Hamish Hamilton and Jonathan Cape, London, 1975, p. 31, entry for 27 October 1964.

14. *A Strategy for the South East*, South East Economic Planning Council, HMSO, London, 1967.

15. 'New city: "Scrap it or concentrate on it" – Mr Benyon', *Bletchley Gazette*, 13 December 1968.

CHAPTER FIVE

1. 'Single-centre city will be opposed', *Wolverton Express*, 4 August 1967.

2. Letter signed Campbell of Eskan to Councillor Dr D. Hall, dated 4 August 1967, MKDC, Board meeting, 25 September 1967: Appendix A(ii) to Agendum 10.

3. 'New city interim plan to be ready in 1968', *Beds and Bucks Reporter*, 26 September 1967.

4. 'Roads-of-the-future plan leads way to the still bigger Bletchley', *Bletchley Gazette*, 22 December 1967.

5. 'Bletchley: Suggested town development and future road pattern', MKDC, Board minute 15 H, 5 January 1968.

6. 'Terms of reference of Bletchley study', MKDC, Board minute 96, 27 May 1968.

7. MKDC, Establishment and Appointments Committee paper (EA/18/69), 1 December 1969.

8. MKDC, Establishment and Appointments Committee paper (EA/24/70), 30 November 1970.

9. 'Office accommodation', MKDC, Board minute 145, 30 November 1970.

10. Frederick Gibberd, 'The master design; landscape; housing; town centres', in Hazel Evans (ed.), *New Towns: The British Experience*, Charles Knight, London, 1972.

11. Frank Schaffer, *The New Town Story*, Macgibbon & Key, London, 1970, p. 53. (Schaffer was head of the new-towns division of the Ministry of Housing and Local Government 1959–65.)

12. MKDC, Lord Llewelyn-Davies' postscript to Board seminar review, 14 March 1968.

13. Richard Crossman, *Diaries of a Cabinet Minister*, vol. 1, Hamish Hamilton and Jonathan Cape, London, 1975, p. 24, entry for 22 October 1964.

14. MKDC, Board seminar, Park Lane Hotel, London, 4–5 December 1967.

15. Llewelyn-Davies Weeks Forestier-Walker & Bor, 'Milton Keynes: Goals and opportunities', 11 March 1968.

16. 'Lord Campbell's review of Board seminar, 14 March 1968', MKDC, 22 March 1968.

17. Gordon Cullen and Richard Matthews, *A Town Called Alcan*, Alcan Industries Limited, 1964.

18. 'Master plan', MKDC, Board minute 77, 29 April 1968.

19. 'Master plan progress report', MKDC, Board minute 133, 30 September and 2 October 1968.

20. Fred Pooley, 'North Bucks new city', Buckinghamshire County Council Departments of Architecture and Planning, Aylesbury, 1966, pp. 50, 97.

CHAPTER SIX

1. Italo Calvino, *Invisible Cities* (trans. William Weaver), Pan Books, London, 1979, p. 101.

2. 'Master plan progress report', MKDC, Board minute 133, 30 September and 2 October 1968.

3. MKDC, Board minute 133, 30 September, 2 October 1968. 'Master plan progress report', Llewelyn-Davies Weeks Forestier-Walker & Bor and '*Aide-mémoire* on discussion of master plan progress report'.

4. ibid.

5. ibid.

CHAPTER SEVEN

1. 'Master plan progress report', MKDC, Board minute 154, 25 and 28 October 1968.

2. 'Interim report on the master plan', MKDC, Board minute 170, 16 December 1968.

3. 'We can afford Milton Keynes – new city "chief"' and 'Push-button buses will be target for vandals says traders' president', *Chronicle & Echo*, 5 February 1969.

4. 'MK: New city for the south-east', *Architects' Journal*, vol. 149, no. 6, 5 February 1969, pp. 361–76.

5. Reyner Banham et al., 'Non-plan: An experiment in freedom', *New Society*, no. 338, 20 March 1969, pp. 435–43.

6. Hugh Roper, 'To plan or not to plan: Some interim thoughts on Milton Keynes', *Journal of the Town Planning Institute*, May 1969, vol. 55, no. 5, pp. 206–10.

7. Subcommittee of the Central Housing Advisory Committee, *The Needs of New Communities* (The Cullingworth Report), HMSO, London, 1967.

8. 'City man's bombshell', *Wolverton Express*, 21 February 1969.

9. 'UDC complains about city centre', *Wolverton Express*, 11 April 1969.

10. 'Meeting with local authorities in the designated area', MKDC, Board minute 86, 30 June 1969.

11. 'Overall proposals for physical planning and transport', MKDC, Board minute 89, 30 June 1969.

12. 'Scrap idea for new city at Milton Keynes', *Buckingham Advertiser*, 12 September 1969.

13. 'Judge the city on need', *Wolverton Express*, 19 September 1969.

14. 'Ratepayers warned of "large burden" from city', *Wolverton Express*, 27 March 1970.

15. 'Analysis of objections to the plan for Milton Keynes information paper 9/70', MKDC, Board minute 60, 4 May 1970.

16. 'Public inquiry', MKDC, Board minute 82, 29 June 1970.

17. Frederic J. Osborn and Arnold Whittick, *New Towns: Their Origins, Achievements and Progress*, Leonard Hill, 1977, p. 237.

CHAPTER EIGHT

1. 'Open University', MKDC, Board minute 179, 16 December 1968.

2. Interview with Lord Campbell, Nettlebed, 23 February 1991. MK/TB tape 4.

3. John Ferguson, *The Open University from Within*, University of London Press, London, 1975, pp. 11–15.

4. 'Open University', MKDC, Board minute 18, 28 February 1969.

5. Interview with Lord Campbell, 23 February 1991. MK/TB tape 4.

6. John Ferguson, *The Open University from Within*, pp. 19–20.

7. Commission on the Third London Airport, *Report*, HMSO, London, 1971.

8. 'Third London airport', MKDC, Board minute 85, 30 June 1969 and 'Draft case for submission to the Roskill Commission: Milton Keynes and the siting of the third London airport', MKDC paper MK. 56. 69.

9. *A Strategy for the South East*, Report by the South East Economic Planning Council, HMSO, London, 1967.

10. Commission on the Third London Airport, *Report*, paras 6.5, 6.17 and 6.44.

11. Letter from Campbell of Eskan to the Bishop of Buckingham, 12 June 1969.

12. 'Third London airport – Roskill Commission', MKDC, Board minute 12, 16 January 1970.

13. Speech by Lord Campbell at Wilton Hall on 17 March 1970.

14. 'Airport "would ruin Milton Keynes"', *The Daily Telegraph*, 21 March 1970.

15. 'The third London airport', MKDC, Board minute 4, 8 January 1971.

16. Commission on the Third London Airport, *Report*, 'Note of dissent by Professor Buchanan'.

CHAPTER NINE

1. 'The chairman's meeting with the permanent secretary', MKDC, Board minute 31, 22 February 1971.

2. Interview with Fred Roche by Jane Chapman, the corporation's press officer, MKDC, Media review of the 1970s, 1979.

3. 'Annual survey of development', MKDC, presented to the board by the general manager, 5 November 1971.

4. Speech by Lord Campbell to the corporation staff, MKDC, 11 February 1972.

5. 'Reductions in public expenditure', MKDC, Board minute 139, 3 August 1973.

6. 'Three-day week', MKDC, Board minute 6, 4 January 1974.

7. 'Public expenditure cuts', MKDC, Board minute 7, 4 January 1974.

8. 'Public expenditure cuts', MKDC, Board minute 34, 4 March 1974.

9. 'Minister's review of new-town policy', MKDC, Board minute 76, 3 May 1974.

10. 'The Minister's policy review', MKDC, Board minute 96, 7 June 1974.

11. 'The future of new towns', MKDC, Board minute 8, 7 February 1975.

12. 'New-town chairmen's meeting with the Minister', MKDC, Board minute 88, 6 June 1975.

13. 'Chairmen's meeting with the Minister', MKDC, Board minute 170, 7 November 1975.

14. 'New-town chairmen's meeting with the Minister', MKDC, Board minute 88, 6 June 1975.

15. 'New-towns conference', MKDC, Board minute 83, 4 June 1976.

16. 'Minister's conference with the new towns', MKDC, Board minute 117, 30 July 1976.

17. 'Public expenditure cuts', MKDC, Board minute 118, 30 July 1976.

18. 'Public expenditure cuts', MKDC, Board minute 146, 1 October 1976.

19. 'Chairmen's conference', MKDC, Board minute 145, 1 October 1976.

CHAPTER TEN

1. 'The frame for London's overspill', *Financial Times*, April 1967.

2. 'Milton's master, trailing laurels', *Guardian*, 6 June 1970.

3. Interview with Derek Walker, Milton Keynes, 11 December 1990.

4. Jeff Bishop, *Milton Keynes: The Best of Both Worlds?*, School for Advanced Urban Studies, University of Bristol, 1986.

5. Tom Wolfe, *From Bauhaus to Our House*, Farrar, Straus & Giroux, New York, 1981, pp. 31–2.

6. Richard Crossman, *The Diaries of a Cabinet Minister*, vol. 2, Hamish Hamilton and Jonathan Cape, London, 1976, p. 460, entry for 4 September 1967.

7. Richard Llewelyn-Davies, 'Changing goals in design: The Milton Keynes example', in Peter Self (ed.) *New Towns: The British Experience*, Charles Knight, London, 1972.

8. Roger Kitchen, 'The social aspects of design and the development of new communities' in 'Social engineering at Milton Keynes', *Architectural Association Quarterly*, vol. 6, nos 3/4, 1974/5.

9. Interview with Fred Roche, Brickhill, Milton Keynes, 21 February 1991. MK/TB tape 3.

10. 'Housing for rent, Fullers Slade', 'Housing for rent, Stanton High Site 2 (Bradville 2)', MKDC, Board minutes 152, 6 August and 178, 1 October 1971.

11. Interview with Michael Murray, chief executive, Milton Keynes Borough Council, Milton Keynes, 21 February 1991. MK/TB tape 1.

12. 'Beanhill housing for rent', MKDC, Board minute 160, 6 April 1973.

13. Christopher Knight, 'Housing at Neath Hill, Milton Keynes', *Architects' Journal*, 15 April 1981.

14. 'Great Linford grid square', MKDC, Board minute 186, 2 November 1973.

15. Interview with Fred Roche, 21 February 1991.

16. Interview with Derek Walker, 11 December 1990.

17. Philip Opher and Clinton Bird, *British New Towns: Architecture and Urban Design. Milton Keynes*, Oxford Polytechnic, Oxford, 1981.

18. MKDC, *New City Milton Keynes*, 1975.

19. Rowan Mactaggart, 'Newcomers to Milton Keynes: Getting their housing priorities right', in *Architectural Design*, vol. XLV, December 1975, pp. 764–6.

20. Camillo Sitte, *City Planning According to Artistic Principles* (trans. G. R. and C. C. Collins), Phaidon Press, London, 1965.

Chapter Eleven

1. Interview with Derek Walker, Milton Keynes, 11 December 1990.

2. Jeff Bishop, *Milton Keynes: The Best of Both Worlds?*, School for Advanced Urban Studies, University of Bristol, 1986, p. 1.

3. *Architectural Design*, vol. XLV, December 1975, pp. 728–35.

4. *Domus*, December 1974, No. 541. 'Milton Keynes Development Corporation, Central Milton Keynes' and 'Minale/Tattersfield/Provinciali: Grafica a Milton Keynes'.

5. MKDC, *New City: Milton Keynes 1974* and *New City Milton Keynes 1975.*

6. 'The flexibility of the plan 1975', MKDC, Board seminar minutes, 7 July 1975.

7. 'Energy projects progress report 1976–81', MKDC, Board minute 300, 4 December 1981.

8. Interview with Frank Henshaw, Milton Keynes, 28 February 1991. MK/TB tapes 5/6.

9. 'Energy projects future work', 'Energy centre', MKDC, Board minutes 70, 5 March 1982 and 6, 10 January 1986.

10. Christopher Warman, 'Wrapped up for winter', *The Times*, 5 December 1990.

11. 'The energy regulations: Part two – city savers', *Building*, issue 14, 6 April 1990, pp. 76–7.

12. Interview with Lord Chilver, 21 February 1991, Milton Keynes. MK/TB tape 2.

13. Interview with Bill Benyon, MP for Milton Keynes, Westminster, 6 March 1991. MK/TB tape 5.

14. Interview with Errol Ray, former town clerk of Bletchley Council and former chief executive of Milton Keynes Borough Council, Milton Keynes, 21 February 1991. MK/TB tape 1.

Chapter Twelve

1. MKDC, Fourth Annual Report for the Year Ended 31 March 1971.

2. MKDC, Fifth Annual Report for the Year Ended 31 March 1972.

3. 'Stanton High, housing costs', 'Yardstick', MKDC, Board minutes 98, 27 July 1970 and 129, 2 June 1972.

4. Patrick Dunleavy, 'Unit 26 public housing' in Stephen Potter (co-ordinator), *Block 6. State Intervention II; Urban Public Services and State Investment*, Open University Press, Milton Keynes, 1982.

5. MKDC, Fifth and Sixth Annual Reports for the Years Ended 31 March 1972 and 31 March 1973.

6. 'The quality of the housing programme', MKDC, Board minute 103a, 8 June 1973.

7. MKDC, Seventh Annual Report for the Year Ended 31 March 1974.

8. Frank Henshaw and Derek Walker, 'Milton Keynes: The housing dilemma', *Architectural Association Quarterly*, vol. 6, nos 3 and 4, 1974/5, pp. 15–19.

9. 'Terrace housing', MKDC, Board minute 151, 17 July 1972.

10. Interview with Lord Campbell, Nettlebed, 23 February 1991. MK/TB tape 4.

11. 'Higher-quality housing', MKDC, Board minute 115, 8 July 1974.

12. 'Garages', 'Car parking and garages: Areas of rental housing', MKDC, Board minutes 96, 6 June and 150, 3 October 1975 (DoE Circular 24/75).

13. MKDC, Ninth Annual Report for the Year Ended 31 March 1976.

14. Richard Crossman, *The Diaries of a Cabinet Minister*, vol. 1, Hamish Hamilton and Jonathan Cape, London, 1975, p. 126, entry for 11 January, 1965.

15. 'Local authority liaison, (b) A common housing policy', MKDC, Board minute 49, 2 April 1976.

16. 'Common housing policy working group', MKDC, Board minute 69, 1 April 1977.

17. Interview with Lord Chilver, Milton Keynes, 21 February 1991. MK/TB tape 2.

18. 'Local authority liaison BMK and MKDC consultative group', MKDC, Board minute 230, 7 December 1979.

19. Interview with Michael Murray, chief executive, Milton Keynes Borough Council, Milton Keynes, 21 February 1991. MK/TB tape 1.

20. Interview with Bill Benyon, MP for Milton Keynes, Westminster, 6 March 1991. MK/TB tape 4.

21. Interview with Fred Roche, Bow Brickhill, Milton Keynes, 21 February 1991. MK/TB tape 3.

22. 'The corporation's rental housing, a) Future requirements', MKDC, Board minute 78, 3 October 1986.

23. 'The corporation's rental housing, c) Ultimate disposals', MKDC, Board minute 78, 3 October 1986.

24. 'External liaison: BMK and MKDC consultative group (4 March 1988)', MKDC, Board minute 23/8, 4 March 1988.

25. Interview with Michael Murray, 21 February 1991.

26. Interview with Erroll Ray, former clerk, Bletchley Urban District Council and former chief executive, Milton Keynes Borough Council, Milton Keynes, 21 February 1991. MK/TB tape 1.

27. 'County in bid to keep corporation in power', *Milton Keynes Gazette*, 13 December 1990.

28. Interview with Bill Benyon, 6 March 1991..

29. Interview with Lord Chilver, 21 February 1991.

CHAPTER THIRTEEN

1. 'Marketing strategy and private housing', MKDC, Board seminar minute 9, 7 October 1977.

2. Robert Maxwell, 'Milton Keynes the beautiful city', *Architectural Association Quarterly*, vol. 6, nos. 3 and 4, 1974/5, pp. 4–14.

3. 'The plan for Central Milton Keynes', MKDC, Board minute 201, 6 October 1972.

4. 'British Rail station', MKDC, Board minute 47, 7 March 1975.

5. 'CMK progress report', MKDC, Board minute 122, 4 July 1977.

6. 'Railway station', MKDC, Board minute 92, 30 June 1978.

7. 'CMK railway station, concourse and offices', MKDC, Board minute 190, 2 October 1979.

8. 'The city club', MKDC, Board minute 79, 6 April 1973.

9. 'Central Milton Keynes, city club and stadium', MKDC, Board minute 61, 5 April 1974.

10. 'The city club', MKDC, Board seminar, 13 September 1974.

11. 'CMK progress report', MKDC, Board minute 122, 4 July 1977.

12. 'City retailing strategy'; 'Milton Keynes arena'; 'Arena'; MKDC, Board minutes 25, 4 February 1983; 34, 2 March 1984; 104, 5 October and 126, 7 December 1984.

13. 'Arena', MKDC, Board minute 66, 12 July 1990.

14. Interview with Bob Hill, MKDC Commercial Director, Milton Keynes, 4 June 1991.

CHAPTER FOURTEEN

1. Terence Bendixson, *The Peterborough Effect*, Peterborough Development Corporation, Peterborough, 1988, p. 159.

2. 'Shopping: Terence Conran talks to Derek Walker and Chris Woodward', *Architectural Design*, vol. XLIV, 8/1974, p. 508.

3. 'Central Milton Keynes: Shopping building and D1.4 offices', MKDC, Board minute 53, 5 April 1974.

4. 'CMK progress report', 'CMK shopping building', MKDC, Board minutes 138, 1 August 1975 and 75, 7 May 1976.

5. 'CMK progress report', MKDC, Board minute 122, 4 July 1977.

6. 'CMK shopping building', MKDC, Board minute 20, 3 February 1978.

7. 'Marks & Spencer', MKDC, Board minute 166, 3 November 1978.

8. 'Prime Minister's visit', MKDC, Board minute 173, 2 October 1979.

9. Interview with Lord Campbell, Nettlebed, 23 February 1991. MK/TB tape 4.

10. MKDC, Thirteenth Annual Report for the Year Ended 31 March 1980.

11. 'CMK shopping building promotion', MKDC, Board minute 79, 6 April 1979.

12. 'CMK users' survey', MKDC, Board minute 233, 7 December 1979.

13. 'CMK shopping entrance doors', MKDC, Board minute 215, 2 November 1979.

14. 'CMK shopping building entrance doors' and 'CMK shopping building award', MKDC, Board minutes 151 and 152, 1 August 1980.

15. 'CMK shopping building entrance doors', MKDC, Board minute 72, 6 March 1981.

16. 'CMK shopping building entrance doors', MKDC, Board minute 122, 1 May 1981.

17. 'Central Milton Keynes shopping building doors', MKDC, Board minute 147, 5 June 1981.

18. 'Central Milton Keynes shopping building', MKDC, Board minute 203, 31 July 1981.

19. 'Central Milton Keynes shopping building', MKDC, Board minute 301, 4 December 1981.

20. 'Central Milton Keynes shopping building trading performance', MKDC, Board minute 36, 5 February 1982.

21. 'City retailing strategy', MKDC, Board minute 61, 6 March 1981.

22. 'Retail strategy progress report', MKDC, Board minute 295, 4 December 1981.

23. 'City retailing strategy', MKDC, Board minute 302, 5 November 1982.

24. Interview with Frank Henshaw, Milton Keynes, 28 February 1991. MK/TB tape 5/6.

25. 'Food centre', MKDC, Board minute 4/3b, 4 January 1985.

26. 'Food centre,' MKDC, Board minute 4/3b, 4 January 1985 and 'Central Milton Keynes food centre', MKDC, Board minute 40/4a, 29 March and 52/3a, 3 May 1985.

27. 'Kingston district centre', MKDC, Board minute 31, 15 March 1990.

CHAPTER FIFTEEN

1. 'Household survey 1973', MKDC, Board minute 95, 7 June 1974.

2. 'Quarterly progress report', MKDC, Board minute 33, 7 March 1975.

3. MKDC, Board seminar minutes, 1 October 1976.

4. Stephen Potter, 'Unit 27 the transport policy crisis' in *Block 6, State Intervention II: Urban Public Services and State Investment*, The Open University, Milton Keynes, 1982.

5. 'Notes and preliminary thoughts on a public transport system for Milton Keynes', MKDC, Public Transport Working Party, October 1973.

6. 'Public transport', MKDC, Briefing note for study visit of the House of Commons Expenditure Committee's Environment and Home Office Sub-Committee, 12 December 1973.

7. 'Public transport', MKDC, Board minute 26, 1 February 1974.

8. 'Public transport', MKDC, Board minute 107, 7 July 1975.

9. 'Public transport liaison', MKDC, Board minute 48, 2 April 1976.

10. Interview with Wayne Perdue, Milton Keynes Transport Management Limited (and MKDC transport unit manager 1979–86), Milton Keynes, 22 February 1991.

11. 'Public transport', MKDC, Board minute 174, 4 November 1977.

12. MKDC, Board seminar minutes, 2 February 1979.

13. 'Public transport review: Paper 1 summary with recommendations', MKDC, Executive management committee, 29 April 1987.

14. Interview with Wayne Perdue, 22 February 1991,

15. Interview with Ian Alston, MKDC transport co-ordinator, Milton Keynes, 22 February 1991.

16. Interview with Wayne Perdue, 22 February 1991.

17. Interview with Ian Alston, 22 February 1991.

18. Interview with Wayne Perdue, 22 February 1991.

Chapter Sixteen

1. Kevin Lynch, *The Image of the City*, MIT Press, Cambridge, Mass., 1960, p. 119.

2. Jeff Bishop, *Milton Keynes: The Best of Both Worlds?*, School for Advanced Urban Studies, University of Bristol, 1986, p. 151.

3. Philip Opher and Clinton Bird, *British New Towns: Architecture and Urban Design: Milton Keynes*, Oxford Polytechnic, Oxford, 1981, p. 6.

4. Jeff Bishop, *Milton Keynes: The Best of Both Worlds?*, p. 150.

5. MKDC, Minutes of board seminar, 1 October 1976.

6. 'Tall buildings and landmarks', MKDC, Board minute 107, 1 June 1979.

7. MKDC, Minutes of board seminar, 7 October 1977.

8. 'Neath Hill and Pennyland local centre', MKDC, Board minute 50, 7 April 1978.

9. 'Fixed-track reservations', 'Ad hoc committee; fixed-track reservations', MKDC, Board minutes 195, 1 December 1978 and 187, 3 October 1980.

10. MKDC, Minutes of board seminar, 2 February 1979.

11. Derek Walker, 'Grid roads: A look at what is emerging' in *The Architecture and Planning of Milton Keynes*, Architectural Press, London, 1982, p. 30.

12. Interview with Neil Higson, Milton Keynes, 28 February 1991. MK/TB tape 6.

13. 'Das Freiflachensystem von Milton Keynes' (The Milton Keynes Park System), Neil Higson, Garten + Landschaft, Munich, 6/1982, pp. 441-53.

14. Interview with Neil Higson, 28 February 1991.

15. MKDC, Board seminar minutes, 7 October 1977.

16. Philip Opher and Clinton Bird, *British New Towns: Architecture and Urban Design: Milton Keynes.*

17. 'City structure', MKDC, 1980.

18. 'Redway', MKDC, 1980.

19. 'City structure', MKDC, 1980.

20. 'West Milton Keynes district plan', MKDC, *Milton Keynes Insight*, Winter/Spring 1989.

21. 'Proposed 132kV electricity line north of Bletchley', MKDC, Board minute 145, 30 September 1968; 'East Claydon to Bletchley 132kV overhead line', minute 103, 12 October 1989; '132kV line', minute 110, 16 November 1989.

22. Jeff Bishop, *Milton Keynes: The Best of Both Worlds?*, pp. 149–50.

23. Interview with Derek Walker, Milton Keynes, 11 December 1990.

Chapter Seventeen

1. 'Quarterly progress report', MKDC, Board minute 27, 4 February 1977.

2. 'Chairmen's conference', MKDC, Board minute 145, 1 October 1976.

3. Interview with Peter Shore at the House of Commons, 20 February 1991. MK/TB tape 1.

4. 'Chairmen's conference', MKDC, Board minute 145, 1 October 1976.

5. 'Chairmen's meeting with Mr Peter Shore', MKDC, Board minute 165, 5 November 1976.

6. 'London and Milton Keynes', MKDC, Board minute 6, 2 January 1976.

7. 'Quarterly progress report', MKDC, Board minute 168, 5 November 1976.

8. 'Public expenditure cuts', MKDC, Board minute 7, 7 January 1977.

9. Interview with Peter Shore, 20 February 1991.

10. 'Public expenditure cuts', MKDC, Board minute 24, 4 February 1977.

11. 'Secretary of State's review of new town targets', MKDC, Board minute 48, 4 March 1977.

12. MKDC, Meeting with Peter Shore, 10 March 1977. 1. '*Aide-mémoire* for Chairman/GM.' 2. '*Aide-mémoire*: Milton Keynes new city; future population targets.'

13. 'Revised population targets', MKDC, Board minute 82, 6 May 1977.

14. 'Household and employers surveys 1976', MKDC, Board minute 83, 6 May 1977.

15. 'Household and employers surveys 1976', MKDC, Board minute 95, 3 June 1977.

16. 'Population targets', MKDC, Board minute 127, 29 July 1977.

17. 'Implementation programme 1978–85', MKDC, Board minute 31, 3 March 1978. Also 'The Implementation Programme 1978–85', MKDC, February 1978.

18. 'Local authority liaison', MKDC, Board minute 88, 30 June 1978. Also letter from the chairman to all board members, 7 July 1978, covering note sent to Bucks County Council.

19. 'Quarterly progress report, for three months ending 31 December 1978', MKDC, Board minute 31, 2 February 1979.

20. Interview with Fred Roche, Bow Brickhill, Milton Keynes, 21 February 1991. MK/TB tape 3.

21. 'New towns policy', MKDC, Board minute 196, 1 December 1978.

CHAPTER EIGHTEEN

1. 'Public expenditure cuts', 'The construction industry', MKDC, Board minutes 129 and 135, 29 June 1979.

2. 'New towns' finance', MKDC, Board minute 154, 27 July 1979.

3. 'Chairmen's conference', MKDC, Board minute 174, 2 October 1979.

4. 'Sir John Garlick', MKDC, Board minute 231, 7 December 1979.

5. 'Finance', MKDC, Board minute 51/1, 5 June 1987.

6. 'Management accounts 1981', 'Chairmen's meeting with ministers', MKDC, Board minutes 64, 6 March and 265, 6 November 1981.

7. 'Public expenditure cuts', 'Quarterly progress report', MKDC, Board minutes 69, 28 March and 89, 2 May 1980.

8. 'Mr John Stanley MP Minister for Housing', MKDC, Board minute 121, 7 July 1980.

9. 'Chairmen's conference', MKDC, Board minute 179, 3 October 1980.

10. 'Mr Heseltine's visit', 'Mr John Stanley's meeting with chairmen', MKDC, Board minutes 221 and 222, 7 November 1980.

11. MKDC, Progress and Achievement, 1987 and 'General Manager's Report', MKDC, Board minute 63, 1 August 1986.

12. 'Mr John Stanley's meeting with chairmen', MKDC, Board minute 222, 7 November 1980.

13. 'Third generation new towns', MKDC, Board minute 49, 6 February 1981 and MKDC, Fourteenth Annual Report for the Year Ended 31 March 1981.

14. Interview with Frank Henshaw at Milton Keynes, 28 February 1991. MK/TB tapes 5 and 6.

15. Interview with Bill Benyon, MP, at the House of Commons, 6 March 1991. MK/TB tape 6.

16. 'Borough of Milton Keynes and MKDC consultative group', MKDC, Board minute 295, 5 November 1982.

17. 'Quarterly progress report July–September 1981', 'Milton Keynes: Continuing prospects for growth' and 'Meeting with Mr John Stanley', MKDC, Board minutes 267, 6 November; 297, 4 December 1981 and 89, 2 April 1982.

18. 'Chairmen's conference and meeting with the minister', MKDC, Board minute 296, 5 November 1982.

19. 'Chairman-designate', 'Lady Campbell' and 'Chairman's farewell message', MKDC, Board minutes 49, 50 and 51, 4 March 1983.

CHAPTER NINETEEN

1. Interview with Erroll Ray, former clerk of Bletchley Council and former chief executive of Milton Keynes Borough Council, Milton Keynes, 21 February 1991. MK/TB tape 1.

2. 'Central business exchange', MKDC, Board minute 108, 6 June 1980.

3. 'Central business exchange', MKDC, Board minute 233, 7 November 1980.

4. Interview with Fred Roche, Bow Brickhill, Milton Keynes, 21 February 1991. MK/TB tape 3.

5. Interview with Lord Campbell, Nettlebed, 23 February 1991. MK/TB tape 4.

6. 'Central business exchange', MKDC, Board minute 93, 2 April 1982.

7. 'Central business exchange', MKDC, Board minute 339, 3 December 1982.

8. 'Hotel', MKDC, Board minute 32/1, 2 March 1984.

9. 'Hotel', MKDC, Board minute 76/3a, 6 July 1984.

10. 'Hotel', MKDC, Board minute 89/3a, 3 August 1984.

11. MKDC, Twentieth Annual Report for the Year Ended 31 March 1987.

12. MKDC, Twenty-third Annual Report for the Year Ended 31 March 1990.

13. 'Car parking in CMK', MKDC, Board minute 247e, 5 December 1980.

14. 'Central Milton Keynes car parks', 'Central Milton Keynes car parking', MKDC, Board minutes 69, 5 March and 341, 3 December 1982.

15. 'Beds and Bucks survey: Milton Keynes', *Estates Times*, 5 October 1990.

16. 'Parking policy for Central Milton Keynes', MKDC, Board meeting 15 February 1990, Paper MK.19.90.

17. 'Parking in Central Milton Keynes', MKDC, Board minute 16, 14 February 1991.

18. Interview with Keith Revill, Milton Keynes, 4 June 1991.

19. Ruth Gledhill, 'Multi-faith church to raise the roof in Milton Keynes', *The Times*, 11 December 1990.

20. Telephone conversation with Frank Henshaw, 23 January 1991.

CHAPTER TWENTY

1. Interview with Lord Campbell, Nettlebed, 23 February 1991. MK/TB tape 4.

2. Simon Midgley, 'A free-market Tory in the driving seat', *Independent*, 30 March 1989.

3. Interview with Lord Campbell, 23 February 1991.

4. Carol Kennedy, 'Profile: Lord Chilver – business and the academic world', *Director*, vol. 42, no. 5, December 1988, pp. 66–70.

5. Interview with Lord Chilver, Milton Keynes, 21 February 1991. MK/TB tape 2.

6. ibid.

7. 'Milton Keynes development opportunities', MKDC, Board minute 103, 5 October 1984.

8. Simon Midgley, 'A free-market Tory in the driving seat'.

9. Interview with Lord Chilver, 21 February 1991.

10. 'Implementation strategy 1984-91', MKDC, Board meeting, 7 December 1984, Paper MK. 98.84.

11. 'Design for the new era', *Independent*, 24 November 1986.

12. 'Corporate development priorities review', MKDC, Board meeting, 18 April 1986, Paper MK. 29.86.

13. 'Implementation strategy 1987', MKDC, Board minute 91, 2 October 1987.

14. Consortium Developments, 'Report on the plan for small new country towns', London, May 1988.

15. 'Responsibilities for public and private', *Town and Country Planning*, vol. 55, no. 11, 1986.

16. 'Chris Patten turns down Foxley Wood', Department of the Environment, News release 714, 20 December 1989.

17. 'Large residential development opportunity', MKDC, Board minute 115, 4 December 1987.

18. 'Large development opportunity', MKDC, Board minute 25, 4 March 1988.

19. 'Emerson Valley North: Large development opportunity', MKDC, Board minute 56, 11 May 1989.

20. 'Plans announced for Emerson Valley North', MKDC, *Milton Keynes Insight*, Summer 1990. Also 'Consortium Developments Ltd', MKDC, Board minute 99/7, 12 October 1989.

21. 'Employment', 'Implementation strategy', MKDC, Board minutes 91/4, 7 October 1988 and 17, 3 February 1989.

22. Interview with Lord Chilver, 21 February 1991.

23. 'Implementation strategy – progress report', MKDC, Board minute 18, 15 February 1990.

CHAPTER TWENTY-ONE

1. 'Milton Keynes: Brief for master plan', MKDC, 20 June 1967.

2. Interview with Derek Walker, at Milton Keynes, 11 December 1990.

3. MKDC, Fourth Annual Report for the Year Ended 31 March 1971.

4. MKDC, Speech by Lord Campbell to corporation staff, 11 February 1972.

5. 'Design philosophy and control', MKDC, Board minute 169, 19 October 1973.

6. 'The flexibility of the plan 1975', MKDC, Board seminar minutes, 7 July 1975.

7. MKDC, Board seminar minutes, 7 October 1977.

8. 'Seminar with industrialists', MKDC, Board minute 42, 7 April 1978.

9. 'Housing demand and the means of provision', MKDC, Board minute 44, 29 March 1985.

10. 'Housing programme' and 'Housing for sale', MKDC, Board minutes 185 and 181, 2 October 1979.

11. 'Shared ownership', MKDC, Board minute 228, 7 November 1980.

12. 'Housing initiatives', MKDC, Board minute 107/3, 1 November 1985.

13. 'Residential development strategy: 1984 review', MKDC, Board meeting, 3 August 1984, Paper MK.70.84.

14. 'Residential development strategy: 1985 review', MKDC, Board minute 76, 28 June 1985.

15. 'Residential development strategy: 1987 review', MKDC, Board minute 52; Paper MK.48.87, 5 June 1987.

16. Paul Woodfield, *A Guide to the Historic Buildings of Milton Keynes*, MKDC, 1986.

17. '1988 residential development strategy', MKDC, Board meeting, 4 March 1988, Paper MK.22.88. 'Affordable housing', MKDC, Board minute 36, 8 April 1988.

18. 'Affordable housing', MKDC, Board minute 36, 8 April 1988.

19. MKDC, Twenty-first Annual Report for the Year Ended 31 March 1988. Twenty-second Annual Report for the Year Ended 31 March 1989.

20. 'Housing', MKDC, Board minutes 39/7, 10 May and 51/6, 14 June 1990.

21. 'Tattenhoe: Large development opportunity', MKDC, Board minute 52, 14 June 1990; 'Housing', minute 78/6, 13 September 1990; 'Housing development', minutes 108/4, 13 December 1990 and 14/4, 14 February 1991.

22. 'Housing development: Disposal arrangements', MKDC, Board minute 88/5, 11 October 1990.

CHAPTER TWENTY-TWO

1. Roger Brunet, *Les Villes Européennes*, DATAR/RECLUS, La Documentation Française, Paris, 1989.

2. MKDC, Letter (F. Lloyd Roche) to the Department of the Environment (A. Flexman), 19 May 1975.

3. Department of the Environment, Letter (A. Flexman) to MKDC (F. Lloyd Roche), 17 June 1975.

4. 'Shopping and office development at Bletchley', MKDC, Board minute 4, 4 January 1974.

5. 'Employment promotion', MKDC, Board minute 168a, 7 November 1975.

6. 'Marketing and promotional strategy', MKDC, Board minute 95, 30 June 1978.

7. 'Employment development strategy 1980', MKDC.

8. 'Advance factory units', MKDC, Board minute 90, 30 June 1978; 'Design Centre exhibition', minute 113, 28 July 1978; 'Employment strategy', minute 163, 3 November 1978; 'General Motors Limited', minute 197, 1 December 1978.

9. 'Employment growth and marketing', MKDC, Board minute 29, 2 February 1979.

10. 'Marketing in Japan', MKDC, Board minute 120d, 7 July 1980.

11. 'Employment growth and marketing', MKDC, Board minute 29, 2 February 1979.

12. 'Employment development strategy', 'Overseas marketing', MKDC, Board minute 251 and 252, 5 December 1980.

13. 'Unemployment', 'Youth unemployment', MKDC, Board minutes 35, 6 February and 68, 6 March 1981.

14. 'Employment development strategy', MKDC, Board seminar, 18 June 1981.

15. 'Pineham employment area', Board minute 266, 6 November 1981; 'Heliport', minutes 294, 4 December 1981; 160, 4 June 1982; 12, 7 January 1983.

16. 'Facilities', MKDC, Board minute 29/3, 3 March 1989.

17. 'Employment development strategy', MKDC, Board minute 53, 11 May 1989.

18. '1990 Milton Keynes employment survey', MKDC.

19. Interview with Lord Chilver, Milton Keynes, 21 February 1991. MK/TB tape 2.

20. ibid.

21. 'Polytechnic MK update', MKDC, *Business Insight*, March 1991.

CHAPTER TWENTY-THREE

1. 'City image: Public relations policy review', MKDC, Board minute 132, 7 May 1982.

2. 'Image – Strategy review', MKDC, Board minute 161, 1 August 1983.

3. 'Milton Keynes' businesses growing furiously', *Japan Times*, 9 May 1985.

4. Dave Rimmer, 'The non-place urban realm', *Harpers & Queen*, February 1986.

5. 'Efficiency drive must continue says PM', *Energy Management*, October 1986.

6. Interview with Bill Benyon, MP for Milton Keynes, House of Commons, 6 March 1991. MK/TB tape 6.

7. ibid.

8. 'Demographic trends', MKDC, Board minute 66, 3 July 1987.

9. 'SERPLAN: Draft south-east planning strategy', MKDC, Board minute 43, 10 May 1990.

10. 'Visit of Secretary of State for the Environment on 11 January 1985', MKDC, Board minute 15, 1 February 1985.

11. MKDC, Letter from Sir Henry Chilver to the Rt Hon. Patrick Jenkin, MP, Secretary of State for the Environment, 22 February 1985.

12. MKDC, Letter from Sir Henry Chilver to the Rt Hon. Kenneth Baker, MP, Secretary of State for the Environment, 4 October 1985.

13. 'Development corporation's future', MKDC, Board minute 53, 4 July 1986.

14. 'Corporate plan', MKDC, Board meeting, 3 April 1987, Paper MK.30.87.

15. 'Development programme', MKDC, Board minute 90/2, 2 October 1987.

16. 'Planning', MKDC, Board minute 137, 5 February 1988.

17. Interview with Lord Chilver, Milton Keynes, 21 February 1991. MK/TB tape 2.

18. Interview with Lord Campbell, Nettlebed, 23 February 1991. MK/TB tape 4.

19. 'Community-related assets', MKDC, Board minute 72, 1 July 1988 and Paper MK.61.88.

20. 'Community-related assets – linear parks and city road landscapes', MKDC, Board minute 31, 3 March 1989.

21. Interview with Michael Murray, chief executive, Milton Keynes Borough Council, Milton Keynes, 21 February 1991. MK/TB tape 1.

22. Dorothy Stroud, *The South Kensington Estate of Henry Smith's Charity: Its History and Development,* The Trustees of Henry Smith's Charity, London, 1975.

23. Interview with Lord Chilver, Milton Keynes, 21 February 1991, MK/TB tape 2.

24. Interview with Michael Murray, 21 February 1991.

25. ibid.

26. 'Consultation on corporation's winding-up date', MKDC, Board meeting, 13 December 1990, Paper MK.101.90.

27. 'Ensuring the successful completion of Milton Keynes: County and borough councils seek government assurances', Buckinghamshire County Council, undated statement [issued on 24 October 1990].

28. 'Milton Keynes Development Corporation wind-up date confirmed', Department of the Environment, News release 189, 29 March 1991.

CHAPTER TWENTY-FOUR

1. T. J. Maslen, *Suggestions for the Improvement of Our Towns and Houses,* Smith, Elder, London, 1843. (Quoted in Walter L. Creese, *The Search for Environment,* Yale University Press, New Haven and London, 1966, p. 319.)

2. Richard Llewelyn-Davies, 'Town design', in David Lewis (ed.), *Urban Structure,* Elek Books, London, 1968, pp. 44–8.

3. 'Milton Keynes – safeguarding the future', Buckinghamshire County Council and Milton Keynes Borough Council, draft joint response to the Secretary of State for the Environment on the wind-up of Milton Keynes Development Corporation, 24 October 1990.

4. MKDC, 'Facts on Milton Keynes' as at 31 March and 30 September 1991.

5. Richard Llewelyn-Davies, 'Town design'.

Appendix 5

ACKNOWLEDGEMENTS AND CREDITS

Terence Bendixson and John Platt would like to thank Julian Hunt and Alan Marshall of the Buckinghamshire County Reference Library for their help in finding documents and illustrations; Pat Mortimer, director of Milton Keynes City Discovery Centre, for permission to make use of his unpublished thesis; the Open University Library and the City Discovery Centre for their help in finding documents; and Michael Pratt, Keith Revill and Derek Walker for lending slides.

CREDITS FOR ILLUSTRATIONS
(The numbers in the list below refer to pages in this book.)

Bendixson, Terence: 180
Bernard Engle and Partners, *Evening News and Star*, 3 December 1965: 30
Buckinghamshire County Council, Milton Keynes Archaeology Unit: front end paper
Buckinghamshire County Council Planning Department: 66
Buckinghamshire County Reference Library: 12, 81
Commission on the Third London Airport, HMSO, 1971: 78, 79
Conran Roche: 222
Cullen, Gordon, *A Town Called Alcan*, Alcan Industries Limited, 1964: 49
Department of Transport: 7, 23
de Soissons, Louis, in Hazel Evans (ed.), *New Towns: The British Experience*, Charles Knight, London, 1972: 219
Donat, John: 8, 17, 28, 41, 44, 61, 68, 73, 84, 268
Guildhall Library (The), Corporation of London: 134
Home Office Prison Service: 215
Jacoby, Helmut: 98, 106, 110, 123, 138–9

Jellicoe, Geoffrey, *Architects Journal*, 18 November 1945: 16
MacCormac Jamieson Pritchard: 120-1, 232
Markham, Sir Frank, *History of Milton Keynes and District*, White Crescent Press, Luton, 1973 (by kind permission of Lady Markham): 14
Michael Ellard Design Associates: 254-5
Milton Keynes Development Corporation: front and back of jacket, ii, ix, 4 (Ian Strang), 10, 36, 53, 59, 71, 76, 87, 89, 97, 99, 100, 103, 104, 108, 112, 114, 116 (John Donat), 124 (John Donat), 128, 135, 137, 144, 146, 148, 151, 152, 161, 164, 169, 172, 173, 175, 176, 185, 187, 189, 192, 197, 199, 202, 204, 206, 209, 216, 217, 220, 229, 231, 236, 240, 243, 245, 246, 247, 248, 252, 256, 260, 262, 270, 271, 272
Milton Keynes Development Corporation, *The Plan for Milton Keynes*, 1970: 39, 47, 55, 56, 58, 62, 130, 132, 156
Ministry of Housing and Local Government, *Northampton, Bedford and North Bucks Study*, HMSO, London, 1965: 34
Ministry of Housing and Local Government, *The South East Study*, HMSO, London, 1964: 26, 27
Open University, *Block 6, State Intervention II: Urban Public Services and State Investment*, Open University Press, 1982: 94
Planning Design Development: 211, 235
Pooley, Fred, *North Bucks New City*, Buckinghamshire County Council, 1966: 20, 50
Pratt, Michael: 24
Runcorn Development Corporation: 158
South East Economic Planning Council, *A Strategy for the South East*, HMSO, London, 1967: 82
Walker, Derek, *The Architecture and Planning of Milton Keynes*, Architectural Press, London, 1982: 170
Wolverton Express, 14 January 1961: 2

Maps on the following pages are based on Ordnance Survey material, with the permission of the Controller of Her Majesty's Stationery Office, Crown copyright: ix, 2, 10, 20, 27, 34, 39, 55, 56, 71, 78, 79, 82, 87, 135, 158, 256, 262, 271, 272, rear end paper

Index

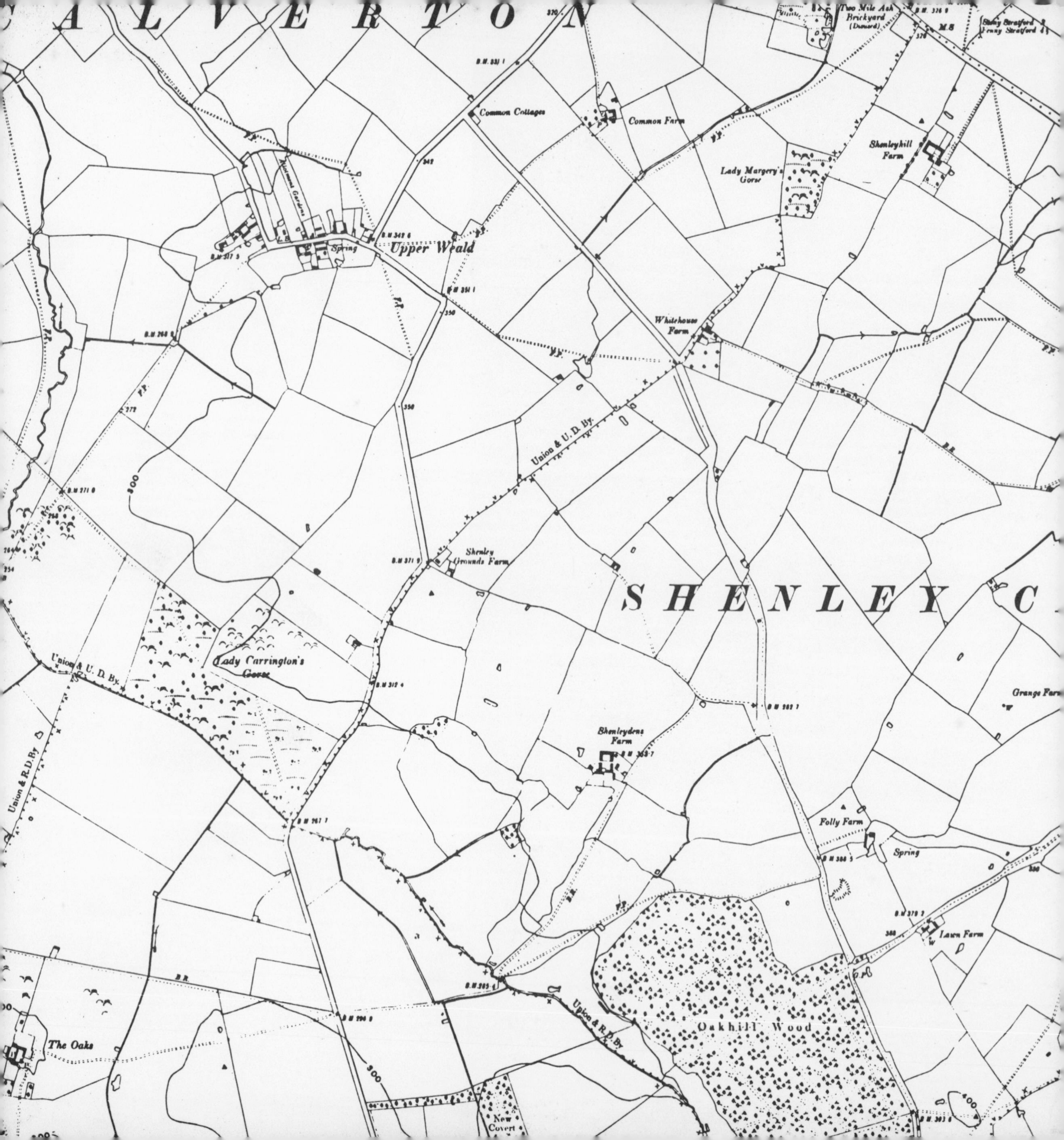

CALVERTON
Two Mile Ash Brickyard (Disused)
Common Cottages
Common Farm
Shenleyhill Farm
Lady Margery's Gorse
Upper Weald
Spring
Allotment Gardens
Whitehouse Farm
Union & U. D. By.
Shenley Grounds Farm
SHENLEY C
Lady Carrington's Gorse
Grange Farm
Shenleydene Farm
Union & R. D. By.
Folly Farm
Spring
Lawn Farm
Oakhill Wood
The Oaks
New Covert